INTRODUCTION TO
FORENSIC SCIENCES

SECOND EDITION

EDITED BY
WILLIAM G. ECKERT

CRC Press
Boca Raton   New York

Publisher:	Robert B. Stern
Editorial Assitant:	Jean Jarboe
Project Editor:	Helen Linna
Marketing Manager:	Greg Daurelle
Direct Marketing Manager:	Bill Boone
Cover design:	Dawn Boyd
PrePress:	Kevin Luong
Manufacturing:	Sheri Schwartz

Library of Congress Cataloging-in-Publication Data

Eckert, William G.
    Introduction to forensic sciences, second editon/ William G. Eckert
    Originally published: New York: Elsevier, 1992
       Includes bibliographical references and index.
       ISBN 0-8493-8101-0
       1. Forensic sciences. I. Eckert, William G.. II. Title.
    QR749.H64G78 1996
    616′.0149—dc20
    for Library of Congress   96-54316
                                                                   CIP

Table of Contents

Preface

This work is dedicated to students at all levels of education, who are interested in the fascinating field of forensic science. The contents of this book, by outstanding contributors, provides the reader with information on the various fields of forensic science that may help them make a career choice or add to their present knowledge. Entry into this field offers a new and rewarding challenge to students who can apply the latest in laser and computer technology to help solve the forensic problems of today.

The new edition of this book has been completely updated. Information is now included on the latest techniques in DNA typing and new information on clinical forensic medicine. Many of the chapters, such as those dealing with forensic science and the law, as well as the historical background chapters, have also been completely rewritten.

Forensic science not only benefits the scientific minded, but has applications in law enforcement. It brings a more practical use of these techniques and a confidence in the results as never before seen. Everyone has potential for making discoveries in this field. The first thing is to identify what the problems are and then to apply common sense and team work to solving them.

William G. Eckert, M.D.

The Editor

William G. Eckert, M.D., a forensic pathologist, was in the first group to be certified in this specialty by the American Board of Pathology in 1959. He has practiced this specialty in New Jersey, Florida, Virginia, New Orleans, Kansas, and California in both coroner and medical examiners' offices and as a private consultant for both prosecution and defense attorneys.

He has done extensive research in multiple areas of forensic science such as accident investigation, child abuse, serial murders, jail deaths, street gangs, and clinical forensic medicine to name a few, and his expertise has been called on to consult on numerous high-profile cases He consulted on the Charles Manson case, the Robert Kennedy case with Dr. Thomas Noguchi of Los Angeles, California, the DC-10 crash in Chicago, and the John Wayne Gacy case with the late Dr. Robert Stein of Chicago, Illinois. Dr. Eckert also consulted for the U.S. Department of Transportation on the jumbo jet crash in the Canary Islands.

The International Reference Organization in Forensic Sciences and Medicine, INFORM, was founded and edited by Dr. Eckert for a number of years. He established the Milton Helpern Center for the Forensic Sciences at Wichita State University which serves as a database for 120 countries. The *American Journal of Forensic Medicine and Pathology* was founded by Dr. Eckert in 1979 and he served as the editor of this important journal for 12 years. Dr. Eckert founded the Asian Pacific Society in 1983 as well as the Pan American Association for Forensic Sciences.

Dr. Eckert also been very active in the field nationally and internationally. He is a past president of the National Association of Medical Examiners; is past president of the International Association of Forensic Sciences, and he was a secretary and vice president of the American Academy of Forensic Sciences.

Among Dr. Eckert's publications are a three-volume text, *Forensic Medicine* with Dr. C. Tedischi and Dr. L. Tedischi and *Interpretation of Blood Stain Evidence at Crime Scences* with Stuart H. James. Dr. Eckert has published over 50 articles and a large number of bibliographies and monographs.

Contributors

Mark L. Bernstein, M.D.
Department of Surgical and
  Hospital Dentistry
School of Dentistry
University of Louisville
Louisville, Kentucky

George T. Duncan, M.S.
Broward County Crime Laboratory
DNA Unit
Fort Lauderdale, Florida

William G. Eckert, M.D.
General and Forensic Pathology
Simi Valley, California

Charles F. Edel
Broward County Sheriff's Office
Ft. Lauderdale, Florida

M. Yasar Iscan, Ph.D.
Department of Anthropology
Florida Atlantic University
Boca Raton, Florida

Stuart H. James, B.A.
Forensic Consultants, Inc.
Fort Lauderdale, Florida

Susan R. Loth, Ph.D.
Department of Anthropology
Florida Atlantic University
Boca Raton, Florida

Alphonse Polkis, Ph.D.
Departments of Pathology and
  Pharmacology and Toxicology
Medical College of Virginia
Virginia Commonwealth University
Richmond, Virginia

William H. Storer, M.S.
Examiner of Questioned Documents
St. Louis, Missouri

Martin L. Tracey, Ph.D.
Department of Biological Sciences
International University
Miami, Florida

Ronald N. Turco, M.D.
Beaverton, Oregon

Cyril H. Wecht, M.D., J.D.
Department of Pathology
St. Francis Central Hospital
Pittsburgh, Pennsylvania

Ronald K. Wright, M.D., J.D.
Fort Lauderdale, Florida

Acknowledgments

Those scientists who helped make this work a success have to be acknowledged and thanked, especially the authors of the last six chapters. They took the time to make our specialty understood and demonstrate a sincere appreciation for the forensic sciences.

Since starting this book, we have lost two men who were not only friends, but teachers of this science: Dr. Robert Stein, Chief Medical Examiner of Cook County and Chicago, Illinois, and Dr. Tom Krauss, a forensic dentist from Kansas. Dr. Krauss was a well-known investigator in the application of photography at crime scenes and the study of trauma from bite marks as forensic evidence of identification.

I would like to express my appreciation to the many educators of forensic sciences in departments of criminal justice, administration of justice and the schools of law enforcement (academies) in America and overseas. These teachers must be recognized for their continuing efforts in providing considerable leadership in improving knowledge and interest in this field.

I am especially thankful that we have had the opportunity to present the newest specialty of forensic science—clinical forensic medicine. This specialty involves the evaluation of trauma in the living—murder suspects, who have injuries which can be related to those seen on the victims and injuries which are also comparable with victims of assault such as children, the elderly, or spouses. This has been an unknown possibility for prosecutors and defense attorneys in cases.

It has been very fortunate that I have had the advice of two strong supporters of this book, namely, my son and attorney Bill Eckert of New Orleans, and Mr. Robert Wachendorf, an experienced and now retired attorney from New Jersey, who supplied the medicolegal aspects.

This book was written for young people who are starting out in the field of forensic sciences. I sincerely hope we have achieved our hope of giving them an insight into a fascinating and rewarding field.

Introduction to the Forensic Sciences

1

WILLIAM G. ECKERT

From the earliest times, the primary tools in the investigation of forensic cases have been observation and interpretation of physical evidence. In the second half of the nineteenth century, science was first applied by advancing the manner in which cases were investigated, and this improved the validity of the conclusions drawn from the investigation by responsible authorities.

A few attempts were made to organize special areas within police departments for processing evidence. Investigating authorities individually obtained scientific information from academic departments of chemistry or pharmacology, which had knowledgeable scientists and technical instruments such as microscopes. Law enforcement authorities had to locate such resources and deliver the evidence for processing by those institutions.

In some instances, scientific laboratories within the police organizations evolved from identification functions. Bureaus of identification developed as the number of criminals rose with population increases. Law enforcement could no longer depend on the memory of shrewd police officers who knew the felons and their gangs so well that they could tell with accuracy whose handiwork was involved in a particular case. Initially, identification bureaus used Bertillon's identification method, which was based on anthropologic measurements supported by photographic documentation. Bertillon's technique was later replaced by the far more accurate technique of fingerprinting. The processing of fingerprints then became coupled with new responsibilities for handling physical evidence such as biological stains, hair, soil, and other materials left at the scene of a crime.

The seeds of modern forensic science were sown in the last quarter of the nineteenth century. Progress from that time has been slow but steady. American forensic scientists are now organized into the American Academy of Forensic Sciences (AAFS); this organization was established in 1948 by many pioneers in the field who were enthusiastically led by Dr. R. H. Gradwohl of St. Louis, Missouri. The American Academy of Forensic Sciences includes the following specific areas of expertise: pathology and biology, toxicology, criminalistics, questioned documents, forensic odontology,

0-8493-8101-0/97/$0.00+$.50
© 1997 by CRC Press, Inc.

anthropology, jurisprudence, psychiatry, and a general section. Other sections are developing in such fields as engineering, geology, and microscopy.

Special Areas of the Forensic Sciences

Pathology

The discipline of forensic pathology is a specialty of medicine and a subspecialty of pathology. It was developed to study the problems related to unnatural death and various types of trauma to the living. The pathologist is a doctor of medicine who has had at least 4 years of training in pathology after medical school and 1 additional year of activity in handling medicolegal autopsies involving unnatural, suspicious, violent, or unexpected deaths. The forensic pathologist may administer a system of medicolegal investigation. The two systems of medicolegal investigation customary in the U.S. are the medical examiner system and the coroner system.

The categories of death to be examined are established by statute and classified according to the cause and manner of the death. In the state of New York, for instance, deaths occurring during medical treatment, all violent and suspicious deaths occurring to individuals under custody in public or private institutions, or deaths occurring to individuals working in industrial hazards are investigated. The investigation may be followed by a postmortem examination during which the pathologist establishes the cause and manner of death. This often requires on-the-scene investigation before an autopsy is performed. Evidence from the body may be referred for further examination to other experts such as the toxicologist, serologist, criminalist, dentist (odontologist), or anthropologist.

Biological testing of evidence includes blood typing and identification of stains for their content. The comparison of blood types is done in paternity cases. In rape cases, saliva and semen, which can be transmitted to another person, may be examined to determine the blood group of the assaulting individual. Distinguishing between human and animal blood is also a part of the pathologist's investigation. Expertise in biology is needed in cases that involve botanical or entomologic evidence. Plant and insect life, for example, may be an important concern in establishing how long a body had been in the place where it was found.

The most helpful information resource in medical areas for the newly graduated lawyer may be the director of the local hospital laboratory. Most hospitals over 150 beds have a pathologist in residence, and laboratories of smaller hospitals are directed or supervised by pathology groups from larger cities so that, for the most part, pathologists are easily accessible. Pathologists are primary initial resources, because their major activity is dealing with problems presented daily by specialists from every medical field. This makes pathologists excellent sources for referrals to those specialists who can clarify and interpret the significance of clinical tests.

The pathologist's experience with examination for injury is beneficial in establishing the possible cause of injuries to living victims. For example, in cases of potential police brutality, the age of an injury is important. Also, pathologists may evaluate the injuries of a young child to determine if the child has been abused.

Tissue and chemical analyses of living persons are performed to establish possible exposure to environmental hazards in industry or the home. Such testing can demonstrate the presence of carbon monoxide, drugs, and harmful metals such as mercury and lead with which the individual may have come in contact. Chemical complications from an overdose of drugs, either accidentally in a child or abuser, or due to a suicide attempt are also subject to analysis in pathologist-directed laboratories.

Malingering and the demonstration of self-injuries is an extremely interesting and relatively recent area of investigation. The rate of discovery of self-injury is directly proportional to the degree of suspicion and awareness of the examining emergency room physician and nurse. In one recent case of self-injury, an individual put her foot into a lawn mower; in another, an infection was produced requiring amputation. Individuals have produced a bloody cough, bloody vomiting, or hematuria by use of instruments that produced the appearance of an emergency requiring hospitalization. Self-destructive patterns are often focused on a solitary area of the body.

Iatrogenic problems are complications that result directly from medical treatment. They may derive from drug complications, new forms of therapy, surgery, or new medical instrumentation. They add liability to the responsibilities of the health care professional and the hospital. The pathologist is often the first to see this type of problem.

Examination of the Dead

Part of the pathologist's general responsibility is to deal with examination of deceased persons. In the case of a hospital death, this is done at the request and with the permission of the family of the deceased. A hospital death may be brought to the attention of the pathologist to document the cause of death, the effect of medical treatment, and the presence or absence of unusual complications or unexpected disease processes. An autopsy is a scientific procedure. Dissection is followed by examination of tissue; chemical or bacteriologic examinations may be required, and the results are documented in a written report and photographs.

In medicolegal cases, permission for body examination is obtained through the authorization of the coroner, who is required by statute to establish the cause of death. The purpose of the autopsy is to document the identification of the victim, any injuries, and the characteristics of such injuries to determine whether activity might have followed a lethal injury. An autopsy also documents the presence or absence of possible sexual problems related to the case, as well as determining the cause and manner of death. This is an extremely important responsibility of the coroner, who is aided by the pathologist. The question of whether a death was accidental, homicidal, suicidal, or of undetermined cause must be answered on the death certificate.

There are occasional cases for which disability and worker's compensation claims may add importance to an autopsy investigation. In some instances where an autopsy was not performed, disinterment of the body and an autopsy must be carried out because of terms of life insurance or claims from workman's compensation. Interment is not always a deterrent to an examination. In the Plains states, for instance, the dryness leads to excellent body preservation and disinterments after up to 5 or 6 years are performed without any major problem. In damper climates, decomposition may be a factor.

Living Cases

Alcohol intoxication is one of the most frequent causes of accidents presented. The problems related to this particular area include accuracy of testing, specimen taking, validity of the results, problems caused by delay in taking the specimens, and variations in the level of alcohol due to the time a blood sample was taken in relation to the time of the accident. The individual's history of alcoholism, serious disease of the liver or kidneys, and metabolic disease such as diabetes are all important in cases of alcohol use, since they have some influence on the metabolism of ethyl alcohol. In possible intoxication cases that involve a low alcohol measurement and a person's apparent inability to handle the task of driving, one must consider the possibility of drug use or of some combination of alcohol and medication. The frequency of this occurrence has led to routine alcohol and drug testing in both living and deceased persons.

Cases of a sexual nature involving living persons frequently require examination for semen stains on clothing, bedding, rugs, or seat covers. This test is important in cases involving incest, carnal knowledge, and rape or sexual assault. In the absence of an available criminalistic laboratory, the hospital laboratory tests smears for spermatozoa and performs chemical testing for acid phosphatase, an enzyme in male secretions. The examination of the victim is usually carried out in the emergency room or doctor's office. In a rape case, advance testing may be also done on the fluid washings from the victim for the presence of blood from the assailant. The hospital laboratory may also be called upon to determine the gender of a young child where there is immature development or lack of development of sexual organs. This is done through chromosomal studies and examination of blood for characteristics of gender.

The examination of surgical tissue is a routine activity for pathologists in a hospital laboratory, and the findings may be used as evidence in cases of medical or product liability. Injuries produced by chemical reactions due to products implanted in the body, such as contraceptive intrauterine devices, may also require documentation by the pathologist. The pathology department also has authority over organ transplantation, which may require specific documentation.

The examination of injuries on suspected murderers, rapists, and assaulting persons opens a large area for trained forensic pathologists who are called upon to collect information from the examination of these people to identify offensive and defensive injuries which they may have sustained in their activity of injury production. Many such people may be identified by the means by which they produce injury and their peculiar manner of selection of their victims and the weapons they use. The examination of victims of child sexual and physical abuse, spouse abuse, and abuse of the elderly at home or in nursing homes is also important in identifying the assailants.

The decision must be made as to whether an alleged victim may not have produced an injury by their own actions. Self injury to an area not usually used in a death attempt may be suspect for the injury to have been produced by the person's own devices.

Toxicology

Toxicology deals with the detection of toxic substances and drugs in body tissues and fluids. The toxicologist analyzes biological fluids and tissues from victims who are thought to have been poisoned accidentally or purposely. The toxicologist, as distinct from the forensic chemist, primarily handles biological materials and can detect poisons in blood, urine, spinal fluid, gastric contents, bile, and tissues.

Anthropology

Forensic anthropologists are experts in the identification of bones and skeletal remains. Their studies provide information about sex, race, age, and time of death. They may also lend support to investigations concerning living cases such as a mix-up of children in a hospital nursery or skeletal identification of persons involved in immigration problems. The forensic anthropologist may be extremely helpful in mass disasters with considerable skeletal remains or in cases of mass burials. A recent application of this expertise was reconstructing the face of a skeletonized head.

Odontology

The odontologist, or dentist, provides information through examination of teeth and dental prostheses. Victims of a disaster or homicide may be identified by a comparison of their dental charts and X-rays to the dental evidence from the victims. Bitemarks in apples, cheese, chewing gum, and other media, as well as on a victim's body, may be studied by these scientists. This form of expertise may also be used in living cases, as the examination of teeth is helpful where there is a possibility of a hospital mix-up of children, as such examinations may depend upon the presence on inherited characteristics in teeth.

Engineering

The investigation of accidents involving vehicles in traffic, recreational vehicles, or aircraft or industrial, fire, electrical, or metal fatigue accidents has brought into the picture those who develop and apply engineering principles to the solution of the cause of accidents. Thus, forensic engineering has been added to the other areas of the forensic sciences.

Biology

The examination of plant life, insects, soil, trees, dirt, seeds, and pollen, as well as blood analysis, can be a means of developing new resources to a forensic investigation.

Geology

This field provides information on rocks and geological material which can offer a very important advance to forensic investigation where evidence of this nature is found on a car. Geological principles can be used to determine where the car has traveled or where a murder victim with dirt or rocks on her clothing may have been murdered or taken.

Psychiatry

The psychiatrist is vital in solving many forensic problems. Psychograms, which analyze behavior personality and psychiatric problems, can offer a profile of an assailant to law enforcement officers. Suicides may require a so-called psychological autopsy. Developed by the coroner's office of Los Angeles under Dr. Thomas Noguchi and other forensic scientists, the psychological autopsy consists of a review by psychologists, psychiatrists, and the pathologist of the events and behavior leading up to a person's death. This in-depth investigation may bring out predisposing behavior, suicidal traits, or financial or alcoholic problems important in establishing causes contributing to the manner of death.

It is extremely important that the accused person be properly investigated from a psychiatric standpoint if the cause of his behavior is a medical problem. There are occasions when the psychiatrist may actually evaluate a testifying witness. In the Alger Hiss case, Whitaker Chambers was evaluated by a battery of psychiatrists in the courtroom. Psychiatrists may use thiopental sodium (truth serum) with people who suffer temporary amnesia due to serious accidents.

Questioned Documents

Questioned document (QD) examinations were reported as far back as Roman times, when cases of forged documents were described. The modern use of typewriters and computer printers has added significantly to the activities of questioned document examiners. The QD examiner's work includes the examination of handwriting, ink, paper, typewriter or printer impressions, or any other form of writing or printing that may have been used in a case. This expertise includes detection of counterfeiting and various types of fraud involving government paper, checks, forms, money, and credit cards or the possible falsification of entries in a ship's log. The investigation of computer fraud may also examine the validity of printout material.

Criminalistics

Criminalistics requires several types of expertise. Criminalists in small departments and laboratories handle a general workload; in larger departments they are more specialized. A large criminalistics laboratory may have sections specializing in firearms and explosives examination, toolmark examination, document examination, biologic examination, physical analysis, chemical analysis, soil analysis, and identification.

The firearms section examines bullets from the body of a homicide victim and compares the condition of these bullets to one fired from the suspected weapon. This is done with a comparison microscope and by weighing and examining the cartridge, bullet, shell, and wadding. Firing pin and ejector marks are also examined. The evidence is documented and recorded for presentation in court; during testimony, the firearms expert presents the results of the examination.

Examination of explosives is increasing in volume in large laboratories. The explosives examiner is responsible for the collection of evidence on the scene, examination in the laboratory, reconstruction of the device, and determining the type of accidental or suspect explosion. The evidence is often fragmentary and may include a timing device, detonation device, explosives, and the package in which the explosives were found. Explosives examiners may have to reconstruct the bomb and possibly detonate it in order to demonstrate its similarity to the crime scene evidence. In fatal explosion cases, cooperation with the pathologist is essential, as part of the explosive may be embedded in the body of the deceased.

Forensic chemistry is responsible for chemical testing of drugs and other substances found as evidence. This includes illicit drugs, alcohol, accelerants used in arson, and residual explosives after a bombing. This section may be responsible for the testing program of blood alcohol and breath alcohol evidence in drunk driving cases.

In the crime laboratory, forensic scientists in the serology section deal with identification of blood and seminal fluid. This requires a high degree of expertise and experience in biologic techniques. Soil analysis requires experience, as it combines chemical and physical testing with considerable skill in the use of the microscope. Microscopy itself is the mainstay of a crime laboratory. A private organization, the McCrone Institute of Microscopy in Chicago, is a major resource in this specialized field for research and practical investigation of problems related to soils and other fragmentary trace evidence.

Identification problems provided the impetus for developing scientific laboratories as a section of law enforcement agencies. Identification departments are now a mainstay of modern criminalistic laboratories. They play a role in the identification of fugitive felons through photographic records, composite drawings, or fingerprint comparison. They may also be used in cases of skeletal remains or of fragmented bodies from disasters. Many techniques including X-ray films, photography, fingerprinting, dental comparison, and blood typing may be used in identification laboratories. Voiceprint comparison is a recently developed specialty of crime laboratories.

The application of physics plays a major role in the investigation of minute trace evidence and accident cases in a major crime laboratory. This requires the use of instruments that perform neutron activation analysis, which is a nondestructive method of testing. X-ray diffraction instruments may also be used in a well-equipped laboratory. In the laboratory investigation of an automobile accident, tires may be examined for failure.

Jurisprudence

The expertise of the professional scientist can be of little value unless it is properly presented in a court of law. Consequently, the American Academy of Forensic Sciences (AAFS) has developed an area concerned with jurisprudence, which offers the practicing attorney the opportunity to learn what may be obtained from the insight and testimony of an expert, so that there can be more definitive preparation and utilization of the expert witness. Annual meetings permit attorneys to attend programs in all areas of the AAFS to gain broader exposure to the knowledge and proficiency of related forensic disciplines.

Medicolegal problems include an infinite number of areas for potential litigation. Basically, legal medicine deals with areas related to the health care and welfare of a patient. It is extremely important for the attorney to understand the medical problems of a case and to know the type of physician or specialist who can provide pertinent information as well as future testimony to support his case. Cases involving both living and deceased persons are handled under such statutory areas as medical liability, institutional liability, workman's compensation, product liability, and environmental protection.

Documentation is extremely important, and pathologists have three major means of documentation: by photograph, diagram, and dictation of a protocol. The autopsy protocol, in most instances, does not include any interpretations or opinions, merely the findings. It is important that all other records be placed in the autopsy file. These should include the chemical analyses for poisons, drugs, and foreign material, the blood group findings, the examination for spermatozoa and acid phosphatase, the dental examination report, and the report of the anthropologist in the event of a skeletonized body. The photographic evidence may be kept with the hospital's coroner or in the police department's files of the case. Any medical evidence should be kept with the autopsy protocol in case the police files are transferred to remote storage after a period of time.

In many instances, the forensic expert's conclusions are based on practical experimentation with problems presented by the evidence. This may require reconstruction of the evidence or a reenactment of an event, as in a arson or a bombing. One of the more practical and basic experimental activities over the past two decades has been the work of Professor H. MacDonell of Corning, New York who has studied the flight characteristics of blood and can evaluate blood spatter evidence obtained from photographs or from an intact crime scene; this evidence can be used to reconstruct the events of a crime.

The development of identifying victims and potential murderers who have transmitted DNA-laden material via semen to the victim's vaginal cavity or blood from the victim to the clothing of the rapist will revolutionize investigations of living as well as dead victims.

The FBI initiative of having all known sexual deviates and jailed murderers documented for their DNA findings may be an important advance to discovery of their participation. Advances in finding minute amounts of blood on scenes by Lumilite and Luminol spotting also make a great deal more evidence available.

The field of the forensic sciences offers many ways in which the young scientist can apply standard methods and scientific disciplines. The field is open to new concepts and offers unlimited potential for physical, biological, and social scientists to participate in service and educational and research activities in an important and practical area of community service.

Summary

This brief overview of some of the activities of the forensic sciences indicates how various sciences can be applied to the documentation of evidence and to the solution of criminal and civil problems in any part of the world where such specialists are available and of their enormous value to law enforcement and justice.

Historical Development of Forensic Sciences

2

WILLIAM G. ECKERT

Modern forensic sciences and their practical applications originated in the middle of the nineteenth century. Previously, because of lack of sophistication in chemistry, physics, biology, and medicine, investigation of trace evidence and suspicious poisoning deaths was largely subjective, which led to great controversy and legal challenges during court trials.

1. The development of photography into a mobile form of documentation, applicable to both crime scenes and laboratories.
2. The evolution of chemistry as a science, predominantly in Germany, and application of these new techniques and instruments to the analysis of chemical evidence, including poisons in body fluids and containers.
3. The refinement and application of the microscope to the routine study of plant and animal tissues and trace evidence from the crime scene, victim, or suspect.
4. The advances in medical pathology enabling definitive knowledge and documentation to be obtained from routine dissection and analysis in cases of unnatural death.

Progress in the forensic sciences has not been uniform throughout the world. In some European countries there has been a century of development, predominantly in forensic centers devoted to the education of physicians, lawyers, and law enforcement officials. Forensic medicine developed quite rapidly from the beginning. The study of questioned documents also emerged in this era. With the further development of laboratory instruments and techniques, forensic toxicology and serology became important at the beginning of the twentieth century. Criminalistics as a science arose less than 65 years ago, paralleling the recognition by the major police departments in the 1920s that they should have a branch devoted to highly technical examinations by skilled specialists. Forensic odontology and anthropology are relatively recent forensic specialties, although there were isolated instances of their forensic application in the past.

Education in the various fields of the forensic sciences varies from on-the-job training in bench work in a small law enforcement department's crime laboratory to a year of special training in forensic pathology and special certification for pathologists already board certified in general pathology.

Specialized education for forensic pathologists has been available for less than 30 years. Certification is the final acknowledgment of training and experience. This has only recently been achieved in forensic toxicology, forensic odontology, and forensic psychiatry through the establishment of boards of certification by the Forensic Science Foundation, established by the AAFS.

Medicolegal Investigation

Colonial Period

It was clear to early American colonists that investigation of certain questionable, suspicious, and violent deaths had to be carried out following the coroner system to which they had been accustomed in their native England. Early reports were quite interesting. In 1635, a coroner's inquest in the colony of New Plymouth, New England, ruled that John Deacon died as a result of bodily weakness caused by fasting and extreme cold.[1]

In 1637, Governor Leonard Calvert of Maryland appointed Thomas Baldridge of St. Mary to be sheriff and coroner, with authorization to "Doe all and everything...the office of sheriff and coroner of any county in England doe."[2] Shortly after he was installed as coroner, Baldridge impaneled a jury of 12 men to hold an inquest over the body of John Bryant. The verdict was, "John Bryant by the fall of a tree had his bloud bulke broken; and hath two scratches under his chinne of the left side, and so that by means of the fall of the said tree upon him the said John Bryant came to his death."[3]

The duties of a coroner in Maryland were defined as follows:[3]

"Upon notice or suspicion of any person that hath or shall come to his or her death entirely within the limits of that hundred as you conveniently may to view the dead body and to charge the said persons with an oath truly to inquire and true verdict to grant how the person viewed came upon his or her death according to the evidence."

In 1647, autopsies were already carried out in Massachusetts when the general court of Massachusetts Bay showed concern with the teaching of medical students by authorizing that "an autopsy should be made on the body of a criminal once in four years." In Talbot County, Maryland, an autopsy was recorded in 1665 to support the coroner's investigation of the death of a servant, Samuell Yeoungman. The report of the coroner absolved the accused in this manner:[4]

> Wee the Jury haueing viewed the Corpse of Samuell Yeoungman and finding a depression in the craneum in on Corrupted, and with all findings Corrupt between the Dura and Pia matter, and the braine and several other bruises in the head and body therefore our verdict in that want of Looking after the above said wounds, were the Cause of his death.

In 1666, coroners in Maryland were appointed by county. In Massachusetts the coroner system was already well established. There are a few early cases reported of the investigations of unnatural deaths; one of these was reported by Dr. Timothy Leary in his chapter on the system of medicolegal investigation in Massachusetts found in the 1928 publication of the Rockefeller Foundation, titled *Methods and Problems in Medical Education.*[5]

A case report from the records of the Court of Assistants of the Massachusetts Bay in 1654 states:

> We whose names are under ritten; being called to venue the Body of Matthew Kehnige and to make in Quiery of the siddiness of his dith and the cause thereof, by searching of his body we finde on his heade on the left side a wounde which wounde we saw oppened and ther was corrupt blude: and the towe small holes out of which wounde Blude Eissued forth and by what we sawe and by the witnesse Brought in on oth we finde that the wounde on his heade as neare as we can judge was a cause of his death. (Followed by 12 signatures, 3 by marks.)

Early records collected by Dr. Jaroslav Nemec in his chronology of medicolegal activities[6] mention the dissection of bodies by physicians and regulation of the practice of medicine in the colonies. In the colonial period, dissection was often carried out by anatomists. The discipline of pathology developed later. There was no recorded teaching of medical jurisprudence in the eighteenth century, although Dr. Benjamin Rush of Philadelphia practiced during this period and later wrote up his lectures on this subject for his medical students. During the precolonial period, postmortem examinations were described in the journals of Jacques Cartier[7] and Samuel de Champlain[8] on cases of scurvy in an effort to learn the mysteries of this incapacitating malady.

In the early colonial period leading physicians dissected the bodies of deceased patients with interesting cases for purposes of learning the characteristics of disease and for anatomical study. Deaths by gunshot were of great interest because of their frequency and importance for treatment. Many autopsies were performed as a part of medicolegal investigation. In one case, involving the death of Governor Henry Sloughter of New York in 1691, an autopsy was ordered by the Provincial Council. The circumstances of the death were suspicious as he suddenly died shortly after he took office, following a very tense political period in which he had approved the execution of a political rival. The symptoms and suddenness of his illness suggested poisoning. The postmortem examination was performed by a Dr. Johannes Kertbyle and was witnessed by five local physicians appointed to assist him. The abstract of the autopsy published in the minutes of the Provincial Council dated July 30, 1691, reads:

> The Doctors and Chirurgeons appointed to view the late Governours Body, pursueant to the order of this board returned under their hands and seales, that the late Gouvernour dyed of a defect of his blood and lungs occasioned by some glutinous tough humor in the blood which stopped the passage thereof and occasioned its settling in the lungs, which by other accidents increased until it carried him off in a sudden and further satisfaction to the council made oath that they knew no other cause of death.[9]

This case is important because it indicated an established recognition of forensic pathology and the role of pathologic anatomy in determining the cause of death. The main objectives of the postmortem examination were to determine the cause of death at a time when the systematic dissection of a body was infrequent and then only following the death of a condemned criminal or social inferior, which provided an opportunity to satisfy anatomical curiosity.

Witchcraft and its mysteries called for investigation of deaths related to suspected conjuring by a witch. In these instances surgeons were enjoined by authoritative governing bodies to look for evidences of witchcraft in the bodies examined.[10] Cotton Mather suspected witchcraft on noting the findings in the autopsy of his son. The child died at 4 days of age and had an imperforate anus. This was also true in the autopsies performed by Dr. Bryan Rossiter of Guilford in Connecticut; these were described in two reports on Connecticut medical history in 1692.[11,12]

In the eighteenth century, autopsies became both more frequent and more informative. Dr. Cadwallader Colden of Philadelphia urged legislation for universal postmortem inspection. His writings and correspondence are well preserved.[13] He advised that postmortem examinations include complete examination of all organs and that an effort be made to correlate anatomic findings with the clinical findings about the deceased patient. Philadelphia became the major center of medical learning in colonial America, with the first medical school being developed at the University of Pennsylvania. Colonial physicians were often trained in London, Edinburgh, and Leyden.

The Republic

In the early years of the nineteenth century, medical students first began receiving education in medical jurisprudence. Dr. James S. Stringham came to New York from Edinburgh and worked at Columbia University, first as professor of chemistry and later of medical jurisprudence and chemistry in a combined program at both Columbia and the College of Physician and Surgeons. His duties included lectures on the handling of bodies of victims of violence. The first quarter of the nineteenth century also saw the development of a chair in midwifery and medical jurisprudence at Harvard University which was held by Walter Channing. A lectureship in medical jurisprudence was established at the College of the Western District of the State of New York at Fairfield. The lecturer was Dr. Theodore R. Beck, who together with his brother John wrote the widely used and authoritative work *Elements of Medical Jurisprudence* published in 1823 and continuing publication through a dozen editions over the following half century. This was an important acknowledgment of the need for adequate postmortem examination of unnatural deaths and unexpected sudden deaths.[14]

Philadelphia continued to be an important center for medical jurisprudence through the efforts of Moreton Stille and Francis Wharton. They collaborated in two works: the *Treatise on Medical Jurisprudence at the University of Pennsylvania* and *Medical Jurisprudence and Toxicology.*

The first major change in medicolegal investigation in America occurred in Massachusetts in 1877, when the state became the first in the country to come to grips with the inherent deficiencies of the coroner system. This system allowed an untrained person, serving by political appointment, to decide the cause of unnatural death on the basis of whatever evidence he could obtain without physical certification. Massachusetts abolished the office of coroner and replaced it with that of medical examiner, who was a qualified physician. Boston's first medical examiner was Dr. Frank W. Draper, Professor of Legal Medicine at Harvard University, who authored a textbook in legal medicine in 1905. This work was based on the experiences he had during the handling of more than 8,000 cases in 28 years of experience. Draper was followed by Dr. George B. Magrath and Dr. Timothy Leary, who jointly covered populous Boston and neighboring Suffolk County. Magrath taught legal medicine and pathology at the Harvard University Medical School, while Leary taught at Tufts Medical School.[5]

With the development of the Massachusetts system there was need for a means of communication between the medical examiners of the state. This was accomplished by the creation of the Massachusetts Medicolegal Society soon after the system was created in 1877. Its purposes were to elevate the status of the medical examiner's office to assist him in the discharge of his duties, to collect and utilize such facts as have medicolegal value, to excite a general interest in the subject of forensic medicine, and to promote its successful cultivation. Every member was required to forward to the corresponding secretary a full and complete report of each case which received his full attention; these transactions were published. In reviewing these transactions covering the period from 1878 to 1936 we can gain insight into many of the problems that confront us today. In the first decade, communications addressed such problems as methods of reporting cases, life insurance, dying declarations, time of death, professional testimony, and activities of the chemist. Later, questions of suicide, homicide, identification of skeletal remains, serologic and toxicologic testing, and problems of intoxication or poisonings were thoroughly discussed.

Prior to the developments in Massachusetts, the only previous mention of the physician and coroner operations was in the Maryland code of Public General Laws in 1860, which authorized the coroner or his jury to require the attendance of a physician in cases of violent death. The choice of physician was left to the coroner. In 1868, the Maryland legislature authorized the governor to appoint a physician as sole coroner of the city of Baltimore.

The Twentieth Century

The spread of medicolegal investigative systems in America was slow and tended to be localized to the populated centers of major cities and counties until the first statewide system developed in Maryland. Some states retained the coroner form but took advantage of having a physician serve as coroner.

New York System

In 1915, the medicolegal investigations in New York City changed from a coroner system to the medical examiner system. This came about after the Wallstein Commission reported many serious defects in the coroner system. Dr. Charles Norris was appointed chief medical examiner;[15] he was given authority to order an autopsy when in his judgment it was necessary. Appointment of the medical examiner by the mayor from a civil service list provided the first civil service appointment in the annals of American medicolegal investigation. The early Massachusetts law did not allow the medical examiner to perform autopsies without the authority of the district attorney. It was not until 1945 that the Massachusetts law was amended to make performance of autopsies discretionary with the medical examiner.

The New York medical examiner system actually took effect in 1918 and was also the American birthplace of the discipline of toxicology, with the establishment of a toxicology laboratory under the direction of Dr. Alexander Gettler. Supporting Dr. Norris were Dr. Thomas A. Gonzalez (later to succeed Dr. Norris as chief medical examiner), Dr. Manuel E. Marten, and Dr. B. M.

Vance. Following Dr. Gonzalez as chief medical examiner was Dr. Milton Helpern. In 1937, Gonzalez, Vance, and Helpern published a major work in forensic medicine titled *Legal Medicine and Toxicology*. This was the most important text in this field in America during the first half of the twentieth century. The second edition appeared in 1954. This book reviewed the subjects of legal medicine and toxicology based on the vast experience of the New York medical examiner's office and its forensic scientists.

The office of the chief medical examiner was located in the pathology building of Bellevue Hospital on First Avenue in Manhattan. Assistant medical examiners performed field investigations throughout Manhattan and the other boroughs. The office of the Chief Medical Examiner of New York was moved to a new building in 1960. When it was dedicated, an international meeting was held in the New York University Medical School Center adjacent to the office.

A medical examiner's office was set up in neighboring Newark, New Jersey, under the direction of Dr. Harrison S. Martland, who had worked in the New York medical examiner's office and had earned renown for his work in the study of radium poisoning in watch-dial painters in the early 1920s. He was recognized by his peers as one of the greatest minds in legal medicine.

California

In some counties of California the offices of coroner and sheriff have been combined, which seems like a step backward for medicolegal investigation. As another variation to the forms of medicolegal investigation, Oakland County medicolegal investigation is done on a contract basis by the Institute of Forensic Sciences, developed from the Western Laboratories established in the 1930s by Dr. Gertrude Moore and Dr. Bobby Glenn. This group no doubt was involved in some cases investigated by Edward O. Heinrich, the "Wizard of Berkeley," during his heyday in the Bay area. In San Francisco city and county, the coroner investigations were supported by the services of the pathologist Dr. Jesse Carr until 1946, when Dr. Henry Moon took over these responsibilities. Dr. Carr went on to develop the Department of Legal Medicine in the University of California Medical School in San Francisco, which continued until his retirement in 1972 and was thereafter included within the Department of Pathology.

The Los Angeles County system developed from the coroner's system and later became a medical examiner system. The director, known as chief medical examiner/coroner, was Dr. Theodore J. Curphey, who worked as a medical examiner on Long Island, New York. Curphey was followed by Dr. Thomas T. Noguchi, who has developed a major office that is a model for others in America.

The Midwest

The coroner's office of Cuyahoga County, Ohio, was studied in 1912 by a committee of the bar and medical societies and by the criminal justice system in Cleveland in 1921. The development of the office into a leading American medicolegal investigative center can be attributed to the industry and administrative abilities of Dr. Samuel Gerber, who found a balance between community and academic environs and set up his office on the campus of Case Western Reserve University with the support of Dr. Lester Adelson, a leading American forensic pathologist. This office has been renowned for its contributions to the field from its beginning. Gerber's industry has been manifest also through his activities with organized forensic medicine. He has served as secretary and president of the AAFS and is currently serving as the executive secretary of the International Association of Coroners and Medical Examiners, which is an organization active in scientific advancement in the field of medicolegal investigation of medical and lay investigators.

Chicago has had a rather unique history in medicolegal investigation, with both peaks and valleys over the years. This mass killing known as the St. Valentine's Day massacre and investigated by coroner Herman Bundeson led to the development of the first crime laboratory in America, under Calvin Goddard. It might have developed further to include forensic pathology if there had been better understanding locally. Dr. Sam Levinson was a prominent pathologist performing coroner autopsies during the 30 years preceding the 1970s.[16] In 1977, the first formal medical examiner system was implemented in Cook County, lead by Dr. Robert Stein, who practiced in Chicago as a pathologist for many years and was trained and certified in forensic pathology. Two previous attempts to establish a medical examiner system in Chicago were made by Dr. Joseph Campbell of Philadelphia and later Dr. William Sturner. Both were faced with the long entrenched coroner system, an environment in which they had little authority to recommend changes. Thus, if a series of deaths was directly related to a community health hazard, the medical examiner did not have the authority to recommend changes to protect the living.

The South

The office of the coroner has held a high place in the government of each parish in Louisiana since the early days of colonization. Today each parish has a physician coroner and an active state coroner's association, providing cohesiveness and effective communication among coroners. New Orleans, in Orleans Parish, has a coroner system whose records antedate the Civil War. Early handwritten French records offer interesting views of the activities of this office and an insight into the problems that followed that war. Suicides, depression, and complications of wounds were well documented in these records. Local pathologists' support of the Orleans Parish coroner's offices was established more reliably under the administration of Dr. Nicholas Chetta in the 1950s when the local medical schools formally agreed to provide pathologists to handle the workload of this office. This tradition of support from each pathology department continues, providing a mutually satisfactory arrangement of providing pathologic material beneficial to teaching medical students and to research projects based on work in the coroner's office on the one hand and coverage for pathologic services on the other hand.

The history of medicolegal investigative systems has largely been the story of strong, dedicated individuals. This was the case in South Carolina, where pathologists Dr. Arthur Dreskin and Dr. Strother Pope in Greenville and Dr. Gordon Henninger, Dr. Charles Garrett, and Dr. Joel Sexton in Charleston successfully established medical examiner systems in their counties. Their appreciation of the importance or proper medicolegal investigation for their state has motivated their continued efforts to have a system implemented throughout the entire state. Dr. Henninger, as chairman of the Department of Pathology of South Carolina University's medical school, supported forensic pathology by having his residents take 3 months' training in this area. He helped Dr. Garrett institute a 22-hour lecture elective and a full-time rotation in forensic pathology for 3 months at the medical school. Dr. Henninger helped Dr. Sexton institute teaching programs in forensic pathology at the Law School of the University of South Carolina in Columbia and at the police academy in Columbia.

Many excellent medicolegal investigative centers are to be found in major cities or counties of America, primarily east of the Mississippi River. These include those in New York State in Rochester and Buffalo and in Suffolk, Westchester, and Nassau counties. Each is run by a chief medical examiner who is trained as a forensic pathologist and has support from toxicology as well as other forensic fields, including dentistry and anthropology, upon request. Pennsylvania's two largest cities, Philadelphia and Pittsburgh, have excellent medicolegal investigative offices. Philadelphia has a medical examiner system, while Pittsburgh has an elected coroner who is a forensic pathologist by training. Typically these offices are responsible for teaching medical students and providing continuing education for medical, legal, and law enforcement authorities. They also act as consultants in medicolegal problems for other counties in their state.

Many excellent programs exist in other large metropolitan areas including Miami, Cincinnati, Indianapolis, Milwaukee, Minneapolis, St. Louis, Kansas City, Denver, Phoenix, Seattle, Detroit, and Pontiac, Michigan. Texas has a medical examiner office joined with the county criminalistics laboratory in forming an institute of forensic sciences to advance cooperation between medicolegal and law enforcement investigators.

Statewide medicolegal investigative systems exist in Maryland (the first such system founded, 1939), Delaware, Virginia, North Carolina, New Jersey, Connecticut, Rhode Island, Vermont, Maine, West Virginia, Arkansas, Oklahoma, New Mexico, Utah, Hawaii, and Oregon. These consist of a centralized office administrated by the chief of medicolegal investigating officers generally called a medical examiner. These officials are forensic pathologists responsible for the investigation of all suspicious, unexpected, or unnatural deaths occurring in their jurisdiction. The local medical examiners report their cases to the central office and may refer cases for autopsy to the central or regional office or to a local pathologist qualified to perform medicolegal cases. The Virginia medical examiner system, organized in 1946, has been a model for the statewide systems of America. Developed from a central office in Richmond, complete laboratory services are available, including those of a toxicology laboratory. Regional laboratories have developed in Norfolk and Roanoke and in the Washington area in northern Virginia. The strength of his system is the liaison the central office maintains with the medical school, which orients the medical students to activities of the program and provides a recruiting base for future medical examiners.

A general analysis or requirements for medicolegal investigation was set forth in 1967 in a report by the American Medical Association's committee on Medicolegal Problems.[17] This committee calculated that for each 100,000 inhabitants in a given geographic area, 250 of a total 1,250 deaths per year should be investigated.

Forensic Pathology

In America the teaching of forensic pathology as a subspeciality of pathology began in 1937, when the Chair of Legal Medicine was established at Harvard University Medical School. It was named after George Burgess Magrath, and its first professor was Dr. Ian Moritz. The Rockefeller Foundation supported the establishment of residency-type training appointment for young pathologists in forensic medicine. A program of seminars in homicide investigation was established in 1945 through the support of Frances G. Lee and it received her name; this program continued until 1967 when Harvard closed the department of legal medicine. The seminar program has been continued in Baltimore, Maryland, as an important activity of the Maryland medical examiner's office. The seminar program is supported by the Maryland Medical Legal Foundation and the Department of Pathology of the University of Maryland Medical School.

Certification in forensic pathology arose from a request by the College of American Pathologists in September 1954 for the establishment of certification examination by the American Board of Pathology.[18] The American Board of Pathology formally established a specialty board in forensic pathology in October of the following year. Dr. Alan R. Moritz became the official representative of forensic pathology on the board.[19] The first exams were held in 1959.

Forensic pathology provides an excellent example of the degree of refinement all other fields of the forensic sciences can reach with understanding and proper development on a solid scientific basis. It symbolizes what has been accomplished by the application of medical jurisprudence by S. E. Chaille.[20]

Forensic Toxicology

Since prehistoric times when plants were first used for their poison content, man has used various forms of plant, mineral, and synthetic material for fishing, hunting, and destroying animal and human enemies. Through the ages, great knowledge has been accumulated regarding the actions and use of poisonous substances. Early Indian and Egyptian writings included references to poisons and antidotes. Greek and Roman literature reported the use of poisons and venoms from plant sources used for suicidal and homicidal purposes. In 339 B.C., Socrates was executed by a poisonous extract of hemlock. In 331 B.C., a mass poisoning occurred in Rome. In 300 B.C., Theophrastus wrote a history of plants and mentioned vegetable poisons and their actions. Before and during the Renaissance, poisoning became an art, with European court histories filled with deaths by poisoning of kings, popes, and nobility. Guards tasted the food and drank the wine destined for the regal table. Professional poisoning occurred until the nineteenth century. Henry III in England punished a poisoner by boiling to death. The most common poisons during this time were hemlock, aconite, opium, arsenic, and corrosive sublimate.[21]

Autopsies and chemical analyses were rarely performed until Plenck stated in 1781, "The only certain sign of poisoning is the chemical identification of the poison in the organs of the body." Mathieu Orfila of France wrote a treatise on poisons that marked the beginning of modern experimental and forensic toxicology. In 1821, Orfila proposed the classification of poisons as: "irritants, narcotics, narcotico-acrids, and putrefiants."[22]

Noteworthy events in the early development of chemical toxicology include the development of a test for the detection of arsenic by James Marsh in 1836, based on Scheele's observation in 1775 that when zinc and acid act on arsenic, a gaseous compound is released which when burned, deposits metallic arsenic. The first extraction of arsenic from human tissue was accomplished by Orfila in 1836. Fresenius and von Babo devised a scheme for the systematic search for all mineral poisons by a wet ashing with chlorine. In 1850, Stras-Otto developed a method for the extraction of alkaloids from cadavers. Selmi, in 1874, detected a morphine-like ptomaine or cadaveric alkaloid.[22] Up to the time of these developments, toxicologic analysis in the early nineteenth century was primarily gastric analysis; the tests were qualitative and crude. An 1832 publication by Henry Coley titled *Poisons and Asphyxia* reviews most aspects of poisoning, including test methods, which were all qualitative and poor. Analysis for metals in organs had to be accomplished by ashing and applying the Marsh test for arsenic and the Reinsch test (developed in 1842) for arsenic and mercury. Qualitative tests were developed for carbon monoxide, alcohol, chloroform, and alkaloids in the mid- and late nineteenth century.

The first quantitative determinations began with tests for metals in 1850, first through chemical means and later by electrolytic deposition. Titrimetric methods came much later. Alcohol testing based on the reduction of chromic acid was the basic method until present times. Quantitative methods have been developed for alcohol demonstration in blood urine, spinal fluid, tissues, and expired air.

Toxicologic analysis of organs in human bodies rarely was done before 1900 because of the primitive development of the system for medicolegal investigation. Elected coroners were laymen with little scientific knowledge. It took the change in the system of medicolegal investigation in Massachusetts in 1877 and in New York City in 1918 to reintroduce the importance of adequate postmortem toxicology to medicolegal investigation. If a case received notoriety and an examination for poison was needed, the coroner sought the services of a professor of chemistry. During the 1890s, Dr. Alexander O. Gettler noted in his review of the history of toxicology[21] that it took one of these professors 20 months to analyze the organs of one postmortem case.

Gettler, the major force behind the development of forensic toxicology in America, began work in the field in 1910 in New York City's Bellevue Hospital where he was a laboratory pathologic chemist. He joined Dr. Charles Norris as toxicologist for the New York medical examiner's office when it was established in 1918. From that time until his retirement in 1959, Gettler's role as a teacher and inventive methodologist was unparalleled. His students have carried on the Gettler spirit of innovation and research and have made outstanding contributions to the advancement of modern forensic toxicology.

Gettler taught most of the major forensic toxicologists of the next generation. These include Dr. Sidney Kaye, the toxicologist in the Virginia Medical Examiner System and later the Chief Toxicologist of Puerto Rico;[25] Dr.

Charles Umberger, the chief Medical Examiner of New York City;[24] Henry Freimuth of the Maryland Medical Examiner's office; Irving Sunshine of the Cleveland Coroner's Office; Leo Goldbaum of the A.F.I.P. in Washington; and Frederic Rieders, currently a leading forensic toxicologist. Many others became students of Gettler's students.

During the 1920s and 1930s, active toxicologists included Dr. D. W. McNally at the University of Illinois and Dr. Walter Camp in Chicago. Professor Rolla Harger at the University of Indiana became prominent as a pioneer in breath testing. Dr. Ray Abernathy was the most prominent toxicologist in the western U.S.

Following the end of World War II, the era of instrumentation began. Instrumentation enabled more accurate quantification of toxic substances in tissue and multiple testing using automated equipment. Combining the automated equipment with computers allowed multiple analysis, calculations, and printing and storage of the results.[25]

Criminalistics

The early development of criminal sciences took place primarily in the last half of the nineteenth century. Except for basic observations, little was done before this time in the examination of physical evidence. Departments of identification had developed in Europe, specifically in France, where Alphonse Bertillon initiated a system of anthropometric measurements for personal identification. This system was adopted by the Paris police in 1882. Despite the development of the fingerprint identification systems, France did not replace the Bertillon system until after his death in 1914. Fingerprint identification developed following its original introduction in Argentina by Vucetich, becoming rapidly accepted in England and on the continent of Europe. Later it was accepted in the U.S. following usage abroad and after the "Will West" case, a classic instance of misidentification by Bertillon.[26]

Advances in chemistry, microscopy, and photography were the stimulus for the development of the early phases of modern criminalistics. One of the early pioneers in the fields of forensic sciences and its laboratory application was Dr. Edmond Locard of Lyon, France. He supported police investigation with many basic techniques. His broad interests included the identification of documents, handwriting, and the study of trace evidence. His philosophy was referred to as the "exchange principle," which holds that when any two objects come into contact there is always a transfer of material between them. Locard was the first person to be identified as a criminalist. His fellow countryman Victor Balthazard was an early researcher in differentiating animal and human hair. In addition, Balthazard developed methods of photographic comparisons of bullets and cartridge cases, which served as an early foundation for this field. In addition to anthropometric identification, Bertillon was also involved with various means of documentation by photography, which he developed to a fine science for criminalistics when he photographed crime scenes and formulated a technique of contact photography to demonstrate erasing on documents. He employed casting techniques for tool marks and used comparison methods to establish the identity of tools. In 1902, he contributed to the "latent print technique" by utilizing chance fingerprint impressions found at crime scenes to identify robbers. His activities were not all successful as evidenced by his misidentification.

European Developments in Criminalistics

Many German-speaking countries were successful in applying basic science to the administration of justice. One such scientist was Dr. R. A. Reiss, trained in chemistry and physics at Lausanne University. He contributed heavily to the use of photography in the forensic sciences and established one of the world's earliest crime laboratories that served the academic community and the Swiss police. His interests included photography of crime scenes, corpses, and blood stains. He made a trip to Brazil in 1913, where his experience in criminalistics was presented to the western hemisphere for the first time.[27]

Four German men in the early 1900s were instrumental in advancing the forensic sciences. Paul Jeserich, developer of forensic chemistry and active in toxicology, studied blood stains by applying the precipitin test of Uhlenhuth to identify human blood. Attempts were made to compare bullets in his laboratory as early as 1898. He further investigated textiles and applied spectrographic analysis to evidence examination.

Richard Kockel of Leipzig, Germany, was an early worker in the area of firearms and tool mark identification. He developed techniques for recording detail and circumference of bullets and tool marks and also used ultraviolet light experimentally in forensic medicine.

Carl Popp, a commercial chemist in Germany, developed an interest in the forensic application of chemistry as well as serologic and toxicologic examinations. He further identified fingerprints and applied photography to forensic fields. He was one of the first to analyze debris for evidence in cases involving explosives and arson. The food chemist August Bruning was involved in many cases of toxicologic analysis, firearms, and trace evidence. Robert Heindl worked on personal identification by fingerprints in his laboratory in Germany and established the first police crime laboratory in Germany in Dresden in 1850.

In Italy, Dr. Ottolenghi founded the Scientific Police School of Rome, designated as the first comprehensive school in the world for the instruction of police officers in scientific techniques. He included instruction about physical evidence and established a laboratory to provide scientific analysis for police in 1908. This laboratory served the police of both the country of Italy and the city of Rome.

In England, C. Ainsworth Mitchell was a public analyst interested primarily in questioned documents and the chemistry of inks during the early twentieth century. His countryman Robert Churchill conducted firearms examinations in many cases throughout England.

Austria also contributed two outstanding criminalists. Siegfried Turkel established the first criminalistics laboratory in Vienna in 1918. This was a private laboratory that also did work for the police. Hans Gross was another outstanding Austrian criminalist who founded an institute in the University of Graz.

American Developments in Criminalistics

In 1924, Los Angeles Police Chief August Vollmer included a laboratory in the organization of the department which was directed by officer Rex E. Welch. Welch had a degree in dentistry but was also interested in forensic chemistry. The first crime laboratory was established in 1929 in the Law School of Northwestern University in Chicago. The crime laboratory in Chicago failed after several years of operation, despite the direction of Dr. Calvin Goddard, the famous firearms examiner. It became the crime laboratory of the police department for the city of Chicago following financial problems in the depression years.

Up to the development of the American crime laboratories in the 1920s, most investigations using scientific rather than intuitive means were carried out by individual scientists. These scientists were often called upon by the police as the only source of scientific expertise in a community. Thus, university chemistry department professors or pharmacology department professors in medical schools and physicians, especially pathologists who had microscopes, were called upon as unofficial experts for help. In some instances they became interested in the field and wrote reports of their findings.

One of the major aids to the development of the forensic sciences in the late 1800s was the microscope. In the U.S., local and regional societies of microscopy appeared. Periodicals published by these societies reported their findings on blood, glass, soil, and the contents of pond water. Their help was often sought by local police in investigating trace evidence. There was great interest at this time in the characteristics of blood cells, and dried blood stains were examined to determine whether their origin was animal or human.

The development of criminalistics in the history of the United States up to 1950 was the subject of a doctoral thesis by Dwayne Dillon at the University of California, Berkeley. In his work, Dillon emphasized the fact that any scientific activity involved in a police investigation was a matter of personal initiative by the police officer in charge of the case, who frequently relied upon the chemist, pharmacologist, microscopist, and pathologist, some of whom later became active in the forensic sciences on a full time basis.

One of the earliest applied forensic sciences was photography. It was used as early as 1859 to demonstrate evidence in a California case. Enlarged photographs of signatures were commonly presented in court cases involving forgery. Crime-scene documentation also used photography.

Firearms examination was primarily nonscientific until the development of the comparison microscope in the early twentieth century. There are, however, legal citations from 1876 of cases involving investigation of rifle markings on fatal bullets, of the effect of muzzle flashes on paper and hair, and of various other examinations involving the effect of firearms discharge on clothing. Dr. Albert L. Hall, a medical practitioner in rural New York, was recognized as an outstanding exponent of firearms investigation at the turn of the century. Dr. Calvin Goddard, a physician and an officer in the U.S. Army Ordnance Department, was recognized as a leader in firearms identi-fication. Goddard later worked in New York City, where he had a private firearms analysis laboratory in which the comparison microscope was used. His major recognition followed his examination of firearms used in Chicago's St. Valentine's Day massacre. This impressed the leaders of Chicago to such a degree that a private crime laboratory was set up at Northwestern University Law School in 1929, under Goddard's direction. Goddard remained there until 1932, when his laboratory was moved to Chicago and established as the Chicago police department laboratory. Firearms examination in the Sacco-Vanzetti case made obvious the absolute need of adequate firearms examination.[28]

The FBI developed its own laboratory in 1932, and it became a valuable resource in that organization and for law enforcement departments through-out the country. This laboratory continues to play a major role in the practice of the forensic sciences.

The early decades of the twentieth century were noted for the develop-ment of the general criminalist who handled all forms of criminalistic inves-tigation. Such a person was Luke S. May, who worked on the west coast and did all forms of testing on tool marks, serologic examination, and rape cases, among others. Edward Heinrich, trained as a chemist, worked in his own private laboratory in the California Bay area; he was referred to as the "Wizard of Berkeley." He contributed to advances of scientific criminal investigation and was called upon to study many baffling cases. Heinrich taught at the University of California at Berkeley, and was influenced by August Vollmer, who helped with the development of police administration at the University of California at Oakland. Under the direction of Dr. Paul Kirk, this program became famous as a general criminalist training program resulting in a doctorate program in criminology and general criminalistics.[27]

The diversity of investigations now required of a crime laboratory necessitates dependence on still newer fields, such as immunohematology and immunoserology. The work of Karl Landsteiner, who discovered the ABO blood groups, and of Dr. Alexander Wiener who discovered the Rh type system in blood, served as a basis for modern biologic testing. Professor F. J. Holzer of Innsbruck, Austria, was a student of Landsteiner and pioneered the application of this field in his country and Europe generally.[28]

Forensic Odontology

Forensic odontology deals with application of dental science to the law. Examination of dental evidence and dentures was reported as early as 2500 B.C., when two molars linked together by gold wire were found in a tomb at Giza in Egypt. Impressions of teeth were used in seals for personal identification more than 900 years ago. In A.D. 66, Nero murdered his wife and presented her head on a dish to his mistress; she identified the head by a black tooth located in the anterior position. One of the earlier primary cases in which dental evidence was used for identification in America concerned the death of Dr. Joseph Warren in 1775. A physician and leader of the American concerned with independence, Dr. Warren was killed during the battle of Bunker Hill and was buried in a mass grave. Paul Revere, who had made a denture for him containing a silver and ivory bridge, later identified Dr. Warren's body by means of this bridge. In a similar English case, the Countess of Salisbury, who was burned in Hatfield House in 1835, was identified by her gold denture.

Dr. George Parkman, a professor from Harvard University, was killed by Dr. J. W. Webster in November, 1849. His body was partially burned and dismembered. A charred fragment of a tooth fused to gold was found in the furnace of the house. During the trial the dentist who constructed the denture for Dr. Parkman testified, and his evidence was enough for the jury to give a guilty verdict of premeditated murder against Dr. Webster, who was subsequently hanged. This marked the first time in the U.S. courts that dental evidence was accepted.

Dental examination helped to identify the body of John Wilkes Booth from an unmarked grave in 1866. In 1837, Edmond Sanders proved to the British Parliament during a discussion of legislation regarding child labor that teeth were a better guide to children's ages than height.

The first major mass disaster in which dental expertise was used to identify victims was the Bazaar-de-la-Charitee fire in Paris. Dr. O. Amoedo took part in the identification of 126 victims and became identified as the founder of forensic odontology through his publication titled *L'Art Dentaire-En Medecine Legale,* a classic book which received worldwide recognition.[29]

The first bitemark identification was made from a piece of cheese left at the scene of a crime. When compared to the teeth marks of the suspected burglar, dental evidence provided a conviction in this case at the Cumberland assizes of Carlisle, England in 1906. In a 1909 case in San Diego, California, the murder victim was burned, and a dentist, Dr. Vastarica, found the teeth to be identical to those that had been described as belonging to the victim. In New York City, floating bodies with marked decomposition have been identified by careful examination of teeth and dentures.

Edward Heinrich, the famous California criminologist, determined that dental remains were not those of an alleged victim of a fire in a laboratory. A body had been substituted in an effort to commit an insurance fraud. The murderer had been clever enough to remove the victim's teeth in the same positions as those of his own mouth.

In other interesting cases, a pretender to the identity of the Grand Duchess Anastasia of Russia was proved false in a dental examination by Dr. Kostrisky, dentist to the Czar. The famous Australian "pajama-girl case" murder of 1934 required dental evidence for positive identification of the victim 10 years after the murder. The Ruxton case in England required study involving reconstruction of the skull with superimposition of photographs and dental evidence.

Two English cases in 1943 occasioned favorable comment from each judge on the importance of dental evidence in securing the conviction of a murderer. In one case, the head of a woman was found under a church cellar floor. An attempt had been made to burn and destroy the body; only the upper jaw remained intact. It was suspected that the remains were those of the wife of a man who disappeared under suspicious circumstances 15 months earlier. After carefully examining the upper jaw, the family dentist determined that the findings corresponded accurately with those of the missing woman.[30]

The second significant case in that year occurred near Luton, England, where the body of a decomposed, naked, edentate female was discovered in a stream. Within 90 days, 11 people positively identified the body as that of four different women, none of whom was the victim. The dentist of the suspected victim was finally located, and identification was made through models of the mouth, which had retained the root tip from a difficult extraction.

Odontology has become more sophisticated in areas of classification and compilation of information. In 1946, a computerized system permitted as many as 500 cards with dental data to be sorted in 1 minute. In 1947, the Englishman Dr. Pattersall advocated the Hollerith system of punch cards in compiling dental data.

In cases of disasters, dental expertise is often required, as in the Coconut Grove nightclub fire in Boston in 1942, where 400 or more were killed, and the Barnum and Bailey Circus tent fire investigation in Hartford, Connecticut, in 1944, where 162 of 268 bodies were identified from dental records.

Bitemark evidence is one of the most interesting applications of dental forensic expertise, as it offers an unusual direct link between an assailant and a victim. A 1949 murder case in Tunbridge Wells, England, offers a clear example. Investigation by dental experts revealed that models of the teeth made from bite marks on the victim corresponded to those of her husband.

The Hume case in Chelsea, England, at about the same time, had a unique twist in that the victim had been placed in a drum of sulfuric acid, and only a few fragments of soft tissue, bone, and (most importantly) dentures were found. These were positively identified by dental records, contributing to the identification of the victim and ultimately the conviction of the murderer.

Perhaps the most important and useful application of the expertise of the forensic odontologist is the management of identification of victims in mass deaths, such as aircraft disasters and military wartime deaths. Following World War II, mass graves of war crime victims and of military operations were opened for identification. In one such instance, Strom in Norway identified more than half of 211 Norwegians who had been killed by the Nazis during the occupation.

A new area of investigation for the forensic odontologist is the cracks and wrinkles of the lips and mouth. Quieloscopy was introduced as a possibility in the 1950s by Dr. Lemoyne Snyder, a famous American pathologist and criminologist, and thereafter was thoroughly studied by Japanese investigators, as evidenced by their active reporting in the forensic literature. Three Japanese cases found this technique helpful to the police in identification problems. Professor Suzuki of Tokyo has made detailed studies and developed great expertise in this area. The extension of the sphere of interest to the lips and mouth has resulted in a name change from forensic odontology to forensic stomato-odontology.

Both dental and fingerprint examinations contribute significantly in the identification of transportation accident victims. The importance of the dental examiner was recognized in the late 1960s when dental disaster squads were organized. When jumbo jets crashed at the airport of Tenerife in the Canary Islands in March of 1977, the American and Dutch governments had teams of forensic experts flown out to support local authorities. The early arrival of the Dutch identification team enabled them to collect dental evidence from

Dutch victims by removing the upper and lower jaws. They returned to Holland with this evidence and worked on the identification processing, while Spanish authorities completed their investigation and released the bodies. Much of the identification was completed in Holland by the time the bodies were returned. The American victims were sent to the Dover, Delaware, Air Force base, where American forensic odontologists were excluded by the military. This unfortunate decision prevented the accumulation of further evidence by these experts.

The field of forensic odontology has made remarkable progress during the past two decades. National societies devoted to this specialty have appeared in Japan, Scandinavia, Canada, the U.S., and other countries. It has also resulted in the development of the International Society of Forensic Stomato-Odontology, which meets periodically and communicates regularly with its members. An international journal of forensic dentistry followed the important activities of Dr. Knut Danielsen of Copenhagen, Denmark, who with Dr. Keiser-Nielsen was active in developing a newsletter for the Scandinavian society. Although there have been other textbooks written in this field, the book by Dr. Warren Harvey of England in 1976 has become a classic in the field.

Forensic odontology continues to be an important forensic resource, as it offers an important alternate way to study evidence in the administration of justice. The recognition of this specialty is aided by the most recent development of a board of certification in forensic odontology in America. This was supported by the activities of the Forensic Sciences Foundation, established by members of the AAFS. The main thorn in the side of the experts in this field today is the relative infrequency of cases receiving requests for support from these dental experts.

Forensic Psychiatry

The beginnings of this specialty of the forensic sciences is the M'Naughten case in England,[33] in which an insane person shot a government official and was found guilty by virtue of insanity.[32,35] One of the leaders in this field of psychiatry was Dr. I. Ray, who contributed a treatise on the medical jurisprudence on insanity. Quen had written about earlier historical aspects of forensic psychiatry in America as well.[33,36] The English Court cases are summarized in this field.[34] The development of criminal profiling is another approach in support of police investigation of cases based on a study of the behavior of the serial murderer so that a suspect can be evaluated before and after he has been placed into custody.

REFERENCES

1. Camps F.E. editor: Gradwohl's Legal Medicine, ed. 2, The Wiliams & Wilkins Co., Baltimore, 1968.

2. Browne, W.H. editor: Archives of Maryland, Maryland Historical Society, vol. 3, Baltimore, 1885.

3. Browne, W.H. editor: Archives of Maryland, Maryland Historical Society, vol. 4, Baltimore, 1887.

4. Pleasents, J.H. editor: Archives of Maryland, Maryland Historical Society, vol. 54, Baltimore, 1937.

5. Leary, T.: The Massachusetts medicolegal system. In Methods and Problems of Medical Education, ninth series, Rockefeller Foundation, New York, 1928.

6. Nemec, J.: Highlights of Medicolegal Relations, National Library of Medicine, 1968.

7. Biggare, H.P.: The voyages of Jacques Cartier, Ottawa, Canada, Publications Public Archives, no. 11, 1924.

8. Hektoen, L.: Early postmortem examinations by Europeans in America, J.A.M.A., 86:576, 1926.

9. Toner, J.M.: Contributions to annals of medical progress and medical education in the United States before and during the War of Independence, U.S. Government Printing Office, Washington D.C., 1874.

10. Deetjen, C.: Witchcraft and medicine. Bull. Inst. History Med., 2:164, 1934.

11. Russell, G.W.: Early medicine in Connecticut, Proc. Conn. Med. Soc., 1892, pp. 69–224.

12. Hoadley, C.J.: Early postmortem exams in New England, Proc. Conn. Med. Soc., 1892, pp. 207–217.

13. Jarcho. S.: Infectious fevers: correspondence of Cadwallader Colden, Bull. Hist. Med. 30:195, 1956. (Colden's other papers in New York Historical Society.)

14. Long, Esmond, R.: A History of American Pathology, Charles C. Thomas, Springfield, IL, 1962.

15. Wallstein Report on the New York City Coroners, 1915.

16. Levinson, S.A.: History and progress of scientific work of the Cook County coroner's office, Bull. Coc. Med. Hist. Chicago, 5:208, 1940.

17. Committee of Medicolegal Problems, American Medical Association, The medical sciences in crime detection, J.A.M.A., 200:155, 1967.

18. Larson, C.P.: History of the College of American Pathologists Committee on Forensic Pathology, CAP Pathologist, January: 23, 1976.

19. French, A.J.: The history and significance of the issuance of certificates in forensic pathology by the American Board of Pathology. In Legal Medicine Annual, Wecht, C. editor, Appleton-Century-Crofts, New York, 1969.

20. Chaille, S.E.: Origin and progress of medical jurisprudence 1776–1876, J. Crim. Law Criminol., 40(4):397, 1949. (Reprint from Transactions of the International Medical Congress, Philadelphia, 1876.)

21. Gettler, A.O.: Historical development of toxicology, J. Forens. Sci., 1(1): 1958.

22. Orfila, M.J.: Traite de Medicine Legale, vol. 3, Paris, 1823.

23. Thorwald J.: Century of the Detective, Section 111: The Winding Road of Forensic Toxicology, Harcourt, Brace and World, New York, 1965, pp. 267–413.

24. Umberger, C.J.: Personal communication, 1950.

25. Eckert, W.G. and Alexander O. Gettler: Am. J. Med. Pathol., 4:4, 1983.

26. Thorwald, J.: Century of the Detective, Section 1: The Adventure of Identification, Harcourt, Brace and World, New York, 1965, pp. 1–110.

27. Dillon, D.: History of criminalistics in the United States (1850–1950), doctoral dissertation, University of California at Berkeley, Ann Arbor, MI, 1977. University Microfilms, Inc.

28. Thorwald, J.: Century of the Detective, Section IV: The Drama of Forensic Ballistics, Harcourt, Brace, and World, New York, 1965.

29. Thorwald, J.: Crime and Science, Section I: Forensic Serology, Harcourt, Brace, and World, New York, 1967, pp. 1–208.

30. Harvey, W.: Forensic Dentistry, Henry Kimpton, London, 1976.

31. Amoedo O.: L'Arte Dentaire en Medicine Legale, Masson, Paris, 1898.

32. Ray, I.: A Treatise on the Medical Jurisprudence of Insanity, Little, Brown, Boston, 1838.

33. Quen, J.: An historical view of the M'Naghten case, Bull. Med. Hist. Med., 42:43, 1968.

34. English reports, fol. 8, vols. 8–12, House of Lords containing Clark and Finnelly, William Green and Sons, Edinburgh, 1901, pp. 718–724.

35. Ray, I.: Confinement of the insane, Am. Law Rev., 3:193, 1869.

36. Quen, J.: Historical reflections on American legal psychiatry, Bull. Am. Acad. Psychiatry Law, 11(4):237, 1975.

37. Hazelwood, R.: FBI Academy, Behavioral Sciences, Quantico, VA, personal communication, 1991.

The Role of the Forensic Laboratory

3

WILLIAM G. ECKERT
STUART H. JAMES

Introduction

Forensic or crime laboratories are concerned with the examination of items of physical evidence associated with crime scenes, victims, and suspects. The scientific findings of the laboratory are utilized in conjunction with the other areas of forensic science and criminal investigation in preparation for a legal proceeding or trial.

Physical evidence may be generally defined as any material either in gross or trace quantities that can establish through scientific examination and analysis that a crime has been committed. Physical evidence may be utilized in forensic investigations in the following meaningful areas:

1. **Defining the element of the crime** — This is the proof that a crime has been committed, such as the identification and quantitation of a drug or controlled substance or the determination of the quantity of alcohol in the blood of a person suspected of driving while intoxicated.
2. **Providing investigative leads for a case** — An example of this would be the identification of a vehicle type in a hit-and-run case through automotive paint and glass analysis.
3. **Linking a crime scene or a victim to a suspect** — This link may be provided through analysis of various types of physical evidence such as hair, blood, semen, and fingerprints.
4. **Corroborating or refuting a suspect's statement or alibi** — In a fatal gunshot case, the examination of bloodstain patterns at the scene and on a suspect's clothing may establish whether a victim was struggling with an assailant as may be claimed or conversely show that the victim was in a totally different position or location when the shot was fired. Physical evidence may also assist with the differentiation of a homicide or suicide. Questions, such as could the victim have fired the fatal shot

or could certain bloodstains have been produced by the victim's activity, may be answered by the evaluation of physical evidence.

5. **Identifying a suspect** — The identification of a suspect is not limited to but often established through fingerprint comparison or DNA profiling.

6. **Inducing a confession of a suspect** — In some cases presenting factual information to a suspect established through the examination of physical evidence, such as the victim's blood identified on their clothing or fingerprints identified on a weapon, will encourage the person to admit involvement in a crime.

7. **Exonerating the innocent** — Physical evidence may be found that may prove a person did not commit a crime. This is often referred to as exculpatory evidence. An example of this type of evidence would be the presence of DNA in seminal fluid from vaginal samples of a rape victim that does not match the suspect.

8. **Providing expert testimony in court** — The presentation of physical evidence in court by an expert is the ultimate test of the validity of the evidence. The conclusions drawn by the expert must meet rigorous standards of scientific proof and withstand a vigorous cross examination by defense counsel at trial. The physical evidence and scientific conclusions must be explained to the jurors in an understandable fashion to assist them in arriving at a just verdict in a case.

Documentation and Collection of Physical Evidence

The quality of physical evidence is dependent upon the proper observation, documentation, collection, preservation, and packaging of this evidence at the crime scene, as well as from the victim and suspect. This is governed by the skill and thoroughness of the crime scene investigators, detectives, and pathologists involved in the case, as well as the sophistication of the scientific methods utilized by the forensic scientists. This is achieved through proper training and experience of the crime scene investigators and forensic pathologists, as well as the forensic scientists or criminalists engaged in the scientific examination of physical evidence in the laboratory. The continuity of the chain of custody of the physical evidence must be maintained throughout the entire process including its analysis and subsequent storage. This is necessary to ensure the admissibility of physical evidence in judicial proceedings and at the trial of the accused.

It is necessary to maintain the relationship of physical evidence to the crime scene prior to its collection and packaging. This is usually accomplished through photography, written notes, and diagrams. The collection of physical evidence requires careful attention to the type of evidence encountered with respect to proper packaging. Care must be taken not to alter, distort, or contaminate the evidence prior to its analysis. Items collected should be marked with a sequential number, referenced to the specific location where it was discovered noting the time and date, and initialed by the person collecting the evidence. Biohazardous materials, such as blood and body fluids, should be placed in clearly marked containers. Crime laboratories maintain protocols for evidence collection and packaging which should be adhered to carefully. For example, bloodstained materials such as clothing and bedding should be thoroughly air dried prior to packaging. This avoids bacterial activity which may hinder subsequent analyses. Special containers are required for collection of particles of trace evidence to avoid loss and contamination. Good communication between the laboratory and crime scene technicians is essential to ensure that proper procedures are being followed.

Types of Physical Evidence

Physical evidence may exist in virtually any form or size depending upon the nature and environment of the criminal event. It may exist at the crime scene, or have been transferred between victim and assailant, as well as any other location depending upon the activities of persons involved. The examination and analysis of physical evidence by the forensic scientist involves the physical or chemical identification of materials to the highest degree of scientific certainty possible with current technology. For example, the identification and quantity of a substance present in samples are the goals of alcohol and illicit drug analysis. This establishes the element of the crime in driving-while-intoxicated cases or those involving possession or sale of controlled substances. The examination and analysis of other types of physical evidence, such as blood and hair, may also establish identification of a material followed by comparisons of known and unknown specimens to determine whether they share a common origin. Occasionally, the comparison process involves the physical matching of fragments of objects, such as vehicular components, glass, or clothing, in a jigsaw puzzle fashion (Figure 3 .1). Often the minute size of materials referred to as trace evidence, such as hairs and fibers, require microscopic comparison. Some types of physical evidence comparisons, such as tool mark impressions or projectiles, may only reveal similarities with class characteristics. This means that the evidence can only be associated with a group of similar material and not a unique source. If the examination and comparison of the physical evidence reveals unique features, they are referred to as individual characteristics and there may be a high probability of a common source. Examples of unique or individual characteristics associated with physical evidence comparisons are matching friction ridge detail with fingerprints, individual wear patterns associated with tool marks or footwear

Figure 3.1   Physical match of broken portion of headlight trim of vehicle suspected of involvement in a hit-and-run accident with portion of trim found on roadway.

patterns, striations on projectiles, and matching DNA profiles in blood, semen, or tissue. Statistical analysis may be employed, such as with DNA analysis, to show the relative frequency of a particular profile.

The following is a summary of common types of physical evidence encountered in forensic or crime laboratories:

1. **Body fluids** — primarily blood, semen, or saliva in liquid or dried form often present on clothing or other fabrics or objects (Figure 3.2). These materials are frequently collected on sterile cloth patches or swabs from a crime scene or person for species identification and possible individualization through serological techniques or DNA profiling. The interpretation of bloodstain patterns at the scene of a violent crime and on the clothing of victims and suspects is an additional area of physical evidence examination which is fully discussed in Chapter 10. Other body excretions, such as urine, perspiration, and feces, may be identified in various stains or materials.

2. **Body tissues** — various organ samples collected at autopsy with blood, urine, and stomach contents for toxicological analysis.

3. **Drugs and controlled substances** — plant materials, powders, tablets, capsules, or other preparations for identification and weight (Figure 3.3).

4. **Fibers** — natural occurring (cotton, wool) or synthetic fibers (rayon, dacron) for identification and comparison (Figure 3.4).

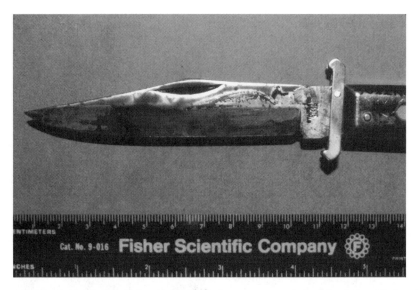

Figure 3.2 Knife blade found in possession of suspect containing blood identified as that of the victim by DNA profiling.

Figure 3.3 Assorted capsules and tablets identified as containing the hallucinogen and controlled substance, lysergic acid diethylamide (LSD).

5. **Finger, palm, and foot prints** — visible or latent prints lifted or casted from various surfaces for identification and comparison. Tire and footwear impressions are often included in this category (Figure 3.5).

6. **Fire and explosive materials** — liquids, solid material, or burned debris for the identification of accelerants and explosive residues.

7. **Firearms and projectiles** — firearms and ammunition for identification, source, and comparison of projectiles and firearm test firings, distance determinations, and operability of firearms.

Figure 3.4 Fibers found on knife blade with the use of the stereo microscope found to be consistent with fibers from the shirt of a victim stabbed to death.

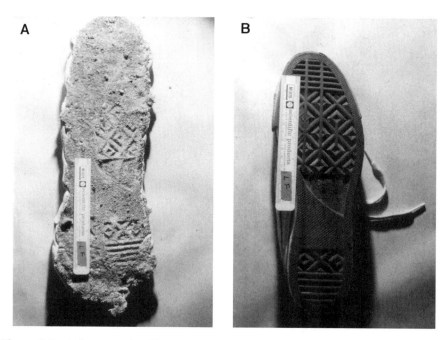

Figure 3.5 (A) Cast made of footwear impression discovered in soil at a crime scene; (B) footwear of suspect showing similarities to footwear impression in (A).

Figure 3.6 Comparison of glass fragments from the scene of accident and the suspect vehicle. The glass originated from a rear window of the vehicle. Note the evidence of heating element in the glass.

8. **Glass** — Trace or large sections. Glass fragments may be associated with a suspect and break-in event or may involve the analysis of glass fractures to determine direction of force applied or sequence of shots fired. Analysis of glass is also utilized for the reconstruction of vehicular crashes (Figure 3.6).

9. **Hair** — Collected from a crime scene, victim, or suspect for determination of species identification (animal or human), race, and the part of body origin. If human, the hair morphological features may be utilized to include or exclude a suspect (Figure 3.7). It is also possible to determine whether the hair was crushed, cut, burned, forcibly removed, or fallen out naturally.

10. **Oils and grease or cosmetic products** — Transferred between objects and individuals and possess unique compositions for comparison.

11. **Paint and paint products** — On various surfaces that may have transferred from one object to another, such as in a vehicular collision. Clothing of pedestrians struck by a vehicle are routinely examined for this type of paint fragment transfer (Figure 3.8).

12. **Serial numbers** — Frequently altered or eradicated on vehicles, firearms, or other objects and through chemical etching may be restored for proper identification.

13. **Soils and minerals, wood, and other vegetation** — Identified and compared as to possible source or location that can be associated with a suspect or victim.

14. **Tool marks** — Impressions or scrapes produced on surfaces that may reveal the type of object that produced them. The object or tool, such as a prybar or screw driver, may possess wear features that can provide

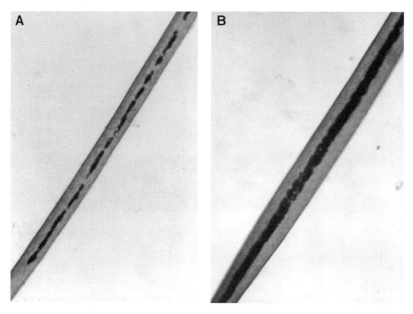

Figure 3.7 (A) A human scalp hair visualized with the compound microscope at approximately × 100 magnification showing the inner medulla and outer cortex of the hair; (B) A human pubic hair from the same individual shown in (A) visualized with the compound microscope approximately × 100 magnification showing the inner medulla and outer cortex. Note the variation in the diameter of the shaft of the hair from the pubic area.

Figure 3.8 Comparison of vehicular paint fragments from the clothing of a hit-and-run victim and a suspect vehicle.

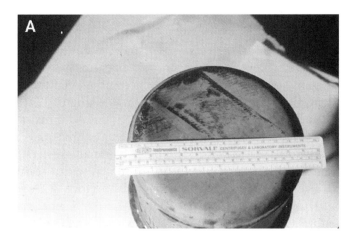

Figure 3.9 Impression created on an underside part of vehicle by victim run over by automobile in fatal hit-and-run accident. The impression was made by jeans and belt of victim; (B) shows area of impact that created impression in (A).

unique characteristics for comparison with the impression. Clothing or fabric impressions may be present on vehicular parts and associated with hit-and-run pedestrian accidents (Figure 3.9).

15. **Questioned documents** — form of physical evidence that may consist of handwritten, typed, copied, or computer-generated materials that are examined for evidence of forgery. The examinations may consist of ink and paper analysis, as well as handwriting comparison, to determine authenticity. Restorative procedures may be utilized in the case of obliterated, physically damaged, or charred documents or materials.

Classification of Laboratories

Forensic or crime laboratories vary in size and capabilities throughout the country and abroad. The federal government operates forensic laboratories in various regions of the country with different specialties. The Federal Bureau of Investigation (FBI) Laboratory in Washington, D.C., is a well recognized crime laboratory. The Drug Enforcement Administration (DEA) maintains several laboratory facilities for illicit drug analysis, and the Alcohol, Tobacco, and Firearms Bureau (ATF) supports criminal investigations involving fires and explosions, as well as those concerned with firearms, alcohol, and tobacco. The U.S. Army operates a crime laboratory in Georgia, as well as in Frankfurt, Germany, and Japan. Many law enforcement agencies operate crime laboratories at the state, county, or local level. The medical examiner's or coroner's offices usually have in-house laboratory facilities. Forensic laboratories are also maintained at colleges and universities, as well as in the private sector. Forensic laboratories may be full service or specialize in one or more areas. For example, the FBI laboratory and most state laboratories are considered full-service operations, whereas many medical examiner's office laboratories concentrate on forensic toxicology or the analysis of body tissues and fluids for drugs, poisons, and other toxic substances. Private forensic laboratories such as National Medical Services, Inc., in Willow Grove, Pennsylvania, offer services in forensic toxicology and criminalistics. Some of the private forensic laboratories are completely specialized in an area of forensic science. The McCrone Research Institute in Chicago, Illinois, performs microscopic analysis of particulate matter, and Cellmark Diagnostics in Germantown, Maryland, provides DNA analysis of blood and other body materials. Whether the forensic or crime laboratory exists in the public or private sector, it should demonstrate a high level of quality control and reproducibility of results through participation in blind testing of samples. Laboratory certification or accreditation is available through organizations such as the Association of Crime Laboratory Directors (ACLD).

Typical Sections of the Forensic or Crime Laboratory

Forensic or crime laboratories that offer multidisciplinary services are usually divided into sections based upon the types of physical evidence examined. Some of the sections require specialized equipment, instrumentation, and training of personnel while other sections may share instrumentation. Criminalists may rotate through various sections of the laboratory depending upon their training, experience, and expertise. Depending upon the size and workload of the particular facility some of the sections may be combined or perhaps further subdivided.

Toxicology and Drug Identification

The toxicology and drug identification section of the laboratory utilizes forensic chemistry and modern instrumental techniques to isolate, identify, and often quantify alcohol, drugs, poisons, and other toxic materials. The material submitted for analysis may consist of bulk quantities of illicit drugs such as marijuana, heroin, LSD, or cocaine which must be accurately weighed, analyzed, and often quantitated to establish the degree of a criminal drug charge. Other liquid, solid, or gaseous materials may be submitted for analysis to determine the presence any toxic or poisonous content. Many crime laboratories analyze blood for alcohol and/or drug content in cases of driving while impaired or intoxicated, as well as perform alcohol, drug, and toxic substance analysis on body tissues and fluids for purposes of death investigation in conjunction with the medical examiner's or coroner's office. Drugs detected may be either of a prescribed or illicit nature. Some commonly encountered toxic substances are carbon monoxide, cyanide, insecticides, and heavy metals. The quantitative blood and tissue levels of these substances, as well as their metabolites, may reveal therapeutic, toxic, or lethal levels present in the body and help determine the role of the substance in the death of the individual. Occasionally, the determination of the absence of a prescribed medication, such as anticonvulsive drugs in victims known to have a seizure disorder, may help to explain their behavior or circumstances of a death.

The procedures utilized in a typical toxicology section of a laboratory may include extraction and purification techniques prior to analysis. Preliminary examination of materials may include chemical spot tests which by color production may indicate the presence of a type of drug or poison. More sophisticated techniques include radioimmunoassay (RIA), thin-layer chromatography (TLC), ultraviolet absorption (UV), infrared absorption (IR), high performance liquid chromatography (HPLC), and gas chromatography (GC).

The application of mass spectroscopy (MS) is now commonly utilized for positive identification of drug and toxic compounds. The reader should refer to Chapter 8 for a more comprehensive overview of forensic toxicology.

Arson Analysis

The detection of accelerants in fire debris samples to help prove arson is a common procedure for crime laboratories. Samples collected by fire investigators from suspected areas of fire origin consist of burned or partially burned wood, carpet, or other materials. Samples of similar materials from unburned areas at the fire scene are also submitted for comparative purposes. Samples of suspected flammable liquids found at a fire scene are also analyzed and in some cases the clothing and shoes from a suspected arsonist.

When these charred materials, unknown liquids, and comparison samples are received in sealed, airtight sample containers and logged at the forensic laboratory, they are subjected to an organized process of isolation or concentration, detection, and identification. Unknown and comparison samples, as well as known laboratory positive standards or controls, are treated in a similar manner. There are four general methods for isolating or concentrating accelerants from fire debris:

1. **Steam distillation** — This technique involves the heating and distilling with steam of the charred material and trapping the distillate with a cold water condenser. The volatile hydrocarbons are collected in a liquid form prior to analysis.

2. **Solvent extraction** — The sample of charred material is extracted by mixing and shaking with a known solvent such as carbon disulfide, methylene chloride, or hexane which dissolves the petroleum distillates and other volatiles into the known solvent. This extract is then evaporated to a small volume which concentrates the sample for analysis.

3a. **Cold head space** — The top of the sample container is punctured and a stopper is inserted in order that a head space vapor sample can be removed with a syringe for subsequent analysis.

3b. **Heated head space** — After the stopper is inserted into the top of the sample container, the vessel is heated in an oven to approximately 100°C or slightly lower. This technique concentrates the head space vapors since the heat drives the volatiles from the charred matrix. This method is popular and more sensitive than cold head space technique.

4. **Vapor concentration on charcoal** — This method utilizes an inert gas purge utilizing nitrogen or air of the heated sample container which carries volatiles through a small tube containing charcoal where they are concentrated. The charcoal is desorbed by heat or a small volume of a solvent such as carbon disulfide and thus prepared for analysis.

The technique of GC is the most commonly utilized for the detection of accelerants in fire debris in forensic laboratories. GC is essentially a separation technique capable of separating mixtures of petroleum distillates and volatile organic compounds into individual peaks which form a pattern for comparison with known standards (Figure 3.10). The introduction of mass spectroscopy coupled with gas chromatography (GC-MS) as well as infrared spectroscopy coupled with gas chromatography (GC-IR) permits specific identification or a "fingerprint" of the molecules to be made. Some forensic laboratories do not possess this advanced capability for identification and utilize the GC pattern recognition of the more common accelerants. Some

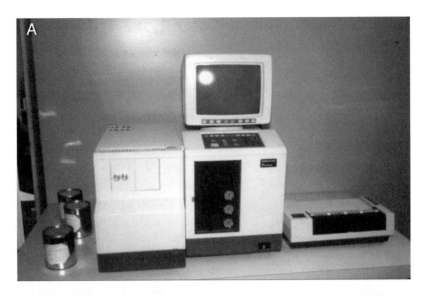

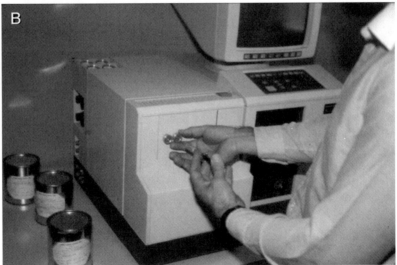

Figure 3.10 (A) Typical gas chromatograph utilized for analysis of alcohol, drugs, accelerants, and other materials in forensic laboratories. (B) Introduction of heated head space sample into injection port of gas chromatograph for detection of accelerants in fire debris.

accelerants are easily recognized by their GC patterns in the absence of interfering substances that may mask them. Examples of these are turpentine, gasoline, kerosene, and the heavier fuel and diesel oils. Those laboratories without GC-MS or GC-IR certainly have the option of further analysis performed by a laboratory with those capabilities if deemed necessary.

Serology

Forensic serology is concerned with the analysis, identification, and individualization of body fluids and tissues, secretions, and excretions. Blood, semen, and saliva are the most frequently encountered types of samples but occasionally samples such as perspiration, urine, gastric contents, and feces may be examined for purposes of characterization. Physical evidence of this type is usually submitted to the laboratory in the form of dried stains on clothing or other materials retrieved from the scene, victim, or suspect. Control samples consisting of clean areas from the surface from which the suspected stains were obtained must be included in the analyses. Standard known samples consisting of victim and/or suspect blood are also utilized for comparative purposes.

The identification of blood or semen on dried, stained materials and subsequent individualization and comparison to known persons for inclusion or exclusion are the major functions of the serologist.

The approach to the identification of a suspected bloodstain begins with a presumptive chemical test to indicate the possible presence of blood. The term presumptive is used to describe these types of tests because they will react with substances other than blood, such as certain metals and plant peroxidases. Common presumptive tests for blood include phenolphthalein, which produces a bright pink color in the presence of blood, and leucomalachite green, which produces a blue-green color in the presence of blood. Luminol is another type of presumptive test for blood which is frequently utilized at the crime scene to locate traces of blood in areas that may have been washed or the blood is not otherwise visible to the naked eye. In these instances the Luminol is sprayed onto suspect surfaces and observed in the dark or near darkness for a bluish-white chemical luminescence which may indicate the presence of blood. This luminescence may be photographed for documentation. If the presumptive test is negative, blood is considered not detected in the sample. If positive, confirmatory tests are performed to prove that the substance is in fact blood, they are followed by species identification to differentiate between human and animal origin. This is accomplished with the use of specific antibodies which will react with the suspect material. Conventional serological procedures for individualization of blood as well as semen include grouping within the ABO system and characterization of polymorphic proteins and genetic markers. In large part these procedures are in limited use with the emergence of DNA profiling which is comprehensively discussed in Chapter 11.

Trace Evidence

The forensic scientist or criminalist responsible for the analysis and comparison of trace evidence must be familiar with a wide range of materials that may be submitted to the crime laboratory in small or trace quantities. The primary tool for the trace evidence analyst is the microscope. A low–medium power stereo microscope usually in the range of × 5–40 is utilized for scanning and sorting many types of physical evidence, such as clothing, for the collection of trace materials. The compound microscope with capabilities up to ×1000 magnification is utilized for the analysis and comparison of hair, fibers, soil, cosmetics, powder particles and residues, and a wide range of particulate matter. A polarized-light microscope is utilized for observation of optical properties and morphology of materials. A comparison microscope is utilized for side-by-side viewing of samples, most commonly hairs and fibers. This is essentially two microscopes connected by a prism arrangement known as a comparison bridge. This permits the field of view from each microscope to be divided into a semicircle so that the two samples can be viewed simultaneously.

The trace evidence analyst may also utilize an array of microchemical tests and instrumental techniques for the identification of paints, glass, oils, and an array of organic compounds. Examples of instruments utilized include GC-MS and techniques of elemental and organic analysis including IR, X-ray diffraction and fluorescence, spectrophotofluorometry, and scanning electron microscopy (SEM). The scanning electron microscope with good resolution and magnification up to ×100,000 is also utilized for the examination of samples of gunshot particles recovered from the hands of persons suspected of recently handling or firing a weapon or being in the immediate vicinity of firearm discharge.

Firearms and Toolmarks

The firearms and toolmark section of the crime laboratory is responsible for the examination of all types of firearms and ammunition, as well as scrapes and impressions on surfaces made by a variety of prying and cutting type instruments.

The examination of pistols, revolvers, rifles, and shotguns determines whether they were in good condition and operable or capable of accidental discharge. Projectiles recovered from a victim or crime scene, as well as fired casings, are examined to determine whether the ammunition was fired from a particular weapon. Most projectiles excluding those fired from shotguns bear impressions referred to as lands and grooves which are reproducible with test ammunition fired in the suspect weapon. If the recovered projectile is not extremely distorted and contains sufficient detail, positive comparisons can be accomplished. In cases where no weapon is recovered, an examination of land and groove detail may indicate the type of weapon utilized to the exclusion of others. Cartridge casings contain firing pin impressions and in some cases ejection marks that can be compared to test casings fired in the

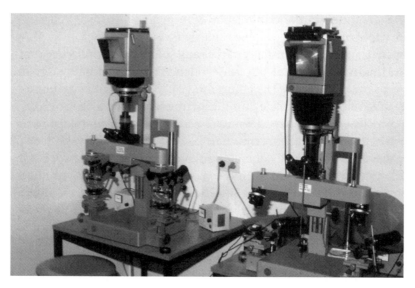

Figure 3.11   Comparison microscopes utilized for projectile and tool mark comparisons.

suspect weapon. A low power comparison microscope with an external light source is utilized for the examination of the features of fired projectiles and casings (Figure 3.11).

The examination of tool marks involves the comparison of impressions created by a hard tool (prybar, screwdriver, knife) created on a softer surface. The impressions left by the tool may show class characteristics indicating the type of tool utilized and possibly individual characteristics due to wearing or nicking of the tool surface that could be considered unique to that tool. Test impressions or cuttings of the suspect tool may be made for study with the comparison microscope.

Fingerprint Identification

This section of a laboratory is often referred to as the latent print section. Partial or complete finger, palm, or foot prints chemically enhanced or lifted from various surfaces at crime scenes, weapons, and other objects are examined, classified, and compared to sets of known or suspect inked sets of prints. This section assists with the identification of the deceased in conjunction with the medical examiner's or coroner's office. Tire and footwear impressions are often examined and compared by personnel in this area of the laboratory.

Forensic Photography

Forensic photography is an important element of crime scene investigation for documentation purposes including the location of the victim and the surrounding area prior to examination by the forensic pathologist and subsequent removal to the morgue. Bloodstains and other items of physical evidence are photographed in place prior to collection and examination. Color film is best suited for these purposes. Videotaping of crime scenes is a technique often employed in addition to photography for documentation purposes. Crime scene units and the forensic pathologist often take their own photographs. Assistance may be requested from the local crime laboratory. The various sections of the crime laboratory may also photograph items of physical evidence and subsequent comparisons and test results to complement their laboratory reports or for courtroom presentation during their testimony. Many laboratories are equipped to develop film and produce enlargements of the photographs. Some special procedures, such as the use of infrared and ultraviolet photography, are employed as well as photography through the various types of microscopes to demonstrate identification and comparison of trace evidence.

Case Presentation 1

Several years ago, during the winter season in a rural college community, a young coed was last seen hitchhiking back to campus. She was reported missing the following day which resulted in an intensive police search for her whereabouts. During the next two weeks, several leads were developed which focused on a known sexual offender living in the area. Further investigation led to the location of the body of the coed in a remote, snow-covered, wooded section of the area. She was in a frozen state, clothed in the apparel she was last seen in while hitchhiking.

Postmortem examination of the victim revealed that she had sustained a fractured skull, with minimal external bleeding as well as bruising in the neck area consistent with manual strangulation. Blood and tissue samples collected for toxicological analysis were negative.

Further examination of the victim revealed a soft contact lens in the left eye with the corresponding right eye lens missing. Vaginal exam by the pathologist revealed evidence of seminal fluid and spermatazoa. The clothing of the victim and the contact lens were submitted to the crime laboratory for trace evidence analysis.

Continued police investigation resulted in the arrest of the suspect identified earlier as a known sexual offender. The suspect's clothing and other possessions were collected and submitted to the laboratory. Scalp and pubic hairs were obtained from the suspect and submitted to the crime laboratory for comparative analysis. A court order was obtained for the search of the suspect's vehicle. Examination of his vehicle revealed fragments of a soft contact lens on the rear floor of the vehicle. Hairs, fibers, and other debris were also recovered from the vehicle. A small bloodstain was collected from the backside of the front passenger seat.

The suspect initially denied any involvement in the death of the coed. Further examination of the physical evidence collected revealed that scalp and pubic hair from the vehicle and the suspect's clothing was consistent with that of the victim. Scalp hair recovered from the victim's clothing was consistent with that of the suspect. The small bloodstain was identified as human blood but could not be further classified. Analysis of the seminal fluid indicated that the suspect could have been a possible donor. The victim's clothing also contained small wood chips. Similar chips were obtained from the car and clothing of the suspect. These were subsequently identified with the SEM as a mixture of pine, maple, and oak chips consistent in size with those produced by a chain saw. The suspect was, in fact, a logger.

The fragments of the contact lens recovered from the suspect's vehicle were further examined at the laboratory. The fragments of the soft contact lens had become hard and brittle due to drying. When reconstituted to their original soft form, they assumed the shape of the contact lens recovered from the victim's eye.

At that time soft contact lenses were exclusively manufactured by a sole lens company and being field tested in a limited college population market. The intact lens as well as the fragment of lens were submitted to the manufacturer for evaluation. The optical company was able to identify both lenses as its product (Figure 3.12). Further analysis by the company revealed the pair of lenses was identical in optical characteristics to the prescription written for the victim. Due to the limited population of soft contact lens users at that time, it was estimated statistically that the probability of the lenses belonging to another individual was approximately 500,000 to one. Upon being confronted with this evidence, the suspect gave a statement claiming that the victim resisted his advances, and he struck her once in the throat, but she jumped out of the car and "must have struck her head at that time." He was subsequently convicted at trial of second degree murder.

This case illustrates the value of physical and trace evidence to link a suspect with the crime scene and victim. Additionally, it demonstrates the value of utilizing the capabilities of a product manufacturer to assist in ultimate identification of evidence obtained. In this case, the contact lens provided an irrefutable link that proved even stronger than wood chips, seminal fluid, or hair comparisons. However, the combination of all physical and trace evidence comparisons provided a solid body of evidence for the jury to consider. This case also illustrates the importance of careful observation and collection of physical evidence at the scene.

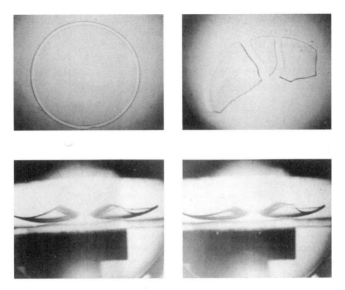

Figure 3.12 Comparison of intact contact lens (left) with fragmented portions of the other lens found in the rear of suspect vehicle (right).

Case Presentation 2

A woman was found dead at her residence by a relative after repeated attempts to reach her by telephone had failed. The postmortem examination revealed that she had sustained severe lacerations to the head and underlying skull fractures consistent with a hammer type of weapon. Bruises and lacerations of the chin and lip with evidence of a broken tooth were noted. The scene of the death was the living room of her residence, where she was found on the floor near a couch. Bloodstain patterns close to the floor on the couch and adjacent wall indicated that several blows were struck while the victim was in a prone position. Bloody footwear impressions led away from the victim through the kitchen to a rear exit. Further examination of the scene in the area around the body revealed a bloodstained gemstone (Figure 3.13A).

Police investigation led to the estranged husband as a suspect. A search warrant was obtained for his premises. Bloodstained clothing discovered in a hamper was submitted to the laboratory. Medium velocity impact bloodstain patterns with a blood type consistent with the victim on the lower trouser legs indicated proximity to forceful impact. The front right pocket of the trousers contained a ring with bloodstains present on the surface. These bloodstains were determined to be consistent with that of the victim. It was noted that the stone was missing from the ring (Figure 3.13B). The gemstone recovered from the scene was found to fit the empty socket of the ring (Figure 3.13C).

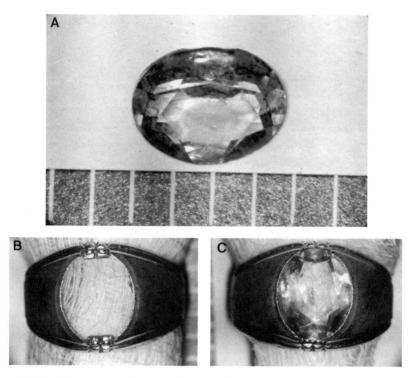

Figure 3.13   (A) Gemstone from ring found at the homicide scene; (B) ring with missing stone found in pocket of suspect; (C) ring of suspect with gemstone fitted into place.

The ring was identified by relatives as a type worn by the suspect. The hammer type weapon was never located. The shoes of the suspect were compared to the shoe prints in blood from the scene and found to possess similar class characteristics; however, individual characteristics were not demonstrated.

The suspect gave a statement that he and his estranged wife had been involved in an altercation. He remembered striking her with his fist but did not recall attacking her with a hammer. Upon the advice of his attorney, the suspect pled guilty to second degree murder prior to trial. He was sentenced to life in prison. This case illustrates a unique variety of physical evidence comparison and matching that can be utilized to connect a suspect with a scene in conjunction with blood and footwear evidence.

Case Presentation 3

A young woman was operating her brother's motor scooter on a dark, desolate road near her farm. Neighbors reported hearing a crash, then seeing a red Mustang leaving the scene at a high rate of speed. The teenager was discovered lying on the roadside with the crumpled motor scooter, apparently the victim of a hit and run driver. The cause of death was attributed to multiple internal injuries.

A short time later, an abandoned red Mustang was discovered approximately one mile from the scene. Ownership was traced to a resident of the area. He denied any involvement in the accident but appeared to be an unreliable historian at the time due to apparent alcohol intoxication. His vehicle was impounded for examination, and he was placed under arrest for possible driving under the influence of alcohol, vehicular manslaughter, and leaving the scene of an accident.

Examination of the vehicle revealed a fresh indentation at the center of the front bumper which contained apparent rubber residue consistent with a tire (Figure 3.14A). The front grill of the vehicle contained small fragments of a blue and gold sticker-type material (Figure 3.14B). The motor scooter sustained severe front end damage, and portions of a blue-gold decal remained on the front steering post (Figure 3.14C). The decal fragments recovered from the grill of the Mustang were found to have a common origin to the remaining portion of decal attached to the scooter.

The suspect subsequently pled guilty to vehicular manslaughter. This case serves as an excellent example of evidence transfer between objects assisting in the identification of a vehicle involved in an impact.

Training and Education of the Criminalist

Many of the early criminalists were police officers and detectives with varied backgrounds. Many lacked formal training and relied upon on-the-job training from a supervisor. They often worked in areas such as latent print examination, document examination, firearms, photography, and crime scene sketching. Some chemical tests were performed such as color tests for the presence of drugs, presumptive test for blood, and breath tests for alcohol.

The advancements of scientific technology utilized by modern forensic and crime laboratories require knowledge in the natural science areas of biology, chemistry, physics, and mathematics. These laboratories usually require a degree in one or more of these areas for employment at the basic level. Many individuals with masters and doctorate degrees are forensic serologists, toxicologists, and microscopists. There has been an increase in the number of colleges and universities offering undergraduate and graduate degrees in forensic science including criminalistics and forensic toxicology. For example, the John Jay College of Criminal Justice in New York City, George Washington University in Washington, D.C., and the University of

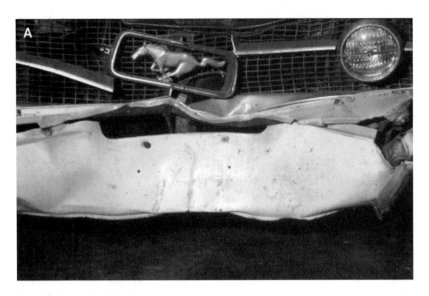

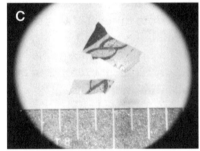

Figure 3.14   Front end of vehicle showing area of impact on bumper and grill; (B) fragments of decal found in grill of suspect vehicle; (C) remainder of decal removed from motor scooter of victim.

New Haven in Connecticut offer degrees in forensic science and criminalistics. St. Johns University in New York offers a degree program in forensic toxicology. For crime laboratory personnel to obtain continuing education, the FBI offers basic and advanced courses in a variety of criminalistics areas and private groups such as the McCrone Institute in Chicago offer courses in microscopy. Herbert Leon MacDonell, an internationally renowned criminalist, instructs basic bloodstain pattern interpretation courses through the Laboratory of Forensic Science in Corning, New York. Many seminars are available through regional and national forensic organizations. The American Academy of Forensic Sciences holds a yearly meeting with the presentation of numerous scientific papers and workshops on a variety of forensic subjects. Additionally, medical examiner offices and crime laboratories as well as private institutions such as the Southern Police Institute (SPI) at the University of Louisville in Louisville, Kentucky, sponsor periodic training seminars and lectures. The forensic or crime laboratory offers an exciting, rewarding career in forensic science and criminalistics for a college graduate who has majored in one or more of the natural sciences.

Suggested Reading

1. DeForest, P.R., Gaensslen, R.E., and Lee, H.C., 1983. *Forensic Science — An Introduction to Criminalistics,* New York: McGraw-Hill.

2. Fisher, B.A.J., 1993. *Techniques of Crime Scene Investigation, Fifth Edition,* Boca Raton, Florida: CRC Press, Inc.

3. Geberth, V.J., 1996. *Practical Homicide Investigation, Third Edition,* Boca Raton, Florida: CRC Press, Inc.

4. Kirk, P.I., 1974. *Crime Investigation, Second Edition,* New York: John Wiley and Sons.

5. Moenssens, A., Starrs, J., Henderson, C., and Inbau, F., 1995. *Scientific Evidence in Criminal Cases, Fourth Edition,* New York: The Foundation Press, Inc.

6. Redsicker, D.R., 1994. *The Practical Methodology of Forensic Photography,* Boca Raton, Florida: CRC Press, Inc.

7. Saferstein, R., 1995. *Criminalistics — An Introduction to Forensic Science, Fifth Edition,* Englewood Cliffs, New Jersey: Prentice-Hall, Inc.

8. Saferstein, R., Editor, 1982. *Forensic Science Handbook,* Englewood Cliffs, New Jersey: Prentice-Hall, Inc.

9. Saferstein, R., Editor, 1988. *Forensic Science Handbook, Volume II,* Englewood Cliffs, New Jersey: Prentice-Hall, Inc.

10. Saferstein, R., Editor, 1993. *Forensic Science Handbook, Volume III,* Englewood Cliffs, New Jersey: Prentice-Hall, Inc.

Forensic Psychiatry

4

WILLIAM G. ECKERT
RONALD N. TURCO

A psychiatrist deals with various aspects of human behavior. In the past century, this expertise has had many applications to courtroom testimony. The investigation, examination, and study of criminals and recommendations for the commitment of psychiatric patients has been the responsibility of the psychiatrist.

A psychiatrist is a trained physician, licensed to practice medicine and surgery in a particular state. Additional training is required for a specialization in the field of psychiatry. Psychiatric residency or fellowship and additional training under an assigned psychiatrist are necessary before certification by the American Board of Psychiatry.[1] Psychiatrists are ethically bound to strict confidentiality. The transactions with a psychiatrist during a therapeutic session are privileged communication; however, during a forensic evaluation they are not, and the examinee is so advised. Psychiatrists have no formal role in criminal investigation and no legal or ethical obligation to use their skill to elicit confessions from criminal suspects.

Forensic psychiatrists have special interests in problems related to courtroom testimony, and some devote their entire practice to the specialty of forensic psychiatry. They may be called upon to help evaluate a defendant whose competence to handle personal affairs, such as the ability to enter into a contract or to execute legal documents, may be in question. They may be asked to testify for the prosecution in a criminal case or for the plaintiff in a civil suit. Occasionally, in unusual and complicated deaths, psychiatrists play a significant role before the trial begins or before the defendant is actually apprehended. Such an instance occurred in Los Angeles when the manner of death of a prominent movie star came into question. During the investigation to determine whether the death was an accident or a suicide, the psychiatrist, pathologist, social worker, friends of the family, and the police acted in concert to find the most likely cause of death. This technique, referred to as a "psychological autopsy", was developed in the 1950s through the efforts of Dr. Theodore J. Curphey and other physicians in Los Angeles.[2,16]

0-8493-8101-0/97/$0.00+$.50
© 1997 by CRC Press, Inc.

The psychiatrist may be called upon during a criminal investigation if there is a question concerning the psychiatric nature of the assailant(s) that may have contributed to the crime. In cases of multiple murders with peculiar sexual activities before or after the victims' deaths or of bizarre mass murders such as the Tate-LaBianca case, a psychiatrist can offer important insight into the murderer's behavior. After a case is reviewed for the type of personality, psychiatric problems, and other peculiarities that the killer may have, a reasonable conclusion as to the behavioral characteristics can be presented. This is a valuable approach in the support of criminal and civil investigations. It is referred to as psychological profiling.[2,3,4,20,24]

Psychiatric evidence in the courtroom is preceded by a thorough examination of the suspect to evaluate his or her mental status and to determine if their state of mind at the time of the offense conforms to the definition of insanity used in the jurisdiction where the crime took place. Psychiatrists can determine the competency of the accused and his or her ability to stand trial. Psychiatric testimony may also be used to counter opposition witnesses in a case involving a psychiatric problem. The psychiatric testimony may be supported by the results of psychological testing. Neurologic examination for organic dysfunction of the brain such as psychomotor epilepsy, may also be used to support the psychiatric examination in assessing insanity and competency.[3] Psychiatrists called by the defense or prosecution may have contrasting opinions depending on their training and theoretical orientation. Far from being a problem, this allows the jury to decide which perspective is more applicable.

Behavioral Disorders

The following disorders may be found in accused persons and be contributing factors in their behavior:

- Acute hallucinations, in which a person hears voices that persecute and abuse the person. This may occur with excessive alcohol intake or drug use. Alcoholism plays a major role in organic brain damage, and drunkenness may lead to a crime.
- Lack of individual adaptation, manifested in many different ways including antisocial personality, which causes a person to be in frequent conflict with society and lack consideration for others.
- Hysterical behavior manifesting emotional instability, marked reactivity, self-dramatization, attention seeking, or a total inadequacy of personality.

- Paranoia, in which a person exhibits rigidity, unwarranted suspicion, jealousy, envy, exaggerated self-esteem, and a tendency to blame others and accuse them of evil motives.
- Schizophrenia, in which a person may exhibit a lack of concentration, withdrawal from society, and eccentricity.

The Forensic Psychiatrist and Personality

Criminal insanity is a legal status based on intent and free will of a person. Legal responsibility for committed acts depends on the presence of free will. There are different tests for sanity, and the resulting differences of interpretation or applications of each test cause many jurisdictions in the U.S. to have different perspectives and guidelines as to what constitutes legal insanity and when a person should be held criminally responsible for his or her actions.

Various tests have been developed to determine the mental state of a person. The M'Naghten test of insanity, developed in England and formulated by the House of Lords, stipulates that an attorney must prove the accused's failure to understand either the nature and the quality or the wrongfulness of his act. The proof of a person's insanity was based on the following questions:

1. Was the accused suffering from a defect of reason resulting from a disease of the mind?
2. Did the accused know the nature of the act?
3. Did the accused know the quality of the act?
4. Did the defendant, at the time of committing the unlawful act, know that he was doing wrong?

"Wrong" as used here had to be further clarified as a "legal wrong", which refers to conscious intent. The act of having an insane delusion could be a defense unless the person realized that in normal society the act would be considered wrong.

Many jurisdictions use the "irresistible impulse" test. This test reveals that an individual may know that an act is wrong but, because of mental illness, is unable to avoid committing it.

The ALI (American Law Institute) test refers to the fact that a person is not responsible for unlawful conduct if it occurs as a result of mental disease or defect. In such cases, the accused lacks substantial capacity either to appreciate the criminality of his conduct or to conform his conduct to the requirements of the law. This is the most commonly used guideline in U.S. courts.

The concept of diminished responsibility, also known as partial insanity, permits the trier of fact to consider the impaired mental state of the defendant even though the impairment does not qualify as insanity under the prevailing tests.

Competency to Stand Trial

Regardless of the mental condition of the accused at the time of committing a criminal act, the accused cannot be tried unless he or she is able to understand the nature and purpose of the proceedings against him and to assist in his own defense. The prosecution of a person who is incapacitated would be a violation of due process. Accused people who become mentally incompetent after conviction may not be subjected to the criminal penalty affixed to the offense. This rule applies to all forms of punishment, including the death penalty. The accused, however, may be incarcerated in a mental hospital for their own and the public's protection.

The psychiatrist's testimony can be given in situations other than where insanity is the question. The psychiatrist may help determine the competency or impeachability of a witness. He may also be asked to determine whether a defendant was competent at the time of a confession or whether there is a question of the admissibility of a confession.

There are many considerations when determining a person's mental state. The major types of disorders are

1. Mental retardation
2. Organic brain syndromes, including senile and pre-senile dementia, alcoholic psychosis, and others of similar nature
3. Psychosis not attributable to physical conditions, including paranoid states, schizophrenia, and affective psychosis
4. Neurosis
5. Personality disorders, including alcoholism, drug dependence, and sexual deviations

Mental retardation may be the result of infection or brain injury. It can also be congenital, when arrested brain development occurs due to a defect in the person's physiologic or biologic system.

The common element in organic brain syndromes is a structural or physical defect or disease. Among the types of organic brain syndromes are those related to the hardening of the arteries, often found in the aged and in syphilis of the brain. This syndrome may also occur following an infection of the brain (encephalitis) or from a virus. Other causes of the organic brain syndrome include multiple sclerosis and brain tumors. Brain tumors can cause bizarre behavior, which may result in the death of a person as a consequence of rage, causing a fatal accident. Organic brain syndrome is associated with alcohol withdrawal in a chronic alcoholic, referred to as delirium tremens. Other chemical substances, including hallucinogens, may produce psychoses resulting in death. There is growing evidence of a chemical (biological, physiological) basis for illnesses such as schizophrenia, affective psychosis, and paranoia; however, research is still in experimental stages.

The Freudian description of functional mental disease considers the complex interplay of environmental, acquired, and instinctual forces that interact with the adaptive and defensive forces of the subconscious mind. The schizophrenic, for instance, is unable to conceive reality, build relationships, or fashion concepts. There may be delusions and hallucinations, and the person's relationships to humans may be lost.

Affective psychosis includes manic depressive illness in which mood swings, illusions, delusions, and hallucinations, precipitated by events that ordinarily would have little effect on a person, are manifested. In the manic phase the person usually shows hyperactivity, optimism, impulsiveness, over-talkativeness, distractibility, irritability, over-interest, and sexual promiscuity. In the depressant state everything looks bleak, the individual is withdrawn, and physical activity slows down.

The paranoid state, a subcategory of functional psychosis, is thought to be rare. In this state, combinations of hallucinations, delusions of grandeur, and persecution problems exist, in which the person feels that "the world is against him."

Neuroses present consistent, recurring anxiety and constant maladjustments, often from very early in life, which may handicap a person attempting to maintain a normal life pattern.

Many types of personality disorders hamper social adjustments. The antisocial personality, a characteristic of the criminal population, is shown by such people's inability to conform to prevailing social norms. Such people cannot form lasting or satisfying relationships. A charming personality; difficulty in relating to people; repeated improper conduct; involvement in alcoholism, drug abuse, or sexual deviations; and distortion of truth are also seen in people with antisocial personalities.

The Psychiatrist's Examination

The need for psychiatric examination is usually determined by the attorneys in cases where a question of insanity arises. In such cases the psychiatrist should be consulted as soon as possible. Competency questions should be raised before the hearing.

The psychiatric examination should be thorough and include a physical examination. The opinion concerning the state of the accused's mind is highly important, and a prolonged, complete examination is essential. The physical examination should give insight into the general appearance, behavior, and emotional state of the person. Sedation or tranquilization of the person at the time of the examination should be noted since sedation can obscure the person's customary behavior. Family background is also very important, because a history of mental illness can be a crucial factor. The personnel record of the person may show instability or behavior patterns characteristic of specific psychiatric disorders. The inability to get along with people may be reflected in poor work or military or police records. As a child the subject may have been exposed to physical or sexual abuse, and such a background could seriously affect them. The physical examination will indicate the standard routine evidences of variation from the normal in the morphology as well as the physiology of the person. Any abnormality of appearance such as ugliness, enlarged nose, ears, or crossed eyes, or traumatic facial disfigurement could be contributing factors to behavioral problems.

Psychological testing — including intelligence tests; psychomotor tests for attention, memory, and conceptual thinking; and personality tests — are used to detect the presence of psychopathologic characteristics. One such test, the Rohrschach, is a projective test that attempts to determine the subject's inner attitudes, fantasies, and defenses. The results of the testing and the clinical examination are summarized into an opinion of the person's mental state; the psychiatrist may also make a recommendation and a prognosis in his report. In addition to the standard forms of testing, the psychiatrist may use narcoanalysis or sodium pentothal in an attempt to reach into the levels of inner consciousness, but this is rarely done in modern times, and hypnosis is held to be unscientific in most courts.

An additional responsibility of the psychiatrist in testing the competency or credibility of a witness by psychiatric examination is to determine if the person suffers from any mental illness that may render them incapable of accurately describing occurrences. A competent witness must be sane both at the time he testifies and at the time of the events about which he or she is called upon to testify. Those who are unable to relate the findings intellectually or to understand the obligation of an oath are also to be considered incompetent witnesses. The psychiatrist's testimony in these cases is important because deep-seated personality disorders may be discerned only by an expert. The paranoid psychotic may appear normal to a lay person. Subjects may also malinger illness to seek relief from legal interventions.

Evaluation of witness competency may be determined before the trial in a pre-hearing examination. The psychiatrist and the prosecuting and defense attorneys may find this evaluation very important if the witness is known to be a drug addict or an alcoholic or is mentally disturbed. In some instances the court may refuse to allow an independent psychiatric examination of the witness, but in other courts a psychiatrist is permitted to remain in the courtroom while the opposition witness testifies. He may then be called to present his opinion of the witness' credibility based on courtroom observation. This was done in the Alger Hiss case, when Whittaker Chambers' testimony was evaluated based on a psychiatric opinion. Examinations of this type, however, are of questionable value.

Psychiatric testimony may be useful in determining the degree to which a confession was volunteered. In this instance, the psychiatrist may determine whether an accused made a knowledgeable or intelligent waiver of his basic rights. The psychiatrist may also be used to negate the accused's capacity to form the requisite intent, which is a necessary element in the conviction for a crime.

Locating the Expert

Locating an expert psychiatrist may be difficult, as not all psychiatrists are experienced or interested in dealing with court and criminal cases. Possible resources for locating an expert psychiatrist are state hospitals or state and community psychiatric organizations. These should be able to find the psychiatrist most qualified to handle a particular situation. Numerous organizations of forensic psychiatry (for example, the psychiatry section of the American Academy of Forensic Sciences) can help. Other organizations devoted to "psychiatry and the law" or to "medicine and the law" are important resources. In most communities, attorneys are aware which psychiatrists are defense or prosecution oriented.

Special Problems Involving the Forensic Psychiatrist

Forensic psychiatrists face special problems that do not concern other forensic experts. Some aspects of the psychiatrist's involvement include the following:

- The right of a patient to treatment
- The right of the patient to refuse treatment
- Confidentiality
- Privileged communication
- Informed consent
- Commitment procedures
- Legal regulation of hospital patient care
- Evaluation of the degree of dangerousness
- The prediction of violence
- The general rights of the patient

Currently, a major problem is the patient's right to treatment. Legal decisions have established that the need for treatment in psychiatric cases is a right. Lack of an insurance provision for mental illness in the Medicare and Medicaid statutes has resulted in a recent consideration to have mentally ill patients returned to community life after an acute episode and after stabilization instead of to the standard mental health facility or hospital. A recent federal court decision has determined that mental institutions are obligated to provide treatment for patients confined by the commitment process.

Problems often arise in the treatment and management of patients in institutions. Among these problems is the psychiatrist's vulnerability to litigations due to complications, injury, or death of the patient associated with electroconvulsive therapy, inadequate or negligent psychotherapy, illegal or involuntary hospitalization, and responsibility for suicide. The commitment of a patient must be based on the presence of a mental illness and a degree of dangerousness to himself and others beyond reasonable doubt.

Other Problems

The general psychiatrist and the forensic psychiatrist may encounter drug abuse. Their concern is the management of drug addiction and abuse. The recent nonmedical trend to place management in the hands of former addicts has resulted from the reluctance of mental-health professionals to adequately involve themselves in treating drug and alcohol users. Despite a profound need for the integration of drug, alcohol, and mental health programs, few well-integrated programs have been instituted although this is changing with the establishment of corporate hospitals specializing in addictionology. Addictionology is also recognized as a medical specialty with guidelines for specific Board Certification. Odyssey House, a private organization operating in several American and Australian cities, handles drug abuse problems by a live-in approach in which rehabilitated drug users help the others. This approach was originated by psychiatrist Dr. Judianne Densen-Gerber. Some of the other approaches have been less successful, and in many respects drug abuse treatment and management depends on individual efforts and community financial resources.

Responsibility in reporting a potential danger poses a problem. The killer of a female student at the University of California at Berkeley had been treated by the university's mental health service. The assailant threatened the life of the victim in statements to a staff psychologist. These threats were reported by letter to the medical authorities and campus police, but a physician caused the letter to be withdrawn. The murder took place two months later and brought about a civil suit by the victim's family against the university; the court ruled for the family. This was a landmark decision.

Child abuse and pornography is another area of interest for the psychiatrist. The use of children in pornographic activities has been a concern of Odyssey House and of Dr. Judianne Densen-Gerber. Those on trial for these offenses generally need psychiatric evaluation, but many have personality disorders and exploit children for personal, financial gain.

Terrorism, hostage taking, and skyjacking are also areas of concern to psychiatrists. The actual management of such cases is an important responsibility for advisors to law enforcement authorities. The solitary skyjacker is thought to be a person who is really trying to commit suicide; unable to complete the act, he depends on others to do it by exposing himself to the hazards of a skyjacking.[4] Political skyjacking is another matter however, and much more complicated.

In terrorist skyjacking cases, the psychiatrist may give guidance to law-enforcement authorities as to handling specific situations. Psychiatrist Dr. Frederick Hacker has been called on to handle many major cases, including the Hearst case and the OPEC hostage situation in Vienna;[5] his guidance has been helpful to authorities.[6,19,21,22]

The psychiatrist may also support police activities by screening candidates for police recruitment. This work tends to eliminate applicants with potentially dangerous psychiatric problems or personality disorders.

Centers of suicidology, or the study of suicide, have been developed by Dr. Robert E. Litman, Dr. Edwin S. Shneidman, Dr. Norman L. Farberow, and Dr. Norman Tabachnick.[6] Important advances in suicide prevention have been due to meetings and communication among experts and lay persons involved in mental health, and a greater understanding of suicide has been developed. The psychiatrist may also be called upon in cases of malpractice involving fellow psychiatrists accused of incompetence or negligence.

The psychiatrist may be called on to evaluate the behavior of historically important individuals. Considerable study of the behavioral patterns of Adolf Hitler has been done; in America, Germany, and Israel, many psychiatrists have handled the aftermath of the Nazi persecution of Jews, and the severe mental injuries suffered by survivors. A study involving the deaths in Jonestown, Guyana, of members of the People's Temple cult. A psychiatric appraisal of the Jonestown situation was carried out by a native of Guyana presently teaching at a U.S. medical school. With a knowledge of the country and the background of the cult, he was able to evaluate the mass suicide. This understanding may lead to better knowledge of similar organizations and the prevention of future tragedies.

Summary

The forensic psychiatrist has the important and expanding role of providing expertise in behavioral evaluation of criminals and noncriminals alike, psychiatric patients, and persons involved in crimes and disasters. The psychiatrist's expertise is a major supporting component of the forensic sciences.

An increasingly important area of civil litigation is the psychiatrists involvement in:

1. Personal injury litigations following industrial accidents or aircraft accidents. In such cases, the psychiatrist attempts to assess the degree of emotional damage sustained by the victim and relate the potential cost of anticipated treatment and disability.[7-10]
2. Sexual harassment lawsuits. The psychiatrist determines the extent of psychological injury sustained by the victim and the future anticipated disability, if any.[14-18]
3. Child sexual molestation and abuse.[1,5]
4. Workmans compensation injuries of a psychological nature such as the development of post-traumatic stress disorder following the witnessing of an industrial tragedy.[11-13]

References

1. Freedman, L., Forensic psychiatry. In *Comprehensive Text of Psychiatry*, Williams & Wilkins, Baltimore, MD, 1967.
2. Litman, R., McCurphy, T., Shneidman, E., Farberow, N., and Tabachnick, N., Investigations of equivocal suicides, *J.A.M.A.*, 184:12, 102, 1963.
3. Moenssens, A., Moses, E., and Inbau, F., Psychiatry, psychology, neurology. In *Scientific Evidence in Criminal Cases*, Foundation Press, Mineola, NY, 1973.
4. Hubbard, D., *The Skyjacker*, Macmillan, New York, 1971.
5. Hacker, F., Crusaders, *Criminals and Crazies*, W.W. Norton, New York, 1976.
6. Farberow, N. and Shneidman, E., *The Cry for Help*, McGraw-Hill, New York, 1961.
7. Wilson, Paul R., Stranger Child-Murder: Issues related to causes and controls. International Journal of Offender Therapy and Comparative Criminology, Volume 31, No. 1, Pages 49–59, 1991. Douglas, J.E. and Burgess, A.E., 1986: *Criminal Profiling: A Viable Investigative Tool Against Violent Crime*. FBI Law Enforcement Bulletin December 1986, Pages 9–13.
8. Bromberg, Norbert, Hitler's Childhood International, *Review of Psychoanalysis*, 1994, Pages 227–244.

9. *The Split Reality of Murder,* FBI Law Enforcement Bulletin 1985, August, Pages 7–11.

10. Elliott F., The Relation of Structural Disorders of the Brain to Abnormal Aggressive Behavior, *Biological Psychiatry,* Elsevier Science Publishing Company, Inc. 1986.

11. Turco, R., Child Serial Murder, The Forum of the American Academy of Psychoanalysis, Volume 37, No. 3, Fall 1993.

12. DeGeneste, Henry et al., Transit Terrorism, *The Police Chief,* February 1996, Pages 44–49.

13. Enelow, Allen, Psychiatric Disorders and Work Function, *Journal of Psychiatric Annals,* 21:1, January 1991. Pages 27-35.

14. Whyman, Andrew D. and Underwood, Robert, J., The Psychiatric Examination in Workers' Compensation, *Psychiatric Annals,* 21:1, January 1991.

15. Panzarella, The Nature of Work, Job Loss, and the Diagnostic Complexities of the Psychologically Injured Worker, *Psychiatric Annals,* 21:1, January 1991. Pages 10-15.

16. Shorter, Edward, From Paralysis to Fatigue, McMillan, Inc., New York, 1992.

17. Wessely, Simon, "Chronic Fatigue and Myalgia Syndromes" in the book *Psychological Disorders in General Medical Settings.* Berne: Hografe & Huber, 1990.

18. Turco, Ronald, The Fibromyalgias: Somatizing Disorders. *Bulletin of the American Academy of Psychoanalytic Physicians,* December 1994, Issue No. 2.

19. Feldman, Marc and Ford, Charles V., *Patient or Pretender,* John Wiley & Sons, Inc. New York, 1994.

20. Simon, Robert, I., The Credible Forensic Psychiatric Evaluation in Sexual Harassment, *Journal of Psychiatric Annals,* Volume 26, No. 3, March 1996.

21. Malmquist, M.D. and Carl, P., The Use and Misuse of Psychiatry in Sexual Harassment Cases, *Psychiatric Annals,* Volume 26, No. 3, 1996.

22. American Academy of Psychiatry and Law. Ethical Guidelines for the Practice of Forensic Psychiatry, Section IV, Adapted May 1987, Revised October 1989 and 1991.

23. Rosenblatt, E.A., Emerging Concepts of Woman's Development: Implications for Psychotherapy, *Psychiatric Clinics of North America,* 1995; 18:95-106.

24. MacKinnon, C., *Sexual Harassment of Working Women,* New Haven, Connecticut, Yale University Press, 1979.

25. Turco, R.N., Psychiatric Contributions to the Understanding of International Terrorism, *International Journal of Offender Therapy in Comparative Criminology,* 1987, Vol. 31, No. 2.

26. Liebert, J., Contributions of Psychiatric Consultation in the Investigation of Serial Murder, *International Journal of Offender Therapy in Comparative Criminology,* 187–188, 1986.

27. Post, J., Notes on a Psychodynamic Theory of Terrorist Behavior. Terrorism: *International Journal of Offender Therapy Comparative Criminology,* Volume 7, No. 3, 1984.

28. Feldman, Theodore, B. and Johnson, Philip, W., The Application of Psychotherapeutic and Self Psychology Priniciples to Hostage Negotiations, *Journal of American Academy of Psychoanalysis,* 23(2), 207-221, 1995.

29. Turco, Ronald, Psychological Profiling, *International Journal of Offender Therapy in Comparative Criminology,* Pages 147–154, Sept. 1990, Vol. 34, No. 2.

Scientific Evidence in Court

5

WILLIAM G. ECKERT
RONALD K. WRIGHT

The culmination of the collecting, cataloging, photographing, investigating, and testing of scientific evidence is its presentation to the trier of fact in court. In the English-American system of law, scientific evidence is thought of as somewhat novel, even though the use of such evidence dates back to the colonial period in the United States.[1] In this chapter we will review briefly the organization of courts in the American system of justice and trace the method by which scientific evidence is admitted into evidence.

Types of Courts: Equitable, Admiralty, Law, Coroner, Grand Jury, State and Federal

To understand evidence and its use in court, it is first necessary to understand differences in types of courts. In England there were two major court systems, equitable and legal, with the rather late development of a third, the admiralty courts. In the United States, these three courts have merged. The coroner court remains in those state jurisdictions which have retained the coroner system. Grand jury courts remain in both the federal and state systems.

Equitable courts come from an ecclesiastic tradition. In England these were the courts of the church. The courts had powers of injunction and mandamus. They could order persons to stop doing what they were doing (injunction) or force them to do what they were not doing (mandamus). The equitable courts were generally maintained after the American Revolution in the United States, but were non-ecclesiastic because of the secular nature of the governments of the United States. In time, states merged the equitable courts with legal courts. The federal government never had separate equitable courts. Today the largest remaining area of strictly equitable court activity is in divorce actions which are always equitable. In equitable courts the trier of fact is the judge sitting without a jury. Because the equitable courts did not have juries before the American Revolution, equitable courts

0-8493-8101-0/97/$0.00+$.50
© 1997 by CRC Press, Inc.

do not have juries today. We will see later in this chapter how this alters the presentation of scientific evidence because of the fear that the jury will be contaminated by being supplied with certain improper information. If there is no jury, there is less of a fear that the judge sitting as the trier of fact will be so easily swayed by improper information.

Admiralty courts were established in England as a separate system, primarily to support the ocean-going trade which developed during the mid- to late-16th century. The courts of law (or common law as it is often called) were deemed too tradition bound and rule ridden to allow easy resolution of the disputes which arose in ocean-going international trade. Thus the courts of admiralty were established, again without juries, as juries were thought to lack the sophistication to understand these novel and complicated issues. Following the American Revolution, the federal court system assumed the role of the admiralty courts in England, retaining the judge as the sole trier of fact.

Courts of common law were the courts dealing with citizen disputes and matters brought by the King of England against his subjects who had disturbed the King's peace. The former actions were considered civil and the latter were considered criminal. These courts were always secular and at least from the 11th century on relied upon juries to hear the evidence and make a decision concerning the questions of fact raised by the parties to the litigation.

Following the American Revolution in the United States, another division of courts occurred with the creation of the federal court system. The U.S. Constitution established the judiciary as a completely independent branch of the government.[2] Further, it established that the jurisdiction of the court would be cases and controversies arising in law and equity, clearly merging the two courts. Judicial administration was an important part of the Bill of Rights, the first ten amendments to the Federal Constitution which were appended to the originally ratified constitution. Of the ten amendments, five dealt explicitly with the courts, with the fourth, fifth, sixth, and eighth dealing with criminal matters as opposed to suits in common law.

Types of Courts of Law: Civil and Criminal

The constitutional distinction between common-law suits and criminal matters reflected an increasing appreciation of differences between civil and criminal cases. This distinction has become increasingly codified, driven in large part because of the criminal matters included within the first ten amendments of the U.S. Constitution. Initially, the rights enumerated in the U.S. Constitution to the defendant in criminal matters, such as the right to counsel, the right to not testify, the right to be secure from unreasonable searches and seizures, and the right to confront witnesses, applied only to the federal criminal courts. Although state constitutions often contained language similar to that in the U.S. Constitution, the U.S. Constitution's guarantee of rights could not be applied to the states. Only those rights found in the individual state constitutions as interpreted by the individual state courts were applicable to criminal actions in state court. However, the 14th amendment to the U.S. Constitution asserted that the states could not deny due process to their citizens. In *Mapp v. Ohio*,[3] decided in 1961, the U.S. Supreme Court held that the right against unreasonable searches and seizures was applicable to the states and that illegally obtained evidence would be excluded from the trial. The court arrived at this conclusion because "due process" was interpreted to include exclusion of illegally seized evidence, and the 14th amendment made this right applicable to the states.

In *Miranda v. Arizona*,[4] the court held that the accused must be advised of the right against self-incrimination, the right to assistance of counsel, and the right to have counsel provided by the state if the defendant is indigent.

These defendant rights have had a significant impact upon the introduction of scientific evidence in criminal cases. Indeed, the collection of physical evidence is a seizure and therefore if the physical evidence belongs to the defendant or is contained within property controlled by the defendant, then either consent must be obtained from the defendant or a properly executed search warrant must be obtained before the item may be used as the basis of evidence.

Other matters which impact the introduction of scientific evidence include the concept of the "Fruit of the Poisonous Tree" first developed in *Wong Sun v. United States*.[5] Basically, the courts have held that illegally obtained information, whether by illegal interrogations, illegal searches and seizures, or illegal arrests which then results in the finding of legally obtained evidence, shall result in the exclusion of the derivative evidence.

In civil matters, those involving the potential loss by the defendant of property but not of liberty or life, the requirements for due process have been interpreted much more loosely. Thus in civil litigation, the requirements of unanimous jury verdicts, right to confront witnesses, exclusion of tainted evidence, and myriad other matters are not applicable.

Coroners and their courts are a fourth distinct court system in the United States, or at least in some parts of the United States. The coroner represents the vestige of Roman law which was introduced to England during the Norman period. The coroner is a judicial officer, operating from the administrative branch, who applies an inquisitional system of justice which is the norm in French-, Spanish-, and German-speaking countries, but which is unusual in English-speaking ones. Because of its non-adversarial, inquisitional nature, coroner's courts lack evidentiary rules.

There is one other inquisitional institution other than the coroner and that is the grand jury. The grand jury must return an indictment before federal criminal charges may be brought, and in most state courts, the grand jury must return an indictment for capital crimes. Lesser charges generally do not require the grand jury to indict before a prosecution may be brought. The grand jury operates under the judicial branch of government, but is inquisitional. Thus there are no evidentiary rules for the grand jury as well.

Evidence — Testamentary and Demonstrative or Physical

Having reviewed the distinctions between various courts and civil and criminal law, we may now turn our attention to evidence in general. Evidence is anything perceptible to the five senses when submitted to court or jury, if competent.[6] Historically, and generally, the jury has heard evidence as opposed to seeing, touching, smelling, or tasting. However, all senses may be employed. Thus substantive items may become evidence, although generally most information is conveyed by the testimony of witnesses, and in the case of criminal trials, this testimony must be live to comply with the confrontational clause of the sixth amendment.

Testamentary evidence is what the witness says. Testamentary evidence is absolutely required to prove any contested fact in the trial. A witness must be sworn to tell the truth. Then using nonleading questions, propounded by the side calling the witness, the witness may say what he or she saw, heard, touched, smelled, or tasted. This is called direct testimony. The opposing side may then ask leading questions, ones which contain within the question the expected answer such as, "Isn't it true that…," to try to impeach the testimony given in direct testimony. This is called cross-examination.

Demonstrative or physical evidence is something which may be seen, heard, touched, smelled, or tasted by the jury itself. It is necessary that the physical evidence be introduced by a person who is presenting testamentary evidence. Physical evidence cannot be introduced without a testamentary witness. Thus physical evidence is always derivative of some sort of testimony.

Evidence is presented by direct examination by the attorney calling the witness. Direct examination must include questions which do not supply the answer to question in the question. "What, if anything, did you do next?" is a perfect nonleading question to ask during direct examination. "Did you pick up the gun?" is an example of an impermissible leading question on direct.

Following direct examination, the attorney for the other party may ask questions on cross-examination. During cross-examination leading questions are permissible and indeed are expected. There is a limit to leading questions, however. "Have you stopped beating your spouse?" is just such an impermissible question. If the witness had not been beating his or her spouse, both yes and no are improper answers. Generally, the attorney calling the witness will object to this sort of question. It is also proper for the witness to give a nonresponsive answer by saying, "I have never beaten my spouse." Good attorneys are adept at cloaking the spouse beating question in difficult-to-recognize formats.

Relevance, Materiality, Credibility, Competence

Before evidence may be presented to the trier of fact, a threshold matter concerns the relevance, materiality, credibility, and competence of the evidence. These are threshold matters which the judge may be asked to rule upon either as pretrial motions or by objection after the witness is called. As with everything having to do with trials, rights are not self-executing. A party may call an incompetent, incredible, immaterial, and irrelevant witness and if the other side fails to object by motion or by timely objection, then the evidence will come in. In the U.S. system of justice, the judge generally is not expected to limit testimony or the introduction of physical evidence unless asked.

Relevance and materiality have to do with whether the testimony or physical evidence shall assist the trier of fact to make a decision concerning the issues in the litigation. These questions are always dependent upon the facts and circumstances of a particular trial. To explain, let us use as an example a criminal trial where the state is bringing charges of murder. The defendant has denied all of the elements of the murder charge. The state wishes to call a witness who will testify concerning the television programs which were on a certain channel on the day of the murder. On its face, it seems difficult to understand how telling the jury what was on television is relevant to the elements of murder. Thus the defense may object to the testimony on the grounds that it is irrelevant and immaterial to any issues in the trial. It is then up to the state to explain to the judge that subsequent witnesses will show that the victim was in the habit of watching a certain program, and at all other times had the television set off, and that when the body was found, the television was on — this then having an important implication as to the time of the attack which was at issue. The judge may admit the evidence presented by the first witness, pending the second testimony making the television testimony relevant. The judge may make the state call the habit witness first and then call the television witness. If the judge allows the testimony of the first witness and then subsequent testimony fails to make the television witness's testimony relevant and material, then the testimony may be stricken from the record and the jury instructed to disregard any of the testimony.

The matters of credibility and competence have to do with more matters of degree than of inadmissibility in modern courts. Historically, only adult males were considered competent to testify, hence the word testify is derived from the same root as testes, the male reproductive organs. Absence of testes made for incompetence to testify. In an effort to present the trier of fact with as much relevant and material information as possible, the threshold question as to credibility and competence usually arises in fact witness testimony in the case of very young children or the severely retarded or if the witness was not in a position to perceive anything concerning the place and event at issue.

Relevance and materiality, and to a lesser extent credibility and competence, are threshold matters and must be established by answers to preliminary questions of the witness. These are predicate questions which establish the relevance and materiality and credibility and competence of the witness. For instance, asking a witness his or her name, and then asking, "Did you see the defendant strike Mr. Jones?", should have the other side objecting that the question is improper because it lacks the proper predicate. These predicate questions must first be asked to show that the witness can see, that the witness was at the place of the event at the time of the event, and that the witness knew who Mr. Jones was or came to know his name. All of these questions are required to lay the predicate for the question concerning the battery which the witness observed.

On this question of competence to testify, or of matters of materiality as well, the attorney opposing the introduction of the evidence may ask for *voir dire* of the witness out of the presence of the jury. The phrase means "speak the truth" and is preliminary questioning whereby an inquiry may be made into any of the objections to allowing the witness to testify. At that time, the opposing attorney can move the court to exclude the witness.

Types of Testamentary Witnesses

Fact Witnesses

Generally, witnesses may only testify concerning what they themselves experienced by the operation of their five senses and their current recollection. Testimony concerning their opinion of what they observed, or more impossible their opinion based upon the observations of others, is not allowed. Clearly there is no bright line between opinion and observation. Indeed, even the use of the term opinion may not mean the testimony is opinion testimony. For instance, asking the question, "In your opinion was it raining at that time, if you could tell?", is actually a question which calls for direct observation.

The question, although unartful, is permissible from a fact witness and should be allowed by the judge. Again, in trial, any question is allowable if not objected to by the other side. Generally, a question of a fact witness containing the word opinion will prompt an objection by the other side.

The distinction between fact and opinion may become even more obscure in questions dealing with more complex observations. The question, "Was the car moving or not?", would seem to be completely proper question of a fact witness. However, "How fast was the car moving, if it was moving?", is a closer question, although most courts have recognized that estimating speed from direct observation of movement over time seems to be a direct observation of the moving vehicle. On the other hand, estimating the speed of a vehicle from the length of the skid marks would seem clearly to be testimony which requires an expert.

Expert Witnesses

An expert is a person who by training, education, experience, or a combination is able to assist the trier of fact by offering opinion testimony concerning matters in dispute. The same rules of materiality and relevance apply to the expert witness as to the fact witness.

Many times a person who is involved in testifying concerning scientific evidence is both a fact and expert witness. Some of the information may have been obtained by direct observation and then from direct observation opinion testimony is made. For example, if an investigator actually measured the length of the skid marks in an accident, he or she may testify to the length, obviously after the proper predicate questions are asked. At this time, the attorney may want to ask the question as to how fast the car was traveling based upon the length of the skid mark. This is clearly expert testimony which may be given only by an expert.

The preliminary matters which must be obtained from an expert witness are the training, education, and experience that the expert has. With experienced and well-trained experts, the other side may concede that the expert is an expert, thereby saving the court and jury's time, as well as, of course, depriving them of learning how qualified the expert is. Generally, the side calling the expert will request to be allowed to go into the expert's background, and at some point the judge will be asked to rule whether the witness is an expert. If the judge decides that the witness is an expert, then questions which are relevant and material to the issues before the court and which are within the expertise of the witness are allowed which require an opinion, and which are based upon observations which were not directly made by the witness, but are presented as hypothetical questions.

Hypothetical Questions

Experts in the field of scientific evidence often did not make the observations which are required to arrive at opinions concerning matters which are relevant and material to the trier of fact. Let us return to the motor vehicle collision again. One of the parties has called an expert in accident reconstruction who, if allowed, will testify that the speed of the automobile involved was 80 miles per hour based upon the skid mark length and an examination of photographs taken of the vehicle following the crash. The expert did not measure the skid marks nor make the photographs. The predicate questions here will concern the reliability of the science of kinetics and an explanation that if one knows the mass of a vehicle, the coefficient of friction which is created at the time of locking up the vehicles tires on the type of roadway involved, and the collision velocity at the time of contact which can be estimated from the static deformation of the vehicle, then the speed at the moment the brakes were applied may be estimated. All of the above being established, the witness would also be asked if the amount of crush damage may be ascertained from examination of photographs and if this is routinely done by experts in the field. Assuming the photographs have been properly introduced by another witness, then the expert may be properly asked a hypothetical question. The hypothetical question should track the evidence which has been or will be presented at trial by the fact witnesses concerning the road conditions, the road surface condition, the deviation from horizontal of the road, the temperature of the air, the tire treads, the brake examination, the length of the skid marks, the weight of the vehicle at the time of the accident, and any other matters which the expert feels relevant to his or her analysis. These facts used in the hypothetical must have been proved or will have to be proved prior to the conclusion of the attorney's part of the trial. If they are not, then the opinion testimony of the expert is subject to be stricken and the jury instructed to disregard it.

Cross-examination of an expert witness will often include hypothetical questions as well. However, the hypothetical presented by the cross-examining attorney will contain the facts that the attorney feels he or she may be able to prove. Again, hypothetical should not contain facts which have not or will not be proved. However, in the case of cross-examination questions, most judges allow greater leeway as to whether or not the factual elements must be proved. This often leads to confusion of the witness and the jury, which can be a legitimate object of cross-examination.

Physical or Demonstrative Evidence

A fact witness may introduce into evidence physical objects which are material, relevant, credible, and competent. In criminal trials such items as the weapon, or the drugs, or the bloody clothing are all subject to becoming physical evidence. The rules are essentially the same for physical as for testamentary evidence. However, physical evidence must meet materiality and relevance tests in its own way. Particularly with an item which is fungible, meaning a thing which cannot be differentiated upon physical characteristics alone, there must be predicate questions which link it explicitly with the events and issues concerning it in the trial.

This process is usually thought of as "chain of custody" or "chain of evidence". It is but one way, and the most commonly utilized way, of introducing physical evidence or of introducing results of testing done on physical evidence. Fact witnesses will have to be called who can show that there was an unbroken chain from the location of the item when it was first obtained, through whatever handling it received, until it was tested or was introduced as evidence or both. Breaking the chain, being unable to trace the location and condition, of the material generally will result in the testing and/or the introduction into evidence being disallowed. Again, the process is one of determining materiality and relevance. Obviously if there is more than a remote possibility that the item in question is not related to the issues in question, then it is immaterial and irrelevant. Again, the process may entail pretrial motions or *voir dire* to determine these threshold questions of admissibility.

One special type of physical evidence often used in criminal as well as in civil trials is photographic and videographic evidence. In cases where there is injury, and where the photographs show those injuries, then another test as well as those previously described is required. The materiality, relevance, and competence questions are generally handled by asking an eyewitness whether the photographs "truly" and accurately display the scene, body, car, or whatever as it was at the time of the crime, accident, event, or whatever. The next question is, "Would these photographs aid you in showing to the jury the scene, body, etc. which you witnessed?" These are leading questions, but generally allowed in direct. The first question satisfies competence; the second satisfies relevance. They may be asked in the alternative and they are no longer leading as in, "Do or do not these photographs ...?" Most jurisdictions have a third test to be considered by the judge. This is whether the photographs' inflammatory value exceeds their probative value. There is always a fear that in the case of injured persons that the shocking nature of injuries will cause such an emotional state in the jury that it will be incapable of rationally deciding the issues. With the current state of motion picture and television depictions of violence, these concerns have become lessened.

Hearsay

Finally, a word about hearsay. As a general rule, hearsay is inadmissible. Thus a question which will elicit hearsay is improper. The question, "And then what if anything did Mr. Smith say?", is on its face improper and will almost always prompt an objection from the attorney on the other side. The point of this exercise being that if Mr. Smith has something to say which is relevant and material, as well as competent, then Mr. Smith should be sworn in as a witness and asked direct questions and then be available for cross examination.

However, there are myriad exceptions to the hearsay rule. These are exceptions which because of convenience or need make the hearsay evidence necessary for the proper administration of justice.

The most common exception to the hearsay rule is the confession in criminal cases. A confession is hearsay. It was not made in court, after the witness had been sworn, with the opportunity for direct and cross-examination. Thus it is inadmissible, except if it is within an exception to the hearsay rule. Such an exception is that admissions against penal interest are exceptions to the hearsay rule. Thus, if the person has said things which implicate him in a crime, then they are admissible hearsay.

There are at least 40 exceptions to the hearsay rule. Thus although hearsay is not allowable by the general rule, often an exception can be found which allows hearsay to come into evidence.

Competence

A special test for competence is required with scientific evidence. The question is whether the science or the scientific tests employed are of such a level of validity as to be allowed into evidence. Historically the test was whether the science was "generally accepted" as being valid. This test of "general acceptance" was first enunciated in 1923 in *Frye v. United States of America,* a criminal case in which the United States wished to introduce polygraph evidence.[7] Evidence of validity included published reports in peer-reviewed journals. In rapidly advancing fields such as so-called "DNA testing", the delay in publication often threatened to limit truly valid science from trial. The so-called "Frye test," at least in federal court, has been changed allowing rapidly advancing science to be introduced. In *Daubert v. Merrell Dow Pharmaceuticals,* the U.S. Supreme Court introduced a four-part test to replace Frye:

1. Whether the type of evidence can be and has been tested by scientific methodology
2. Whether the underlying theory or techniques has been subjected to peer review and has been published in the professional literature (although this is not a *sine qua non*)
3. How reliable the results are in terms of potential error rate
4. General acceptance (the old Frye test) can have a bearing on the inquiry[8]

Role of the Judge

The role of the judge in U.S. courts, is to see that the issues to be tried are as limited as possible, to preside over the trial, to limit evidence to the issues that are to be tried, and to instruct the jury on what they should consider in arriving at decision concerning the issues at trial.

The judge rules on pretrial motions which limit and attempt to simplify the evidence. In trial, the primary job of the judge is to rule upon motions presented before questioning is begun and upon objections made to questions after they are asked. The witness should listen to each question asked and make certain that the opposing attorney has had the opportunity to object to the question prior to answering. Failure to do so will generally lead to an admonition from the judge and at worst could lead to a mistrial, if impermissible information is presented to the jury.

Objections may be made to answers as well as questions. The most common is that the answer is unresponsive to the question asked. Occasionally, the answer may contain information which the attorney feels is impermissible to be known by the jury. Under such circumstances, the attorney may make a motion to strike the testimony and will often move for a mistrial.

Summary

Scientific evidence is demonstrative and testamentary information using the techniques of science to assist the trier of fact to decide which of two or more theories explain what, why, who, and when something happened which is the object of contention in a trial.

The evidence must be relevant and material. It must be probative and its introduction should be limited to situations where the probative value exceeds the inflammatory nature if any. Scientific evidence is introduced by one side or the other in its case in chief by direct testimony. Hypothetical questions may be used by the attorney of either party to clarify or alternatively impeach the scientific evidence. Although historically novel testing was limited from introduction, the majority of courts now allow science on the border of invention. Expert testimony is almost always required in presenting scientific evidence.

References

1. Howel, State Trials, 687 (1665); reference in Moenssens, A.A., J.E. Starrs, C.E. Henderson, and F.E. Inbau, *Scientific Evidence in Civil and Criminal Cases,* The Foundation Press, Westbury, NY, 1995.

2. United States Constitution, Article III.

3. Mapp v. Ohio, 367 US 643 (1961).

4. Miranda v. Arizona, 384 U.S. 436 (1966).

5. Wong Sun v. United States, 371 U.S. 471 (1963).

6. In re: Fischers' Estate, 47 Idaho 668.

7. Frye v. United States, 293 Fed. 1013, 1014 (DC Cir 1923).

8. Daubert v. Merrell Dow Pharmaceuticals, 113 S.Ct 2786 (1993).

Legal Medicine and Jurisprudence

6

CYRIL H. WECHT

This chapter introduces the field of expertise in which the law and medical science interface: legal medicine. Enormous opportunities exist in this relatively little known but burgeoning scientific area. However, the sacrifices necessary to become an expert in legal medicine are considerable. To be truly qualified, a person must earn degrees in a scientific specialty and law. Once the person has obtained the requisite credentials, battle must be done with anachronistic political systems and methods of investigation in order to use the hard-learned modern techniques.

The picture is not, however, bleak. Substantial and satisfying rewards accrue to the successful practitioner. The medicolegal expert will be increasingly in the forefront as society grapples with the wide multiplicity of new problems encompassed by this discipline. Only with the combined knowledge of the medical and legal professions can these problems be solved.

Investigative Systems

To one degree or another, all civilizations have recognized the need for medicolegal investigation in their civil and criminal justice systems. *The Code of Hammurabi*, written in 2200 B.C., dealt in part with what is now called medical malpractice.[1] The ancient Egyptians developed a system to determine whether a death was natural and what its causes were. The Chinese compiled a volume titled *Hsi Yuan Lu* (the washing away of the wrong), describing different procedures for investigating suspicious deaths.[2]

In the Middle Ages, medicolegal investigation developed within two major systems. In continental Europe, medicolegal investigation always maintained itself free from political influence; objectivity and true expertise were maximized by the resultant autonomy of the discipline. By the eighteenth and nineteenth centuries, many European universities developed curricula in legal medicine.

0-8493-8101-0/97/$0.00+$.50
© 1997 by CRC Press, Inc.

In sharp contrast, the English system of medicolegal investigation was always an integral part of the political system. The office of coroner was established in 1194. Although initially not one of its functions, the investigation of death soon became a function of the coroner. For a time the duty was usurped by the justices of the peace but was reacquired in late nineteenth century. At that time the jurisdiction, which continues today, was first defined, and the coroner was to investigate the sudden, violent, or unnatural deaths and all deaths of prisoners.[3]

Exercising their early numerical superiority in the "new land", the English established the coroner system in the U.S. The heritage of being related to government naturally caused the coroner's position in the democratic U.S. to be an elected one. In many instances this has been unfortunate. Few jurisdictions have any requirement for this office. Therefore, a large number of elected coroners often have absolutely no legal or medical qualifications! Furthermore, some of the above-mentioned anachronisms can be attributed to political influence in coroner's positions. As in many areas where government is involved, the coroner's office is slow to change. By not adopting rapidly changing science and technology, coroners do not provide all the knowledge and services that modern forensic science can provide. This inherent inertia found in many elected coroner systems is compounded by the fact that even if lay coroners were so disposed, most of them simply lack the background to master existing technology, let alone emerging techniques.

Starting in Suffolk County in Massachusetts in 1877, and New York City in 1915, the antiquated, politically oriented coroner system has been slowly yielding to the more appropriate medical examiner system, which is patterned after the nonpolitical European systems of objective scientific investigation. Medical examiners are appointed rather than elected and must have certain professional qualifications. In fact, under most state laws modern medical examiner systems are professionally oriented nonpolitical offices, headed by board-certified forensic pathologists.

The *Model Medical Examiner's Act*, promulgated by the National Municipal League with the help of Dr. Richard Ford (then Medical Examiner of Suffolk County, Boston), described the role of the medical examiner. Jurisdiction is to be assumed in all cases of sudden, violent, suspicious, unexpected, unexplained, and medically unattended deaths. Medical examiners also assume jurisdiction in cases of perioperative deaths, fatalities occurring in industrial employment, all motor vehicular accidents, and all deaths arising from known, suspected, or alleged criminal acts.

It is truly a travesty of justice to allow so crucial a position to be staffed by people untrained in the complex and ever-expanding field of forensic pathology. Fully half of the elected coroners in the U.S. have no scientific background. Examining the earlier mentioned jurisdiction of medical examiners and even coroners, it becomes apparent just how important and complex medicolegal investigations can be. Two examples will illustrate the impact of a coroner's or a medical examiner's findings.

In December 1970, 38 coal miners died in an explosion in the Hyden Mine disaster in Leslie County, Kentucky. A physician at the scene of the accident determined that five of the miners survived the initial explosion and later succumbed to carbon monoxide poisoning. However, the physician's findings were never admitted into evidence because she was not called to testify. Instead, the findings of the Leslie County coroner were heard at the hearing conducted by the U.S. Bureau of Mines. The coroner, a funeral-home operator, listed all the deaths as resulting from the original explosion. The significance of the disparity between the physician's and the coroner's findings came out at the hearing: the mine's operators had not supplied their employees with adequate "self-rescuers", which are small gas masks that give the wearer about an hour's extra breathing time. Had the doctor's testimony been admitted, the mine operators may well have faced criminal sanctions for their failure.[4] Such testimony would have strongly indicated the propriety of an action in tort for wrongful death, pain and suffering of the trapped miners, and other civil damages.

A more famous example of the consequences of a poor medicolegal investigation occurred after the assassination of President Kennedy; in my opinion, a woefully inadequate autopsy was performed on the President's body, and the entire postmortem report is a textbook example of how not to conduct a medicolegal investigation.

It must be noted that simply changing the system from that of a coroner to a medical examiner does not guarantee expert service; nor should it be assumed that the coroner system precludes the highest grade of medicolegal investigation. Cuyahoga County in Ohio (Cleveland) and Allegheny County in Pennsylvania (Pittsburgh) are examples of well run medicolegal investigative units that still function as elected coroner's systems.

The thrust of the above discussion of coroner vs. medical examiner is that the coroner system offers less probability that the needed forensic experts will be provided. Causes of death have become as subtle and complex as society itself. Only a medically trained person has the expertise required to function competently in the position of either medical examiner or coroner. Going one necessary step further, the medical examiner/coroner must also be well versed in the law in order to determine the legal cause of death, as physical and legal causes of death do not always coincide. The best solution is a medical examiner system headed by a qualified forensic pathologist. The medical examiner should have broad authority to decide when he is to assume jurisdiction, rather than wait for another party to request his intervention as is common in coroner systems. The medical examiner, however, will be most effective if he retains the coroner's power to subpoena and swear in witnesses. He should also keep the procedure and legal power of the coroner's inquest as an aid to solving the complex problems with which he is faced.

Medicolegal Issues

A practitioner of legal medicine can expect exposure to a wide range of complex, fascinating, and intellectually challenging scientific issues. The number and variety of problems confronting legal medicine is growing all the time, and it is from this vibrancy that the medicolegal expert derives his greatest satisfaction.

He will find himself outside the laboratory dealing with the explosive and important contemporary bioethical issues: abortion, birth control, artificial insemination, sterilization, organ transplantation, environmental control, human research and experimentation, the definition of death, euthanasia (right-to-die; physician-assisted suicide) medical malpractice, health care delivery, public health and preventive medicine, industrial hazards, mental health, AIDS, and drug abuse.

These problems call for a cross-fertilization of ideas, programs, and solutions from the traditional academic disciplines and professions with which he is familiar. In addition, they demand a synthesis of opinions from the community at large in order to promulgate solutions that deal with the many social, moral, ethical, and religious concerns. It is the medicolegal expert who possesses the unique training and expertise to best coordinate the attack on these problems.

A plethora of legal and ethical questions arose with human heart transplants. In response, an interdisciplinary committee was established at Harvard University in 1969 to develop medicolegal ground rules to govern the transplant process. The rules have been overwhelmingly successful because they are based on sound medical concepts. The Uniform Anatomical Gift Act descended directly from these guidelines; within 2 years the Act was adopted by every jurisdiction in the country.

Similarly, seemingly overnight, the U.S. was confronted with a drug abuse problem of previously unimagined proportions. Through another cooperative effort, a variety of effective programs was developed to deal with this problem. While a great deal remains to be done in this area, once again the medicolegal practitioner is uniquely suited to deal with it in the preventive, curative, and rehabilitative stages.

Another sensitive, although less widely publicized, medicolegal issue is human experimentation. No doubt such work yields valuable information to scientists, physicians, and drug manufacturers; however, there is just as little doubt that it is attended by grave moral and legal dilemmas. In our society, there are considerations more basic than medical or scientific advancement, and these must not disappear behind a misguided quest for knowledge. Someone must balance the information to be gained against the legal, moral, and ethical considerations; unfortunately, experimentation gone wild is not unheard of.

In 1971, it was revealed that the U.S. Public Health Service was deliberately allowing 400 black men in Tuskegee, Alabama, to go untreated for diagnosed syphilis in order to study the disease's progression. Experimentation in Nazi concentration camps during World War II represents the extreme in loss of control; even if there had been an advance in knowledge in those experiments, it is painfully obvious that the circumstances were unconscionable. Experiments at the Hamburg State School and Hospital in Eastern Pennsylvania presented a less clear-cut imbalance of ethical and scientific considerations: up until 1973, mentally retarded children were injected with an experimental meningitis vaccine. Although the hospital had obtained a broad consent from the children's parents, the exact nature and inherent risks of the experiment were never disclosed. The consent hardly qualified as informed consent as recognized by the courts.[5]

Speculating that the information from such experiments might be useful, what are the legal, ethical, and moral ramifications vis-a-vis the subjects? What authority decrees that some persons are to be subjects so that others may benefit? Who will be tomorrow's subjects? Although some forms of human experimentation must continue, someone must deal with these questions and restrain science without stifling it. That someone is the medicolegal expert.

Manageable standards for environmental health must be promulgated. On the local level, how much pollution can we permit and still maintain a reasonable level of health? What is a "reasonable level of health"? Do certain levels of sulfur dioxide, aromatic hydrocarbons, particulate materials, and other potentially toxic substances result in identifiable morbidity and mortality when present over a prolonged period of time? The future health of much of the civilized world can hinge on the answers to these questions.

Industrial hazards are an area into which legal medicine has only recently ventured. With new manufacturing processes constantly being developed and new products being introduced, previously unknown health hazards are also appearing. The dangers of chromium, asbestos, beryllium, and silica dust are only now becoming fully understood. An autopsy performed by a skilled forensic pathologist, corroborated by scientific studies, may identify the toxic propensities of these and other industrial substances and lead to appropriate safety measures.

Medical malpractice is no doubt a most pressing and controversial problem today. It seriously hinders the development of positive interprofessional relationships between physicians and attorneys. It produces hostility, resentment, and anxiety in physicians. It has helped drive medical costs beyond realistic bounds. Here again, the medicolegal expert is needed right in the middle — both sides of a lawsuit need an expert conversant with medical procedures and results as well as their legal significance. In fact, in most jurisdictions medical malpractice is almost impossible to prove without expert testimony. The medicolegal expert also has a moral obligation in the area of medical malpractice. As a physician, he must take affirmative action to police his own ranks; he owes it to his profession and to the public. With his unique background the medicolegal expert must also contribute to other methods of reducing the costs of medical malpractice. Among the solutions being explored are arbitration panels, screening panels, "no fault" schemes, elimination of lay juries, limitations on contingency fees, and ceilings on awards.

Obviously, legal medicine has a growing and exciting vitality. Increasingly it takes the lead in dealing with many complex and current social problems. The practitioner can hope to derive great satisfaction from addressing and solving the issues mentioned.

The Forensic Expert

So far this chapter has referred only obliquely to the areas of specialty within forensic science; there are many. This section will describe several of these specialties, concluding with a discussion contrasting hospital and forensic pathology.

A forensic anthropologist attempts to determine biological and physical information about a deceased, such as age, sex, stature, race, and culture. Sources for such data are usually the complete or fragmented skeletal remains but may also include burned bodies and semiskeletal remains. Skilled forensic anthropologists can differentiate between postmortem changes and those that took place before death. These skills are often crucial in identifying mysterious remains and determining whether the death was caused by foul play.

Forensic odontologists compare antemortem dental records to present observations of a body's dental characteristics. The major significance of these studies is in identifying an otherwise unrecognizable body. Forensic odontology takes the general identification made by the forensic anthropologist, and specifies exactly who the body belongs to. This specialty comes into play primarily with burn victims and other bodies whose physical characteristics have been significantly altered.

Forensic toxicology deals with detecting and interpreting organic and toxic materials. A forensic toxicologist works with physicians, pathologists, and police in investigating suspicious deaths. He makes on-the-scene investigations to determine the source of a toxin, which in turns helps him identify the toxic material. New and rapidly growing areas of investigation for the forensic toxicologist are environmental pollution, industrial toxins, chemical and radiologic hazards, and drug and alcohol abuse. His perspective in analyzing a complex cause-of-death case is invaluable. For instance, had the earlier-mentioned U.S. Bureau of Mines investigation of the Hyden, Kentucky, mine disaster included a toxicology report, a different conclusion as to the cause of death of several miners would have been reached, since the blood of at least five contained lethal levels of carbon monoxide.

Within such a wide range of expertise the forensic toxicologist assumes the role of monitoring our environment and technology and educating the public on these areas.

To date, of all the forensic specialties only forensic pathology and forensic psychiatry are consistently and uniformly accorded professional recognition by the courts. In fact, forensic psychiatrists are often compelled by courts to wend their way through "gray" semantic and legal areas with respect to criminal responsibility, ability to stand trial, and danger of mental illness. Perhaps the most difficult concept with which they must deal is the defense of insanity in criminal cases. Several jurisdictions in the U.S. adhere to an English definition of insanity formulated in 1843; the M'Naughten definition states, "It must be clearly proved that, at the time of the committing of the act, the party accused was laboring under such a defect of reason, from a disease of the mind, as not to know the nature and quality of the act he was doing, or if he did know it, that he did not know he was doing what was wrong."[7] Only if each component of this definition can be proved (or disproved, from the prosecution's point of view) will the defense of insanity be successfully raised. As can be seen by reading the definition, the forensic psychiatrist must go beyond the bounds of legitimate medical testimony and express quasi-judicial, social or moral opinions.

Forensic psychiatry has enormous impact in the areas of alcohol and drug addiction. Those addicted are now regarded as "sick" instead of "wrong"; today, addicts are subjects for psychiatric rehabilitation rather than incarceration.[8]

Forensic psychiatrists work in civil as well as criminal cases. For example, they may be asked for expert opinions in divorce and annulment proceedings, child custody cases, questions of mental health or fitness of a parent to raise children, wills contested with regard to the deceased's mental capacity at the time a will was made, or personal injury claims with regard to psychological or emotional damages.

Forensic pathology must rank as the major and best known specialty of forensic science. Although a medical subject for formal board certification only since 1959, modern forensic pathology dates back to the Renaissance in Europe and at least two centuries in England. To qualify to take the national certification examination, a physician must meet the following requirements:

1. Undergo standard training in anatomic pathology
2. Complete a one-year residency at one of 25 recognized training centers in forensic pathology
3. While at such a center, perform at least 300 autopsies

Contrasting hospital pathology with forensic pathology will illustrate the significance of the latter. A hospital pathologist rarely develops an understanding of the medical, philosophical, and legal problems related to the determination of the manner of death, because most hospital autopsies involve natural deaths. In other words, hospital pathologists concern themselves with what morphologic changes can be found in a body and their significance with respect to the person's demise. Forensic pathology, on the other hand, has as its major concern why a death occurred and what caused it. Such determinations require that a death be placed in the context of surrounding events before and after. A hospital pathologist simply does not use an "environmental" approach. As a result, a hospital autopsy report frequently omits information that could be crucial in civil or criminal actions.

"Perspective" contributes enormously to the effectiveness of a forensic pathologist. In medical malpractice situations, for instance, his investigation is not hampered by geographical (i.e., the hospital) proximity to the defendant-physician. For the same reason, the forensic pathologist is less susceptible to misplaced professional loyalty with fellow physicians. Scientific determination of the truth and the welfare of the patient and society represent the primary responsibilities of forensic pathology.

"Ignorance" also lends objectivity and integrity to the investigations of a forensic pathologist. Unlike a hospital pathologist, he often has no access to the medical history, or even the identity, of the deceased. The investigation therefore begins without prejudice or preconceived notions. The following basic determinations are the essential beginning points for a forensic pathologist:

1. Who is the victim (sex, race, age, distinguishing characteristics)?
2. When did death and the injuries occur?
3. Where did death and the injuries occur?
4. What injuries are present (type, distribution, pattern, path, and direction)?

5. Which injuries are significant (major vs. minor, time vs. artefactual or postmortem injuries)?
6. Why and how did the injuries and death occur (mechanism and manner of death)?

The difficulty of obtaining answers to these questions can be compounded by postmortem changes in a body or by thermal and mechanical mutilation. Thus, by beginning with a clean slate and given the inherent difficulty of such an investigation, the objective, pursuit of truth becomes intensified. All this contributes to intense, objective, and thorough investigation.

The attitudes of the two mentioned branches of pathology toward time and cause of death probably represent their greatest point of divergence. The forensic pathologist, because of his familiarity with the law, recognizes the crucial importance in terms of criminal or civil liability of what caused a death or injuries and when they occurred. Consider the following: A and his wife B are killed simultaneously in an accident. Their state has no statute covering simultaneous death situations. In his will, A left his estate to B, if she survived him. If not, his children, C and D were to inherit. Due to a family altercation, B would not leave either child a cent. In her will, B leaves her meager estate to the Society for Unwed Mothers. Hoping to prove that B survived A, if even by an instant, so that they might inherit A's fortune through B, the Society brings an action against A's estate. The job of the forensic pathologist is to determine who survived whom.

An integral step in an investigation to determine answers to questions such as these is a visit to the scene of the event. The forensic pathologist makes such visits in order to evaluate the death in the overall context of the victim's milieu. Situations at a scene that may seem inconsequential to others often provide crucial information to the forensic pathologist, and inconsistencies that may otherwise have gone unnoticed are considered. These visits contribute to a major goal of the forensic pathologist: developing an accurate mental picture of what took place. Hospital pathologists, of course, derive their name from the site of their work; they do not make visits to the scene of a death.

Hospital pathologists primarily attempt to explain the signs and symptoms of disease through their findings of morphologic changes in the body. Forensic pathologists are more attuned to the pathology of trauma. While a medicolegal investigation begins with a careful external examination of the body, a hospital autopsy stresses internal organs. Thus, a hospital pathologist tends to detect natural disease, while a forensic pathologist is more alert to unnatural deaths.

Another difference in the two branches of pathology appears in the reporting of findings. The forensic pathologist's report will be used at trial and by insurance companies. It must therefore be written in relatively simple language, comprehensible to lay people. It must also express opinions as to the probable cause of any trauma, time of occurrence, and so on. Hospital reports are couched in medical terminology and generally articulate only the cause of death and the actual changes that led to the "cause of death" conclusion.

Familiarity with legal concepts makes the testimony of the forensic pathologist critical in both civil and criminal litigation. He must be able to discern the difference between the medical and the legal cause of death. For instance, extraneous contributing factors to a death do not necessarily change the legal cause. If the victim of a gunshot wound in the abdomen subsequently dies of surgical complications, the death is still a homicide. Legally, the person firing the shot caused the death. A hospital pathologist in such a case would list the cause of death as the morphology changes caused by surgical complications. It is easy to see how this situation would also apply to malpractice deaths.

To recap, the forensic pathologist integrates all the information concerning a death into his findings: toxicology reports, forensic odontology and anthropology reports, circumstances at the scene of death, etc. He then goes beyond merely determining the medical cause of death to a determination of the time, manner, and legal cause of death. The totality of his investigation and application of legal knowledge to the resultant information makes the forensic pathologist's findings unique in the world of law and medicine.

Education and Employment

Legal medicine involves the interprofessional relationships between law and medicine. Of course, medical school must be completed, and the best direction to follow then is a residency training program before law school. One of the following medical specialties should be pursued: pathology, internal medicine, surgery, or psychiatry. Specialization is recommended because the sheer volume of information in each area precludes expertise in all.

Upon completion of this rigorous education, several employment options are open: forensic pathologist or forensic toxicologist in a coroner/medical examiner's office, forensic psychiatrist in charge of a behavior clinic, or internist functioning as a medical director for an insurance company or pharmaceuticals maker. Teaching possibilities in legal medicine unfortunately are widely available; a severe shortage of qualified instructors and programs currently hinders the development of legal medicine. This seems to stem from the medical hierarchy's lack of awareness of the discipline and of its importance. It is, therefore, the duty of every forensic scientist to actively promote medicolegal education and participate in teaching.

The importance of legal medicine is best understood by attorneys. It has been estimated that 70 to 80% of all civil cases need some medical or scientific proof, either in pretrial preparation or expert testimony in the courtroom.[9] Attorneys, insurance agencies, and government constantly need the unique expertise of forensic scientists. An aspiring medicolegal practitioner must realize, however, that educational background alone will not meet the requirements of an effective expert witness. Command of the English language and the ability to clearly and simply present complicated medical findings are also essential. In addition, the desirable expert witness will express firm opinions on the witness stand; undue vacillation can be fatal to a particular legal endeavor.

The most common and important forum for a medicolegal expert continues to be the criminal courtroom. The testimony of a forensic expert may be the determining factor in a case of homicide, involuntary manslaughter, voluntary manslaughter, first or second degree murder, or in other criminal actions. In a case in which I was involved, a man was charged with the serious crime of rape. Testing showed that the accused's blood type was O, while the seminal fluid removed from the victim fell into a type AB group. These findings conclusively proved that the accused was not the rapist. Although not always as dramatic, the forensic expert's findings often contribute to the direction of a criminal trial.

As society grows more complex and new civil causes of action appear, the demand for experts will continue to increase. Demand will also increase as forensic scientists enlarge their sphere of influence here, as they have in the industrial and environmental areas. The need for forensic scientists is great; our task is to increase the available educational opportunities and upgrade and then maintain the quality of available employment opportunities.

References

1. Harper, B.: *The Case of Hammurabi,* 2nd ed., 1904, pp. 77–81.
2. Oliver: *Legal Medicine in Europe and America,* A B A J, 18:405, 1932, and Smith: The development of forensic medicine and law-science relations, *J. Pub. L.,* 3: 304–306, 1954.
3. An Act to Amend the Law Relating to Coroners, *Geo. C.,* 59: 16–17, 1926.
4. *The New Republic,* Feb. 13: 15, 1971.
5. Cobbs vs. Grant, Cal. Rptr., 104: 505, 1973, and Canterbury vs. Spence, 404: 772, 1972.
6. *New Republic,* 164: 15, 1971.

7. M'Naughten's Case, *Eng. Rep.*, 8: 718, 1843.

8. Robinson vs. California, 370 U.S. 660 (1961), and Powell vs. Texas, 392 U.S. 514 (1967).

9. Curran, W. and Shapiro, F.: *Law, Medicine and Forensic Science*, Vol. VIII, ed. 2, 1970.

Recommended Reading Material

Forensic Sciences (4 Volumes), Edited by Cyril H. Wecht, M.D., J.D., Published by Matthew Bender & Company, Inc., New York (1982).

Scientific Evidence in Civil and Criminal Cases by Professors Andre A. Moenssens, James E. Starrs, Carol E. Henderson, and Fred E. Inbau, Published by The Foundation Press, Inc., Westbury, New York (1986).

Health Law by Professors Barry R. Furrow, Thomas L. Greaney, Sandra H. Johnson, Timothy Jost, and Robert L. Schwartz, Published by West Publishing Co., St. Paul, Minnesota (1995).

Forensic Pathology

RONALD K. WRIGHT
WILLIAM G. ECKERT

7

Forensic pathology is probably the oldest branch of the forensic sciences, and, indeed, until the first quarter of the twentieth century, virtually all forensic sciences were a branch of the medical examination of forensic problems. Since then, the explosive expansion of criminalistic techniques has taken the forensic sciences in numerous directions away from their medical beginning. Perusal of older textbooks of legal medicine will show that many of the areas now dealt with by criminalistics laboratories were then within the purview of forensic medicine. With the specialization leading to movement from the medical arena, there remain two broad areas which are still in the medical sphere today, clinical forensic medicine, which will be covered in other chapters, and forensic pathology.[1]

The word "pathology" is derived from a combination of two Greek words, *pathos* meaning disease and *logos* meaning the study of. Thus, pathology is the study of disease. Pathology concerns itself primarily with the scientific diagnosis, as opposed to the treatment, of disease. It is the study of the illnesses and injuries which cause disease.

Although historically, dating back to the mid-nineteenth century, pathology was a single specialty, from the mid-twentieth century a number of subspecialties of pathology have developed. First is anatomic pathology. This is the specialty primarily involved in the study of disease by examination of tissues removed at surgery or at autopsy. The second is clinical pathology specializing primarily in the diagnosis of disease by laboratory testing. Most general pathologists in the United States are trained in both anatomic and clinical pathology, although many are trained in only one of these two primary areas.

A tiny minority of persons who are general pathologists continue their training and become forensic pathologists. To become a forensic pathologist in the United States requires a year of training in an approved training program or two years of experience, both after becoming trained as a general pathologist. Thus the training in forensic pathology requires completion of a baccalaureate degree, usually requiring four years; completion of medical school, generally requiring another four years; completion of postgraduate training in pathology for an additional four years; and then one or two additional years. For most forensic pathologists in the United States the minimal training requirement is 13 years after high school graduation.

Forensic pathology concerns itself with the intersection of the legal world and the pathologic world. Thus, there is a bias of forensic pathology toward the pathology of injury as opposed to illness, as injury is so frequently involved in civil and criminal litigation and thus of great importance to the legal world. However, many illnesses are of importance to forensic pathologists, especially if there is concern that a previous exposure to injurious agents may have caused an illness.

In the United States, forensic pathologists are most often employed by state and local governments and are involved in the investigation into the cause of deaths. This death bias, however, is not definitional of the specialty, and although the examination of bodies of persons who have died is often thought of as the only basis of forensic pathology opinions, this is not true. The investigatory techniques of forensic pathology are equally applicable in the determination of the cause of injury or disease irrespective of whether the person is alive or dead.

Great overlap exists between general pathologists and forensic pathologists, primarily because in most countries, there are woefully too few trained forensic pathologists to perform forensic pathologic examinations. Therefore, the general pathologist, either as part of professional duties or as an additional area of private practice, commonly indulges in forensic pathology. In a few countries, mainly on the continent of Europe, there is a much more rigid distinction between the practitioners of legal medicine and the general pathologist. In the United States and Great Britain, more forensic pathology is performed by general pathologists than by full-time forensic pathologists.

Role of the Forensic Pathologist

Leaving aside clinical forensic medicine for the moment, a primary function provided by most forensic pathologists is the examination of the dead body. Indeed, currently in the United States it is estimated that the number of forensic to non-forensic autopsies is 10:1 or greater.[2] Generally, although the exact statutory language varies from state to state in the United States and from country to country elsewhere, unexplained or suspicious deaths must be investigated by some legal process. In countries with separation of the judicial and the executive function, death investigation may be done by either or both processes.

Generally, in the English-American system of law, the judicial function is noninquisitional. The judge sits to listen to evidence presented by two or more parties involved in a case or controversy. In the Roman system of law, practiced in most non-English speaking countries, the judge is empowered to investigate and thus inquire; therefore, there is an inquisitional system of administration of justice.

The coroner in the English-American system is an exception to the above. The coroner is a judge, or a quasi-judicial official, who has authority to inquire into the cause of death of persons whose deaths were unexplained or suspicious. Thus the coroner is the only inquisitional judge or quasi-judicial officer in the English-American system of law.

Currently in the United States another system of death investigation also exists — the medical examiner system. Under this system, the medical examiner, with more or less the same investigational powers as the coroner, investigates deaths as well. In some states, both systems are used, with the medical examiner often empowered in the more populous urban areas. The primary distinction between the medical examiner and coroner is the general lack of training or experience required of the coroner. The sole requirement to become coroner is to be popularly elected. Medical examiners are generally required to be physicians, often are required to be pathologists, and are sometimes required to be forensic pathologists.[3]

In the majority of deaths, a physician who cared for the deceased while alive is empowered to certify the death. The physician should be confident that the person is deceased, that the person died of an illness without medical-legal significance, and that the cause of death is relatively apparent from the history, physical, and laboratory testing done during the life of the deceased.

Unfortunately, the practice of having attending physicians sign out deaths without autopsy has been shown to be fraught with major errors in cause of death determination most of the time.[4] Indeed, the reason for this is that physicians receive either no training in death certification or less than a few minutes during their medical education and training.[5]

If the physician does not feel confident or if there are circumstances which make the case fall within the category of a noncertifiable death, the appropriate law officer (coroner, medical examiner, or equivalent) must be notified of the death. In some countries death investigation is executed by the police. In those countries with Roman legal tradition, death investigation is by an inquisitional judge or magistrate. On consideration of the facts of the case, this law officer will decide that the case may be signed out as a natural death or that it requires further investigation often including autopsy examination.

Specific Activities

"Autopsy" is an unfortunate word coming from the Greek *auto* meaning self and *opsy* meaning to look. Thus autopsy means to look at one's self. When referring to a deceased person, this is not terribly accurate, meaning probably that it is man looking at man. A better word is "necropsy" which comes from the Greek *necros* meaning death and of course *opsy*. This being similar to "biopsy" which comes from the Greek *bios* meaning life and *opsy*.

Another term is "postmortem examination," which is often shortened to "post." However, the word "autopsy" is commonly used in the United States and this convention will be adhered to in this chapter.

The autopsy in the medicolegal sense is directed mainly at determining the cause of death and at detecting, describing, and interpreting any signs of injury or disease that may be present which may be useful in understanding as much about how the person came to be deceased as possible.

Forensic pathology is very much involved in the pathology of trauma or injury, especially in homicidal, accidental, and suicidal cases where bodily damage may be the major finding. Similarly, poisoning cases are really injury, but the injury is chemical or toxic rather than mechanical. Even where natural diseases are concerned, the causes may often be termed "injurious," as in the chest tumors associated with asbestos exposure or the bladder tumors associated with aniline dyes, both of which may have profound medicolegal significance in the civil sense and are due to long-term injuries from toxic substances. In addition, a large part of the autopsy workload consists of the investigation of sudden death due to natural causes that cannot be certified by a physician. However, the major concerns of forensic pathologists are with mechanical trauma, either with criminal connotations as in homicide by shooting, stabbing, or punching or in civil matters such as road, rail, and air accidents and suicide.

Indeed, generally only the medicolegal officer is allowed to determine whether the death is homicidal, suicidal, accidental, or natural. This four-part system of death classification is utilized worldwide. It has a theocratic historical base, with accidental and natural deaths being God's doing and homicidal and suicidal deaths being the work of man.

In practice, natural deaths are those due solely to disease without any violence or injury. The other three are deaths resulting from some sort of injury. Accidental deaths are those that result from injury where there was no intent to harm the person. Homicidal and suicidal deaths are ones resulting from some intent to cause injury or death. In homicide the actor is a person other than the deceased. In suicide the actor is the deceased.

Attendance at the Scene of Death

Under the medical examiner system, deaths, especially those that are sudden, unexpected, suspicious, or frankly criminal, are visited by a doctor with medicolegal experience. The body is commonly seen where it was found, and the medical examiner from his or her experience will decide whether the circumstances merit further investigation, which almost always includes an autopsy.

Where the medical examiner system does not exist, the attendance of a pathologist at the scene of the death is dependent on the suspicion index of the police, and this may vary greatly from place to place. In some areas, visits to the scene of a death by a forensic doctor are virtually unknown, whereas in more enlightened (and perhaps wealthy) jurisdictions the police will be aware of the advantages to be gained by asking the pathologist to come out to see any death about which the officers are not entirely satisfied.

There are considerable advantages to the pathologist seeing the body at the locus of the death. In many cases, the initially suspicious circumstances may be dispelled by the pathologist, who with extensive experience may recognize some noncriminal circumstance. Many natural deaths, accidents, and suicides may look suspicious to a police officer if he or she has not encountered a similar case before, but the forensic pathologist, due to his or her familiarity with a wider range of unusual circumstances, may well rapidly perceive the true nature of the death.

The advantage of having a pathologist visit the scene of a homicide is that he or she can get a total picture of the circumstances that a written description and photographs cannot convey as completely. The position of the body, the position of any weapon present, the distribution of blood splatter, and myriad other factors help the pathologist build up a mental picture which will allow the correlation and interpretation of the later autopsy findings. The experienced forensic pathologist is aware of many details at the scene almost subliminally, and although not actually intuitive, allows the pieces to be fit together in the mind like a puzzle so that an overall appreciation of the circumstances of the death can be built up in a way that no other reconstructive method can offer. It is far better for a pathologist to be called unnecessarily to borderline cases than not to be called to a serious case. Many of the most notorious criminal cases in medicolegal history have started as "just another death," and it is frequently in the first few hours or even minutes of an investigation that errors are made that echo through the courts for years. Thus, every case must be handled with the utmost care and seriousness, because pathologists never know which case is to become the cause cerebre.

The pathologist should have near prime access to the scene of a suspicious death. The body should not be moved or touched by investigating officers until the pathologist arrives. The only other persons who should approach the body are paramedics who have been called to ensure that life is extinct. Although prime consideration is given to preserving the scene of a crime, this of course takes second place if there is any possibility that the victim is not dead and might benefit from emergency medical attention. Unfortunately, paramedics tend to err on the side of finding signs of life often when these signs are invisible to all others. This leads to conflicts between paramedics and death investigators. As time progresses and the futility of out-of-hospital cardio-pulmonary resuscitation of trauma victims becomes more clearly understood, the paramedics will respond, fail to perceive signs of life, and then immediately leave the scene to the expert pathologist.

The only other investigating officer who should have priority over the pathologist is the photographer, and in many jurisdictions the detective officers and pathologists have a system worked out in advance to ensure that priorities are in the right sequence.

At the scene the main function of the pathologist is to look and observe, making such notes and taking such photographs as are appropriate. Another function is to try to make some estimate of the time since death by feeling the body's heat and degree of stiffness and possibly by taking the temperature at the scene.[6] The pathologist usually has the responsibility of moving the body in order to look underneath at the previously covered surface. Seeing that the body is properly transported to a mortuary without the loss of any trace evidence or any interference that would negate the subsequent examination is usually the responsibility of the pathologist.

Autopsy

As stated, the primary (but not sole) function of the pathologist is to determine the cause of death, the extent of the injuries, and the presence of natural disease or poisoning and, apart from making a factual record of these matters, to offer deductive opinions as to the mechanism and possible time of the action. He or she should confine himself or herself to the medical aspects and not "play detective," which is the function of the rest of the team. However, the pathologist is entitled to offer any deductions he or she thinks valid, subject to the provision that he or she delineates his or her limits of error as clearly as possible. For instance, the detective officers will inevitably ask the time of death. This should be given with a "bracket" of the limits within which the death probably could not have happened and the possibility of death having occurred out of these ranges.

The autopsy itself follows a standard pattern and should be a full autopsy in every case.[7] The practice of examining only the obvious injuries or only the diseased organs is to be deprecated, because the experienced pathologist never fails to be surprised at the multiplicity of unexpected injury and disease that is found in so many cases.

In criminal cases, especially those due to mechanical violence, the external examination of the body is frequently as important — if not more important than — the more classic dissection. Where someone has been beaten with a blunt instrument or stabbed many times, a description of the external appearances is vital. The same holds true for gunshot wounds, where much information concerning distance and direction of the weapon to the body is to be gained from an external examination rather than from internal dissection of the organs.

Thus, the first part of the autopsy will be a careful evaluation of the body surface, but even before this there are important preliminaries. First, the identity of the body must be confirmed. If the pathologist has attended the scene of the crime he or she knows that this is the body that was examined at the scene. However, at some point in time the actual identity of the deceased must be established by someone who knew the person in life.

The reason for this step is that should the death come to criminal trial, in the United States the prosecution must prove beyond and to the exclusion of every reasonable doubt that the person is deceased and that the death was caused by criminal design. The pathologist shall be an important witness in the proof of the criminal design part of the prosecution's case. However, unless the pathologist knew the deceased personally, he or she cannot testify about the autopsy until it is shown that the deceased autopsied is the deceased the defendant is charged with killing. Until the above is proved, the testimony of the pathologist is irrelevant. Historically, someone who knew the deceased was shown the body and made a formal identification. Then that person could come to testify that he or she saw the deceased at the mortuary and made an official identification. Then the pathologist could testify that the body so identified was the one he or she was now testifying about. On non-decomposed bodies, this process of formal identification has become much less necessary with the use of photographs and unique case numbers.

Before the external examination is begun, the body should be carefully measured, both the height from heel to crown of head and the weight. These matters are relevant in many cases, especially where there is some argument as to whether a small assailant could have damaged a large victim or where the height of injuries above the ground in stabbing, gunshot, and transportation injuries are at issue. It also helps to assist in the identification of the body if the postmortem dimensions can be compared with the known physical characteristics of the deceased when alive.

An examination of the deceased's clothing by the pathologist is often of great importance, although it will be minutely examined by the criminalistics laboratory as well. However, it is within the pathologist's authority to look for bullet holes or stab perforations and compare these with the position of the wounds on the body. It is also appropriate for the pathologist to examine for powder residues on the clothing of gunshot wound victims so as to better correlate the autopsy findings in estimating the range and direction of the gun from the deceased at the time of the gunshot. Other examinations of clothing may be made for the presence of blood, vomitus, semen, fecal material, and many other features which, although they will be subjected to subsequent detailed study by the forensic laboratory, have definite medical aspects that can be incorporated into the opinions and interpretations expressed by the pathologist.

The general physique and state of nutrition of the deceased should be evaluated, with the extremes from obesity to emaciation noted. These observations may be of importance in a number of cases, especially in children or handicapped adults for whom neglect to the point of starvation may be a point at issue. Also, the general cleanliness of the body may be important, as in self-neglect, child neglect, mental disorders, drug dependency, and senile dementias; there may be considerable neglect of the skin surface, with dirt, skin infections, and parasite infestations noted.

All injuries, whether recent or old, must be carefully noted, described, and photographed. The size of such injuries must be measured, and their location on the body noted, so that later reading of the report can pinpoint their position. The usual method is to give the distances, usually in metric units, from major anatomical landmarks. For instance, a stab wound of the chest may be described by its length and breadth and also by its distance right or left of the midline of the body and its location below the top of the head or above the heel. Distances from such landmarks as the nipple, sternal notch, umbilicus, chin, and nose are also helpful additions, but the most important are the distances which allow one to estimate the position in relation to the world as well as in relation to the deceased.

The state of the body regarding stiffness (rigor mortis) should be noted. However, it is much more important to know the state of rigor when the body was first found than when it is in the mortuary some hours later.

Post mortem hypostasis, which is generally and somewhat inaccurately called livor mortis or lividity, is the discoloration of the most dependent parts of the body where blood settles after death due to the force of gravity. It is of some use in determination of the time of death.[8] Sometimes hypostasis may be an indicator that the body was moved after death if some or all of the discoloration is found in a non-dependent position. The color of hypostasis is useful, as well as it may indicate carbon monoxide or cyanide poisoning

or poisoning by strongly reducing compounds which produce methemoglo-
bin in susceptible individuals.

When injuries or other abnormalities are present on the body surface
the forensic pathologist will record them by words, drawings, and photographs. Preprinted body diagrams are commonly employed upon which the
position and size of various injuries or abnormalities may be recorded. Well
taken photographs should also supplement these diagrams. The ease of use
and inexpensive nature of modern color photography has made photography
routine. Digital images are replacing chemically developed photographic film
as the preferred medium.

Radiographs (X-rays) are frequently used in the practice of forensic
pathology. In cases where there is body mutilation, in all cases of gunshot
wounds, and in all knife wounds, radiographs are routinely taken before any
internal examination is made. The radiograph will document the relationship
of internal organs to any metallic foreign body. The prediction of the path
and final resting place of a bullet is extremely difficult from an external
examination alone. Countless hours and excessive mutilation of the body can
be avoided by the use of radiographs. In addition, in cases of possible elec-
trocution, the X-ray examination of possibly defective electrical equipment
is invaluable.[9] In all cases of child deaths, complete skeletal X-rays should be
taken to find subtle evidence of old trauma such as is seen in the battered
baby syndrome.

Finally, the external examination may reveal surface fragments of material that may be trace evidence, such as paint flakes in injuries from traffic
accidents, glass fragments from windshields, fibers, blood, semen, and extraneous hairs present on the surface or embedded in wounds on the body. In
assault cases, foreign material may be present under the fingernails and may
include hair, fiber, skin fragments, or blood from the assailant. These may
be vital to the investigation, and normally the fingernails are either trimmed
off with sharp scissors and retained in separately labeled containers or they
are scraped out by means of a sharpened clean instrument such as a tooth-
pick, the contents again being separately retained and labeled. Ordinarily the
criminalistic laboratory will handle the analysis of these materials, although
commonly the forensic pathologist will photograph and examine any suspicious material. The yield from fingernail scrapings is distressingly low. However, with polymerase chain reaction (PCR) amplification of any deoxyribose
nucleic acid (DNA) containing materials, it is possible from submicroscopic
amounts of tissue to positively identify an assailant, if there has been transfer
from the assailant to the victim and if it is properly collected and analyzed.

Such DNA evidence is more commonly found in sexual offenses where
the pubic hair of the victim may have hair from the assailant as well as transfer
of blood and semen. Careful search, collection, and preservation of these

materials may lead to the identification of the assailant using analysis of the DNA molecule. Pulled hair with the bulb or base, as well as all bodily fluids, generally have sufficient DNA to amplify with PCR and analyze for individually unique areas. With blood and semen, if the amount is visible to the eye, it is usually not necessary to perform PCR amplification but direct analysis, thus reducing the probability of contamination. All of these techniques, however, are based upon careful identification, collection, and preservation, which is done by the forensic pathologist.

The internal examination follows and is basically a detailed exercise in morbid anatomy, a name applied to the exposure and recognition of abnormal morphologic features within the body. In the first instance, this is done by dissection and naked-eye inspection. Further examination is conducted by microscopic examination of the tissues along with toxicologic, biochemical, biologic, or immunologic investigation as may be appropriate.

As stated before, a full autopsy should be conducted in every case and no shortcuts taken merely because the cause of death seems obvious from the history or appearances. Although the cause of death is important, it is not the only issue, and matters such as the collateral presence of natural disease that might have contributed to the death and other more subtle injuries or poisonings may be equally or even more important. For instance, in a case where a person dies during a fight, the assailant may already have been arrested and charged with murder. However, a careful postmortem examination can alter the legal aspects of the case considerably. Although at first the body may show signs that a severe injury is present on the back of the head, internal examination may reveal a recent heart attack that may have caused the deceased to collapse and strike his or her head even before any significant injury was caused by the fight. Alternatively, there may be signs of brain membrane hemorrhage due to the rupture of a natural ballooning or aneurysm of one of the blood vessels at the base of the brain, a relatively common occurrence. Although, in these cases the legal aspects may not completely absolve the alleged assailant, the gravity of the charge may well be reduced from murder to manslaughter or even less.

To ascertain all these facts, a standard autopsy is performed. This entails opening the front of the body from the neck region to the pubis. In the United States, it is common to make a "Y" shaped incision to avoid any visibility of the incision when the body is viewed and to preserve the large arteries in the neck for use to inject embalming fluid. In Europe, it is more common to take the incision on the front of the neck up to the larynx (voice-box). In either case the object is to examine the contents of the head, neck, thorax, and abdomen for abnormalities. In addition, the brain is examined by cutting the scalp over the vertex of the head from behind each ear, the cut traversing the upper part of the scalp. The scalp is reflected back from the skull, and the top of the skull sawed and removed exposing the brain for examination.[10]

After all of the cranial, neck, thoracic, and abdominal organs have been examined, they are replaced, and all of the incisions are sewn closed leaving no disfiguration of the body. After a completed autopsy, the fact that an autopsy was done is not discernable by persons viewing the clothed body.

Samples of blood are taken in all deaths. Blood samples are preferably taken from peripheral veins such as those at the armpit or groin or in the neck. Blood should not be taken from the general pool in the chest or abdomen, as this area may be contaminated by substances from the intestines or stomach. After death the walls of the alimentary canal become permeable, and therefore some substances such as alcohol and barbiturates may diffuse passively into adjacent organs such as the heart chambers, so that blood taken from these sites may have a false-positive level of chemical substances which were not present during life.[11]

Blood is usually taken for chemical and serologic purposes. For the latter, refrigerated, unpreserved blood is preferred. For alcohol analysis it is routine to collect the blood in a tube containing sodium fluoride, which reduces microbiologic action that may increase or reduce the alcohol content after collection. It has been shown that after death, microorganisms — especially yeast and some bacteria — may produce appreciable quantities of alcohol, and thus create an artificially high level of alcohol. This is particularly true if the interval between death and autopsy (the post-mortem period) is prolonged. Fluoride causes the process to be slowed following the collection of the blood, although of course nothing can be done to avoid alcohol production within the body.[12]

Stomach contents are frequently taken, both for toxicologic analysis and sometimes to identify the nature of the last meal. This is done by recognition of muscle fibers, starch grains, vegetable cellular elements, and other features. In passing, it should be noted that estimation of the time of death from the state of digestion of the stomach contents is unreliable. The digestion process can be completely arrested when some severe injury, or even emotional shock, occurs; this happens most notably in cases of coma from head injuries. I have seen the stomach contents of a motorcyclist who had been in a coma for five days following an accident. The contents appeared as fresh as if the food had been just swallowed. The value of examining stomach contents apart from chemical and toxicologic analysis is to ascertain the nature of the last meal so that if it was known that a person had eaten rice and beans at a particular meal and if these elements were recognized, it would be logical to suppose that death had occurred after that meal, but before a subsequent meal.

Other samples taken at autopsy may be samples of head, pubic, eyebrow, and eyelash hair. These are necessary for use as negative controls in distinguishing between foreign hair found on the body and the deceased's hair.

Urine, if available, is an important sample and is usually collected as part of the autopsy examination. Generally it is drawn into a syringe directly from the exposed bladder. Urine being nearly free of protein is an extremely good sample to use for screening for drugs of abuse.

Ocular fluid, the clear fluid found within the eye, is extremely important as a sample. Analysis of ocular fluid for chemical constituents provides the closest estimation of values near the time of death.

Bile, drawn from the gall bladder with a syringe, is also commonly taken for toxicologic testing. Both urine and bile tell more about what drugs were taken in the days prior to death than what was intoxicating a person at the moment of death. Ocular fluid is a reasonable representation of drugs and alcohol a few hours before death.

All of the organs are studied by the naked eye (macroscopically) for the presence of injuries or natural disease, and, as stated, it is customary to take specimens for microscopic examination. In criminal cases, or potentially criminal cases, this is done routinely by most forensic pathologists even if the organ showed no macroscopic abnormality. It is always safer to take tissues that are not needed than not to take tissues that later become an important medicolegal issue. Microscopic examination is performed after the tissue is processed in the histology laboratory, and the report is generally appended to the macroscopic autopsy report. Similarly, the results of toxicologic and serologic reports are appended. The final autopsy report may have to be delayed until the results of all of the ancillary examinations are completed, so that a complete overview of the case may be made and a reasoned interpretation and conclusion offered.

The autopsy report varies greatly in length according to the nature of the case. A simple unexpected death from natural disease may require merely completing a page or two. However, in criminal deaths or cases where there is civil litigation it is preferable to write a report with all of the details, including negative findings of normal organs. It is unsatisfactory to fail to mention normality, because the long delay between the autopsy and the subsequent court proceedings may make it impossible to remember details of the examination. A blank in the report may be taken to indicate that the organ was normal, or alternatively that it was not examined or that it was examined but was not reported upon. It is therefore essential that negative findings be noted. This can be done without making excessively long reports by merely reciting a list of normal organs and noting that they were examined, weighed, and found to be normal.

After a description of all injuries, abnormalities, and disease and ancillary investigation, a cause of death is listed. In some deaths, the exact cause of death cannot be ascertained after complete investigation and autopsy. In such cases this is noted in place of the cause of death.

In addition to the cause of death, separately recorded and identified, should be a report concerning an interpretation of all of the investigation and autopsy findings to try to explain why the death occurred. This is often the most important part of the report, in that the pathologist's training and experience is called into play to interpret the findings for the benefit of the reader of the report.

The pathologist is cautious not to over-interpret findings. The opinions must be backed up by fact and established science in the field of legal medicine and must not extend into speculation or fantasy. The opinions may well be challenged by expert witnesses called by an opposing party. The expectation of this tends to make the forensic pathologist more cautious and more painstaking in reaching conclusions. This is a healthy situation and a vindication for the adversary system used in the English-American legal system. This method is often criticized by those from the inquisitional system where reliance is placed upon a consensus of expert opinion given independently to the court without further challenge.

This, then, is the primary function of the forensic pathologist, to see every aspect of a case from attendance at the scene of the death through completion of a report and presentation of evidence in court. The duty is onerous and not to be undertaken lightly. When the expert witness rises in court to give testimony, he or she is usually questioned concerning his or her training, experience, and aptitude for the job. The weight of the evidence, as far as the court and jury are concerned, will be modified by the experience and training. In fact, major cases often become the "battle of the experts," with numerous expert witnesses of varying degrees of fame being called to prove or disprove some of the controversial aspects. In this respect, care must be taken to identify the correct fields of expertise, because a most eminent professor of general pathology may not know much at all about forensic pathology. The opposing expert witness may be a relatively obscure but proficient assistant medical examiner whose knowledge of medicolegal matters may far exceed that of his prominent general colleague. Unfortunately, not all juries understand the distinction, and the attorneys may not take pains to point out the difference. With a declining number of full-time forensic pathologists, more and more general pathologists are becoming involved in medicolegal issues, and although many are competent, this is by no means a uniform situation.

In any event, the pathologist must present the truth no matter which side of a case calls him or her as a witness. The pathologist should be there to help the judge and jury to arrive at a just decision. The pathologist must reveal all of the facts of the case, even those which are disadvantageous to the party calling him or her. Any attempt to bend, distort, or conceal relevant evidence will only lower his or her status in the eyes of the judge, jury, and professional colleagues. The worst condemnation of an expert is that his or her opinion may be bought by the highest bidder.

The forensic pathologist, by education and training, is entrusted to utilize science to understand the cause of disease or injury and is called upon to explain this to judges and juries.

References

1. Eckert, W., The development of forensic medicine in the United Kingdom from the 18th Century, *Am. J. For. Med. Path.,* 13(2) 124-131, 1992.

2. Wright, R.K. and Tate, L.G., Forensic pathology: last stronghold of the autopsy, *Am. J. For. Med. Path.,* 1:57-60, 1980.

3. Wadee, S.A., Forensic Pathology: a different perspective: investigative medicolegal systems in the United States, *Med. Law,* 13(5-6) 519-30, 1994.

4. Marwith, C., Pathologists request autopsy revival, *JAMA,* 273(24):1889-1891, 1995.

5. Adams, V.I. and Herman, M.A., The medical examiner: when to report and help with death certificates, *J. Fla. Med. Assn.,* 82(4):255-260, 1995.

6. Jones, M.D., James, W.S., Barsai, S., and Nokes, L.D.M., Post-mortem electrical excitability of skeletal muscle: preliminary investigations of an animal model, *For. Sci. Int.,* 76:91-96, 1995.

7. Hutchins, G.M., Practice guidelines for autopsy pathology: autopsy committee of the College of American Pathologists, *Arch. Path. Lab. Med.,* 118(1), 19-25, 1994.

8. Vanezio, P. and Trujillo, O., Evaluation of hypostasis using a colorimeter measuring system and its application to assessment of the post-mortem interval (time of death), *For. Sci. Int.,* 78, 19-28, 1996.

9. Wright, R.K. and Gantner, G., Electrical injuries and lightning, In: Froede, R.C., ed., *Handbook of Forensic Pathology,* Northfield IL: College of American Pathologists; 1990.

10. Katelares, A., Kencran, J., Duflon, J., and Hilton, J.M., Brains at necropsy: to fix or not to fix, *J. Clin. Path.,* 47(8), 718-720, 1994.

11. Takayasu, Tatsunori et al., Experimental studies on post-mortem diffusion of ethanol-d-6 using rats, *For. Sci. Int.,* 76:179-188, 1995.

12. Takayasu, Tatsunori et al., Post-mortem degradation of administered ethanol-d-6 and production of endogenous ethanol: experimental studies using rats and rabbits, *For. Sci. Int.,* 76:129-140, 1995.

Forensic Toxicology

8

ALPHONSE POKLIS

Introduction

Toxicology is the study of poisons. More specifically, toxicology is concerned with the chemical and physical properties of toxic substances and their physiological effects on living organisms, qualitative and quantitative methods for their analysis in biological and nonbiological materials, and the development of procedures for the treatment of poisoning. A poison may be regarded as any substance which, when taken in sufficient quantity, will cause ill health or death. The key phrase in this definition is "sufficient quantity". The ingestion of large amounts of water over an extended period of time has been known to cause fatal electrolyte imbalance. This seemingly bizarre behavior — ingestion of massive amounts of water — is known as psychogenic polydipsia and occurs in certain forms of schizophrenia. Conversely, minute quantities of arsenic, cyanide, and other poisons may be ingested, causing no apparent toxicity. As the 16th century physician Paracelsus observed, "All substances are poisons; there is none which is not a poison. The right dose differentiates a poison from a remedy."

Recently, the science of toxicology has expanded to include a wide range of interests, including the evaluation of the risks involved in the use of pharmaceuticals, pesticides, and food additives, as well as studies of occupational poisoning, exposure to environmental pollution, the effects of radiation, and, regretfully, biological and chemical warfare. However, it is the forensic toxicologist who has held the title of toxicologist for the longest period of time. The forensic toxicologist is concerned primarily with the detection and estimation of poisons in tissues and body fluids obtained at autopsy or, occasionally, in blood, urine, or gastric material obtained from a living person. Once the analysis is completed, the forensic toxicologist then interprets the results as to the physiological and/or behavioral effects of the poison upon the person from whom the sample was obtained. In the case of tissues collected at autopsy, the analytical results may reveal that the decedent

0-8493-8101-0/97/$0.00+$.50
© 1997 by CRC Press, Inc.

died from poisoning. In living persons, the presence of a drug in a blood or urine sample may explain coma, convulsions, or erratic behavior.

The complete investigation of the cause or causes of sudden death is an important civic responsibility. Establishing the cause of death rests with the medical examiner, coroner, or pathologist, but success or failure in arriving at the correct conclusion frequently depends upon the combined efforts of the pathologist and the forensic toxicologist. Poisoning as a cause of death cannot be proven beyond contention without toxicologic analyses that demonstrate the presence of the poison in the tissues or body fluids of the deceased. Most drugs and poisons do not produce characteristic or observable lesions in body tissues, and their presence can be demonstrated only by chemical methods of isolation and identification. If toxicological analyses are avoided, death may be ascribed to poisoning without definite proof, or a death due to poisoning may be erroneously attributed to some other cause.

In instances where death is not due to poisoning, the forensic toxicologist can often provide valuable evidence concerning the circumstances surrounding a death. The erratic driving behavior of the victims of automotive accidents is often explained by the presence of alcohol in blood or tissues. Psychoactive drugs, those which affect behavior, often play a significant role in circumstances associated with sudden or violent death. The detection of alcohol, narcotics, hallucinogens, or other drugs may substantiate the testimony of witnesses as to the aggressive, incoherent, or irrational behavior of the decedent at the time of a fatal incident. Conversely, negative toxicology findings may dispel stories of the decedent's drug use. Negative findings are also significant in persons who should be regularly taking medications to control pathological conditions. In the case of epileptics, negative or low drug concentrations may indicate the decedent was not taking his medication in the prescribed manner and as a result experienced a fatal seizure.

History of Forensic Toxicology

Until the 19th century, physicians, lawyers, and law enforcement officials harbored extremely faulty notions about the signs and symptoms of poisoning. It was traditionally believed that if a body was black, blue, or spotted in places or "smelled bad" the decedent had died from poison. Other mistaken ideas were that the heart of a poisoned person could not be destroyed by fire, or that the body of a person dying from arsenic poisoning would not decay. Unless a poisoner was literally caught in the act, there was no way to establish that the victim died from poison. In the early 18th century, a Dutch physician, Hermann Boerhoave, theorized that various poisons in a hot, vaporous condition yielded typical odors. He placed substances suspected of containing poisons on hot coals and tested their smells. While Boerhave was not successful in applying his method, he was the first to suggest a chemical method for proving the presence of poison.

During the middle ages, professional poisoners sold their services to both royalty and the common populace. The most common poisons were of plant origin (such as hemlock, aconite, belladonna) and toxic metals (arsenic and mercury salts). During the French and Italian Renaissance, political assassination by poisoning was raised to a fine art by Pope Alexander VI and Cesare Borgia.

The murderous use of white arsenic (arsenic trioxide) became so widespread among the general population that the poison acquired the name "inheritance powder". Given this popularity, it is small wonder the first milestones in the chemical isolation and identification of a poison in body tissues and fluids would center around arsenic. In 1775, Karl Wilhelm Scheele, the famous Swedish chemist, discovered that white arsenic was converted to arsenous acid by chlorine water. The addition of metallic zinc reduced the arsenous acid to poisonous arsine gas. If gently heated, the evolving gas would deposit metallic arsenic on the surface of a cold vessel. In 1821, Sevillas used the decomposition of arsine to detect small quantities of arsenic in stomach contents and urine in poisoning cases. In 1836, James M. Marsh, a chemist at the Royal British Arsenal in Woolwich, used the generation of arsine gas to develop the first reliable method to determine an absorbed poison in body tissues and fluids, such as liver, kidney, and blood.

The 1800s witnessed the development of forensic toxicology as a scientific discipline. In 1814, Mathieiv J. B. Orfila (1787–1853), the "father of toxicology", published *Traité des Poisons* — the first systemic approach to the study of the chemical and physiological nature of poisons. Orfila's role as an expert witness in many famous murder trials, and particularly his application of the Marsh Test for arsenic in the trial of the poisoner Marie Lafarge, aroused both popular and scholarly interest in the new science. As Dean of the Medical Faculty at the University of Paris, Orfila trained many students in forensic toxicology.

The first successful isolation of an alkaloid poison was performed in 1850 by Jean Servials Stas, a Belgian chemist, using a solution of acetic acid in ethyl alcohol to extract nicotine from the tissues of the murdered Gustave Fougnie. Modified by the German chemist, Friedrich Otto, the Stas-Otto method was quickly applied to isolation of numerous alkaloid poisons, including colchicine, conin, morphine, narcotine, and strychnine; the method is still used today.

In the second half of 19th century, European toxicologists were in the forefront of the development and application of forensic sciences. Procedures were developed to isolate and detect alkaloids, heavy metals, and volatile poisons.

In America, Rudolph A. Witthaus, Professor of Chemistry at Cornell University Medical School, made many contributions to toxicology and called attention to the new science by performing analyses for New York City in several famous poisoning cases: the murders of Helen Potts by Carlyle Harris and of Annie Sutherland by Dr. Robert W. Buchanan, both of whom used morphine. In 1911, Tracy C. Becker and Professor Witthaus edited a four-volume work on medical jurisprudence, *Forensic Medicine and Toxicology*, the first standard forensic textbook published in the U.S. In 1918, the City of New York established a medical examiner's system, and the appointment of Dr. Alexander O. Gettler as toxicologist marked the beginning of modern forensic toxicology in America. Although Dr. Gettler made many contributions to the science, perhaps his greatest was the training and direction he gave to future leaders in forensic toxicology. Many of his associates went on to direct laboratories within coroner and medical examiner systems in major urban centers throughout the country.

In 1949, the American Academy of Forensic Sciences was established to support and further the practice of all phases of legal medicine in the U.S. The members of the toxicology section represent the vast majority of forensic toxicologists working in coroners' or medical examiners' offices. Several other international, national, and local forensic science organizations, such as the Society of Forensic Toxicologists and the California Association of Toxicologists, offer forums for the exchange of scientific data pertaining to analytical techniques and case reports involving new or infrequently used drugs and poisons. The International Association of Forensic Toxicologists, founded in 1963, with over 750 members in 45 countries, permits worldwide cooperation in resolving technical problems confronting the toxicologist.

In 1975, the American Board of Forensic Toxicology was organized to examine and certify forensic toxicologists. One of its stated objectives is "to make available to the judicial system, and other public, a practical and equitable system for readily identifying those persons professing to be specialists in forensic toxicology who possess the requisite qualifications and competence". In general, those certified by the Board must have an earned Doctor of Philosophy or Doctor of Science degree, have at least 3 years full-time professional experience, and pass a written examination. At present, only about 200 toxicologists are certified by the Board.

Deaths Investigated by Toxicologists

Accidental Poisoning

Most accidental poisonings occur in the home. Children, due to their innate curiosity and adventurous nature, may gain access to and ingest prescription drugs, detergents, pesticides, and household cleaners. Fortunately, public awareness of the safe storage of household chemicals, safety top containers, the availability of poison control information centers, and better emergency-room procedures for treating child poisonings have all contributed to a marked decrease in this type of death. Accidental poisoning in adults is usually the results of mislabeling, storage of a toxic substance in a container other than the original one. As often as not, the improper container is an old whiskey bottle! Arsenic, weed killer, strychnine, cyanide, cleaning solutions, and numerous other deadly poisons have been eagerly and mistakenly drunk from cider jugs and old whiskey bottles. An open container of cyanide next to a tin of sugar on a basement work bench has been known to sweeten a final cup of coffee.

Accidental poisonings may occur in industry due to carelessness or mishaps which expose workers to toxic substances. While the potential for accidental poisonings in industry is great, safety standards and regulations and the availability of emergency medical services today prevent industry from being a source of many fatal intoxications.

Deaths from Drug Abuse

Drug abuse, the nonmedical use of drugs or other chemicals for the purpose of changing mood or inducing euphoria, is the source of many poisonings. Drug abuse may involve the use of illicit drugs such as heroin or phencyclidine; the use of restricted or controlled drugs such as cocaine, barbiturates, and amphetamine; or use of chemicals in a manner contrary to their intended purpose — such as inhaling solvents and aerosol products. Since the development and glorification of the "drug culture" in the mid-1960s, deaths due to illicit drug use are the most common fatal poisonings investigated by toxicologists, particularly in large urban areas. Table 8.1 presents the drugs most commonly encountered in death investigations; note the high incidence of cocaine, alcohol, and heroin/morphine.

In a broader sense, drug abuse may also include the excessive use of legal substances, such as alcohol and prescription drugs. The use of alcohol is the biggest drug problem in the U.S. Alcohol plays a significant role in violent deaths. Of the 40,000 automobile accident deaths that occur annually in the U.S., 50% involve drinking drivers, and 60% of pedestrians killed have significant blood alcohol levels. Of urban adults who were admitted to a hospital with a fractured bone, 50% fractured the bone during or after drinking. Significant blood alcohol levels are found at autopsy in 35% of all persons committing suicide and in 50% of all murder victims. Also, many people die each year due to many pathologic conditions directly attributed to alcohol or complications of other pathologic conditions aggravated by alcohol consumption. Alcohol is a self-limiting poison:

**Table 8.1   Drugs Most Frequently Encountered
in Medical Examiners Cases, 1991[a]**

Rank	Drug Name	Number of Mentions	Percent[b] of Total Episodes
1	Cocaine	3,020	45.75
2	Alcohol — in combination	2,436	36.90
3	Heroin/Morphine	2,333	35.3
4	Codeine	783	11.86
5	Diazepam	587	8.89
6	Amitriptyline	437	6.62
7	Methadone	430	6.51
8	Nortriptyline	379	5.74
9	d-Proxpoxyphene	325	4.92
10	Diphenhydramine	241	3.65

[a] Drug Abuse Warning Network, National Institute on Drug Abuse data from 27 metropolitan areas.
[b] Percent of total episodes may exceed 100%, as a single case may involve more than one drug.

people usually lose consciousness before a lethal dose is ingested. Therefore, overdose deaths due to the ingestion of excessive quantities of alcohol are uncommon. However, numerous accidental deaths occur from the concurrent ingestion of potent prescriptions drugs and alcohol.

Suicidal Poisoning

Suicide is a common manner of death in cases of poisoning. In general, about twice as many men successfully commit suicide as women. However, twice as many women attempt to commit suicide with poison as men. The most common suicidal agent is carbon monoxide, a gas generated by the incomplete combustion of carbonaceous compounds. Automobile exhaust contains a substantial concentration of carbon monoxide. Allowing a car motor to run in a closed garage is the usual method used by those who commit suicide with carbon monoxide. While cyanide, arsenic, and other well known poisons may be occasionally used as suicidal agents, most deaths result from prescription drugs. Persons suffering from depression and other emotional disturbances usually have available a supply of potent and, if taken in excess, deadly drugs to combat the symptoms of their psychological disorders. Today, most suicidal poisonings involve multiple drug ingestion; usually three to seven different drugs are ingested at one time. By analyzing the gastric and bowel contents, blood, urine, and the major organs of the body, the toxicologist can determine the minimum quantity of the poison ingested. In suicides, the results of such analysis demonstrate that a massive quantity was taken; this establishes beyond doubt that the decedent could not have accidentally taken such a dose.

Homicidal Poisoning

Accidental and suicidal poisonings are common today; murder by poison is rare. Determining that a person died as the result of homicidal poisoning is often the most difficult type of investigation for law enforcement officers and medical experts. The general evidence of poisoning is obtained from a knowledge of the symptoms displayed by the decedent before death, the postmortem examination of the body by the pathologist, and the isolation and identification of the poison by the toxicologist. For successful prosecution of a suspect, law enforcement officers must establish that the perpetrator had access to a supply of the poison, that the suspect was aware of the lethal effects of the poison, and that the suspect had opportunity to administer the poison to the decedent.

When the victim is attended to, before death, by a physician, the doctor seldom, if ever, considers poisoning as a cause of the patient's ills. Only if the patient's occupation brings him into contact with toxic substances (works in a refinery, chemical, or smelting plant; works on a farm and uses pesticides and herbicides) will the physician suspect a chemical intoxication. Murder by poison most commonly occurs within the home, and the physician will seldom suspect a bereaved husband, wife, son, or daughter of poisoning another family member. Also, there is rarely any symptom of poisoning which cannot equally well be caused by disease. Vomiting, diarrhea, rapid collapse, and weak pulse, all symptoms of arsenic poisoning, may also be due to a ruptured gastric ulcer or an inflammation of the pancreas or appendix. Likewise, both strychnine and tetanus cause convulsions. Contracted pupils and narcosis may be from narcotic drugs or brain lesions. However, there are circumstances which render a diagnosis of poisoning moderately certain. The onset and progression of symptoms to rapid death immediately after eating or drinking indicate acute poisoning, since bacterial food poisoning has a delayed onset of symptoms.

The pathologist can recognize the effects of certain poisons at autopsy. Strong acids and alkalis may cause extensive burns around the mouth or the surface of the body, with severe destruction of the internal tissues. Metallic poisons may cause intensive damage to the gastrointestinal tract, liver, and kidneys. Phosphorus, chlorinated hydrocarbons, and poisonous mushrooms cause gross fatty degeneration of the liver. However, most poisons do not produce observable changes in body tissue; hence, in many instances of poisoning, the value of the pathologist's examination of the body is establishing that death was not due to natural causes or traumatic injury and that there is no evidence for cause of death except from possible poisoning. In most cases, toxicological analysis produces evidence for murder by poison.

Toxicological Investigation of a Poison Death

The toxicological investigation of a poison death may be divided into three steps:

1. Obtaining the case history and suitable specimens
2. The toxicological analyses
3. The interpretation of the results of the analyses

Case History and Specimens

Today, there are readily available to the public thousands of compounds that are lethal if ingested, injected, or inhaled. The toxicologist has only a limited amount of material on which to perform his analyses; therefore, it is imperative that, before beginning the analyses, he or she is given as much information as possible concerning the facts of the case. The toxicologist must be aware of the age, sex, weight, medical history, and occupation of the decedent, as well as any treatments administered before death, the gross autopsy findings, drugs available to the decedent, and the time interval between the onset of symptoms and death. In a typical year, the toxicology laboratory of a medical examiner's office will perform analyses on tissues for such diverse poisons as prescription drugs (analgesics, antidepressants, hypnotics, tranquilizers), drugs of abuse (hallucinogens, narcotics, stimulants), commercial products (antifreeze, aerosol products, insecticides, rodenticides, rubbing compounds, weed killers), and gases (carbon monoxide, cyanide). Obviously, the possible identity of the poison prior to analysis would greatly help.

The collection of specimens for toxicological analysis is usually performed by the pathologist at autopsy. Specimens from numerous body fluids and organs are necessary as drugs and poisons display varying affinities for the body tissues (see Table 8.2). Drugs and poisons are not distributed evenly

Table 8.2 Exhibits Collected at Autopsy for Toxicological Analysis

Specimen	Quantity	Toxicant Sought
Adipose tissue	200 g	Insecticides, thiopental
Bile	All available	Codeine, morphine
Blood	15 ml	Alcohols, carbon monoxide
Brain	500 g	Volatile poisons
Kidney	One whole organ	Heavy metals
Liver	500 g	Most toxicants
Lung organ	One whole	Methadone, gases, inhalants
Stomach and intestinal contents	All available	All toxicants taken orally
Urine	All available	Most toxicants
Vitreous humor	All available	Digoxin, electrolytes, glucose

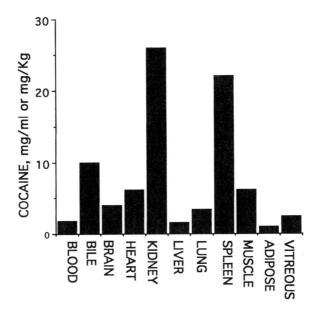

Figure 8.1 Distribution of cocaine in cases of fatal intravenous injection. (Data from Poklis, et al., *J. Anal. Toxicol.*, 9, 227, 1985. With permission.)

throughout the body, and the toxicologist usually first analyzes those organs expected to have the highest drug concentrations, Figure 8.1. A large quantity of each specimen is needed for thorough toxicological analysis because a procedure which extracts and identifies one compound or class of compounds may be ineffective in extracting or identifying others.

In collecting the specimens, the pathologist labels each container with the date and time of autopsy, the name of the decedent, the identity of the sample, and the signature of the pathologist. The toxicologist, when receiving the specimens, gives the pathologist a written receipt and stores the specimens in a locked refrigerator until analysis. This procedure provides an adequate chain of custody for the specimens which enables the toxicologist to introduce his results into any legal procedures arising from the case.

Specimens should be collected before embalming, as this process may destroy or dilute the poisons present and render their detection impossible. For example, cyanide is destroyed by the embalming process. Conversely, methyl or ethyl alcohol may be a constituent of an embalming fluid, thus giving a false indication of the decedent's drinking prior to death.

Toxicological Analysis

Before beginning the analysis, the toxicologist must consider several factors: the amount of specimen available, the nature of the poison sought, and the possible biotransformation of the poison. Because he is working with a

limited amount of specimen, the toxicologist must devise an analytical
approach which will allow the detection of the widest number of compounds.
Figure 8.2 outlines a schema for the isolation of poisons when the offending
compound is not known. In cases involving oral administration of the poison,
the gastrointestinal contents are analyzed first, since large amounts of residual
unabsorbed poison may be present. The urine may be analyzed next, as the
kidneys are the major organ of excretion for most poisons and high concentrations of toxicants are often present in urine. Following absorption from
the gastrointestinal tract, drugs or poisons are first carried to the liver before
entering the general systemic circulation; therefore, the first analysis of an
internal organ is conducted on the liver. If a specific poison is suspected or
known to be involved in a death, the toxicologist chooses to first analyze
those tissues and fluids in which the poison concentrates.

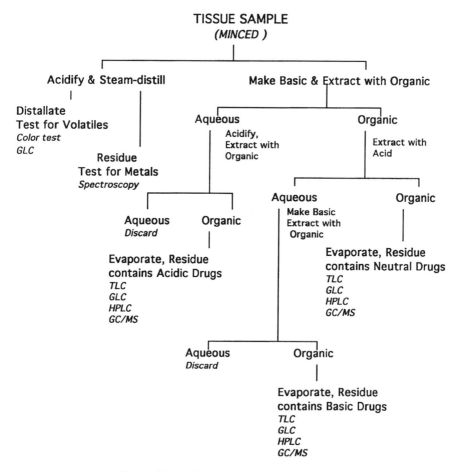

Figure 8.2 Schema for isolation of poisons.

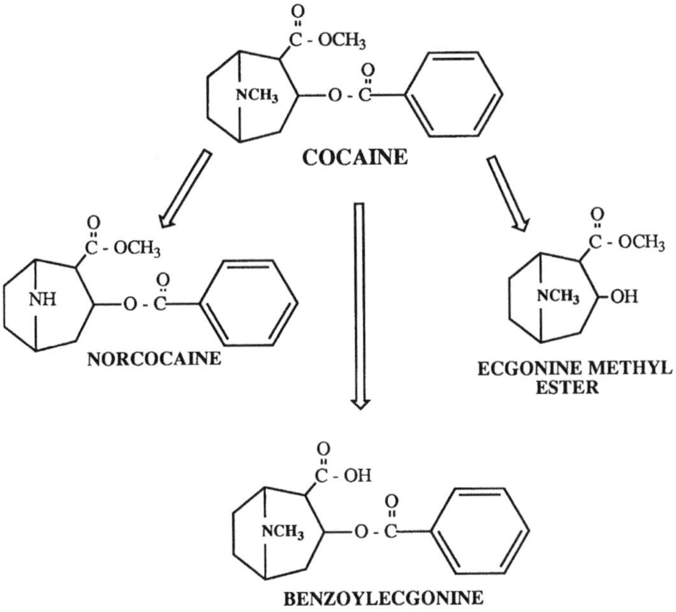

Figure 8.3   Biotransformation of cocaine.

Biotransformation is a term used to denote the conversion by the body of a foreign chemical to a structurally different chemical. The new compound is called a metabolite. Biotransformation of a drug or poison usually, but not always, results in formation of a physiologically inactive substance which is more readily excreted from the body than the parent compound. Figure 8.3 presents the biotransformation of cocaine. Metabolites may be physiologically active or inactive and nontoxic, less toxic, or more toxic than the parent compound. Cocaine exemplifies this process as norcocaine is physiologically active, while benzoylecgonine and methylecgonine have no physiologic action (Figure 8.3). Thus, the toxicologist must have an understanding of biotransformation reactions. In some instances, the metabolites are the only evidence that a drug or poison has been administered. Evidence of heroin or cocaine use is indicated by the presence of their respective metabolites, morphine and benzoylecgonine.

The toxicologist must be aware of the normal chemical changes which occur during a body's decomposition. The autopsy or toxicological analysis should be started as soon after death as possible, as natural decomposition processes may destroy a poison initially present at death or may produce substances or compounds with chemical or physical properties similar to those of commonly encountered poisons. For example, during decomposition, phenylalanine, an amino acid normally present in the body, is converted to phenylethylamine, which has chemical and physical properties very similar to amphetamine. The ethyl alcohol and cyanide content of blood may be decreased or increased depending on the degree of putrefaction and microbial activity. However, many poisons, such as arsenic, barbiturates, mercury, and strychnine, may still be detectable many years after death.

In the investigation of a poisoning, it is first necessary for the toxicologist to isolate and identify the poison. Therefore, forensic toxicologists group poisons according to the method used to isolate the substances from body tissues or fluids.

Group I: Gases

Most gases of toxicological significance are not detectable in autopsy specimens. However, some may be isolated from blood or lung tissue by aeration processes. Usually, air samples are collected at the scene of exposure.

Group II: Steam Volatile Poisons

Compounds in this group are isolated by steam distillation. The sample (blood, urine, or a tissue homogenate) is made acidic with hydrochloric acid or basic with solid magnesium oxide. A stream of steam is passed through the sample and the volatile poisons are distilled off in an aqueous distillate. Poisons distillable from an acid medium include carbon tetrachloride, chloroform, cyanide, ethanol, methanol, phenols, nitrobenzenes, and yellow phosphorus. Poisons distillable from a basic medium include amphetamine, aniline, meperidine, methadone, and nicotine.

Group III: Metallic Poisons

Metals are isolated from tissue by destroying all the organic matter comprising the tissue. The tissue may be destroyed by excessive heat (dry ashing) or by boiling with concentrated acids or strong oxidizing agents (wet ashing). Various methods may be used to identify specific metallic poisons remaining in the ash.

Group IV: Nonvolatile Organic Poisons

This group contains most of the drugs of interest to toxicologists in the U.S. today. Compounds in this group are usually present in tissues only in minute quantities. Some drugs (e.g., barbiturates) may be directly extracted from tissue homogenates by organic solvents. However, many compounds are often separated from the bulk of the tissue matrix by preparing a protein-free filtrate of tissue. This filtrate is then subjected to selective extraction with organic solvents under varying conditions of acidity. Using such techniques, drugs are isolated into five subgroups.

1. Strong acids (e.g., chlorothiazide, salicylates)
2. Weak acids (e.g., acetaminophen, barbiturates)
3. Neutrals (e.g., meprobamate, methaprylon)
4. Bases (e.g., codeine, phenothiazines, quinine, strychnine)
5. Amphoterics (e.g., hydromorphone, morphine)

Group V: Miscellaneous Poisons

This group includes all poisons not classified in the previous four groups. The substances included in this group are inorganic anions (e.g., bromine), highly water soluble organic ions (e.g., curare, fluoroacetate, paraquat), and organic compounds insoluble in water or alcohol. Generally, specific techniques must be used to isolate and identify these compounds from biological samples.

In performing an analysis, the toxicologist has available all the techniques of modern analytical chemistry. If the poison which caused the death is known, a specific analysis may be performed; however, if the agent is not known, or more than one toxicant is suspected, the toxicologist must first perform a series of analyses to determine which toxicants are present and then determine by quantitative analysis the amount of each toxic substance present in the various specimens. While numerous chemical methods are available to the toxicologist, only a few of the more common procedures are discussed. All of these methods can be applied to qualitative (identification) and quantitative (concentration) analysis.

Color Test

A color test is a chemical procedure in which the substance tested for is acted on by a reagent which causes a change in the reagent, thereby producing an observable color or color change. Color tests may be used to determine the presence of specific compounds or a general class of compounds. The procedures are usually rapid and easily performed. The greatest utility of color tests in toxicology is the rapid screening of urine specimens, as the urine may be analyzed directly without time-consuming extraction procedures. An example of color test is the "Trinder's test" for the detection of salicylates in blood or urine. A reagent of ferric nitrate and mercuric chloride is mixed with 1 ml of blood or urine; if salicylates are present, a violet color is observed. As in all other toxicology testing, the presence of salicylates must be confirmed by another method of analysis. A positive Trinder's test is observed for salicylic acid (a metabolite of aspirin), salicylamide, and methyl salicylate. A false-positive, that is the development of a color when no salicylate is present, may be observed in urine of diabetic patients excreting acetoacetic acid and in patients receiving high therapeutic doses of phenothiazine drugs. The toxicologist must be aware of the limitations of the tests he performs and particularly the sources of false-positive reactions.

Microdiffusion Test

Microdiffusion analysis is used for the rapid isolation and detection of volatile poisons. A simple microdiffusion apparatus consists of a small porcelain dish with two separate compartments, an inner well surrounded by an outer well formed between the periphery of the wall of the inner compartment and the higher outside wall of the dish. The outer well is the sample cell, to which a small quantity, 1 to 5 ml, of blood, urine, or tissue homogenate is added. To the inner well an "absorbent" is added. The absorbent is a reagent or solvent in which particular volatile substances will readily dissolve. After the sample and absorbent are added to the proper cell, the dish is sealed with a viscous sealant material and a ground-glass cover plate. If allowed to sit at room temperature or gently heated, the volatile poison will diffuse from the sample into the atmosphere of the dish and be entrapped by the absorbent solution, which often is a color reagent. As the poison is liberated from the sample, the toxicologist may observe a color formation or color change in the absorbent in the inner well. Numerous volatile poisons and gases may be detected by microdiffusion techniques; they include acetaldehyde, carbon monoxide, cyanide, ethanol, fluoride, halogenated hydrocarbons, and methanol.

Chromatography

Chromatography is a separation technique. The components of a sample mixture are distributed between two phases, one of which is stationary while the second one, the mobile phase, percolates through a matrix or over the surface of a fixed phase. The components of a sample mixture exhibit varying degrees of affinity for each phase, and as they are carried along by the mobile phase, a differential migration occurs. Some components are retained on the stationary phase longer than others, producing a separation of the compound. The retention of a component by the stationary phase depends on several factors, including the chemical and physical nature of the stationary and mobile phases, as well as the experimental conditions, such as temperature or pressure. It is essential, therefore, that pure reference standards be chromatographed under the same conditions as the unknown materials. Compounds are tentatively identified by comparing their retention on the stationary phase with that of the reference standards. Following chromatography, the identity of the compounds must be substantiated by other methods of analysis. There are many varieties of chromatographic analysis; however, only the three most commonly applied by toxicologists will be briefly discussed. These are thin-layer chromatography (TLC), gas liquid chromatography (GLC), and high-performance liquid chromatography (HPLC).

Thin-Layer Chromatography.   In TLC, the stationary phase is a "thin layer" of an absorbent, usually silica gel, which is spread on a solid support, such as a glass plate. Concentrated sample extracts and drug standards are applied as a series of spots along the bottom of the plate and allowed to dry. The plate is then placed in a closed tank, in which the absorbent layer makes contact with a "developing solvent" (mobile phase) below the applied spots. The solvent moves up the plate by capillary action, dissolving and separating the components of the extracts. When the solvent has reached the top of the plate or ascended a predesignated distance, the plate is removed from the tank and the solvent evaporated from the plate. Each individual drug in the standard mixture and in the extracts will separate during migration, producing a series of spots or narrow bands extending from the bottom to the top or solvent front on the plate. The migration of compounds is expressed by the retention factor (Rf) which is defined as the ratio of the distance moved by the compound to the distance the mobile phase ascends the plate from the point of application of the compound. The presence of a drug is visualized by spraying or dipping into the plate various reagents which produce colored reactions with particular components. Several sprays may be used in sequence to aid in identification of compounds. Some drugs will react with certain reagents but not with others. For example, in screening urine extracts for the presence of drugs of abuse, the toxicologist may first spray the chromatogram with ninhydrin, which produces a red or pink color with primary amines such as amphetamine or ephedrine. Next, he may apply ethanol in sulfuric acid, which produces a series of brightly colored pink, orange, blue, or green spots with phenothiazine tranquilizers and their metabolites. The plate may then be sprayed with iodoplatinate, which reacts with all nitrogenous bases. There are numerous TLC spray reagents to choose from, but the toxicologist must be guided by the chemical nature of the compounds it is desired to identify. If a compound from the extract migrates the same distance and reacts to the applied sprays in the same manner as the reference drug, the toxicologist then has a tentative identification of the compound, which must be confirmed by another chemical test; however, he has ruled out all compounds which do not migrate the observed distance in this TLC solvent system and do not react in the same manner to the spray reagents. Table 8.3 presents the Rfs and reactions with visualization reagents of several drugs commonly sought in toxicology screening.

Gas Liquid Chromatography.   In GLC, the mobile phase is an inert carrier gas (e.g., helium, nitrogen) which flows through a column packed with a solid support coated liquid stationary phase (packed column) or over a stationary phase coating the walls of narrow column (capillary column). Numerous types of liquid materials are available, and the toxicologist varies the stationary phase depending upon the nature of the compounds or groups of compounds he wishes to separate and identify. Extracted samples are

Table 8.3 Thin Layer Chromatographic Data of Some Drugs of Toxicological Interest

| Drug | Rf | Spray Reagent | | | | |
		Ninhydrin	Diphenyl-Carbazone in Mercuric Sulfate	Heat	U.V. Light	Iodoplatinate
Morphine	0.15					Blue
Phenylpropanolamine	0.27	Red				Light brown
Codeine	0.30					Brown
Quinine	0.38				Blue	Brown
Amphetamine	0.39	Pink				
Phenobarbital	0.53		Purple			
Amobarbital	0.75		Purple			
Chlorpromazine	0.78			Red	Brown	Brown
Thioridazine	0.78			Blue		Dark brown
Diazepam	0.88				Yellow-green	Red-brown
Amitriptyline	0.98				Blue	Light brown

1. Developing solvent: ethyl acetate, 170 ml; methanol, 20 ml; ammonium hydroxide, 10 ml. (B. Davidow et al., *Am. J. Clin. Pathol.*, 38, 714, 1968.)

vaporized and carried through the column by the gas. As the components are eluted from the column, they are carried by the gas stream to a detector, which produces an electronic signal that is amplified and displayed on a recorder. The migration of a compound through the column is usually expressed by the retention time (Rt), which is defined as the time elapsed between injection of the sample and the detection of the compound. The retention time provides a tentative identification of the compound, and the strength of electronic signal to the recorder may be used to determine the quantity of the compound present in the sample. An extract of a specimen chromatographed under the same conditions as reference drugs and producing a peak at the same time would be tentatively positive for the reference drug in the specimen. The height of the peak and the area under the peak are directly related to the concentration of the drug present. Gas chromatography is particularly suitable for the analysis of volatile substances such as alcohols (Figure 8.4).

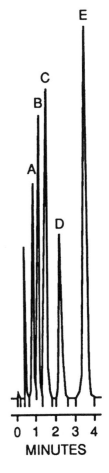

Figure 8.4 Gas chromatographic separation of common volatiles: (A) methanol, (B) acetone, (C) ethanol, (D) isopropanol, (E) butanol.

High-Performance Liquid Chromatography.   In HPLC the mobile phase is a liquid which flows through a column packed with solid stationary phase under continuous pressure. Numerous types of stationary materials are available, and the toxicologist may use almost any solvent or numerous aqueous mixtures as the liquid phase. Therefore, specific procedures can be developed for separating compounds which are not easily resolved by other chromatographic methods. The method is particularly suited for heat liable compounds, which may decompose when volatilized for GLC separations. As with GLC, eluted drugs are identified by their Rt, and detector responses are proportional to the concentration of drug present in the sample.

Spectroscopy

Spectroscopy concerns the absorption or production of radiant energy. The absorption of radiation is a characteristic of all molecules; however, the wavelength of the absorbed radiation may vary from X-rays through ultraviolet, visible, and infra-red and on to microwave and radio frequencies. Therefore, the interaction between a chemical compound and radiation is dependent on its molecular structure and the wavelength of the radiation. When the absorption of radiation by a compound is determined relative to the wavelength of the radiation, an absorption spectrum is observed which is characteristic of that compound. The specificity of the spectrum is related to the region of absorption. For example, numerous compounds have identical ultraviolet (200 to 350 nm) spectra while infra-red (2.8 to 25 M) spectra are extremely specific "fingerprints" of a given compound. Also, there is a direct relationship between the magnitude of the absorption of radiant energy and the quantity of absorbing material present. This applies to the absorption of any radiant energy, from X-rays to radio waves. By experimentally choosing the wavelength of maximum absorption, the concentration of a compound present in a sample can be determined.

The spectrophotometer used to measure the absorption of radiant energy consists of a radiation source, a sample cell through which the radiation passes, and a detector for measuring the absorption of the radiation. The wavelengths most applicable to toxicological analysis are the ultraviolet, visible, and infra-red. The commercial instruments used for measuring the absorption of these forms of light may vary from simple colorimeters, used to measure absorption in the visible range, to highly sophisticated spectrophotometers employing monochromatic light and sensitive electronics to detect, amplify, and record low levels of radiation. While various forms of spectroscopic analysis may be applied to forensic toxicology analysis, only ultraviolet spectrophotometry will be discussed here.

Absorption of ultraviolet (UV) light may result in electronic transitions in organic molecules, causing the promotion of electrons from low-energy to high-energy orbitals. The actual wavelength of maximum absorption will depend on the chemical groups present in the molecule, the solvent in which the compound is dissolved, the pH, and the temperature of the solution. Aqueous and alcoholic solutions are the most common solvents used by toxicologists. Plotting or electronically graphing the absorbance of a compound vs. wavelength (210 to 350 nm) results in an ultraviolet absorption spectrum. The majority of drugs of toxicological interest absorb light in the ultraviolet region. The UV spectrum is characteristic of a compound under the experimental conditions and may be used for tentative identification of the presence of a given drug. However, identification is not unequivocal as numerous compounds display the same UV spectrum. For example, amphetamine, ephedrine, methamphetamine, phenylethylamine, propoxyphene, and many other drugs possess UV absorption maxima in acidic solution at 263, 257, and 252 nm. Also, if other UV absorbing compounds are present in a sample, a mixed spectrum (that is, the composite spectrum of all compounds) will be observed. Today, these limitations may be overcome by separating compounds by HPLC and then recording the UV spectrum as the isolated drugs elute from the column. The concentration of the drug may be determined by comparing the magnitude of absorption at the maximum wavelength of absorption to that of a series of concentrations of pure drug standards analyzed under the same experimental conditions.

Mass Spectrometry

In mass spectrometry, a sample is bombarded with a beam of electrons which produces a charged molecule or shatters the sample into ionic fragments of the original sample. The assortment of charged particles is then separated and detected according to their atomic masses. A "mass spectrum" is a display of the different mass-to-charge fragments produced and their relative abundance. Under experimental conditions, the fragmentation patterns of complex molecules yield a characteristic spectrum that is highly specific and often establishes an unequivocal identification. A typical fragmentation pattern of triazolam, a hypnotic drug used to treat insomnia, is presented in Figure 8.5. Identification of triazolam is based upon the molecular ion at 343, the characteristic mass-to-charge (m/e) fragmentation pattern, and the relative abundance of each ion. For example: 313 m/e, abundance 100; 238 m/e, abundance 87; 75 m/e, abundance 60; 342m/e, abundance 50; and so on. Generally, seven matches of an unknown sample compared to a reference standard are sufficient for identification. While simple in principle, the instrumentation used to produce mass spectra is highly complex.

In toxicological analysis, drugs or poisons are usually first separated by gas chromatographic analysis. As the compounds elute from the column, they are carried into the bombardment chamber of the mass spectrometer.

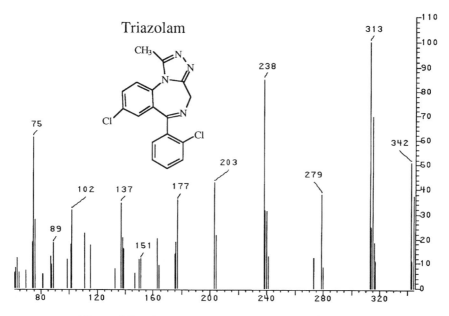

Figure 8.5 Electron impact mass spectrum of triazolam.

A computerized system displays the resultant mass spectrum and automatically searches stored spectra of known compounds to identify the unknown samples.

Immunoassay

Immunoassay is a technique which requires antibodies that bind tightly to the drug of interest and only weakly or not at all to other substances. At present, there are three commercially available systems, widely used in forensic toxicology: enzyme multiplied immunoassay technique (EMIT), fluorescent polarization immunoassay (FPIA), and radioimmunoassay (RIA). An immunoassay consists of a mixture of the drug-specific antibody and a "labeled drug" for which the antibody was prepared. The "label" may be a radioactive atom (RIA), or chemically attached fluorescent compound (FPIA), or an enzyme (EMIT). When a sample containing the drug of interest is added to the mixture, it competes with the "labeled drug" for binding to the antibody. The presence of the drug sought is indicated by a change in radioactivity (RIA), fluorescence polarization (FPIA), or enzyme reaction rate (EMIT). These techniques may be used for both qualitative and quantitative analysis. The techniques are rapid and often simple to apply, and samples may be analyzed directly without prior extraction. Therefore, immunoassay techniques are extremely useful in the rapid screening of specific toxicants in biological specimens such as urine. These techniques are highly specific for a given drug or class of drugs, as the drug is the only antigen which will react or bind with the prepared antibody. Any drug for which a specific antibody can be produced can theoretically be analyzed by immunoassay techniques.

Interpretation of Findings

Once the analysis of the specimens is completed, the toxicologist must interpret the findings as to the physiological effects of the toxicants on the decedent at the concentrations found. Specific questions as to route of administration, whether or not the concentration of the toxicant present was sufficient to cause death or to alter the decedent's actions so as to contribute to his death, must be answered. Assessing the physiological meanings of analytical results is often the most difficult problem faced by the forensic toxicologist.

In determining the route of administration, the toxicologist notes the results of the analysis of the various specimens. As a general rule, the highest concentrations of a toxicant will be found at the site of administration. Therefore, the presence of large amounts of drugs and/or poisons in the gastrointestinal tract and the liver indicate oral ingestion, while higher concentrations in the lungs compared to other visceral organs indicate inhalation, and high toxicant concentrations in tissues surrounding an injection site will indicate a fresh intramuscular injection. Intravenous injection introduces a drug directly into the systemic circulation, thus bypassing the initial effect of concentration in the liver. An examination of the relative drug concentrations in multiple tissues may indicate intravenous rather than oral injection (Figure 8.6).

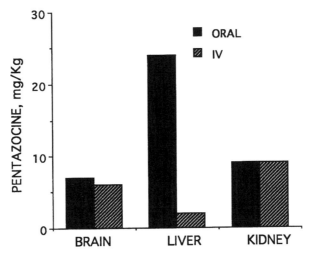

Figure 8.6 Comparison of the tissue distribution of pentazocine following oral and intravenous administration.

The presence of a toxic material in the gastrointestinal tract, no matter the quantity, is not sufficient evidence to establish that agent as the cause of death. The toxicologist must demonstrate that absorption of the toxicant occurred and that it has been transported by the general circulation to the organ where it has exerted a fatal effect. This is established by blood and tissue analysis. An exception to the rule is strong corrosive chemicals which exert their deleterious effects by directly digesting the tissues, thus causing hemorrhage and shock. Examples are concentrated hydrochloric and sulfuric acid, lye, and phenol.

The results of urine analysis are often of little benefit in determining the physiological effects of a toxic agent. In general, urine results establish only that sometime prior to collection of specimen a toxicant was present in the body. Correlation of urine values with physiological effects is poor, due to various factors influencing the rate of excretion of specific compounds and urine volume.

The physiological effects of most drugs and poisons correlate with the concentration in the blood and establish that absorption has taken place. Therefore, blood concentrations are often the best indicators of toxicity; consequently, blood is a most valuable specimen to the toxicologist.

To interpret blood or tissue levels properly, the toxicologist must consider all factors which influence obtaining a given toxicant concentration in a specimen. Interpretation of blood or tissue values may be divided into three categories: (1) normal or therapeutic, (2) toxic, and (3) lethal. A normal value is that concentration of a substance found in the general population and which has no toxic effect on the body. For example, cyanide is usually readily identified as a highly poisonous chemical; however, minute quantities of cyanide are generated following the ingestion of certain foods. Also, small amounts of cyanide are generated and absorbed during tobacco smoking. Therefore, small amounts of cyanide are a normal constituent in the body and low concentrations are tolerated without toxicity. Many heavy metals, such as arsenic, lead and mercury, which are not essential to normal body functions, are present in the general population due to environmental con-tamination. A therapeutic value is that concentration of a drug present fol-lowing a therapeutically effective dose — the sufficient amount of drug necessary to treat a medical disorder, but not enough to cause toxicity. A toxic value is a concentration of a compound which is associated with harm-ful effects which may or may not be life threatening. A lethal value is that concentration of a toxicant whose effect as the cause of death is consistently established in well documented and investigated cases. A comparison of normal and lethal tissue values for arsenic is presented in Figure 8.7.

In certain instances, the toxicologist may differentiate acute from chronic poisoning. For example, hair is the preferred specimen for the diagnosis of

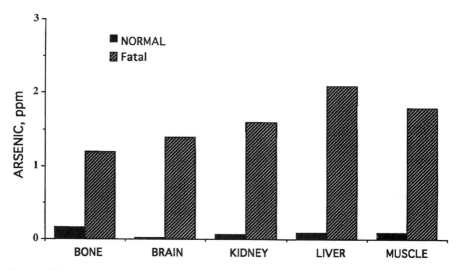

Figure 8.7   Arsenic tissue concentrations found in the normal population compared to those in a case of fatal poisoning.

chronic arsenic exposure. The analysis of sequential sections of hair provides reliable correlation to the pattern of arsenic exposure. Arsenic circulating in the blood is deposited in the hair follicle, where it is trapped by keratin and carried up the follicle in the growing hair. The germinal cells of the hair are in relatively close equilibrium with the circulating arsenic, and as arsenic concentrations in blood rise or fall, so does the amount of arsenic deposited in the growing hair. Hair grows approximately 0.4 to 0.5 mm/day or about half an inch (12.5 mm) per month. Therefore, analysis of 1.0-cm segments or less provides a monthly pattern of exposure. Normal arsenic content of hair varies with nutritional, environmental, and physiological factors; however, the maximum upper limit in persons not exposed to arsenic is about 5 ppm. Once an individual is removed from the source of arsenic exposure, hair values return to normal within several weeks. The profile of arsenic in the hair of a murder victim presented in Figure 8.8 is consistent with chronic arsenic poisoning. The murderer prepared the victim's meals the last 2 months of his life. The victim was in the hospital the third through the fifth months prior to death, and with the murderer before that time.

Factors which may influence the response of an individual to a given toxicant concentration include age, sex (normal status), body weight, maturity, and nutritional, genetic, and immunological status. Also, the presence of disease or specific organ pathology and central nervous system activity (depression, stress, etc.) must be considered. An additional factor which often complicates interpretation is the pharmacological phenomenon of "tolerance". Tolerance is a state of decreased responsiveness to a toxicant as a result of prior exposure to it or its chemical congener, usually over a long period

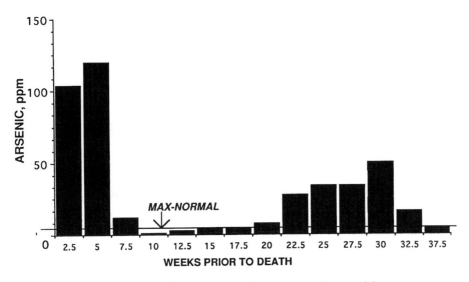

Figure 8.8 Distribution of arsenic in hair from a case of homicidal poisoning.

of time. There are several physiologic mechanisms for the development of tolerance; however, cellular adaptation is the most troublesome to the toxicologist. Cellular adaptation is a form of tolerance in which ever-increasing blood or tissue levels of a drug are necessary to elicit the desired pharmacological response. For example, narcotic addicts may regularly take doses of methadone which for them do not produce central nervous system depression, while the same dose may cause death in someone not regularly receiving opiates.

Factors that influence a given blood or tissue concentration following the administration of a toxicant are related to both the nature of the compound and the biological makeup of the individual. The chemical composition and physical characteristic of a material often affects its toxicity. For example, the hydrochloride or oxide salts of certain metals are much more soluble in the gastrointestinal tract and, hence, more rapidly absorbed than their sulfide salts. In general, the faster the absorption of an agent, the higher the blood concentration. Pharmaceutical preparations may be formulated in such a way that, following oral ingestion, the drug is absorbed either rapidly or extremely slowly. The biological factors primarily affecting blood concentration are its binding to tissue proteins and the rate of biotransformation of the toxicant. The rate of biotransformation of a substance is genetically controlled and is often subject to significant individual variations. If several individuals are given the same dose of drug per body weight, the blood concentration of each may vary greatly due to a difference in their rates of biotransformation of the drug.

Toxicants are eliminated from the body by various routes. Gases such as carbon monoxide are removed by the lungs in expired air. Others, such as toxic metals, DDT, and morphine, are primarily eliminated through the bile and, hence, feces. While these are not major routes of excretion, most poisons are present to some degree in all body secretions: milk, sweat, and tears. The major route of elimination of most toxicants is through the urine. The rate of elimination of toxicant by urine greatly affects the amount present in blood or tissues at any time. However, urinary excretion is often highly variable, depending upon the volume and acidity of the urine. Theoretically, it is possible to produce a tenfold change in rate of elimination of weakly acidic or basic drugs by changing the acidity of urine one pH unit.

Only after reviewing the case history, taking into account all the above factors of toxicity, distribution, and biotransformation and comparing the analytic results with similar cases reported in the professional literature or similar cases from his own experiences, does the toxicologist write his final interpretation of a case.

The Toxicologist as Expert Witness

The forensic toxicologist is often called on to testify in court as to his or her analytical findings and their interpretation. Although few toxicologists have medical degrees, they are frequently permitted to state in court the effects of drugs or poisons on the human body. When questioned as to his analytical findings, the toxicologist must first establish that he has maintained a proper chain of custody of all specimens analyzed. The written chain of custody establishes that all specimens received were from the stated decedent and were stored before, during, and after analysis in a manner which prevented unauthorized persons from tampering with the specimens. The toxicologist must be completely familiar with the principles, procedures, and limitations of all tests which he performed. His interpretation must reflect a knowledge of the professional literature, as well as his own experience with similar cases. Although he may disagree with other experts in the field, all his conclusions must be based on sound scientific or medical knowledge. As with all expert witnesses, the forensic toxicologist must present all testimony with honesty and integrity. If he does not know the correct answer to a question, he should state that he does not know. No one knows all things about any given field of medical or scientific endeavor. At best, a successful testimony in court may further the ends of justice; at worst, it may serve as an educational experience.

SUGGESTED READINGS

1. *Clarke's Isolation and Identification of Drugs in Pharmaceuticals, Body Fluids and Post-mortem Material,* 2nd ed., A. C. Moffat, Senior Ed., Pharmaceutical Press, London, England, 1986.

2. *Disposition of Toxic Drugs and Chemicals in Man,* 3rd ed., R. C. Baselt and R. H. Cravey, Yearbook Medical Publishers, Chicago, IL, 1990.

3. *Poison Detection In Human Organs,* 4th ed., A. S. Curry, Charles Thomas Publisher, Springfield, IL, 1988.

4. *Medical Toxicology, Diagnosis and Treatment of Human Poisoning,* M. J. Ellenhorn and D. G. Barcelous, Elsevier Science Publishing, New York, 1988.

5. *Introduction to Forensic Toxicology,* R. H. Cravey and R. C. Baselt, Biomedical Publications, Davis, CA, 1981.

SERIES

1. *Advances in Analytical Toxicology,* R. H. Baselt, Ed., Yearbook Medical Publishers, Boca Raton, FL.

2. *Methodology for Analytical Toxicology,* Vol. 1, 2, and 3, I. Sunshine, Ed., CRC Press, Boca Raton, FL.

Questioned Documents　9

WILLIAM H. STORER

Death, drugs, and disaster; bodies and blood, guns and glass; semen and saliva; bullets, bombs, and bite marks; tool marks and trauma; poisons, homicides, safe paint, footprints, fingerprints and psychoses. These are the kinds of events and evidence that challenge forensic scientists. These are the things that keep forensic laboratories working 7 days a week. And when the general public thinks of forensic science, these are the things that usually come to mind.

But there also are nonviolent — very subtle — tools of crime. They do not bruise, batter, slash, or shoot. Yet they are used to steal our money or threaten our security more often than guns, knives, pry bars, or bombs. They are just pieces of paper. In the forensic business, these paper weapons are called questioned documents.

They can be hold-up notes, extortion notes, or ransom notes; fake, burned, or altered business records; bogus checks and counterfeit $100 dollar bills. They can be venomous anonymous letters that divide and destroy business and family relationships. They can be the writings of a psychopathic killer: taunting obscenities that he has printed in lipstick on his victim's walls, mirrors, or even on the victim's body. They can be documents needing proof of genuineness or forgery, such as wills, contracts, deeds, charge slips, lottery tickets, insurance forms, or medical records.

So, as you review the various forensic science careers, consider also this unique career: forensic document examiner.

If you become a document examiner, you will not conduct crime scene searches, street investigations, interviews, or interrogations. These face-to-face encounters with the street reality of crime and its victims, witnesses and suspects are not the work of forensic document examiners. Document examiners are laboratory investigators — not field investigators — most of the time.

But know this, as a document examiner you will not be bored. Be assured, you will not find your work routine or mechanical. As document examiner you will be challenged constantly by the inconspicuous, often deceptive, and frequently invisible clues that hide in questioned documents. To find them and to fully evaluate them you will need plenty of supervised apprentice training and several years of hands-on laboratory experience. And you will need to develop a nagging self-discipline that keeps asking, "Have I discovered all there is?" — because questioned documents must always be challenged as well disguised and deceptive traps.

As document examiner you will usually work your cases solo — just you and the documents. In most cases you will not use quick chemical tests or sophisticated computerized instruments. Instead, you will use your eyes, your intellect, your experience, and optical tools such as the stereo-binocular microscope and camera. Solutions to most of your document problems will come from what you have detected with your eyes, microscope, camera, and other electronic tools. The accuracy of your conclusions will come from your very specialized apprentice training and from your experience in working a vast variety of questioned document cases.

Examining questioned documents is a personal and mostly subjective decision-making business. If you happen to work in a large laboratory with other document examiners, you will have the opportunity to discuss with them your findings and conclusions. But when the examiner's name on the report is yours, you alone will be responsible for the findings and conclusions. Your signature at the end of the report means that the conclusions are yours, not a committee's. And you will be expected to show judges and jurors why you believe you are right. And you will do it alone.

A word about conclusions. Lawyers call them opinions. Lawyers on the other side of the case always call them mere opinions, implying that your conclusions are no more than guesses. And you can count on being asked by opposing lawyers discrediting questions such as: "Isn't it possible that you are wrong?" "How many times have you been wrong?" "Isn't it possible that some other document expert will disagree with your opinion?" "How many times have you been opposed in court by another document expert?" and "Can you be wrong in this case?"

So as a forensic document examiner you will usually have two basic problems to resolve: (1) solving the evidence puzzle itself and (2) convincing judges and jurors that your opinions (conclusions) are correct.

Photographs can be powerful tools for convincing judges and jurors that you are right. Photographs convert opinion verbiage into visual demonstrations of your findings and conclusions. And photographs can convert disparaging cross-examination questions into pointless harassment. That is why document examiners must also be good photographers.

What you say and demonstrate in criminal court can often be the push that sends a defendant to prison, sometimes to death row. What you say and demonstrate in civil court can make or destroy a litigant's financial future. And what you report to investigators and to prosecutors can be the crucial evidence that rescues an innocent suspect from possible prosecution. So, if you can live with decision making that is invariably subject to attack, and if you want responsibility that directly affects the lives, liberty, and finances of others, then consider a career as a forensic document examiner.

What Is a Forensic Document Examiner?

The American Board of Forensic Document Examiners defines forensic document examination as follows:

> "Forensic document examination is the practice of the application of document examination to the purposes of the law. Forensic document examination relates to the identification of handwriting, typewriting, the authenticity of signatures, alterations in documents, the significance of inks and papers, photocopying processes, writing instruments, sequence of writings and other elements of a document in relation to its authenticity or spuriousness."

You will probably get a better idea of what document examiners do by a review of what they are asked to do. Later in this chapter you will see some questions that civil attorneys, prosecutors, defense attorneys, investigators, and assorted clients put to document examiners, but first…

Who Should Not Consider a Career in This Field?

Here are some considerations that might eliminate your choosing this forensic career. First, you must have good vision. Your eyes will be your basic tool for finding and recognizing evidence and for comparing things such as writing features and typeface designs.

You will be comparing colors, sizes, shapes, and inconspicuous microscopic items that only good vision can detect. You will constantly be looking at things close up, so you cannot have eye defects that go beyond correctable vision defects. Your precision, your accuracy, and your credibility will depend on what you see and on how well you interpret what you see.

If you are color blind, this is not the career for you. And if you cannot detect gross and subtle differences in sizes and shapes of things (the defect is called form-blindness), then this is no career for you. When you apply as an apprentice you can expect to be tested for color-blindness and form-blindness.

If public speaking freezes your senses, then maybe this career is not for you. Remember, you will sometimes testify in court. Judges and jurors are tough audiences. They will judge how you look, what you say, and how you say it. And, for certain, opposing lawyers will make vigorous assaults on your findings and conclusions; that is what they are hired to do. And, sometimes your ethics, objectivity, and motives will also be assaulted.

If you are the outdoor type that hates to sit at a lab desk for long periods, and if the microscopic world really does not interest you, then you probably will not like questioned document work.

Where Do You Receive Training?

Securing appropriate — emphasize *appropriate* — training in forensic documents is a difficult but not impossible goal. Unlike most of the forensic science disciplines, there are no colleges that offer a degree in forensic document examining. That leaves only one legitimate option: serving a lengthy apprenticeship in a questioned document laboratory.

Although some criminal justice curricula and a few seminars offer an introduction to forensic document work, they provide only a starting place for the interested student. A dedicated attempt by one criminal justice college to offer a full-time program in forensic documents failed after several years because of low enrollment. An indication, perhaps, that a desire to enter this forensic specialty lies not with college-bound forensics students but rather with people who are already employed in or out of the justice system.

A degree in criminalistics or a related laboratory science can get you started; it can be the key to employment in a law enforcement laboratory. That can be the first step to securing apprentice training in the forensic laboratory's questioned documents section.

Many aspiring examiners are beyond the usual college age. Some are looking for a job change; some are looking for an income or retirement supplement; some are people who purport to identify personality and behavioral traits from handwriting analyses; some are from academia who smugly believe that their current laboratory science or social science credentials when supplemented with some textbook reading are more than adequate credentials for hiring out as questioned document experts. Be assured, a lack of full-time supervised apprentice training does not discourage any of these aspiring examiners. They join the legions of the self-trained and self-certified who boldly operate in the civil sector where each practitioner can set his or her own credential standards. Knowledgeable heads of law enforcement agencies and prosecutors' offices who are aware of appropriate credentials do not deal with these self-trained practitioners. Thus, these people operate in the civil sector where they can easily hire out as experts just because they say they are.

Self-trained (which means not adequately trained) document examiners and other self-trained forensic identification specialists are a menace to fact-finding and justice. Which simply means that apprenticeship in a forensic document laboratory is the only appropriate training process.

So what is wrong with being a self-trained, self-made document examiner? Plenty! Consider that all trainees make mistakes; that is part of learning. But trainees with no full-time supervisors make mistakes that slip by undetected and uncorrected. That breeds faulty techniques, incompetence, and future mistakes. Remember: what document examiners say in reports and in court (and this applies to all forensic scientists) directly affects the liberty, the wealth, and even the life sometimes of the case's litigants, defendants, victims, and innocent suspects. Mistakes cannot be tolerated. Examiners cannot call back their mistakes like manufacturers of defective goods. And the potential for making mistakes is ballooned if the trainee is also the teacher.

Trainees need the personal presence of experienced examiners to show them how to see, how to interpret, how to evaluate, and how to reason. On-the-spot, full-time supervision is needed to critique and to correct. Trainees need face-to-face instruction on how to avoid making mistakes in judgments that so seriously affect others. Trainees need a wide range of training cases. These exist only in the files of established laboratories, not in books, short courses, seminars, or the annual get-togethers of other unqualified, self-certified, would-be examiners. And, of course, books, short courses, seminars, and the trainee herself or himself cannot evaluate or cultivate the trainee's own ethical thinking and standards.

Where Are These Training Laboratories?

You will find them in large-city police departments, state law enforcement agencies, federal law enforcement agencies, military services, and the private sector.

Today most legitimate training is available only at law enforcement laboratories. To repeat, this is because (1) there are no colleges or private schools that offer the absolutely necessary and appropriate 2-year forensic training in questioned document work, and (2) only large law enforcement labs have the staff and other resources necessary to support the trainee's study and money needs during a 2-year training period. Most legitimate examiners in private (civil) practice do not have the time or financial resources to support the apprenticeship needs of the trainee who produces no income.

You will find that many examiners now in private practice received their own training while on the staff of a law enforcement laboratory. Know also that there are well qualified examiners who hold no baccalaureate degree, but they have served an appropriate apprenticeship in a document lab.

Regarding the Credentials of Those Purporting to be Experts in any of the Forensic Science Disciplines

The courts (and forensic scientists themselves) usually equate minimum forensic credentials to college credentials. But the absence of available college training in questioned document work means that the courts and others have no universally accepted minimum standards (such as college or apprenticeship) for accepting or rejecting the credentials of purported document experts. Thus, the forensic documents discipline is one of the few that is open to anyone wishing to hire out as an expert, regardless of their training history. Fortunately, enlightened law enforcement agencies that maintain forensic labs now require that their document examiners meet the standards of and be certified *specifically* by the American Board of Forensic Document Examiners (ABFDE). Thus, the law enforcement sector is not an employment target of self-trained examiners. But the courts and lawyers in the civil sector either ignore or are not even aware of these ABFDE standards that expose and identify the nonapprenticed and undertrained. That is why the would-be's have formed organizations whose lesser standards will accommodate and "certify" those who cannot meet ABFDE standards.

The civil sector offers a tempting money-making vocation to anyone with a table, a magnifying device, and membership in a group that will "certify" its members on the basis of the group's own accommodating definition of training and experience. Some groups even use the term "board certified" to imitate and exploit the ABFDE's prestigious pioneering and valid "Board Certified Diplomate" rating. *Caveat emptor!!*

Today most legitimate trainees come directly from the ranks of a law enforcement agency's own field investigators or crime laboratory staff. So if you are thinking about a career in forensic documents, you should inquire now at the various law enforcement laboratories (federal, state, city, military) regarding their selection of document examiner trainees.

Here are some federal government agencies that maintain questioned document laboratories:

1. Federal Bureau of Investigation
2. U.S. Postal Inspection Service
3. U.S. Secret Service

4. Bureau of Alcohol, Tobacco, and Firearms
5. Internal Revenue Service
6. Central Intelligence Agency
7. U.S. military services

What Schooling and General Qualifications Should a Trainee Applicant Have?

Here are some qualifications you will want to meet. They are part of the qualifications and requirements for certification in forensic document examination as established by the ABFDE. While these qualifications apply to certification of already trained document examiners, they should be part of every trainee's career planning:

1. General qualifications:
   Applicants must be persons of good moral character, high integrity, and good repute and must possess high ethical and professional standing.
2. Educational qualifications:
   Applicants must possess an earned baccalaureate degree from an institution acceptable to the Board. Acceptable institutions are those accredited by regional accrediting commissions recognized by the U.S. Office of Education, and other institutions in the discretion of the Board.

When your training is completed and you have acquired some experience, you will want to apply for certification by the ABFDE. Here are some of the Board's professional requirements and qualifications for certification:

1. Forensic document examination is the practice of the application of document examination to the purposes of the law.
2. Forensic document examination relates to the identification of handwriting, typewriting, the authenticity of signatures, alterations in documents, the significance of inks and papers, photocopying processes, writing instruments, sequence of writing, and other elements of a document in relation to its authenticity or spuriousness.

As a trainee you will want to consider applying for membership in the questioned documents section of the American Academy of Forensic Sciences. Membership in the appropriate section of the Academy should be seriously considered by all career people in any of the forensic science disciplines.

Consider also membership in the American Society of Questioned Document Examiners.

Membership in either or both of these high-caliber professional organizations is not a professional requirement, but it does reflect an interest in the profession. Membership keeps you in touch with what is going on in your field and lets you make some contributions to your profession.

What Special Courses Should You Take in College?

A baccalaureate degree in one specific science area is not required. But you are strongly urged to consider at least a minor in one of the laboratory sciences, such as chemistry. Some document examiners have a degree in criminalistics.

As document examiner, you will be doing laboratory work with laboratory tools, so your schooling should be laboratory oriented. Laboratory science credits that include microtechniques will be your armor for your head-on battles with opposing lawyers in court.

You can expect trouble from judges and opposing lawyers if your chemical test findings are not supported with college chemistry credits. Because some judges will not allow you to testify about chemical tests without chemistry credits, your college chemistry and other science credits are, in effect, your "license to practice" in court.

So seek out laboratory science electives that will enhance your science skills and credentials. Following are are some suggestions:

Microchemical Analysis

Almost all of your work in document examining will be microscope oriented. The microscope will be your basic tool. Granted, as examiner, you will not do much chemical analysis unless you go to work in a document laboratory that does a lot of ink identifications and ink comparisons. But, your training in microchemical techniques will prepare you for doing ink analyses, for working with the microscope, and for handling microscopic evidence with disciplined precision. When you work with questioned documents, you are dealing with microscopic evidence, so take courses that include extensive use of microscopes and micro-techniques.

Writing

You cannot escape report writing. As document examiner, you will have to write reports that describe your findings and conclusions. You will want to write reports that preclude a reader's need to ask, "What do you mean by that?". Almost anyone can write a report filled with muddy verbiage and insider jargon. But investigators and clients want to read in specific but simple words what you found, what you concluded, and why.

Find a "news writer's" course. It can show you how to write non-wordy reports. And it can show you how to write technical papers (for other examiners to read) that are not filled with stuffy academic verbiage. If you are not acquainted with the keyboard of a computer and the use of computer programs for other than just word processing, then add that skill goal to your list.

Law

Forensic means that which deals with the courts and the law. So, as an expert working in the justice business (criminal and civil) you will be dealing directly on a daily basis with the rules of evidence, with the courts, with lawyers, and with law enforcement officers. As a trainee applicant you will do well to bring with you (or plan on earning) some course credits in civil law, criminal law, and the rules of evidence.

Photography

If you cannot take pictures with cameras having adjustable shutter speeds and lens apertures and if the following photographic terms are foreign to you, then you should consider some courses in basic and advanced photography: f/stop, exposure index, focal length, fine grain, guide numbers, filter factors, infrared photography, ultraviolet photography, macrophotography, microphotography.

Cameras are necessary investigating and reporting tools. You will use cameras to discover and decipher erasures, eradications, and obliterations on documents. You will use cameras to decipher and record invisible entries on burned documents. And you will use your camera for nondestructive (nonchemical) discovery of fraudulent ink entries and for the detection of differences between inks.

If questioned documents cannot be brought to your laboratory, then sometimes you must go to them. That means you will have to photograph them to make a record of what you saw and to allow more study of the evidence at your laboratory.

The presentation of video evidence and testimony at criminal and civil trials is increasing. And its usefulness in the questioned document lab is limited only by the document examiner's ingenuity and skill in using a video device. So, the document examiner trainee should acquire a knowledge of video recording devices, and a skill in video camera techniques and video presentations.

You will use cameras and darkroom tools and video devices to make presentations at trials, to show the jury what you saw, and to demonstrate the reasons why you know your conclusions are correct. Very simply, you cannot be a first-class document examiner unless you are a skilled photographer.

Identifying Handwriting

Forensic document examiners deal with handwriting most of the time. The act of writing employs our vision, our brain, and the movements of our muscles and nerves. We first learned to write by copying examples shown by instructors and copybooks. As beginners, our writing looked a lot like our classmates' because we all tried to copy the same examples. These common copybook characteristics (many of which continue to show in our adult writing) are called *class characteristics*. The writing of many people show similar class characteristics.

As we gained experience in writing and as our volume of writing increased, each of us developed variations of the copybook forms. Our deliberate attempts to change our writing style, our increasing writing skill and age, changing physical condition, and need (or lack of need) for speed and legibility all added uniqueness and individuality to our writing. These unique and often inconspicuous features that we knowingly and unconsciously put into our writing are called *individual characteristics*.

Individual characteristics in combination with class characteristics are the features that help separate one person's writing from another. They are part of our unconscious, automatic, and recurring writing habits. This simply means each of us when writing in our normal and usual fashion will write uniquely the same way tomorrow as we did yesterday and today, allowing for some natural variations.

With practice and increased use, the writing process becomes more and more an automatic unconscious act; habit takes over. We do not consciously need to think about how to form letters and words: our brain and muscles through habit will automatically construct them. So unless we deliberately tell our muscles to do otherwise, they will consistently reproduce our own unique writing characteristics time after time within our own personal range of natural variations.

There are exceptions to these principles, of course; there always are exceptions to general principles. Because of exceptions, every handwriting case must be treated as an unique puzzle. That is why identifying the author of writing, or identifying forgery, requires special supervised training.

You have heard the statement, "I never write the same way twice." That statement is not entirely accurate. To be accurate, the statement should be, "I never write exactly the same way twice." Your handwriting does vary. Thus, you do not write exactly the same way all the time. But under normal writing conditions your writing features remain consistently similar within a limited range of natural variations. The range of these variations can be found by examining appropriate known samples (exemplars) of a writer. When that writer's class characteristics, individual characteristics, and range of variations are pinpointed, and if these features are found to exist in questioned writing, that specific writer can usually be identified as the author of that questioned writing.

The limits of your natural writing variations do not hold if you make a conscious effort to change your writing. For example, right-handed anonymous letter writers might successfully avoid identification by altering their writing by using the awkward (left) hand, by deliberately contriving odd letter constructions, by changing the writing's slant, or by using any combination of these and other deceiving tactics. Physical injury to the writing hand, impaired vision, intoxication, awkward writing position, and illness might also alter a writer's usual writing features. If these conditions are extreme, the writer might not be identifiable. To repeat, the skills needed to recognize and interpret these problems in handwriting identification require plenty of supervised training and practical experience.

Genuine and Forged Writing

First, a few comments on the word "forgery". In the jurisprudence business, the word forgery has a special meaning: forgery is the making, altering, or writing of a document with the intent to defraud. "Intent to defraud" is the important phrase; however, you will find the terms forgery and imitation used interchangeably in this chapter.

To avoid implying that they know a writer's intent, document examiners do not use the term forgery in their reports or testimony. To stay out of lawyers', judges', and jurors' territory, document examiners use the term imitation (or some similar term) to report or testify that a signature or other writings are not genuine. Thus, an examiner's report might read: "The questioned John Doe signature on the contract comprising Specimen Q-1 is not the genuine signature of John Doe. It is a signature written by some other writer who attempted to imitate the genuine signature of John Doe."

Proving or disproving intent to defraud is the lawyer's job. Accepting or rejecting the lawyer's theories of intent is the job of the judge or jury. Providing demonstrable objective evidence is the document examiner's job.

To identify a signature as genuine or imitation (such as a will signature), the examiner needs known genuine signatures of the person whose signature is in question. To identify an unknown writer (as in the case of an anonymous letter writer) the examiner needs known writing samples of suspects. These known samples establish a writer's unique identifying characteristics and variations; the samples are called *exemplars* or *standards*.

The best exemplars are usually those that were not written specifically for comparison purposes, such as the writing on personal letters, business memos, personnel forms, business forms, and checks. These exemplars will most often show the writer's natural writing features and writing variations. Exemplars that are written specifically for comparison purposes, either voluntarily or by court order, can be deliberately contrived (disguised) by the writer in an attempt to avoid identification. Even when written by a person who is not attempting to alter his or her writing, these exemplars that were written for comparison purposes might not show the writer's more natural, casual, and careless writing features and variations.

Most law enforcement agencies have some kind of exemplar writing form that suspects are asked to fill out. The form shows a list of fictitious names, addresses, and numeral combinations. But, a single form usually provides only a meager amount of the needed writing. It usually does not provide enough of the specific letters and letter combinations needed for each specific case. Neither does a single form always reveal the writer's range of writing variations. And of course the suspect can also deliberately alter (disguise) his or her writing when filling out the form. Unfortunately, inexperienced investigators will often secure only one form. And that can produce inconclusive findings and very disappointed investigators.

Exemplars that are written specifically for comparison purposes should consist of many dictated pages of the same or similar text, words, numerals, names, etc. that comprise the questioned writing. It is a time-consuming process, but voluminous exemplars offer the best opportunity for successful handwriting investigations. Failures in many document investigations are caused by inadequate exemplars. To repeat, appropriate exemplars are the very foundation for any successful handwriting investigation.

Here are some of the features of genuine writing: smooth, rapid, nonstop, free-flowing pen movement; sweeping t-crosses and i-dots; sweeping starting and ending strokes; an absence of carefully made repair and correcting strokes; and letter formations and pen movements that show close similarity to the exemplars' letter formations and pen movements.

While the genuine writing of aged, ill, or unskilled writers can be slow, tremulous, and laboriously written, it will usually show a naturalness and consistency that can be recognized by the experienced examiner. These features are not like the slowly drawn, awkward, stop-and-go, inconsistent pen movements and divergent letter formations produced by a forger trying to imitate the writing of someone else. But, differentiating poorly written genuine writing features from the defective writing features of forgery is not always easy or possible. Success depends on many factors, such as the volume of the questioned writing, the volume of the exemplar writing and its closeness in date to the questioned writing, and the conditions under which the questioned and exemplar writings were written. These features of genuine writing and forged writing help examiners answer Questions 1 and 2 that follow.

The Examining Process

Using the unaided eye in combination with the microscope, the examiner compares the obvious and the inconspicuous writing features in the questioned writing with the writing features in the exemplar writing. These features include letter shapes, letter sizes, letter heights, the height relationships of letters, writing slant, the direction and shape of beginning and terminal strokes, letter connections, letter disconnections, pen pressure, and smoothness of pen movement. In brief, the examiner compares all of the features that make up the questioned writing and the exemplar writing.

The examiner looks for combinations of significant similarities and combinations of significant differences between the questioned writing and the exemplar writing. If the examiner finds combinations of significant similarities between the questioned and exemplar writing and if there occur no significant differences, then it becomes increasingly likely that the questioned writing and the exemplar writing were written by the same person. At the end of the study, after all of the evidence has been evaluated, the examiner might conclude that the person who wrote the exemplars was in fact the person who wrote the questioned writing, or in the case of a questioned signature, that the questioned signature is genuine.

But if combinations of significant differences exist between the questioned writing and exemplar writing and if the typical features of forgery exist in the questioned writing, then the examiner might conclude that the questioned writing was not written by the exemplar writer or, in the case of a questioned signature, that the signature is not genuine. These sound like simple principles, do they not? Well, the principles are simple and sound. But applying the principles and their exceptions is far from simple.

Note the terms "significant similarities" and "significant differences". These are subjective terms, are they not? They most certainly are. So who ultimately determines just what is significant and what is not? The examiner, of course. So when making handwriting comparisons, how do examiners objectively and accurately decide which features serve as significant similarities, which serve as significant differences, and which are not significant at all?

These decisions come from the examiner's knowledge and understanding of class characteristics, individual characteristics, and all the forces that can affect the way we write. And to repeat once more, this knowledge and understanding come from supervised training and much practical experience.

There will be times when examiners cannot give definite answers. They will have to report, "I do not know." And that inconclusive statement is not an answer that investigators and clients like to hear. But sometimes the available handwriting evidence will not permit a definite yes or no answer, as in the case of disguised writing or when too few or inappropriate exemplars are submitted.

In some cases, the examiner might decide that the evidence warrants more than just the inconclusive, "I do not know." So the conclusion might be reported as a degree of probability, such as, "It is highly probable that the John Doe signature is genuine." Or, with a lesser degree of probability, "The John Doe signature is probably genuine."

Reporting or testifying in varying degrees of probability can be a dangerous and misleading business. Report readers and jurors can easily misunderstand the examiner's specific meaning of "highly probable" or "probably" or any other terms that embrace degrees of probability. So the examiner must make it very clear in the report's wording or in courtroom testimony that the conclusion is less than certain. Reporting in degrees of probability is truly a subjective gray area. Thus, probability reporting demands very precise, nonambiguous explanations of the examiner's conclusion.

Witnesses in court who can qualify as expert are granted the extraordinary privilege of expressing their opinions (conclusions) based on their examinations of the evidence. But, an expert opinion is not the same as a best guess. Guessing (lawyers call it speculation, a conclusion without supportive demonstrable evidence) absolutely does not belong in written reporting or in testimony.

Reporting or testifying in varying degrees of probability must never be used to pacify a client or as a camouflage for what really is only the examiner's best guess. A probability opinion must never be used to avoid having to report the unwelcome, nonhelpful inconclusive opinion. But, be aware, there are those who take the position that any expert testimony or written conclusions that embody degrees of probability are nothing more than best guesses. If the examiner chooses to use a probability opinion rather than an inconclusive opinion, then the examiner must be prepared to demonstrate why the probability conclusion is more objective and more appropriate than, "I do not know."

Some Document Problems and How They Are Solved

Can document examiners answer all of the following 40 questions all the time? No. But many of the questions can be answered most of the time. Useful answers, of course, depend on the quality of the evidence and the skill, training, experience, and tools of the examiner.

It must be remembered that document examiners can evaluate only the evidence that is submitted. The examiner cannot use hearsay evidence, police reports, eyewitness statements, confessions, admissions, knowledge of other examiners' opinions, signed statements, or even notary affidavits, as elements for forming conclusions. Only the submitted physical evidence as evaluated by the examiner can serve as a basis for the examiner's own reports or testimony.

Following each of the first 23 questions is a brief discussion on how the problem might be solved. Each discussion does not, of course, reflect all the ways that the problem might be solved. Solving the problem (answering the question) can require many approaches combined with the examiner's experience, tools, and innovative skills.

1. **Is the signature on this document genuine or is it an imitation (forgery)?**

2. **Who wrote the signature or other writing on this document?**

Document examiners spend much of their time trying to answer these two questions because most document problems are handwriting problems.

Figure 9.1 shows a forgery on a fraudulent contract. The victim's wife was tricked into signing this contract while it was blank. The victim's own signature was then forged to complete the fraud. In Figure 9.1 you can see tremor and awkward, stop-and-go pen movements in the victim's first name, "Walter". These defects are the typical features of forgery. The victim's last name also showed the same features of forgery.

Figure 9.2 shows the victim's genuine (exemplar) writing. Note the smooth-flowing pen movement in the name "Walter". The victim's exemplar signatures (on canceled checks and other legitimate documents in this same business deal) showed no tremor, no pen lifts, no unnatural stops and starts. Figure 9.2 shows the typical features of genuine natural handwriting. The examiner's photo exhibits helped to convince the jury that the questioned signature was in fact not written by the victim.

When a writer (forger) attempts to imitate the writing of someone else (either by tracing or freehand copying), the forger's own identifying handwriting features are usually eliminated in the forging process. Thus, the writer of the Figure 9.1 forgery could not be identified.

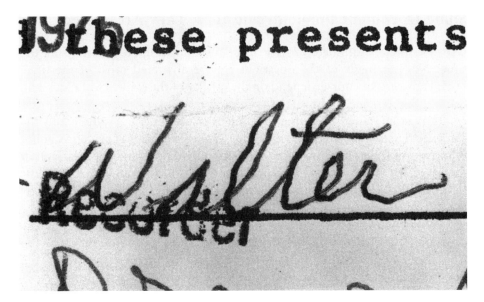

Figure 9.1

Figure 9.2

With regard to Question 2, questioned writings can appear on an infinite variety of documents, such as anonymous notes, purported suicide notes, business records, drug dealers' records, gambling records, medical records, and diaries. Identifying their author can be successful if (a) combinations of unique identifying similarities are found to exist between the questioned writing and the exemplar writing, and (b) no significant differences are found to exist between the questioned writing and the exemplars. And, the typical pen movement features of forgery, such as pen lifts at unnatural places, slow tremulous pen movements, and pen strokes that are added in order to repair or correct the forger's mistakes, must be absent in the questioned writing.

Successful (reliable) identifications depend on the amount of questioned writing, the amount of appropriate exemplars, the circumstances under which the questioned writings and the exemplars were written, and of course the training and experience of the examiner.

3. **Can this suspect be eliminated as the writer of the questioned writing?**

Differences that are found to exist between questioned writings and exemplars do not always signal that the exemplar writer should be eliminated as the writer of the questioned material. Differences can be contrived in the questioned writing by the writer, as in the case of anonymous letters. Differences can be the result of awkward writing positions, writing hand weakness due to illness, writing hand injuries, temporary eyesight injuries, and intoxication. Differences can occur when the exemplars themselves are deliberately disguised by the suspect. Differences can exist because the questioned writing and the exemplars are not of similar time periods. It should be noted that although the writing of some people will show a dramatic change over a long period of time, the writing of all people does not necessarily have to change. A writer might be eliminated when it can be shown that the suspected writer (via appropriate exemplars) did not have the natural writing skill to have written the more graceful, skillfully written questioned writing. You are invited to read the texts listed at the end of this chapter for an in-depth discussion of the nuances, pitfalls, coincidences, and exceptions to the rules that face examiners in the identification and elimination of writers.

4. **Was the document signed or prepared on the document's date?**

Investigations might show that a printed form itself was not in existence on the forms's date. The examiner's reference files might show that the typewriter or printer that produced the questioned entries was not in existence on the document's date. The design of a manufacturer's watermark in the document's paper stock might show that the design was not in existence on the document's date. Chemical analyses, if allowed, might show that the ink formulation (pen) did not exist on the document's date. But ink analyses of this kind require extensive ink sample reference files. Very tremulous exemplar signatures of an aged and ill person that are dated on and near the date of the questioned document can show that this writer did not have the physical ability to have produced the more skillfully written questioned signature. Other features of the questioned signature might show that it is an imitation. If the questioned signature is found to be genuine through exemplars from other dates, then the document's date does not reflect the writer's writing ability on that date. Thus, the document was not signed on the date it bears. Conversely, exemplars showing good writing skill that are dated on and near the date of the questioned document can show that the document's tremulous genuine signature (if it is found to be genuine) was not written on the document's date.

5. **What make of typewriter was used to produce this document?**

6. **Was the typewriter in existence on the document's date?**

The examiner's reference files can help identify the specific make, or the files may indicate several possible makes. Type styles that are similar can be found on typewriters of several different manufacturers, so examiners must be cautious before concluding that the questioned text was produced on a specific make of typewriter. Examiners attempt to maintain reference files that show type style changes that have been made at intervals by the various manufacturers. Thus, the evidence might show that the document exhibits a style or an individual letter or numeral design that did not exist on the document's date.

7. **Was this document prepared on the suspect's typewriter?**

Figure 9.3 shows damaged type characters: the lower case "o" and lower case "p". These were two of several damaged characters that were present on a series of threatening notes. See the notch at the upper left of the "o", and see the upward pointed spur on the lower left serif of the "p". These same two defects (and others) were also present in exemplars of a suspect's business letter (Figure 9.4). The combinations of similar individual characteristics (defects) existing in the questioned and exemplar texts showed that the questioned notes had been typed on the suspect's office typewriter. Of course, the evidence could not identify who typed the notes. Figures 9.3 and 9.4 show the effects of the damaged type characters on different paper surfaces.

8. **Were all the entries on this document typed during the same typing interval or were some entries added at a later time?**

A specially made glass plate, scribed with horizontal and vertical lines to form a grid, can be laid over the typewritten material to reveal alignment or misalignment of the entries.

| Figure 9.3 | Figure 9.4 |

For example, if the first and last typewritten lines on a contract's page are in perfect vertical and horizontal alignment with each other, and if a questioned entry that appears on a line between them is not in the same perfect alignment, the evidence shows that the questioned entry was not typed in sequence with the first and last lines. That is, the questioned entry was added at a later time. Typewritten questioned entries that show a ribbon condition that is different from other entries on the document can indicate or establish that the questioned entries and the other entries were made at different times.

Figure 9.5 shows a portion of a certificate of deposit. It was suspected that the name of another relative had been added (as co-owner) at a much later time. Although the same typewriter had been used, the questioned name (the top entry) shows a misalignment with the lower name. The top entry also shows a cloth ribbon imprint much weaker than the lower entry. The evidence clearly shows that the questioned upper name was added at a later time, when the ribbon was much drier.

9. **Was this document produced on this specific printer?**

10. **What kind of printer produced this document?**

The era dominated by the manual and electric printing machines that we have known as impact typewriters is over. Their dominance as office and home printing machines has passed. Although we will continue to see documents generated on manual and electric typewriters, these machines are rapidly being

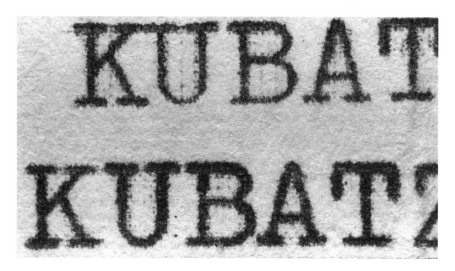

Figure 9.5

replaced in the work-place and home by new computer-controlled printers such as impact dot-matrix printers, inkjet printers, and laser printers.

Figure 9.6 shows the dot pattern of a 9-pin dot-matrix printer; the dot pattern serves to identify the dot-matrix printer. The dot pattern is less discernible in the pattern produced by a 24-pin printer or when a printer is set to "letter quality" mode rather than draft mode. The numerous pins that produce the dot-matrix characters can develop defects. And in some cases, the defects can be sufficiently unique to connect a questioned text to a specific dot-matrix printer. But these pin defects develop far less frequently than do the defects that develop in the typeface characters of impact manual typewriters and impact electric typewriters.

Figure 9.7 shows the imprint made by an ink jet printer. The fast drying ink is ejected onto the paper from tubes in the printer's ink cartridge. Note the feathered edges of the various letters caused by spattering of the ink on impact with the paper. The paper's surface texture can affect the amount of spattering. This spattering is one feature that helps to identify the ink jet printer.

Figure 9.8 was produced by a laser printer. The laser printer product is similar to that produced by a plain paper office copy machine. An image of the laser's keyboard generated text is electronically created on the printer's drum. Powdered toner sticks to the drum where the electronic image was formed. The toner image is transferred to plain paper and the toner is briefly heated so that the toner fuses to the paper: the same process as a xerographic office copy machine.

Viewed under the microscope, the printout of the laser printer is very similar if not identical to that of an office photocopy. Thus, it can be difficult

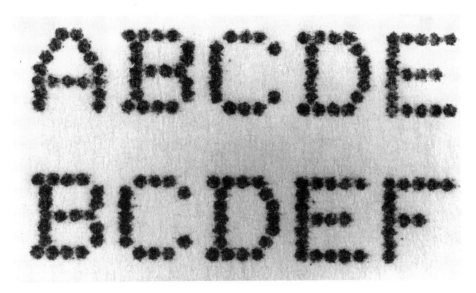

Figure 9.6

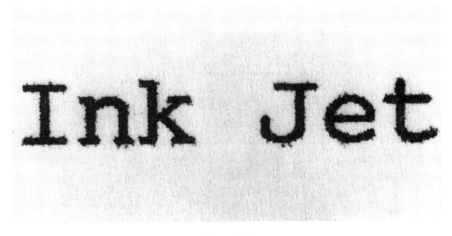

Figure 9.7

to discern the difference between an original document just produced on a laser printer and a photocopy of that original.

Experience to date has shown that ink jet printers and particularly laser printers develop few of the unique imprint defects that can connect a questioned text to one specific make or individual printer. Also, ink jet printers and laser printers have the built-in capability of printing a multitude of different character designs. This feature rarely permits an identification of the printer's manufacturer.

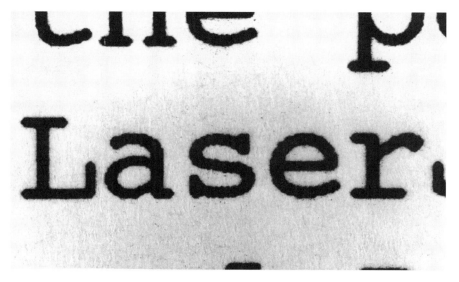

Figure 9.8

In summary, successful identification of a specific make of ink-jet printer or laser printer, or the connecting of a questioned document to a specific ink-jet printer or laser printer is seldom possible.

11. **Can this questioned photocopy be connected to one make of copier and/or to one specific copier?**

The internal paper transport mechanism of some copiers can produce indentations and other markings on the paper as it is being transported through and out of the machine. These class characteristics, when discernible, can in some cases provide an identification of the copier's manufacturer if the examiner has appropriate reference files.

The copy machine can also produce unique and identifying defects on the photocopies it generates. These individual characteristics (defects) can be created by high volume use, by the careless removing of jammed paper (producing scratches on the drum), lack of normal maintenance and repair, and by infrequent cleaning of rollers, drum, corona wires, and platen. These individual characteristics can appear as black or white lines across the paper, as tiny black specks called "trashmarks", as smudges, and a variety of other flaws. If the examiner finds that a combination of similar defects exists between a questioned photocopy and an exemplar photocopy made on a suspect copier, then there might be sufficient evidence to conclude that both were produced on the same copier.

The examiner must always be absolutely certain that the submitted questioned photocopy is in fact the *original* photocopy in question — that it is not a second generation photocopy made from the original questioned photocopy on an intervening copier. The intervening machine could introduce misleading trashmarks and other defects that are not related to the investigation. This same caution applies to the evaluation of the submitted exemplar specimens.

Color copy machines have invited the counterfeiting of paper money, stamps, bank checks, driver licenses, or any documents that will serve the purposes of thieves. Color copies can be identified as such by a microscopic examination of the image. The microscopic examination will disclose the overlaying pattern of the various single colors that in turn produce the various hues in the color image. The rib-like pattern typical of one make of color copier is shown in Figure 9.9.

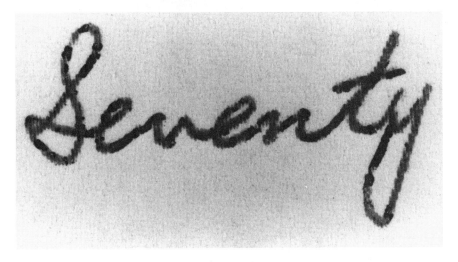

Figure 9.9

12. Have pages been substituted in this multi-page document?

13. Have pen entries been added at a later time to this document?

A page of a multi-page contract or last will and testament that shows a manufacturer's watermark or an ultraviolet fluorescence that is different from accompanying pages can indicate that this page may be bogus, that it has been substituted for the original page.

Mechanical watermarks are logos or designs impressed into paper when it is made; they usually identify the paper's maker. Chemical watermarks can be put on the paper after it is made. These custom-designed chemical watermarks can be the consumer's own company trade name or they can be a personal logo.

Mechanical watermarks are sometimes coded. They are inconspicuously marked or periodically changed by some paper makers for purposes of quality control dating. Thus, these coded watermarks can help to show that a document (the paper stock) was or was not in existence on the date that the document bears. Figure 9.10 shows a manufacturer's watermark bearing a vertical code mark under the second "t" in "cotton".

Figure 9.10

A questioned page that shows fewer staple holes than the surrounding pages is evidence that the questioned page was inserted at a later time.

Ink comparisons made with infrared luminescence techniques, with special viewing filters, or with chemical tests can show that the signature on a questioned page was not written with the same pen that was used to write that person's signatures on the other pages of the multi-page document.

14. **Does this questioned document show indented replicas (impressions) of writings that were written on another document while it was lying on the questioned document?**

Indented writing can be detected when a spotlight or flashlight is directed at a low angle across the document's surface. Figure 9.11 shows a sheet of note paper with the indented impression of a hold-up note. This sheet, if found on a suspect's note pad, could connect the suspect to the robbery.

The low-angle-light technique requires that the light be constantly shifted to different angles in order to decipher the indented text. If the impressions

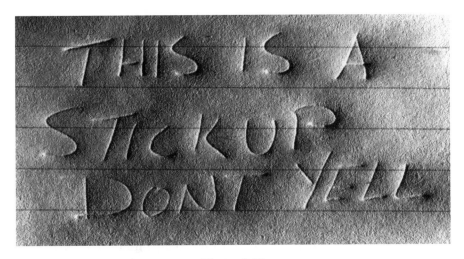

Figure 9.11

are sufficiently deep, this technique is very productive. But if the impressions are very shallow, the attempts to decipher can be very time consuming and futile. Photography is required to record the deciphered impressions, and this also is a very time-consuming process.

A device known as ESDA (electrostatic detection apparatus) is now widely used. The process does not damage the document. In many cases it has the capability of yielding readable texts from very faint indented writing that is not visible at all with low-angle light. To oversimplify the ESDA process: a sheet of very thin polymer plastic is laid over the document, and the two are held in close contact by vacuum. While the two are in the ESDA box (about the size of a desktop printer), the surface of the plastic sheet is electrically charged. The surface of the plastic sheet is then sprayed or dusted with black toner-like material. The indented text is made visible because the toner adheres to the plastic sheet's surface in greater amounts where indentations exist in the underlying document. The plastic sheet bearing the replica of the indented text is peeled from the document and preserved. Although the ESDA process is not always successful, it is usually superior to the low angle light technique because ESDA can produce readable text from very weak impressions, and at the same time ESDA provides an immediate replica of the text for further study and for court presentation. But when an ESDA device is not available, the low angle light technique plus photography can often provide a very satisfactory restoration and courtroom presentation.

The cartoon detective method of rubbing over the surface of the document with a pencil is absolutely not an appropriate method of discovering and deciphering indented writing. The pencil's graphite defaces the document, the graphite can inhibit the chemical development of latent fingerprints, and the pencil's pressure during the rubbing process can smooth out weak impressions that might be made visible with low angle lighting or with the ESDA process.

15. Can you restore or decipher the text of the original entries that have been erased, eradicated, or obliterated on this document?

16. Have the original ink entries on this document been altered by the addition of new ink entries?

17. Can you decipher the entries on these burned documents?

Here are some of the nondestructive methods for detecting, deciphering, or restoring erasures, chemical eradications, obliterations, alterations, and entries on questioned and burned documents: standard infrared photography, infrared luminescence photography, ultraviolet photography, high contrast film photography, black-and-white photography with various colored filters, and viewing with special custom-made dichroic filters. Success in any restoration and deciphering problem can be a trial-and-error process. Training, experience, photographic expertise, the degree to which the document can be defaced, the inherent nature of the alterations or degree of charring, and available equipment can all affect the degree of success.

Figure 9.12 shows the endorsements on a stolen payroll check. The thief apparently realized that he had endorsed the stolen check in his own natural handwriting. So he obliterated this first endorsement with two different pens. He then endorsed the check a second time in a contrived writing style, in an attempt to avoid identification. Infrared luminescence photography revealed the writer's natural writing in the first "Daniel Allen" endorsement.

Infrared luminescence photography, an infrared image converter combined with television viewing, special viewing filters, and chemical analyses are widely used processes for revealing that the entries on a document were made with different pens or that the meaning of an original ink entry had been changed by the addition of pen strokes, or new words, or numerals.

Figure 9.13 shows a standard black-and-white photograph of a check. The question: Did someone alter the original amount of the check by adding the word "teen" and the numeral "1" in order to raise the original amount of $4,000 to $14,000?

Figure 9.14 shows an infrared luminescence photograph of the check. The photograph clearly shows that the word "teen" and the numeral "1" had been added to the check with a different pen. The original entries were written with an ink that exhibited strong infrared luminescence; the second pen (ink) exhibited no infrared luminescence properties.

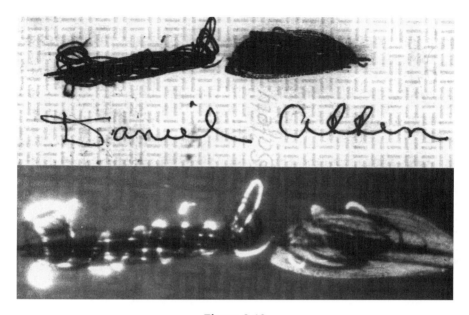

Figure 9.12

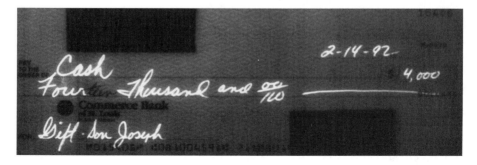

Figure 9.13

Figure 9.14

18. Can faint handwriting, writings that have been overlaid with rubber stamps and other writings, partially erased writings and entries, and other barely discernible features of a document be made visible for identification?

19. Can out-of-focus features in a document's photograph be rendered identifiable?

Special computer programs combined with electronic scanners and other appropriate equipment offer possible means for visually enhancing the texts or images of otherwise nondecipherable features of a document or photograph. Some forensic document laboratories have this capability. This service is also offered in the business sector, so the document examiner whose facilities do not offer this service can refer an inquirer to an appropriate specialist.

20. Can these water-soaked documents recovered from fires, floods, etc. be dried without damage to the documents?

Most forensic document laboratories do not have the facilities or special equipment for handling and restoring massive volumes of water-soaked documents. This service is available in the business sector, so the document examiner can refer the inquirer to the appropriate specialist. Attempts to restore the legibility of water-soaked ink writings are sometimes successful via ultraviolet, infrared, or special black-and-white photography and other processes described under Questions 15, 16 and 17.

21. What is the sex, age, or health status of this document's writer?

The sex of a writer cannot be identified by handwriting. Neither can the specific age or physical condition of a writer be determined solely on studies of handwriting. Unskilled, awkward writing that shows a close similarity to ordinary copybook letter constructions might indicate a youthful writer or an adult writer who has developed few writing skills. Writing that shows tremor and halting pen movements might be the genuine writing of an aged or seriouly ill writer. Or it might have been written by a writer of any age who is afflicted with a tremulous muscular disorder. Attempts to be specific in questions of a writer's age or type of illness via handwriting analysis is speculation that invites error.

22. What was the mental condition of the writer when this document was executed? Was he intoxicated?

While abnormal mental and physical conditions might influence a person's writing, it is not possible for a document examiner to identify these conditions by a study of the questioned writing. Writings done under coercion can seldom be identified as such. Alcohol and drug intoxication and blood-alcohol percentage cannot be identified via handwriting features. Claims of the writer's poor physical condition, poor eyesight, nervousness, excitement, unusual writing positions, or rough writing surfaces are frequently offered by purveyors of fraudulent documents to excuse what really are the defective writing features of forgery.

23.   What can you tell me about the writer's personality?

People who claim skill in identifying personality traits by studying a writer's handwriting are called graphologists or graphoanalysts. Forensic document examiners do not engage in personality identification via a study of handwriting.

Graphologists are not forensic document examiners, although some graphologists claim to be. Some graphologists and other would-be document examiners who have read a few standard questioned document texts and who have attended some lectures boldly hire out as forensic document examiners, a more lucrative vocation than graphology. But their exaggerated credentials are poor imitations of the appropriate credentials recognized by the American Board of Forensic Document Examiners.

Here are a few more document problems (with no discussion of possible solutions) that are submitted to document examiners.

24.   Was the ink signature written over the typewritten entry, or was the typewritten entry typed over the ink signature?

25.   A fold in a document intersects an ink signature. Was the document folded before or after the signature was written?

26.   An ink signature intersects the embossed notary seal on a deed of trust. Was the signature written before or after the seal was embossed?

27.   How long has the ink signature been on the document? What is the age of the ink?

28.   Were the pencil entries on the document written with more than one pencil? How many?

29. Is the signature on this oil painting, lithograph, or watercolor a genuine signature of the artist?

30. Is this a genuine historical document?

31. What is the ethnic background of the writer?

32. Was the writer of the questioned material a right- or left-handed writer?

33. Did a blind person write the questioned material?

34. Does the questioned writing indicate the writer's educational background?

35. Was the questioned signature written by a person, a machine, or is it a rubber stamp?

36. Was the writer's hand guided, assisted, or supported during the writing of the signature?

37. Was the questioned document torn (removed) from this specific writing pad?

38. Was this specific pen used to write the questioned document?

39. Photocopies (machine copies) or facsimile (FAX) copies are the only available questioned documents. Will they provide a basis for determining the genuineness or non-genuineness of the signatures on them?

40. Is this photocopy a contrived composite of several other documents? Is it a pasteup?

These are not the only questions you will be asked to answer as a document examiner. But they will give you an idea of the kinds of document problems you will face. Having seen the scope of these questions, you can understand why document examiners are called *document* examiners, not just handwriting examiners.

Forensic document examiners are expected to know: (1) how to answer these 40 and other questions, (2) whether the questions can be answered at all, and (3) where to go for help if their own technical skills or laboratory tools cannot adequately challenge the problem.

Examiners must assume that the client's (a layman's) question may not truly reflect all of the document's features that need to be investigated in order to completely resolve the problem. So, experienced and appropriately trained examiners will always be prepared to look beyond those document features that are targeted by the layman client.

For example, in a recent case the testator's signature on each of the three pages of a typewritten last will and testament were in question. The questioned signatures were written on a typewritten signature line that appeared above the testator's typewritten name. The client's only question was, "Are the signatures that appear above the testator's typewritten name the genuine signatures of the testator?" The examinations of the questioned signatures revealed that the questioned testator signatures were in fact genuine. That answered the client's question. Further examinations disclosed that the will's three-page typewritten text was in fact typed on the same manual typewriter that produced the testator's typewritten name that appeared under each signature. Witnesses to the will had testified at a deposition that the entire will was typed in the testator's kitchen at one sitting, and that the three pages of text and the typed testator names were typed in normal sequence.

Microscopic examinations of the will's text disclosed that the three-page text was produced with a cloth ribbon that was in near-new condition. But, the typed testator names were produced with a cloth ribbon in a much drier condition and with a different cloth thread pattern. Thus, the evidence clearly showed that the will's text and the typed testator names were typed at different times with different cloth ribbons. It was concluded that the testator had signed three blank sheets of paper for some other purpose. After the testator died, the witnesses who for several years had custody of the typewriter and the three signed but otherwise blank sheets of paper merely typed the text of the spurious will in the blank space above each of the three genuine signatures. In the interval between the typing of the three testator names and the will's three-page text, a new ribbon had been installed.

Wise attorneys welcome the examiner's offer to assist with trial preparations. So, examiners must be prepared to offer guidance and assistance in trial preparations and courtroom presentations of the evidence. Although the examiner must always remain an objective participant, the examiner does have the responsibility to be a forceful advocate of his or her own findings and conclusions. That includes being prepared to suggest the most effective way to present the examiner's findings and conclusions at trial. It means offering to provide suggested questions for use in qualifying the examiner as an expert. And it means being prepared to suggest the most effective way to defend against the conclusions of a purported expert hired by the other side.

So, as you consider the various forensic disciplines in your career planning, consider the questioned documents discipline. Be reminded that legitimate entry into the discipline can be difficult because of the few easily accessible sources for acquiring your appropriate apprentice training. But if you seek a criminal justice career that offers intellectual and technical challenges, and if you seek a forensic laboratory career that frequently matches you to a one-on-one skill contest with the criminal, then consider the questioned documents discipline. Forensic documents examining can offer you the personal satisfaction of knowing that the products of your intellect and investigative skills can make a worthwhile contribution to the goals of the justice system.

Suggested Reading

Aginsky, V.: A microspectrophotometric method for dating ballpoint inks — a feasibility study, *J. Forensic Sci.*, vol. 40 (no. 3), 475, 1995.

Aginsky, V.: Some new ideas for dating ballpoint inks — a feasibility study, *J. Forensic Sci.*, vol. 38 (no. 5), 1134, 1993.

Arbouine, M.W. and Day, S.P.: The use of drum defects to link laser- printed documents to individual laser printers, *J. Forensic Sci. Soc.*, vol. 34 (no. 2), 99, 1994.

Beck, J.: Handwriting of the alcoholic, *Forensic Sci. Intl.*, vol. 28, 19, 1985.

Beck, J.: Sources of error in forensic handwriting evaluation, *J. Forensic Sci.*, vol. 40 (no. 1), 78, 1995.

Black, J.A.: Application of digital image enhancement software with the Macintosh computer to questioned document problems, *J. Forensic Sci.*, vol. 37 (no. 3), 783, 1992.

Blueschke, A. and Lacis, A.: Examination of line crossings by low KV scanning electron microscopy (SEM) using photographic stereoscopic pairs, *J. Forensic Sci.*, vol. 41 (no. 1), 80, 1996.

Bohan, T. and Heels, E.: The case against daubert: the new scientific evidence "standard" and the standards of the several states, *J. Forensic Sci.*, vol. 40 (no. 6), 1030, 1995.

Brunelle, R.L.: Ink dating — the state of the art, *J. Forensic Sci.*, vol. 37 (no. 1), 113, 1992.

Cabanne, R.A.: The Clifford Irving hoax of the Howard Hughes autobiography, *J. Forensic Sci.*, vol. 20 (no. 1), 5, 1975.

Cantu, A.A. and Prough, R.S.: Some spectral observations of infrared luminescence, *J. Forensic Sci.*, vol. 33 (no. 3), 638, 1988.

Conway, J.V.P.: Evidential Documents, Charles C Thomas, Springfield, IL, 1959.

Crown, D.A.: The differentiation of electrostatic photocopy machines, *J. Forensic Sci.*, vol. 34 (no. 1), 142, 1989.

Dawson, G.A.: Brain function and writing with the unaccustomed hand, *J. Forensic Sci.*, vol. 30 (no. 1), 167, 1985.

Ellen, D.M., Foster, D.J., and Morantz, D.J.: The use of electrostatic imaging in the detection of indented impressions, *Forensic Sci. Intl.*, vol. 15, 53, 1980.

Fahy, R.: Can you identify cigarette paper?, *The Quarterly Newsletter of the American Board of Forensic Document Examiners, Inc.*, vol. 6 (no. 1), 7, Houston, TX, 1996.

Farrell, C.S. and Nelson L.K.: Nondestructive differentiation of full-color photocopies, *J. Forensic Sci.*, vol. 36 (no. 1), 145, 1991.

Fisher, J.: The Lindbergh Case, Rutgers University Press, New Brunswick, NJ, 1987.

Flynn, W.: Electronic fonts for document examiners, *The Quarterly* Newsletter of the American Board of Forensic Document Examiners, *Inc.*, vol. 5 (no. 3), 16, Houston, TX, 1995.

Flynn, W.: Some inkjet printer ink is "chromatographically" identical to the ink in bic liquid ink pens, *The Quarterly Newsletter of the American Board of Forensic Document Examiners. Inc.*, vol. 6 (no. 1), 23, Houston, TX, 1996.

Franks, J.E.: The direction of ballpoint penstrokes in left- and right-hand writers as indicated by the orientation of burr striations, *J. Forensic Sci. Soc.*, vol. 22, 271, 1982.

Gerhart, F.J.: Identification of photo copiers from fusing roller defects, *J. Forensic Sci.*, vol. 37 (no. 1), 130, 1992.

Gilreath, J.: The Judgment of Experts: Essays and Documents About the Investigation of the Forging of the "Oath of a Freeman", American Antiquarian Society, Worcester, MA, 1991.

Haring, J.V.: The Hand of Hauptmann, Hamer Publishing, Plainfield, NJ, 1937.

Hicks, A.: Computer imaging for questioned document examiners I: the benefits, *J. Forensic Sci.*, vol. 40 (no. 6), 1045, 1995.

Hicks, A: Computer imaging for questioned document examiners II: the potential for abuse, *J. Forensic Sci.*, vol. 40 (no. 6), 1052, 1995.

Hilton, O.: Scientific Examination of Documents, CRC Press, Cleveland, OH, 1982.

Hilton, O: Detecting and Deciphering Erased Pencil Writing, Charles C Thomas, Springfield, IL, 1991.

Houde, John: Image enhancement for document examination using the personal computer, *J. Forensic Sci.*, vol. 38 (no. 1), 143, 1993.

Hunton, R. and Puckett, J.: Restoring texts of typewriter ribbons: a reliability study of the RAW-1 ribbon analysis workstation, *J. Forensic Sci.*, vol. 39 (no. 1), 21, 1994.

Kelly, J.H.: Classification and identification of modern office copiers (monograph), American Board of Forensic Document Examiners, Houston, TX, 1983.

Kelly, J.S.: Facsimile documents: feasibility for comparison purposes, *J. Forensic Sci.*, vol. 37 (no. 6), 1600, 1992.

Kelly, M.: First challenge of handwriting identification in a daubert hearing, *The Quarterly Newsletter of the American Board of Forensic Document Examiners. Inc.*, vol. 5 (no. 2), 1, Houston, TX, 1995.

Kerr, L.K. and Taylor, L.R.: Linguistic evidence indicative of authorship by a member of the deaf community, *J. Forensic Sci.*, vol. 37 (no. 6), 1621, 1992.

Leung, S.C., Cheng, Y.S., and Fung, H.T.: Forgery I-Simulation, *J. Forensic Sci.*, vol. 38 (no. 2), 402, 1993.

Moon, H.W.: A survey of handwriting styles by geographic location, *J. Forensic Sci.*, vol. 22 (no. 4), 827, 1977.

Morgan, M. and Zilly, P.: Document examinations of handwriting with a straightedge or a writing guide, *J. Forensic Sci.*, vol. 36 (no. 2), 470, 1991.

Moryan, D.: Using the video spectral comparator in the comparison of carbon copies and carbon paper impressions, *J. Forensic Sci.*, vol. 40 (no. 2), 296, 1995.

Moshe, K., Wetstein, J., and Conn, R.: Proficiency of professional document examiners in writer identification, *J. Forensic Sci.*, vol. 39 (no. 1), 5, 1994.

Muehlberger, R.J.: Identifying simulations: practical considerations, *J. Forensic Sci.*, vol. 35 (no. 2), 368, 1990.

O'Hara, C.E.: Fundamentals of Criminal Investigation, 3rd ed., Charles C Thomas, Springfield, IL, 1973.

Oron, M. and Tamir, V.: Development of some methods for solving forensic problems encountered in handwritten and printed documents, *Intl. Crim. Police Rev.*, no. 324, 24, Jan. 1979.

Osborn, A.S.: Questioned Documents, 2nd ed. (facsimile reproduction), Nelson-Hall, Chicago, IL, circa 1985.

Osborn, A.S.: Questioned Documents, 2nd ed., Boyd Printing, New York, 1929.

Osborn, A.S.: The Problem of Proof, The Essex Press, Newark, NJ, 1926.

Pereira, M.: Quality assurance in forensic science, *Forensic Sci. Intl.*, vol. 28, 1, 1985.

Saferstein, R.: Criminalistics: An Introduction to Forensic Science, Prentice-Hall, Englewood Cliffs, NJ, 1977.

Saferstein, R.: Forensic Science Handbook, Prentice-Hall, Englewood Cliffs, N.J., 1982.

Sperry, G.: Platen information revealed: a technique for locating latent text on typewriter (or printer) platens, *J. Forensic Sci.*. vol. 39 (no. 1), 223, 1994.

Stiltoe, L. and Roberts, A.D.: Salamander: The Story of the Mormon Forgery Murders, Signature Books, Salt Lake City, UT, 1988.

Storer, W.: Handwriting experts, *Gateway Net, Amer. Soc. for Indust. Security*, vol. 25, (no. 1), St. Louis, MO, 1995.

Thornton, J.: Courts of law v. courts of science: a forensic scientist's reaction to Daubert, *Shepard's Expert and Scientific Evidence Quarterly*, vol. 1 (no. 3), 475, 1994.

Wenderoth, M.: Application of the VSC/Atari 1040ST image-processing system to forensic document problems, *J. Forensic Sci.*, vol. 35 (no. 2), 439, 1990.

Zimmerman, J. and Mooney, D.: Laser examination as additional nondestructive method of ink differentiation, *J. Forensic Sci.*, vol. 33 (no. 2), 310, 1988.

Bloodstain Pattern Interpretation

10

STUART H. JAMES
CHARLES F. EDEL

Introduction

The examination of blood provides invaluable information to the forensic scientist in many areas of criminal investigation. Information is obtained from blood by the forensic pathologist, toxicologist, serologist, and crime scene investigator.

Blood is studied by the forensic pathologist to assist with the diagnosis of various diseases that may relate to the cause of death, such as AIDS, anemia, leukemia, or malaria, as well as many other conditions. The forensic pathologist also uses blood evidence during the external examination of a victim before autopsy. The degree of postmortem lividity or settling of blood within the body may help establish the approximate time of death or whether the lividity is consistent with the position of the victim at the scene. A cherry-red lividity may suggest carbon monoxide or cyanide poisoning. Blunt trauma often produces external bruising or contusions, which can be identified by the forensic pathologist as either fresh or old. Minute hemorrhages in the eye, referred to as petechiae, are often present in asphyxial deaths.

Blood is examined by the forensic toxicologist in conjunction with other body fluids and tissues to determine the presence or absence of alcohol, drugs, and poisons. The quantitative blood level of toxic agents helps to establish the cause and manner of death or provide evidence of an intoxicated driver. Interpretation of toxicological data may also help with the diagnosis of drug and alcohol abuse or assist with the explanation of erratic behavior of individuals who may injure themselves or other persons.

The forensic serologist examines blood collected from crime scenes to establish that the substance is, in fact, blood and distinguishes human from animal blood. When this has been done, the blood may be typed within the ABO group and other antigenic systems, isoenzyme systems, DNA typing, or other individualization systems. The results are then compared to serological testing performed on victim's and suspect's blood.

0-8493-8101-0/97/$0.00+$.50
© 1997 by CRC Press, Inc.

The crime scene investigator is responsible for the proper documentation of the crime scene through careful observation, photography, measurements, diagrams, and the collection of physical evidence. Blood is one of the most significant and frequently encountered types of physical evidence at scenes of violent crimes. The circumstances and nature of violent crimes involving bloodshed produce a variety of bloodstains and patterns.

The examination of a crime scene for the purposes of bloodstain interpretation should be incorporated into the systematic approach for crime scene examination. Bloodstain interpretation is part of the overall investigation, which includes the documentation, collection, and evaluation of all physical evidence. Physical evidence is defined as any and all materials or items associated with a crime scene which by scientific evaluation help to establish the elements of a crime and provide a link between the crime scene, the victim, and the assailant. The information provided by bloodstain interpretation should be evaluated in conjunction with evidence provided by the postmortem examination of the victim and analyses performed by the crime laboratory.

When bloodstains are studied with respect to their geometry and distribution on various surfaces, they can reveal valuable information for the reconstruction of events that produced the bloodshed.

- Origin(s) of the bloodstains
- Distances between target surface and origin at time of bloodshed
- Type and direction of impact that produced bloodstains
- Object(s) that produced particular bloodstain patterns
- Number of blows, shots, etc. that occurred
- Position of victim, assailant, or objects during bloodshed
- Movement and direction of victim, assailant or objects after bloodshed
- Support or contradiction of version of events given by suspect or witnesses
- Additional criteria for estimation of time of death
- Correlation with other laboratory and pathology findings relevant to an investigation

Bloodstain pattern interpretation uses the sciences of biology, physics, and mathematics. Observations of bloodstains have been used since prehistoric man tracked wounded animals, just as modern hunters do today. The use of bloodstain pattern interpretation in criminal investigations by the German forensic chemist Paul Jeserich was documented in the nineteenth century. In 1939, the French scientist Balthazard presented a treatise of bloodstain pattern experiments at the 22nd Congress of Forensic Medicine in Paris, France. In 1955, the noted criminalist, the late Dr. Paul Kirk of Berkeley,

California, successfully used bloodstain evidence in the case of the State of Ohio vs. Samuel Sheppard. This was a significant milestone in the recognition of bloodstain evidence by the legal system. Further growth and use of bloodstain pattern interpretation is credited to Herbert Leon MacDonell of Corning, New York, who conducted experiments to re-create and duplicate bloodstains observed at crime scenes and wrote the first modern treatise on the subject in 1971, titled "Flight Characteristics and Stain Patterns of Human Blood". MacDonell gave formal instruction in the form of Bloodstain Institutes across the country. As a result, the utilization of bloodstain pattern interpretation at crime scenes and its acceptance by the courts have been greatly enhanced. Interest in research and practical applications of bloodstain pattern interpretation in forensic science has grown considerably in the past 20 years.

Scientific literature on the subject has grown due to the efforts of many people, most of whom are members of the International Association of Bloodstain Pattern Analysts, founded in 1983. This organization publishes a quarterly newsletter. Scientific articles pertaining to bloodstain pattern interpretation are also published in the *Journal of Forensic Sciences*, the *Journal of the Canadian Society of Forensic Science*, and the *American Journal of Forensic Medicine and Pathology*.

Physical Properties of Blood

Blood can be characterized as a fluid consisting of cellular components and plasma which circulates under pressure through the arterial and venous systems of the body. The color of blood is imparted by the presence of oxygenated hemoglobin present in the red cells, which normally comprise approximately 40 to 48% of blood. Arterial blood is a brighter red due to its high levels of oxyhemoglobin, which is less in the venous system due to tissue distribution of oxygen and the return of carbon dioxide to the lungs.

When the circulatory system is disrupted by trauma or disease, bloodshed occurs internally or externally or both. When blood is exposed to the external environment, it is subjected to various forces and will behave in a predictable manner based on the laws of biology, physics, and mathematics. Biologically, the clotting and drying process of blood will be initiated. Observations of the degree of clotting and serum production and extent of drying of blood at a scene may help estimate the time since bloodshed occurred. Being a liquid, blood behaves according to the laws of fluid dynamics. Its physical properties, including viscosity, specific gravity, surface tension, and the forces acting on blood outside the body determine the size, shape, directionality, and location of bloodstains on various surfaces. Experiments performed with human blood subjected to various external forces including gravity have confirmed that blood follows the principles of fluids in motion.

Blood droplets are formed when small masses of liquid separate from a larger mass outside the body. The separation of these drops from the source of blood is caused by gravity and/or impact to the blood source exceeding the forces of surface tension and viscosity of the blood. Surface tension is the result of the molecular cohesive forces that cause the surface of a liquid to resist penetration and separation. Viscosity is the resistance of a fluid to flow or to change form or the position of its molecules due to the attraction of the molecules to each other. As a drop of blood is falling through air, the surface tension of the liquid will minimize its surface area; this will cause the drop to assume a spherical shape rather than the tear-drop shape often used by artists.

Experiments have shown that the volume of a drop of blood varies between approximately 0.01 and 0.16 ml when allowed to drip from various objects; the average volume of a drop of blood is approximately 0.05 ml. The terminal velocity or maximum speed of a free-falling drop of blood in air is achieved when the acceleration of the drop is offset by the resistance of air. MacDonell has established that for a drop size of approximately 0.05 ml the terminal velocity is 25.1 ± 0.5 feet per second. Smaller drop volumes would have lower terminal velocities, and larger drop volumes would have higher terminal velocities. MacDonell demonstrated that a single drop of blood will not break up into smaller droplets by simply falling through air; for this to occur, the drop must either strike an object or be acted upon by an additional force.

Bloodstains are characterized by their appearance on the various surfaces that the blood contacts subsequent to bloodshed. The size, shape, concentration, and distribution of bloodstains depends on many factors. The forces acting upon blood which has exited the body form the basis for the classification of bloodstains into the general categories of low, medium, and high-velocity bloodstain patterns. The surfaces upon which the blood droplets impact also affect the size and shape of the resultant bloodstains. The interpretation of the directionality, origin, or the source of the blood and the activities that produced the bloodshed depends on their size and shape, convergences, and calculation of the angle of impact relative to the target surface, as well as the texture of the target surfaces.

A blood droplet striking a surface at 90° will produce a bloodstain which is essentially circular in shape. A blood droplet striking a surface at an angle less than 90° will be more elongated or oval in shape (Figure 10.1). This is independent of the forces acting upon the blood source, whether it be gravity or impact to the exposed source of blood. The force factors will affect the size rather than the shape of the resultant bloodstains. A bloodstain on a smooth, hard surface will exhibit little if any distortion, but a bloodstain on a rough, textured surface will exhibit spines and peripheral spatter due to

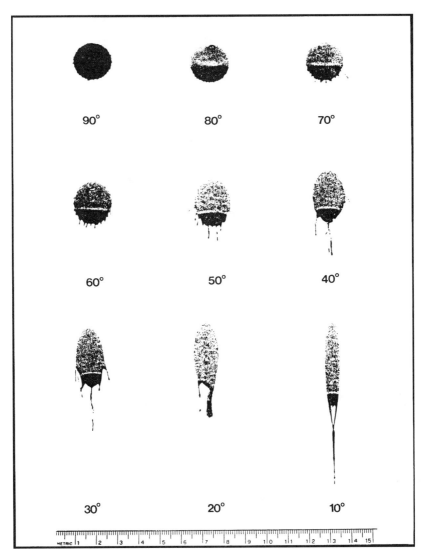

Figure 10.1 Shape of bloodstains relative to decreasing angle of impact of single blood drops falling onto smooth cardboard.

the disruption of the surface tension of the blood droplet upon impact (Figure 10.2). The interpretation of the directionality and angle of impact of such stains may be difficult.

The size or diameter of a bloodstain produced by a free-falling drop of blood increases with the distance from which it has fallen, up to about 7 feet. At distances beyond 7 feet, the diameter of resultant bloodstains does not increase. The diameters of these bloodstains range from approximately 13 to 22 mm (Figure 10.3). Estimation of the distance from which a blood drop

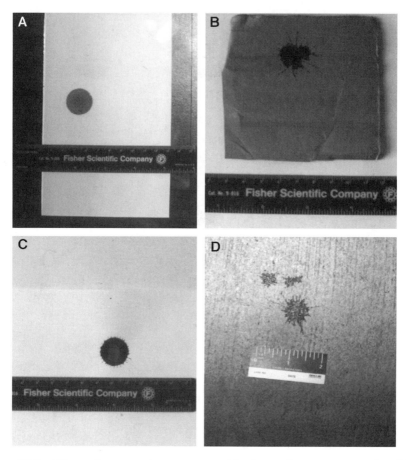

Figure 10.2 Effects of target surface textures on bloodstain characteristics produced from single drops of blood that fell from a height of twelve inches: (A) glossy, smooth cardboard; (B) corrogated cardboard; (c) glass; and (D) rough, painted surface.

has fallen based upon the diameter of a bloodstain must also take into account the volume of the original drop of blood, which may not be known.

Angle of Impact

The angle of impact is defined as the internal angle at which blood strikes a target surface. The angle of impact is a function of the relationship between the width and length of the resultant bloodstain. At an impact of 90°, the resultant circular bloodstain will have an equal width and length, each representing the diameter of the circle. The more acute the angle of impact, the greater the elongation of the bloodstain. Measurement of the width and length of individual bloodstains is taken through the central axis of each

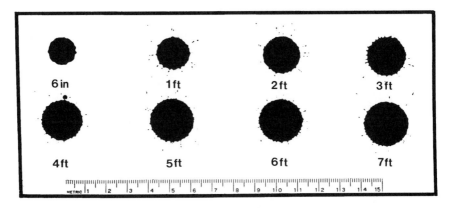

Figure 10.3   Increasing diameter of bloodstains as a function of increasing distance fallen by single drops of blood from fingertip onto smooth cardboard.

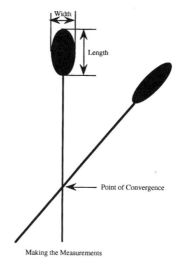

Figure 10.4   Measurement of width and length of bloodstains with point of convergence.

dimension (Figure 10.4). The calculated value of the width to length ratio (W/L) is used in the formula:

$$\text{angle of impact} = \text{arc sin W/L}$$

The arc sin value giving the angle of impact may be determined from trigonometric tables or by using a scientific calculator which has the arc sin function. The impact angle of a bloodstain is a function of its width-to-length ratio as the sine value vs. known angles of impact from prepared standards of bloodstains (Figure 10.5).

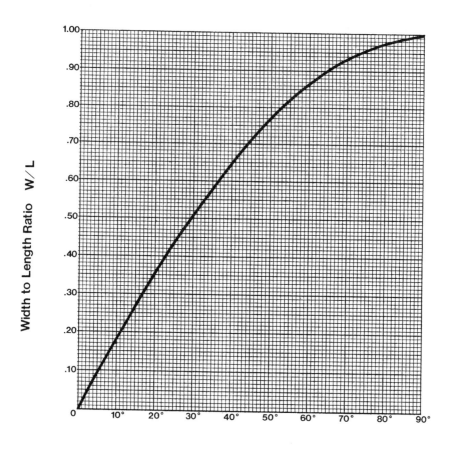

Figure 10.5   Impact angle of a bloodstain as a function of its width to length ration (sine function).

Points of Convergence

Blood droplets may strike surfaces at various impact angles and directionalities. Directionality relates to the direction a drop of blood travelled in space from its point of origin. The tail of elongated bloodstains and their edge characteristics generally point in the direction the blood droplet has travelled. An exception to this is a wave cast-off, which is a small blood droplet that originates from a parent drop of blood due to the wavelike action of the liquid in conjunction with striking a surface at an angle less than 90°. The tail of a wave cast-off bloodstain points back to the parent drop (Figure 10.6).

A point of convergence is defined as a common point to which individual bloodstains in a pattern can be traced or projected on a surface. It is determined by tracing the long axis of well defined bloodstains back to a

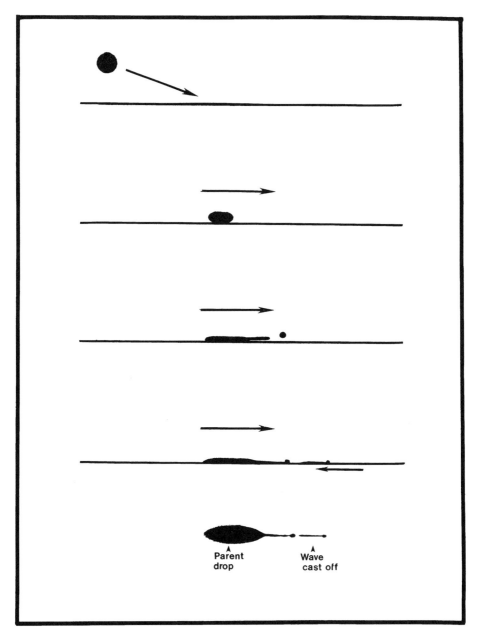

Figure 10.6 Dynamics of wave cast-off formation by a blood drop. The tail of the parent drop points in its direction of travel, whereas the tail of the wave cast-off points back to the parent drop.

two-dimensional common point or points (Figures 10.4 and 10.7). This may be accomplished at the scene by the use of strings extending through the long axis of the bloodstains. The point(s) of convergence may also be represented

Figure 10.7 Determination of the two-dimensional point of convergence of multiple bloodstains.

graphically by measuring the location of the bloodstains and angles of directionality relative to known sets of points.

Point of Origin

The point of origin is defined as the location in space from which the blood which produced the bloodstain originated. It is determined by projecting calculated angles of impact of well defined bloodstains back to an axis constructed through the point of convergence. The point of origin is a three-dimensional representation in space (Figure 10.8). It may be constructed at the scene by the use of a semi-protractor and strings which determine origin in space extended away from the two-dimensional surface along the axis of convergence based upon the angle of impact of the individual bloodstains. The point of origin may be established graphically by plotting the distance of the individual bloodstains from the point of convergence with their angle of impact. The point of origin of bloodstain patterns may represent the distance from a wall, ceiling, or other structure.

Computer programs exist to process the data obtained from the measurement of bloodstains for the determination of convergences and points of origin, but they do not replace the need for accurate measurements of the bloodstains. For example, the STAINER 1.0 software introduced by Forensic Solutions of Nashville, Tennessee, will provide automated calculations of all

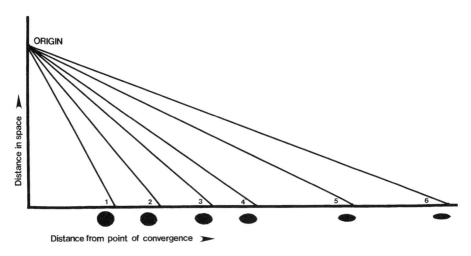

Figure 10.8   Determination of the point of origin of bloodstains by projection of impact angles.

necessary distances with measurements from at least two bloodstains with a common origin. Two points of origin can be combined on two different surfaces which are perpendicular to each other, such as a floor and a wall. The current version of the program is designed for use on IBM PC-compatible systems using the MS-DOS operating system.

Whether the convergences and points of origin are calculated manually or with a computer, the objective of determining the location of the source of bloodstain patterns can be achieved. When conclusions are drawn, they should be expressed within a range of possible flight paths that could produce a similar angle of impact. Frequently, several points of origin can be established which would indicate movement of the source of blood during the deposition of the bloodstains. Impossible points of origin can also be established which may help reconstruct the scene or refute the description of events described by a suspect.

Low-Velocity Bloodstain Patterns

Bloodstains and patterns classified as low-velocity in nature are the group with the greatest variety of shapes and sizes and are usually larger than those produced by medium or high-velocity impact. Bloodstains produced on a surface when the blood source has been subjected to a low-velocity force of approximately 5 feet per second or less are considered low-velocity impact bloodstains. Individual drops of blood falling from a source of blood and subject to only gravity are considered within the low-velocity category.

Free-falling drops of blood can produce elongated bloodstains when subjected to horizontal force or motion. An example of this would be a person

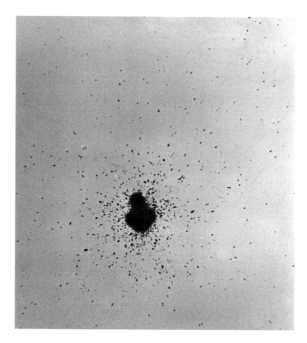

Figure 10.9 Drip pattern produced by drops of blood falling onto each other on surface showing satellite spatter.

walking or running while dripping blood from an object or wound. The direction of travel of these bloodstains may be indicated by the leading-edge characteristics of the stain in the form of a tail, spines, or projections.

Free-falling blood drops often form drip patterns which result from drops of blood falling into previously deposited wet blood on surfaces (Figure 10.9). These drip patterns tend to be large and irregular in shape with small (0.1 to 1.0 mm) circular to oval bloodstains, referred to as satellite spatter, near the central stain. Satellite spatters, are often produced when large volumes of blood fall from a victim's wound or pools of wet blood are disturbed by an object such as a foot stepping into it.

When more than 1.0 ml of blood is subjected to a low-velocity impact or allowed to fall to a surface, a splashed bloodstain pattern will result. Surrounding the large irregular central area will be elongated peripheral spatters contrasted to the more circular stains produced by blood dripping into blood. Quantities of blood over 1.0 ml in volume that are projected in a manner exceeding gravitational forces and low-velocity impact will result in a bloodstain pattern exhibiting streaking elongated peripheral spatters. Vomiting of blood is an example of large-volume projected blood.

Blood exiting the body under pressure, as the result of a cut artery, is a form of projected blood referred to as arterial gushing or spurting. The

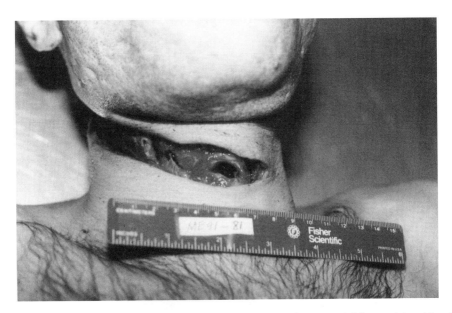

Figure 10.10 Victim of throat slashing with cut carotid artery visible on right side of neck.

resultant bloodstain patterns often show large stains with downward flow patterns on vertical surfaces, or the pattern may be smaller discrete stains appearing as spatters of a generally uniform size (Figures 10.10 and 10.11). If a victim is close to the floor, the arterial spurting may produce a large pooling of blood.

Cast-off bloodstain patterns are produced when blood is projected from a bloody object in motion, such as a blunt object. In many blunt trauma cases, the weapon (bat, crowbar, pipe, fist, etc.) is swung repeatedly at the victim. Knives and other sharp objects can also produce cast-off bloodstains, depending upon the nature of the thrust. Once blood has been exposed at the impact site, blood adhering to an object or weapon will be thrown off and travel tangentially to the arc of the back or side swing and impact on nearby walls, ceilings, or other surfaces. Less blood is cast-off during the down swing of the object. The cast-off bloodstain patterns are often seen as uniformly distributed trails on the target surface, with the more elongated stains more distant from the source. The size of cast-off bloodstains is generally in the 4 to 8 mm range, although larger and smaller stains will be encountered (Figure 10.12). This depends on the type of weapon, amount of blood adhering to it, and the length of arc of the swing. Determination of the angle of impact and convergence of these bloodstains will help determine the position of the assailant swinging the weapon. The number of distinct trails of cast-off bloodstains can be used to estimate the minimum

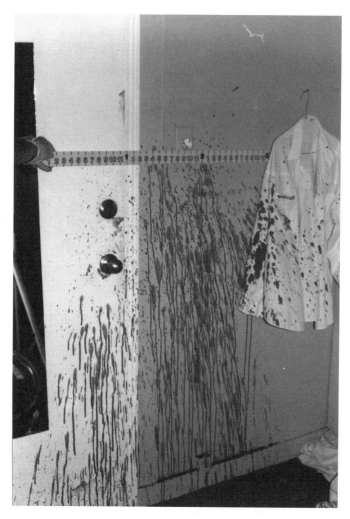

Figure 10.11   Arterial spurt bloodstain pattern produced by victim of throat slashing while standing near door and wall.

number of blows struck plus one, since generally the first blow causing blood-shed would not produce enough blood to adhere to the weapon to be cast.

Flow patterns of blood are easily recognizable and indicate the direction of travel of blood moving horizontally or vertically on surfaces due to gravity. Directional changes are due to impediment by objects along the path of the blood flow, changes in surface angles, and alteration of the position of the source of blood. Flow patterns from a bleeding source on a victim often terminate in a pool of blood. A smudge is a bloodstain that has been altered or distorted by contact with a nonbloody surface, so that further classification of the stain is not possible.

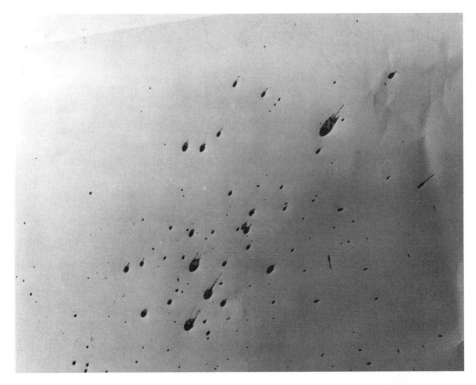

Figure 10.12 Cast-off bloodstain pattern travelling upward on wall surface.

A wipe pattern is characterized as a bloodstain created when an object moves through an existing wet bloodstain, removing blood from the original stain and altering its appearance. Often the direction of the wipe may be determined by the feathering of the edges away from the original stain.

A transfer bloodstain pattern is a bloodstain created when a wet, bloody surface contacts a secondary surface. A recognizable mirror image of the original surface or a portion of that surface may be produced. Examples of common blood transfer patterns are hand, finger, shoe, and footprints (Figures 10.13 and 10.14). Bloody hair swipes on surfaces are also a type of blood transfer pattern. Class and/or individual characteristics may be determined from distinct blood transfer stains. Blood soaking from contact of an object with a wet blood source may occur, for example, when a person kneels in a pool of blood on a floor (Figure 10.15).

Another useful observation of bloodstains on surfaces other than horizontal is the recognition of the dense zone. When a blood droplet of sufficient volume strikes a nonhorizontal surface, gravitational forces continue to act on the wet stain. The lower area or base of the bloodstain will be denser due to the continued accumulation of blood due to gravity. After the bloodstain

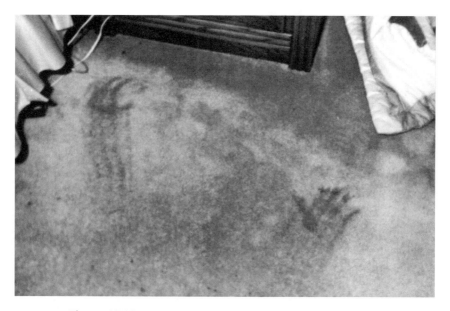

Figure 10.13   Sliding hand print bloodstain patterns on carpet.

Figure 10.14   Partial hand print bloodstain pattern on bed sheet.

has sufficiently dried on the surface, this dense zone cannot be altered (Figure 10.16). Bloodstained objects or surfaces which have been moved after bloodshed may show bloodstains with dense zones inconsistent with their observed position. This observation would indicate an alteration of the scene.

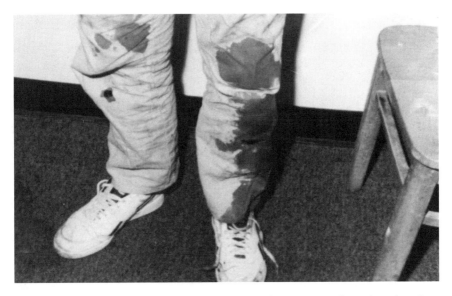

Figure 10.15 Bloods soaking of left knee and leg of trousers resulting from kneeling in blood.

Dense Zone

Figure 10.16 Diagrammatic representation of dense zone at lowest edge of bloodstain produced by the effect of gravity.

Medium-Velocity Bloodstain Patterns

Medium-velocity impact spatter is defined as bloodstains produced on a surface when the exposed blood source has been subjected to a force other than gravity of at least 5 to 25 feet per second up to 100 feet per second. Impact force greater than 100 feet per second would be in the range of high-velocity impact. The energy of the impact causes the blood to be broken up into small droplets. The resultant bloodstains produced on surfaces are usually within the range of 1 to 4 mm in diameter with smaller and larger stains not uncommon (Figure 10.17). Blows administered to a victim with a blunt

Figure 10.17 Medium-velocity impact blood spatter produced by beating.

instrument, as well as a sharp object, will produce medium-velocity blood spatter once the blood has been exposed to receive impact. The distribution of medium-velocity blood spatter and determination of directionality and angle of impact on nearby surfaces assist with the positioning of the victim and assailant during bloodshed. Blood droplets are often radially distributed away from the impact site, and spatters may be seen on the assailant's person and clothing. The quantity and location of blood spatter observed on an assailant depends upon the relative position of the assailant and the victim, as well as the angle and number of blows struck. For example, an assailant delivering blows with overhead swings to a prone victim would likely receive blood spatter on the lower legs as well as the hand and arm wielding the weapon. On the other hand, when the direction of force is away from the assailant, such as with side swings of a blunt weapon, little if any spatter may impact upon the assailant.

Events other than beatings can produce bloodstains in the size range of medium-velocity impact spatter. Examples include coughing and expiration of blood through the nose and mouth, minor events such as the slapping of a hand or object in blood, cast-off blood on some occasions, minor arterial spurting, as well as fly activity. The occurrence of these events can often be recognized and distinguished through careful examination of the entire scene, the victim's injuries, and condition of the body.

An understanding of fly activity at scenes of exposed blood, as well as body decomposition, is essential for proper interpretation of blood spatters. The mouth parts of the common housefly are specialized for lapping and sucking while the horsefly is characterized as a biter. The mosquito is specialized for piercing and sucking. Many flies ingest blood and regurgitate it onto a surface. These surfaces may also show evidence of excretion or defecation of digested or partly digested blood. The blood spatters produced as the result of these activities are usually a millimeter or less in size with no definite point of origin (Figures 10.18 and 10.19). They may be observed on many surfaces at a scene, including the decomposing body and the clothing. Often these surfaces would appear to be protected from receiving impact spatter which occurred during injury to the victim. Conclusions should be conservative and carefully considered when evaluating blood spatter, especially when there is a limited number of stains available for examination.

Regurgitation   Defecation   Swipe Defecation

Figure 10.18 Diagrammatic representation of types of bloodstain produced as the result of fly activity.

Figure 10.19 Bloodstains produced by fly activity on blue jeans of victim.

Figure 10.20 High-velocity impact blood spatter on wall from gun shot exit wound. Note projectile hole in wall.

High-Velocity Bloodstain Patterns

High-velocity impact blood spatter is produced by a high-velocity force striking a source of blood. A high-velocity impact is considered to be approximately 100 feet per second or more and is usually associated with gunshot and high-speed machinery. A mist-like dispersion of minute blood droplets is characteristic of high-velocity impact blood spatter patterns (Figures 10.20 and 10.21). Due to the low mass of these droplets, their distance travelled in space is limited (approximately 3–4 feet). The resultant bloodstains have diameters of 0.1 mm or less. However, bloodstains associated with high-velocity impact are produced in the medium-velocity spatter size range and larger. Due to their greater mass, the larger droplets can travel greater distances.

At crime scenes, evidence of high-velocity impact blood spatter is most frequently associated with gunshot injury. Blood spatter may originate from either an entrance or exit wound, but the blood droplet dynamics differ between the two locations. Spatter from an entrance wound is referred to as back spatter; the blood droplets travel opposite to the direction of the projectile toward the weapon and the shooter. Back spatter is more commonly observed with close-range discharge of a firearm. The amount of back spatter is also affected by the type of weapon and ammunition and the anatomic features of the wound site. It may be absent due to the blocking effect of hair and clothing.

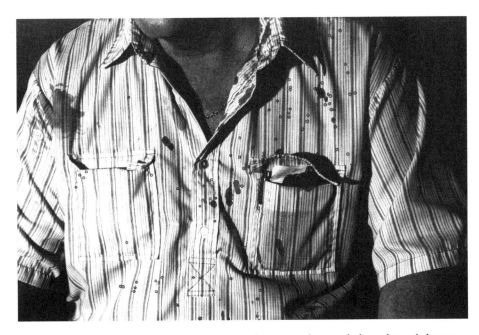

Figure 10.21 Areas of back spatter resulting from gun shot circled on shirt of shooter.

Blood may be drawn back into the barrel of the firearm with close-range discharge in addition to back spatter impacting on the exterior of the weapon and the hand, arm, and chest of the shooter.

Forward spatter is associated with an exit wound, the blood droplets travelling in the same direction as the projectile. The quantity and distribution of forward spatter is generally greater than observed with back spatter. The determination of the point of origin of high-velocity blood spatter assists with positioning of the victim and assailant at the time of discharge of the weapon and initial bloodshed. As with medium-velocity blood spatter, care should be exercised with interpretation of small bloodstains and consideration given to other activities that may have been responsible for the bloodstains.

Photographic Documentation of Bloodstain Patterns

Photographic documentation of physical evidence at the crime scene, including bloodstains, is an essential part of the overall investigative effort and reconstruction. Crime scene investigators responding to death cases and nonfatal violent crime frequently do not appreciate the valuable information available from careful examination and interpretation of bloodstain patterns. As a result, the photographic documentation of the victim, scene, physical evidence, and assailant with respect to bloodstains may be incomplete and lacking in detail for subsequent evaluation and courtroom presentation.

Persons trained in bloodstain pattern interpretation may be consulted on a case for prosecution or defense after the event has occurred and the crime scene is no longer available. Reconstruction of the scene and ultimate conclusions regarding bloodstain patterns in a given case may then be limited in scope, and important details may be impossible to resolve due to poor photographic technique at the time of the original scene investigation. Furthermore, investigators trained in bloodstain pattern interpretation, when testifying in court, depend on good photographic documentation of bloodstains.

The examination and serological studies of bloodstains in the crime laboratory, such as the precipitin test for human origin, ABO grouping, genetic marker profiling, and DNA studies must also include photographic documentation of bloodstains on clothing and other items of physical evidence prior to the removal of bloodstains from the material submitted for examination. Samples of suspected blood that are cut or otherwise removed from articles of clothing or other physical evidence may represent portions of an important bloodstain pattern. Sometimes the bloodstained area may be minute in size and quantity such as with high-velocity impact blood spatter. Complete removal of these small bloodstains for serological testing may be required in many cases. When that occurs, it is extremely important that the bloodstains be photographed properly; otherwise, the interpretative value of those bloodstains is irretrievably lost.

Good photographic documentation of the bloodstains, of both overall bloodstain patterns and individual bloodstains, is crucial. Crime scene photography including documentation of bloodstain patterns is easily and effectively done with the use of a 35-mm camera with a 35- to 50-mm lens for overall photographs, close up or macro lens capability, flash attachment, and high quality color film. Color enlargements of 8 × 10 inches are a good size for analysis and courtroom presentation. Color slides are also very useful for courtroom presentation. Color slides can be made from original scene photographs with a copy stand and photo lamps; good results have been obtained with reflecting the light from white cardboards. This reduces the amount of glare on the subject photograph. Color slide film 100 ASA is used, with the camera set at 125 ASA with the lens setting on automatic. The exposure time is adjusted to 1/15 or the closest setting that will allow a reading of f8 to f11 on the internal light meter of the camera. These parameters have been effective in reducing overexposure of the slides which can be a problem.

Personal experience has shown that Polaroid reproductions have limited value for crime scene work and bloodstain pattern interpretation. Black-and-white photographs are of use with Luminol but generally do not suffice for bloodstain pattern interpretation, since stains other than blood will appear similar to bloodstains and tend to confuse the issues.

A most important tool for the forensic photographer is a measuring device scaled in millimeters and inches to be included in all photographs or slides of bloodstain patterns or individual stains in order to document the size of the bloodstains. Experience has shown that blue or gray 6-inch rulers work well to eliminate glare and provide a good guide for color reproduction.

The Crime Scene

The indoor crime scene is for the most part protected from the elements and easily preserved for extended periods of time, unless the incident occurred in a public place and there is pressure to clean up the scene as quickly as possible. On the other hand, bloodstains present at outdoor crime scenes may be altered in appearance by the terrain and weather. Photography of the outdoor crime scene should be done as soon as possible, to minimize changes or obliteration of bloodstains and other physical evidence due to prevailing conditions. It may be necessary to photograph an outdoor scene at night with a strong light source. A ladder or truck with a boom is useful for overall photographs of an outdoor scene. If weather is not a problem, significant bloodstains should be rephotographed in the daylight hours. Whether indoors or outdoors, it is important to limit access to any crime scene, especially bloody scenes, to avoid unnecessary tracking of wet blood or alteration of existing bloodstain patterns that might compromise proper interpretation.

Bloodstain evidence at the crime scene should be documented with high quality color photographs and/or slides before the body is moved or the scene otherwise altered. A reference scale should be used. It is important to coordinate the photography of the victim and visible injuries with photographs of bloodstains and patterns on the body and clothing. Overall views from above should be taken, as well as close-up photographs of small bloodstains on the body with a ruler in place. Bloodstains on the body should be photographed in conjunction with the bloodstains in the immediate area of the body before the victim is turned or moved. When the body position has been altered, the area should be rephotographed to document any changes of previously formed bloodstains or the creation of new or artifactual bloodstains.

Much of the critical bloodstain pattern photography of the scene relating to walls, ceilings, floors, and other objects is best accomplished after the overall scene photography and photographic documentation of the body have been completed and the body removed. Bloodstain patterns should be photographed with the camera held at 90° to the bloodstains if possible. When individual bloodstains are photographed closeup, the general area of these bloodstains should be recognizable from prior scene photographs so that a point of reference is established. If bloodstain convergences and points of origin are established through measurements and string reconstruction, these procedures should also be photographed.

The bloodstained clothing of a victim should be carefully removed after initial photography at the scene and the postmortem examination. The garments should not be folded or packaged in a damp condition. The best procedure is to hang and air-dry over clean paper before packaging in paper bags; this will minimize the alteration of bloodstains and the production of additional bloodstains or artifacts.

The examination of clothing and bodies of suspects for bloodstains and trace physical evidence often yields valuable evidence to associate that person with a victim. Assailants frequently receive bloodstains and spatters on exposed parts of their bodies, such as on the face and hands; these should be photographed promptly.

The photographic documentation of bloodstains on clothing should be done before any suspect bloodstains are removed for serological testing. The use of a mannikin is helpful in duplicating the proper orientation and location of bloodstains as they were while the victim or assailant wore the garments.

The Use and Photographic Documentation of Luminol

Luminol is a well known chemiluminescent compound and is used as a presumptive, catalytic test for the presence of blood, taking advantage of the peroxidase-like activity of heme for the production of light as an end product rather than a true color reaction. Luminol reagent is applied on objects or areas containing traces of suspected bloodstains. A bluish-white luminescence or light production on the suspected area observed in the dark is a positive test. Luminol is best used for the detection of traces of blood which are not readily observable at crime scenes. This includes light tracking of blood on dark floors and carpeted areas, cracks and crevices in floors and walls, and areas where previous attempts at cleaning bloodstained areas are suspected. The patterns of blood resolved with Luminol may be as important as the detection of blood itself. The sensitivity of the Luminol test is as high as one part in five million, and is effective with aged and decomposed bloodstains. The Luminol test is easy to perform and adaptable to crime scene work. Reagents and supplies are relatively inexpensive and can be obtained from the local crime laboratory. Commercial kits for Luminol testing are more expensive but are packaged in vials for individual use, and reagent preparation is simplified. Although Luminol is a presumptive test for the presence of blood, further analysis of positive areas must be made before the blood can be confirmed. Certain surfaces such as painted walls, porcelain, and metal and cleaning agents such as hypochlorites may also react with luminal.

Many investigators confirm a positive result with an additional presumptive test such as phenolphthalein, which can be accomplished before or after the Luminol spray has been applied. Preferences in procedure for further serological testing of Luminol reactive areas should be obtained from the local crime laboratory.

One of advantages of Luminol is that the procedure lends itself well to photographic documentation and is especially valuable when large bloodstain patterns otherwise not visible are resolved. The following is a general outline of equipment and procedures for the use and photographic documentation of Luminol.

Equipment Required

- Luminol reagent and spraying device
- Luminescent measuring device
- 35-mm camera with 50-mm lens, bulb setting, and wide open lens setting (e.g., f1.8) capability
- Shutter release cable
- Tripod
- Flash unit
- ASA 100 to 400 black-and-white or color film (print or slide)
- Timer
- Appropriate protective clothing, gloves, and eye protection

Procedure

Before the use of the Luminol reagent the surface or object should be photographed in position using a flash unit with the luminescent ruler in place (Figure 10.22). This will assist with the location of the positive luminescent areas against a dark background. With the exception of some overall views, the camera angle should be perpendicular to the surface of interest. The camera lens f-stop should be set at the widest aperture and the exposure setting at the B or Bulb position. With the shutter cable release attached, the equipment is ready for use.

The room or location should be darkened before and during the application of Luminol. A small amount of ambient light will help visualize darkened areas. The Luminol reagent is sprayed with a slow, even motion, avoiding saturation of the surface; as fine a mist as possible is best. The surface can be resprayed during the timed exposure to enhance the reaction. An exposure time of 30 to 45 seconds will generally produce satisfactory results (Figures 10.22 and 10.23). Experimentation with this timed exposure may

Figure 10.22   Area of carpet prior to spraying with Luminol.

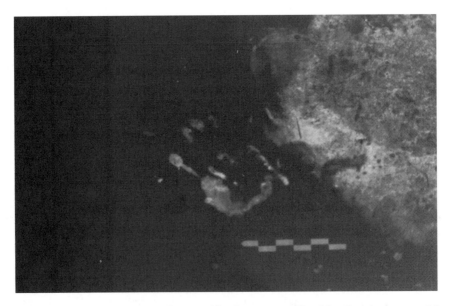

Figure 10.23   Area of carpet showing bloodstains visualized by Luminol spray. Note partial hand print on left. See color plate following page 228.

be desirable. Two to three investigators may be needed for this procedure: one to spray Luminol, a second to operate the camera, and possibly a third to operate the timer and lights.

It is possible to obtain a double image of the Luminol reaction and the object itself. This occurred quite by accident in a recent case when at the end of the exposure time the room lights came on with the bulb setting still activated. The shutter cable was released within a second afterwards and the resulting photograph initially thought to be worthless showed the jacket and luminescence quite well in a single photograph.

Charles F. Edel, formerly of the Broward County, Florida, Sheriff's Office Forensic Services Division published an article in 1989 in the *Journal of the Florida Division of the International Association of Identification,* titled "Let's See What We Are Looking At," demonstrating the use of a light source during the Luminol spray period which permitted visualization of the area being subjected to Luminol, as well as the positive luminescent reaction in the same photograph. A flashlight provided the indirect light source on the surface being sprayed with Luminol, avoiding direct light on the reacting area which would wash out the luminescence.

The value of bloodstain evidence as an important tool for crime scene reconstruction is enhanced by good photographic documentation. Photography provides a permanent record of bloodstain evidence in a case which is easily conveyed to a jury. Photographic evidence must stand up to the scrutiny of opposing experts and counsel, as well as being a visual aid to a jury which must weigh the evidence and reach a verdict in court.

Report Writing

A formal report of a crime scene reconstruction using bloodstain interpretation should be written clearly and concisely. Diagrams and photographs enhance the report's clarity.

The following is a descriptive case report of a blunt force death involving bloodstain pattern interpretation. The suspect was accused of beating his friend to death with a section of a road sign post. He admitted only to finding his friend dead when he returned to their outdoor camp. He pled guilty to murder prior to trial.

Case Study 1

Re: State of Florida vs. C.W.

Case Number: 90-85092

Enclosed is my report of crime scene reconstruction, physical evidence examination, and bloodstain pattern interpretation for the case of the State of

Florida vs. C.W. My conclusions are based upon my review and examination of the following materials and visits to the scene of the homicide of the victim, in this case, W.S.

1. Scene and autopsy photographs
2. Evidence log and scene diagram
3. Report of postmortem examination of the victim, W.S., which was performed on 04/13/90

Examination of physical evidence was conducted on the dates of 04/16/90, 04/23/90, and 05/01/90. Scene examinations were conducted on the dates of 04/16/90 and 04/25/90.

Case History

The location of this homicide was a wooded area west of railroad tracks which run parallel to U.S. 1 south of Hypoluxo Road in Lantana, Florida. The body of the victim, W.S., a 47-year-old white male, was found on the ground close to a makeshift tent of plastic material. The victim had sustained multiple extensive blunt force injuries to the head.

Postmortem examination revealed the victim W.S. to be 76 inches in length and to weigh 235 pounds. The autopsy findings were determined to be as follows with respect to injuries:

1. Multiple lacerations of the skin, frontal area, forehead, and facial areas. Approximately 15 lacerations of the front area of the head are described. Twelve of these lacerations are horizontally oriented, with three showing a vertical orientation.
2. Comminuted depressed fracture of the skull, involving frontal bone, nasal bones, and left orbital area
3. Subarachnoid hemorrhage of the brain
4. Lacerated contusions of the brain, orbital surface of frontal lobes
5. Fracture of the zygoma, bilateral
6. Multiple fractures of the maxilla
7. Fracture of the left body of the mandible with avulsion of left lower lateral incisor tooth

Aspiration of blood was noted, as well as abrasions and bruises of the skin on the upper left anterior chest, abdomen, upper extremities, and lower extremities. The upper extremities also showed superficial lacerations. The cause of death was determined to be craniocerebral injury with contributory aspiration of blood and the manner of death determined to be homicide.

Figure 10.24   Victim at camp site near makeshift tent.

Description of Scene and Bloodstain Patterns

The scene of this homicide was approximately 0.4 mile south of Hypoluxo Road in a group of Banyan trees located approximately 182 feet west of U.S. Highway 1 in Lantana, Florida. The victim was identified as W.S., a 47 year-old white male. Sheriff's Office reports indicated that the victim was found by a friend who reported the homicide.

This scene is best described as a transient campground which is afforded adequate protection from the elements by the group of trees. A makeshift, clear plastic tent is located in the northeast corner of this wooded area. The inside floor area of this tent measured approximately 11 feet, 2 inches, north to south and 6 feet east to west. The openings of the tent were located on the east and west sides. The tent was supported by rope attached to nearby trees and held down by tires on the north and south sides. Large amounts of debris, including beer and wine bottles, were noted to be in the general area of the campground.

The victim is seen lying on the ground at the southwest corner of the tent on his back, face up with his head pointing to the north and his feet pointing to the south (Figure 10.24). The arms are extended outward from the body and flexed inward at the elbow with the forearms parallel to the head. The hands are partially clenched. The victim has sustained massive blunt force trauma to the head area. A section of signpost approximately 26 1/2 inches in length rests laterally across the chest of the victim with one

Figure 10.25   Massive blunt force injuries inflicted to head of victim with metal sign post which lies across chest.

end, on the ground near the right elbow and the other end, which is heavily bloodstained, resting on the chest below the chin (Figure 10.25).

The victim is clad in a brown, blue, and white plaid-type long-sleeved shirt with the sleeves rolled up near the elbows. The shirt is partially unbuttoned in front, exposing an underlying blue shirt. This blue shirt is visible on the partially exposed abdomen. The victim is also wearing blue jeans and a brown belt, with the fly of the jeans partially open. The legs are partially spread with black shoes on the feet.

To the right of the body is an upright plastic container. To the left of the head and left arm of the victim is the plastic covering comprising the southwest corner of the tent. Near the left side of the victim is one of the black tires which is holding down a portion of the plastic tent. A plastic bag is seen opposite the left knee of the victim, and a metal wash bucket is seen to the left of the left foot of the victim. An area of dirt between the shoes of the victim appears to be disturbed.

There is a large quantity of blood which appears to be partially clotted on the victim's face and hair as well as surrounding the victim's head on the ground. Each hand shows heavy blood transfer from contact with a wet source of blood. The shoulders and arms of the victim show extensive

Figure 10.26 Medium-velocity impact blood spatter on left shoulder and arm of victim.

radiating patterns of medium-velocity impact blood spatter, circular to oval in shape, as well as irregularly shaped clotted spatters of blood. A heavy concentration of medium-velocity impact blood spatter is seen on the left forearm (Figure 10.26).

The blood spatters are seen to have extended beyond the left arm of the victim and impacted onto the adjacent outside surface of the plastic tent in the southwest corner to a height of approximately 30 inches above the ground. The average diameters of the blood spatters on the outside plastic tent surface range from 0.5 to 5 mm with smaller and larger bloodstains present. Some of these spatters may represent forceful wheezing or expiration of blood from the victim's nose or mouth. Some of the bloodstains present on the lower portion of the tent surface in this area have been smeared by a hand or other object having contact with that surface while the blood was wet. Irregularly shaped clotted blood spatters are also noted on the plastic tent surface. Also present on this plastic tent surface are several dripped and projected bloodstains with a downward directionality, with the origin above the observed head position of the victim. The medium-velocity impact blood spatter also extends onto the southwest corner of the tent flooring and is seen as oval, elongated bloodstains.

Medium-velocity impact blood spatters have also been deposited on the tread area of the tire near the left chest of the victim, as well as the lower chest area, abdomen, and upper thigh area of the blue jeans. The jeans also show evidence of dripped and projected bloodstains on the left and right thigh which have originated from above the thigh.

The plastic bag to the left of the victim's left knee also shows evidence of medium-velocity impact spatter. The white plastic bleach container shows circular to oval medium-velocity impact blood spatter with diameters ranging from approximately 0.5 to 3.0 mm. Their directionalities are consistent with the container being in its observed position at the time it received the spatters of blood. This bleach container also shows dripped and projected bloodstains on both sides of the container relative to the position of the victim which have originated from above the container. Dripped bloodstains are also seen on the ground near this container.

Medium-velocity impact blood spatters extend on the ground to the north of the victim's head, where it is seen to be present on leaves, broken plates, and a razor, as well as on the surface of a spray disinfectant can.

The radiating pattern of medium-velocity impact blood spatter continues to a tree located approximately 5 feet, 4 inches, to the north of the head of the victim, where the blood droplets have impacted the exposed root of the tree and up the trunk of this tree to a height of approximately 50 inches above the ground. Some cast-off bloodstains may be present here as well (Figure 10.27). On the west branch of the tree are seen irregularly shaped spatters and possibly cast-off bloodstains on the bark surface located approximately 56 inches above the ground.

Within the tent on the floor near the north wall of the plastic covering are seen transfer bloodstains on a yellow and white striped towel. Just to the north of this towel are seen heavy contact bloodstains on the foam rubber flooring which are consistent with having been produced from sustained contact with a wet source of blood. Above this area of contact bloodstaining on the floor of the tent is located a blood transfer pattern on the inside surface of the plastic tent covering with features consistent with a bloody hair swipe which feathers in an upward direction (Figure 10.28). At the east opening of the tent just to the south of the peak of the plastic tent cover is an additional blood transfer pattern with features consistent with a bloody hair swipe which is seen to feather south to north (Figure 10.29). There was no evidence of medium-velocity impact blood spatter seen on the inside surface of the plastic tent covering.

Figure 10.27   Cast off bloodstains on trunk of tree behind victim.

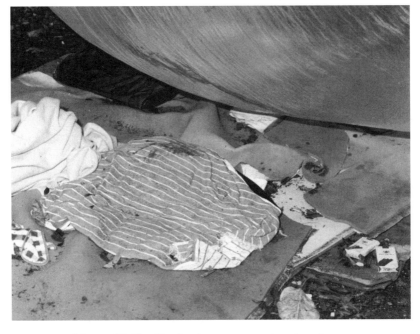

Figure 10.28   Bloodstains present on interior of tent.

Figure 10.29 Bloodstains present on exterior top edge of tent.

To the east of the tent and measured approximately 15 feet, 10 inches, from the feet of the victim is a small clump of trees on the east side of the scene perimeter. Some of the limbs of these trees are down on the ground. On a large tree limb oriented east to west is seen a large contact bloodstain which has resulted from contact with a wet source of blood. Between this limb and a standing tree to the north is seen a green blanket on top of some downed tree limbs. A large quantity of contact bloodstaining is present on the surface of these limbs (Figure 10.30). On nearby leaves are seen drip patterns of blood which have resulted from blood falling from a source above the ground affected only by gravity and dripping into itself from the source. No evidence of medium-velocity impact blood spatter was seen in this area.

Examination of the Physical Evidence

The examination of physical evidence was conducted on the dates of 04/16/90, 04/23/90, and 05/01/90.

Clothing of Victim

1. The shirt of the victim, W.S., consists of a blue, brown, and white plaid long-sleeved shirt size XL, and Bud Burns brand. The rear of this shirt

Figure 10.30   Bloodstains on ground and tree branches to east of victim and tent.

is heavily blood-soaked. The front of this shirt shows considerable medium-velocity impact blood spatter and blood-soaked areas most heavily concentrated on the shoulders and upper arms of this garment. The diameter of these spatters of blood ranges from 0.5 to 4 mm, with some smaller and larger bloodstains present. Many of the blood spatters consist of irregularly shaped impacted clots of blood. The quantity of medium-velocity impact spatter decreases somewhat down the right arms to the cuff, where there are also some blood-soaked areas. The left arm of the shirt shows a denser pattern of medium-velocity impact spatter, clotted spatters, and as some blood-soaked areas. Void areas on the sleeves are due to the irregular bunching of the material while worn by the victim with his sleeves rolled up to the elbows. The front chest area of the shirt shows medium-velocity impact blood spatter and clotted spatters on the left and right front areas, more concentrated on the left side. Additional blood soaking and blood transfer is present on the right side of the shirt. The underside of the right lower front edge of the shirt shows blood spatter and staining on the inner surface due to this surface being exposed at the time of bloodshed to that area. Some plant debris and dirt is also present on this garment.

2. The blue jeans of the victim, W.S., consist of Rustler brand jeans with a brown knitted belt. The rear left leg of the jeans is relatively free of bloodstaining with scattered bloodstains present on the upper rear of the right leg. The front and lateral side of the upper right leg shows a bloodstain pattern consisting of circular to oval and irregularly shaped bloodstains with a range in diameter from 5 to 10 mm which have resulted from dripping and projection of blood from a source above. There are also smaller, 0.5- to 4-mm diameter, circular to oval spatters of blood, some of which consist of clotted blood. The upper front of the left leg of the blue jeans shows an area of dripped blood from above with circular to oval shaped stains as well as some spatters of blood. The left knee shows a blood-soaked area resulting from blood which has soaked through from the inside surface of the fabric. There are scattered areas of spattered blood present on the lower legs of the jeans. Some plant debris and dirt is also present on this garment.

3. The footwear of the victim, W.S., consists of a pair of Athletix brand shoes with a prominent circular sole design. The left lateral side of the right shoe shows some projected bloodstains with a directionality towards the sole of the shoe. A trace of blood is detected on the sole with Phenolphthalein reagent. Similar projected bloodstains are present on the right lateral edge of the left shoe.

4. The undershirt of the victim, W.S., consists of a green short-sleeved Tuxan brand garment. The rear of this shirt is considerably blood-soaked with evidence of plant debris and dirt present. The front of this garment shows blood transfer stains and medium-velocity impact blood spatter on the upper central chest area. Many of these spatters are circular to oval in shape with diameters ranging between 0.5 and 4 mm. Some of these blood spatters consist of small clots of blood. This area of the underlying shirt was exposed during bloodshed due to the outer shirt being partially unbuttoned. The lower front area of this shirt also shows spatters of blood and clotted blood as it extended beyond the lower edge of the outer shirt during bloodshed.

Clothing of Suspect

1. The shirt of the suspect, C.W., consists of a long-sleeved sweatshirt with a crab design on the front chest area and the logo "I've got the Crabs". Below this logo on the front is seen a small area of blood transfer. On the upper right arm of this garment are seen numerous circular to oval shaped medium-velocity impact blood spatters measuring 0.5 to 4 mm in diameter. There are also spatters of clotted blood. Similar medium-velocity impact blood spatters and spatters of

clotted blood are present on the lower right arm extending onto the right cuff. The left arm of this garment also shows similar medium-velocity impact blood spatter and spatters of clotted blood extending from the upper arm area to the cuff. There are some small transfer bloodstains present on the lower back of this garment. The trousers of the suspect, C.W., consist of grayish-green Levi's for Men Action Jeans brand, size 34–36 with a brown belt with silver buckle. The upper rear and upper front of these jeans are relatively free of bloodstains. The right front leg of the jeans measuring from the lower edge of the cuff upward 21 inches just above the knee area show numerous medium-velocity impact blood spatters with the heaviest concentration from the cuff to 12 inches above the cuff from the mid to inner lateral side of the right leg of the garment. Many of these blood spatters range in size from 0.5 to 5.0 mm in diameter, with smaller and larger bloodstains present. Many of the spatters consist of clotted blood which exhibit irregular sizes and shapes (Figures 10.31 and 10.32). The left front leg of these jeans shows numerous medium-velocity impact blood spatters present on the fabric from the lower edge of the cuff upward 23 inches just above the knee, with the heaviest concentration from the cuff to 12 inches above the cuff. Many of these blood spatters range in size from 0.5 to 5.0 mm in diameter, with smaller and larger bloodstains present. Many of the spatters consist of clotted blood of irregular size and shape. The lower right leg of the jeans contains a considerably greater quantity of blood spatters than the left leg.

3. The shoes of the suspect, C.W., consist of black/gray Nike Airline brand running shoes with a crosshatch sole pattern. The left shoe shows blood transfer stains on the laces with some heavier contact staining to the right of the laces. The toe area is relatively free of bloodstaining. There is medium-velocity impact blood spatter present on the inner lateral edge of the sole below the heel with a few scattered bloodstains above this area on the upper portion of the shoe. The right shoe shows scattered irregular bloodstains on the upper front surface, including the laces, with little evidence of bloodstaining on the front toe area. The inner lateral surface shows large transfer bloodstains. Below this area on the inner lateral edge of the sole there is a heavy concentration of medium-velocity impact blood spatter consisting of circular, oval, and irregularly shaped bloodstains, many with diameters of 0.5 to 5.0 mm with some smaller and larger spatters present (Figure 10.33). There is a void area absent of spatter above the visible spatters due to the hang of the cuff of the trousers that previously covered that portion of the shoe.

Figure 10.31   Medium-velocity impact blood spatter on shoes and lower trouser legs of suspect.

The Weapon Found at the Scene

The weapon found at the scene of this homicide consists of a section of iron signpost which appears twisted on the shaft near the grip area. This V-shaped section of post measures approximately 26 ½ inches long, 1 ½ inches deep, and 3 inches wide at the end that rested on the chest of the victim. Due to compression of the metal, the grip portion of the post tapers to a minimum diameter of approximately 1 ¼ inches on the flattened surface and then flares out at the end to an approximate diameter of 3 inches. A trough and row of holes is present down the shaft of the post. The end of the iron post which rested on the chest of the victim is heavily bloodstained from contact with a source of blood. There are also numerous, circular to oval shaped medium-velocity impact blood spatters on the shaft exhibiting diameters from 0.5 to 4 mm, with some smaller and larger bloodstains present. Blood flow patterns are present on the shaft which have travelled from the heavily bloodstained end to the grip area of this iron post.

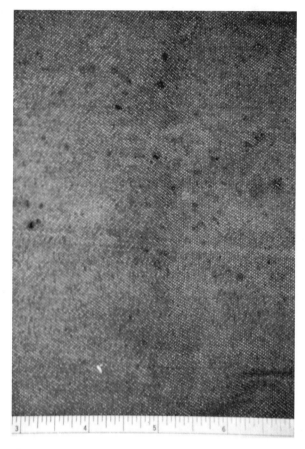

Figure 10.32 Closer view of medium-velocity bloodstains on trousers of victim showing some clotted spatter.

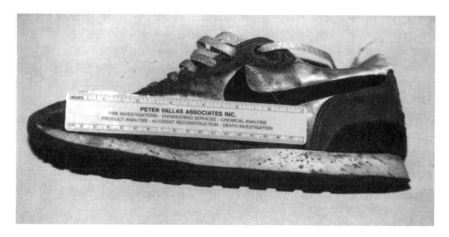

Figure 10.33 Medium-velocity impact blood spatter on right shoe of suspect.

Examination of Photographs of the Hands of the Suspect

Color photographs taken of the hands of the suspect in this case, C.W., by Detective D.S. at the scene on 04/12/90 reveal the palmar surface of the hands to be moderately bloodstained. The bloodstains on the palm of the left hand appear diffuse, with more concentration of blood at the juncture of the base of the fingers and the palm. Several small circular to oval spatters of blood are present near the base of the thumb extending over the juncture of the wrist and the palm.

The palmar surface of the right hand of the suspect, C.W., shows a concentration of contact bloodstaining which extends across the base of the fingers and the adjacent surface of the right palm. This bloodstaining extends towards the wrist along the inner lateral aspect of the hand and is more diffuse along the base of the thumb. This area of described bloodstaining is sharply delineated across the right palm below the base of the fingers and below the little finger towards the wrist. This delineation forms a rectangular-shaped void area free of bloodstaining in the central portion of the right palm which is oriented between the right thumb and first finger and parallel to the extended thumb (Figures 10.34 and 10.35). This area is sometimes referred to as the web of the palm. This void area is consistent with an object being held tightly in the right hand during the time that blood contacted the palm. The tight grip on the object prevented the blood from contacting the central portion or web of the palm and created the sharp outline of the void or gripping pattern of the hand-held object (Figure 10.36).

Conclusions

The victim in this case, W.S., received multiple blunt force injuries to the head with many of the wounds oriented laterally across the head and face. The final blows administered to the victim were delivered while he lay prone in his observed position on the ground near the southwest corner of the clear plastic tent. The radial pattern of medium-velocity impact blood spatter typically produced during a beating of a prone victim is present on the victim and the area in proximity to the position of the victim on the ground. The heaviest concentrations of blood spatter are present on the upper body and arms of the victim, on the lower portion of the southwest corner of the tent, the tree trunk to the north of the victim's head, the tire and plastic bag located to the left of the victim, and the plastic bleach container to the right of the body of the victim. These objects were in their observed locations when they received the blood spatters. The origin of these medium-velocity impact blood spatters is consistent with the observed location of the head of the victim at the scene.

There is no evidence to indicate that the victim was moved subsequent to the fatal beating. However, the presence of projected bloodstains and

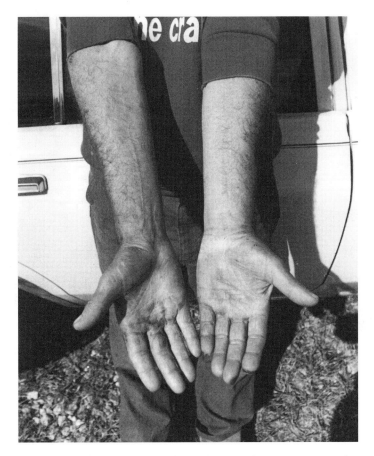

Figure 10.34 Bloodstains on palmar surfaces of hands of suspect. Note void area on right web area.

dripped blood on the outside surface of the tent, the plastic bleach bottle, and ground to the right of the victim are consistent with the victim being erect or semi-erect when that blood was deposited. The drip patterns and projected blood on the front of the victim's trousers are consistent with a head wound shedding blood while victim was in a sitting position. The transferred blood on the hands of the victim is consistent with the victim having hand contact with an exposed source of blood, such as his head, prior to the final blows being struck.

The radial pattern of medium-velocity impact blood spatter is more concentrated on the left arm of the victim, on the southwest corner of the plastic tent cover, and on the lower trunk of the tree to the north of the head of the victim. The blood spatter has also impacted the tire and plastic bag to the left of the victim, his chest, and trunk area. Blood spatter is also present on the white plastic bleach container to the right of the victim as well as the

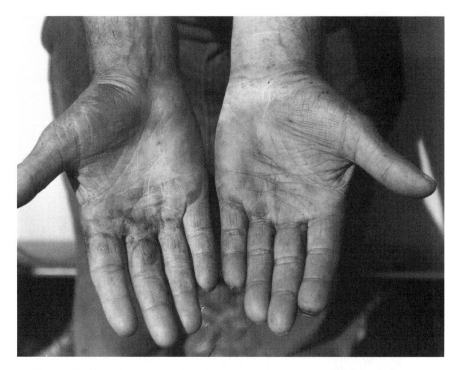

Figure 10.35   Closer view of void area on right palmar surface of suspect.

right arm. Void areas in this spatter pattern exist on the ground to the right of the victim's head.

This is consistent with blows struck to the prone victim by an assailant positioned close to the right side of the victim's head and right arm. The lower legs and shoes of an assailant would intercept the medium-velocity impact blood spatter which would create the void areas on the ground. The position of the weapon on the chest of the victim is also consistent with the assailant being to the right of the victim. Blows struck from this position would produce the laterally oriented wounds across the face of the victim. The vertically oriented wounds on the face of the victim were produced by blows struck with the weapon aligned vertically with the head with the assailant either behind or in front of the head at the time these blows were struck. This orientation may account for the apparent cast-off bloodstains on the upper trunk and limb of the tree to the north of the head of the victim on the ground.

The observed position of the victim represents his final location but is one of three locations at the scene where physical activity involving bloodshed occurred. At a prior time the victim shed blood inside the tent near the north side of the plastic covering. There is evidence of transfer of blood on a towel inside the tent and contact bloodstaining on the floor of the tent. This would

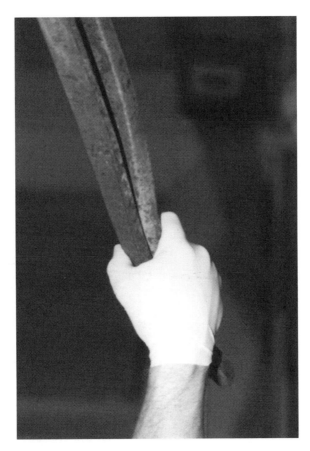

Figure 10.36 Grasping of weapon in right hand to produce void of blood on palmar surface.

indicate that the victim was on the floor of the tent after initial bloodshed occurred. The hair swipe on the inside surface of the north side of the plastic covering are consistent with the victim rising from the floor. The hair swipe on the top of the east opening of the tent is consistent with contact with the head of the victim at a point when he was above the floor of the tent. The absence of blood spatters on the inside walls of the tent indicate that multiple blows were not struck to an exposed source of blood inside the tent. However, the first blow usually does not create blood spatter, since the blood must be exposed when impacted to produce the spatter. Therefore, the location of the victim when the first blow to the head was struck is not revealed by the bloodstain evidence. All that can be said with certainty is that the victim was shedding blood within the tent prior to the final blows being struck. The large accumulation of blood in the clump of trees to the east of the tent on the leaves and downed limbs indicates that the victim was shedding blood

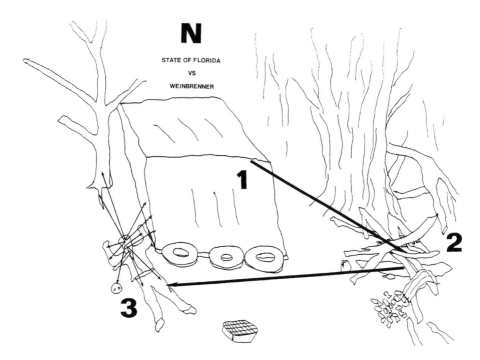

Figure 10.37 Reconstructed path of victim during assault and his final position showing radial pattern of blood splatters produced by final blows to the head.

in that area in a larger quantity than that observed within the tent. This would support the conclusion that he was in this second area after being in the tent. The bloodstain evidence indicates that the victim was bleeding in contact with the tree limbs on the ground for a period of time. There is no evidence of medium-velocity impact blood spatter in this area. If blows were struck to the victim in this area, they impacted areas of the body where blood was not exposed.

There is no evidence to indicate that the victim was dragged to his final location. Disabling injuries may not have occurred at this point during the altercation. It is possible that the victim was able to move from this location in a continuing effort to elude his assailant prior to falling to the ground where the final blows were struck (Figure 10.37).

The presence of clotted blood spatters on the victim and the area of his final position indicates that a significant period of time elapsed between initial bloodshed and the administration of the final blows to the victim. This is consistent with the victim is receiving initial injury and shedding blood in two locations at the campsite prior to his final position. An average time of 3 to 15 minutes for exposed blood to form visible clots may be used as a guideline for this interval.

The trousers of the suspect, C.W., exhibit numerous medium-velocity impact blood spatters on the left and right legs from the cuffs to the knee area. Many of these spatters consist of clotted blood. The blood spatters are more concentrated on the mid- to inner lateral aspect of the right leg. Medium-velocity impact blood spatters are also present on the shoes of the suspect, more concentrated on the inner aspect of the right sole. The shirt of the suspect shows medium-velocity impact spatter on the arms. When prone victims are beaten with a blunt object, medium-velocity impact blood spatters are usually found in the region of the assailant's lower trouser legs and shirt sleeves. The presence of these blood spatters on the clothing of the suspect indicates that he was in close proximity to a physical activity such as a beating with a blunt object involving bloodshed at the time blood was spattered from an exposed source of blood receiving impact close to the ground. The right leg of the suspect's trousers and right shoe were more exposed to the source of blood spatter than were the left trouser leg and shoe. The presence of the clotted blood spatters on the suspect's trousers would further classify the physical activity that produced the blood spatters as one for which there was a significant time lapse between initial bloodshed and spattering of clots of blood.

Blood spatters are also present on the palmar surface of the left hand of the suspect, C.W., near the base of the thumb and edge of the wrist. This is consistent with proximity to a physical activity where exposed blood is spattered.

The palmar surface of the right hand of the suspect, C.W., shows a concentration of contact bloodstaining which extends across the base of the fingers and the adjacent surface of the right palm. This bloodstaining extends towards the wrist along the inner lateral aspect of the hand and is more diffuse along the base of the thumb. This area of described bloodstaining is sharply delineated across the right palm, below the base of the fingers, and below the little finger towards the wrist.

This delineation forms a rectangular-shaped void area free of bloodstaining in the central portion of the right palm which is oriented between the right thumb and first finger and parallel to the extended thumb. This area is sometimes referred to as the web of the palm. This void area is consistent with an object being held tightly in the right hand during the time that blood contacted the palm. The tight grip on the object prevented the blood from contacting the central portion or web of the palm and created the sharp outline of the void or gripping pattern of the hand held object.

The grip area of the iron signpost found across the chest of the victim in this case narrows to a minimum diameter of approximately 1 inches on the flat surface. Blood has flowed down the shaft of the iron post to the area of the grip. The void area on the right palm of the suspect is of adequate diameter to have gripped tightly this iron signpost or object of similar dimension while blood accumulated around the edges of the object while it was being held. The compression of the object in the web of the palm of the right hand of the suspect prevented bloodstaining beneath the object and created the void area.

Case Study 2

In this case, a woman was accused of shooting and stabbing her ex-husband. The investigation indicated that she drove from out of state and appeared at her ex-husband's door armed with a gun. She claimed that he attacked her initially with a knife when he answered the door and dragged her through the house. She sustained a small cut on her right hand. Interestingly, the blood trail leading from the residence was found by DNA analysis to contain a mixture of blood of both the assailant and the victim. This would be consistent with blood from her cut hand mixing with the victim's blood on her person or object (possibly the knife) before dripping onto the sidewalk. The ex-wife was convicted of second-degree murder.

Report of Bloodstain Pattern Interpretation

Re: State of Florida vs. L.M.

On April 9, 1992, the following materials were received:

1. Report of postmortem examination
2. Reports from the regional crime laboratory
3. Sheriff's Department investigative reports and evidence tracking work sheets
4. Transcribed interview of H.M
5. Color photographs of the scene and autopsy

On April 20, 1992, I visited the scene of this homicide and examined items of physical evidence at the Sheriff's Office. At this time, the carpet from the closet adjacent to the master bathroom was tested with the chemical reagent Luminol.

History of the Case

On May 14, 1991, the body of the deceased was found in the master bedroom of his residence. The victim was a 37-year-old white male who measured 6 feet in height and weighed 172 pounds. The postmortem examination revealed that the victim had sustained numerous injuries:

Stab Wounds

1. Left infraclavicular chest involving the left lung
2. Left precordial chest involving the heart
3. Left inferior chest involving anterior mediastinum
4. Right infraclavicular chest involving the pectoralis muscle
5. Left lateral neck involving incision of left internal jugular vein and left common carotid artery
6. Left lower lateral neck involving subcutaneous tissues
7. Soft tissues of posterior left thigh

Incised Injuries

1. Right upper chest
2. Right lower chest
3. Left elbow
4. Posterior left forearm
5. Right index finger
6. Right dorsal hand
7. Left popliteal area

Gunshot Injuries

1. Close-range gunshot to left jaw
2. Close-range gunshot to right posterior shoulder
3. Indefinite range gunshot to anterior right wrist
4. Close-range, through and through gunshot to left upper arm

Mechanical Injuries

1. Superficial abrasion of upper anterior nose
2. Superficial abrasion of mid anterior nose
3. Two abrasion/contusions to mid-upper back
4. Acute contusion to right forearm
5. Irregular abrasion to right distal dorsal forearm

Scene Photographs

Bloodstain Pattern Interpretation

Entrance Way and Exterior of Residence. The main entrance door is located on the east side of the residence. Bloodstains are present on the threshold of the doorway which were deposited when the door was in an

Figure 10.38   Exterior of residence showing sidewalk leading away from front entrance.

open or partially open position. A trail of bloodstains which have been produced by individual falling drops of blood has been deposited on the surface of the outside concrete sidewalk (Figure 10.38). These bloodstains show irregular edge characteristics consistent with the rough surface upon which they have been deposited. Their maximum diameters are approximately ½ inch, with smaller bloodstains present. Many of these bloodstains exhibit elongated spines on the edge of the bloodstain leading away from the front entrance way. These spiny projections indicate the direction of travel of the source of blood above to be away from the entrance of the residence (Figure 10.39).

Just inside the front entrance way of the residence is a small grayish-blue throw rug in the foyer. The floor in this area consists of brown hexagonal tile. To the left and in front of the rug are seen additional circular bloodstains which have resulted from free-falling drops of blood from a blood source

Figure 10.39   Bloodstain created by free falling drop of blood while moving away from front door. Note spines on edge of bloodstain indicating direction of travel.

above striking the floor tile at approximately 90°. These bloodstains possess smoother edges than those on the cement walkway outside and do not exhibit direction of travel; rather, they are consistent with a stationary source of blood above.

Living Room.   The foyer area leads to the north into the living room. The living room appeared to be in normal order with no signs of a struggle. An empty casing was located to the right of the large TV near the north west wall. No bloodstains were seen in the living room.

Kitchen.   The foyer leads to the west into the kitchen area of the residence. The kitchen is elongated in a north-south direction with a counter along the west wall and appliances along the east wall. The counter extends at an angle towards the center line of the kitchen at the south end. The kitchen floor consists of brown hexagonal tile similar to the foyer floor.

Bloodstain patterns on the tile floor of the kitchen consist of bloodstains which are near circular with irregular edges and have been deposited from a source of blood above with impact angles of approximately 90°. At the south end of the kitchen floor there are numerous bloodstains of this type which exhibit satellite spatter. This spatter has resulted from blood droplets falling into a previously deposited wet bloodstain already on the floor (Figure 10.40).

Figure 10.40   Blood drip pattern on kitchen floor of residence.

A trail of similar bloodstains continues on the tile floor in the direction of the dining room to the north near the center of the kitchen floor. Some of these dripped bloodstains exhibit some directionality to the north towards the dining room. Others have been altered while partially wet by an object passing through the original bloodstain.

On the north wall of the kitchen near the left edge of the entrance way to the dining room, approximately 3 feet, 9 ½ inches, above the floor, is a narrow elongated blood transfer stain which is consistent with being produced by the edge of a hand wet with blood at the time of deposit. Below this area on the same wall are seen some projected or cast-off bloodstains with a downward directionality located above the blue waste basket. On the kitchen counter is seen a small blood transfer stain near a measuring tape and dish rack.

Dining Room.   The dining room is located to the north of the kitchen and south of the master bedroom. The floor of the dining room is similar brown hexagonal tile. A blood-drip pattern is concentrated on the floor just to the south of the dining room table and continues to the entrance to the master bedroom. The source of this blood would be above the floor and dropping at approximately 90°. Some of the bloodstains exhibit spiny edges, while others have been altered while partially wet by an object passing through the original bloodstain. The path of the blood-drip pattern is consistent with continuation from the kitchen to the entrance way of the master bedroom.

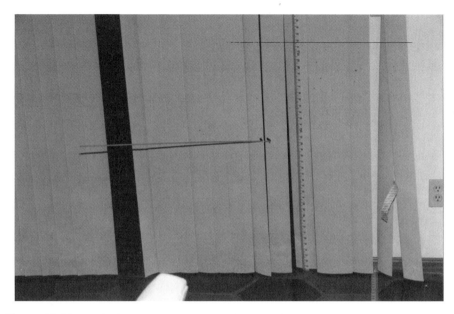

Figure 10.41   Path of projectile into vertical blinds indicated by wooden dowel in hallway of residence.

Some of the smaller bloodstains are consistent with projected blood from a source above.

On the surface of the vertical blinds along the west side of the dining room is seen evidence of a projectile hole (Figure 10.41). Above this area is seen an area of impact blood spatter which could be associated with the exit of a projectile from a source of blood (Figure 10.42).

To the right of the entrance into the master bedroom is a blood transfer stain on the door jamb and adjacent wall. This transfer stain is consistent with having been produced by the side or edge of a hand wet with blood. Below this area is seen a projected bloodstain pattern and drips of blood with a downward directionality (Figure 10.43).

Master Bedroom.   The master bedroom is located at the north side of the residence. The door swings inward and to the left. Additional drip patterns of blood are observed on the carpet just inside the doorway. Some cast-off type bloodstains are seen on the wall behind the door located 2 to 3 feet above the floor. These bloodstains exhibit a downward directionality and are angled toward the hinged side of the door. On this wall above the light switch is observed blood transfer approximately 4 feet above the floor. Blood transfer also extends onto the adjacent vertical blinds which are in front of the west sliding glass doors of the master bedroom. Additional cast-off type bloodstaining is seen near the center of the vertical blinds approximately 2 feet above the floor.

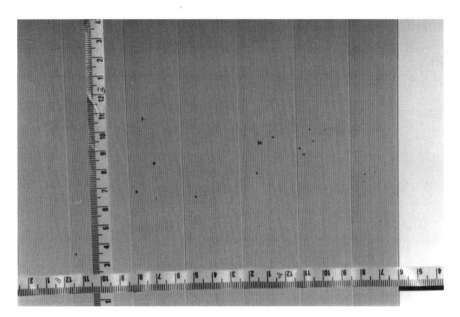

Figure 10.42   Impact blood spatter near projectile hole in vertical blinds.

The victim in this case, K.J., is observed to be lying on the carpeted floor of the master bedroom between the sliding glass door and the water bed (Figure 10.44). The water bed is located near the center of the bedroom with the head against the north wall. There are dripped and projected bloodstains on the carpet between the victim and the entrance way of the bedroom. The victim is situated on the floor with his head near the side of the bed. The body is angled to the southwest, the feet of the victim within the lower edge of the vertical blinds. The feet are crossed right over left, with the right sole bloodstained. Blood transfer, downward flow patterns, and projected bloodstains are seen on the exposed legs of the victim. The victim is clad only in white shorts which are considerably bloodstained. Blood transfer is present on both hands and arms. Drainage of blood is observed from wounds on the chest and neck as well as from the nose.

A large pool of blood which appears to be partially clotted is on the carpet to the left of the victim. Blood-soaked underwear can be seen within the blood pool to the left of the victim's head. The victim's glasses are at the edge of the blood pooling nearest the bed. A void area within this blood pooling shows the location of the victim's left upper arm, indicating that he was turned to his right after bloodshed occurred. The victim was originally positioned on his left side. On the overhanging sheet above and to the left of the victim is seen a blood transfer feathered towards the victim with some small projected bloodstains below this area.

Figure 10.43 Transfer and projected bloodstains on right side of entrance to master bedroom of residence.

Against the south wall opposite the foot of the bed is a dresser with a TV on top. To the left of this dresser on the wall are observed some projected bloodstains. On the floor near three shirts are seen additional projected-type bloodstains and possible transfer of blood. To the east of this area is a lamp with the shade on the floor in the corner. The exposed area of the lamp shade shows elongated bloodstains with a downward directionality. In front of the lamp toward the foot of the bed are seen additional blood-drip patterns and blood transfers on the carpet. A bloody shoewear transfer is visible on the carpet pointed away from the bathroom entrance, which is on the east wall opposite the side of the bed (Figure 10.45). On the east wall between the entrance to the bathroom and the lamp on the floor is a large transfer bloodstain approximately 3 feet above the floor. There are areas of projected bloodstains with a downward directionality on the wall below the transfer.

Figure 10.44 Victim on floor in master bedroom after being rolled to his right by paramedics. Note void produced by right shoulder from original position.

Figure 10.45 Bloody shoe prints on carpet in master bedroom leading away from master bathroom.

Figure 10.46   Knife case with broken glass top. Note impression showing shape of missing knife.

The bedspread has been pulled back over the foot of the bed. A large contact bloodstain and spatters are seen on the exposed portion of the bedspread, which is on the bed. Blood drip patterns and transfer of blood are observed on the exposed portion of the bedspread on the floor. There is evidence of dripped or projected blood on the exposed sheet near the foot of the bed which continues over the edge of the foot of the bed with a downward directionality.

There is a knife case present on the bed on the side nearest the entrance to the bathroom. It is located near the edge of the bed and the pillow. The glass top has been broken with shards of glass present on the top of the case as well as on the surrounding sheet (Figure 10.46). Small circular apparent bloodstains are seen on the sheet to the left of the case and possibly on or beneath a shard of glass on the sheet near the lock of the case. The case contains several types of folding knives and a stellate-shaped instrument. Below the broken glass area, a knife impression is seen near other knives in the case.

Master Bathroom.   Near the entrance way to the bathroom on the east side of the master bedroom are additional individual drips of blood on the carpet. Also seen are blood transfer impressions consistent with having been produced by bare feet. On the edging between the bedroom carpet and the

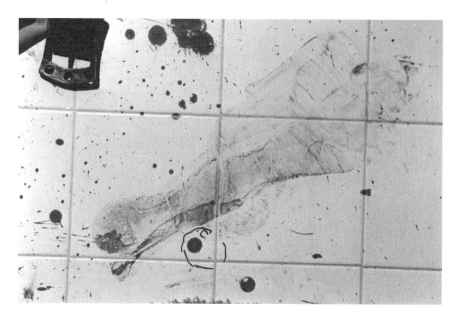

Figure 10.47 Bloody impression created by bare foot on floor of master bathroom.

bathroom tile and onto the tile itself is seen a continuation of stains produced by individual free-falling drops of blood.

A partial shoe print is present on the edging extending onto the bed-room carpet. The area of the tiled bathroom floor between the sink cabinet to the north and the closet to the south shows an array of dripped and projected bloodstains. There are numerous bloody partial shoeprint trans-fers oriented in different directions. Much of this floor area is covered with smeared blood which is consistent with having been produced by bare as well as shod feet (Figures 10.47 and 10.48). A large smearing of blood has travelled across the bathroom floor to the base of the sink cabinet, where a transfer of blood is seen consistent with having been produced by a bare foot. In some areas of the floor, drips of blood have been deposited on top of the smeared areas of blood. A blood-transfer stain is seen consistent with a partial shoe print over a partial hand print. Blood has dripped on top of the edge of the sink and on the front of the sink cabinet, where some projected blood is also noted.

A pair of tan trousers is observed on the bathroom floor and cover some of the deposited bloodstains. The trousers appear to be considerably blood-stained with some bloody shoe transfers present. Blood transfer and dripping of blood extends onto a blue throw rug on the bathroom floor to the east of the closet entrance. Two projectile casings were found on the floor of the bathroom.

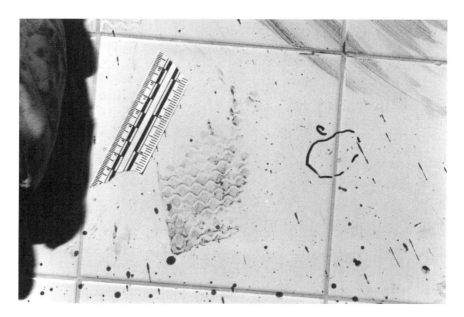

Figure 10.48 Bloody impression created by shoe on floor of master bathroom.

Bathroom Closet.   The entrance to the bathroom closet is on the south side of the bathroom. On the wall to the west of this entrance is a blood transfer consistent with a hand and feathered downward. A transfer of blood is present on the right-side closet door casing above the latch area. There was sufficient blood within this transfer to permit a flow pattern down the casing to the floor below. Additional but lighter blood transfers are present closer to the latch area.

Within the closet there is a large contact bloodstain on the carpet in front of a rack of hanging clothes (Figure 10.49). Projected bloodstains and blood transfers including numerous partial shoe and footprints are seen around this heavily bloodstained area. Projected bloodstains and spatter were present on the south and west walls of the closet approximately 15 inches above the floor. These stains are more apparent when the clothing is removed from the racks (Figure 10.50). Transfer bloodstains are noted on the exposed surfaces of some of the hanging clothing. A picture frame on the carpet exhibited projected and dripped bloodstains both on top of the frame and below. Two projectiles were recovered from the floor of the closet.

Reconstruction and Sequence of Events

The victim in this case, K.J., received gunshot and knife wounds which resulted in considerable bloodshed within his residence during the assault as well as at his final resting position in the master bedroom (Figure 10.51).

Figure 10.49 Blood soaked area of carpet in master bathroom closet.

Figure 10.50 Impact blood spatters on wall close to floor in closet of master bathroom.

Initial bloodshed of the victim has occurred at the south end of the kitchen, where free-falling drops of blood impacted the tile floor. However, the appearance of bloodstains does not necessarily indicate the precise location

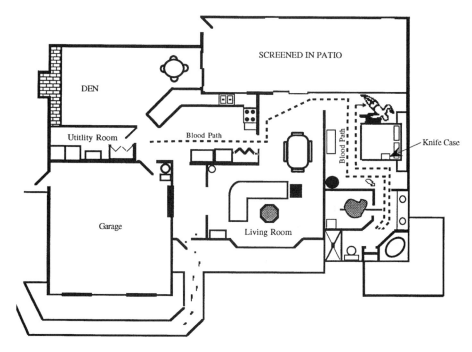

Figure 10.51 Diagram of residence showing path of retreat of victim.

in the residence where the initial injury or injuries occurred to the victim. A trail of dripped bloodstains on the kitchen floor shows directionality to the north into the dining room of the residence. Some of these bloodstains have been altered while still partially wet which indicates a secondary activity having taken place. A blood transfer stain on the kitchen wall to the left of the entrance way to the dining room likely was produced by a hand wet with blood.

The trail of bloodstains from the victim continues to the west parallel to the dining room table and then north into the master bedroom. The victim was likely struck by a projectile while retreating through the dining room into the master bedroom. This projectile exited the victim and re-entered the vertical blinds and sliding glass door casing at the west side of the dining room. Impact blood spatter is noted on the vertical blinds in proximity to the projectile defect.

Dripped bloodstain patterns show continuation of the victim's route to the east around the foot of the bed into the bathroom and into the walk-in closet. Physical activity involving bloodshed has occurred in the bathroom-closet area. In the closet the heavy accumulation of blood on the carpet beneath the hanging clothing is consistent with the victim being positioned on or close to the floor during significant blood loss. Bloody footprints close to the south wall and pointing outward would position the victim close to that area at some point in the sequence. Bloody shoe prints on the opposite side of the large bloodstain on the carpet in the direction of the south wall would position an assailant close to the victim while in the closet. Areas of spattered and projected bloodstains on the south and east walls of the closet are consistent with physical activity involving the victim and assailant while the victim is close to the floor. Evidence of projectiles within the closet would indicate shots fired into that area.

Bloodstains present on the tile floor of the bathroom show transfer and sliding of both shod and bare feet. There is evidence of sliding of a bare foot wet with blood. This is also an area where blood other than that of the victim is identified, indicating a bleeding assailant as well as bleeding victim.

It is concluded that the injured bleeding victim was able to get out of the closet through the bathroom and back into the master bedroom while still alive and able to ambulate. This is based upon the presence of bare footprints in blood leading out of the bathroom. Bloody shoe prints leaving the bathroom in the same direction indicate the departure of the assailant from that area back into the master bedroom. There is no bloodstain evidence to indicate that the victim was dragged back into the master bedroom. Additional physical activity involving bloodshed has occurred in the master bedroom prior to the final resting position of the victim. Contact was made by a bleeding area of the victim on the bedspread with evidence of spatters of blood on that surface as well. Bloodstains beneath the bedspread on the carpet at the foot of the bed indicate that the bedspread had been moved during the struggle. This is also an area where blood other than that of the victim is identified, indicating a bleeding assailant as well as bleeding victim.

The victim sustained significant blood loss on the floor to the west of the bed. It was noted in the autopsy report that the victim had sustained an incision of the left common carotid artery. With sufficient blood pressure, this type of injury produces characteristic arterial spurting patterns on nearby surfaces. These types of patterns are not observed along the retreating route of the victim. An explanation for this is that the incision to the common carotid artery in the neck may have occurred in the final stages of the assault. The accumulation of injuries with external and internal bleeding would likely have lowered blood pressure, lessening the opportunity for large spurting patterns to be produced.

The presence of shards of glass on the bed in the master bedroom on and around the knife case would indicate the case was broken while on the bed. Cutting and stabbing of the victim likely occurred in the closet, bathroom, and master bedroom area of the residence. Outside of these areas, the bloodstain evidence is more consistent with a gunshot wound of the victim occurring in the dining area and his movement retreating from the south end of the kitchen, where his bloodshed was initially observed on the floor.

Bloodstains different than the type of the victim were detected in the master bedroom and bathroom as well as inside the front door. The exit of an assailant from the premises is documented by blood-drip patterns which exhibit a directionality on the sidewalk away from the entrance way of the premises. These bloodstains are likely a continuation of the drip pattern from inside the front door. There is no evidence of a struggle involving forceful bloodshed having occurred in the foyer inside the front door nor at the south end of the kitchen where the victim's blood is initially observed.

Preparation for Trial

Attorneys, whether for the prosecution or defense, may not be as familiar with bloodstain interpretation as with other types of forensic evidence. It is important to establish a rapport with attorneys through pretrial conferences. This will provide opportunity for counsel to become familiar with the expert's qualifications, limitations, and professional demeanor, as well as the field of bloodstain evidence. The expert's testimony should be outlined in detail. It is often helpful for the expert to provide questions in logical order and to suggest the types of demonstrative evidence to be used during trial. The order of presentation of items of physical evidence as well as photographs, slides, video tapes, charts, diagrams, or models should be prepared. The direct examination should include an opportunity for the expert to educate the jury about bloodstain interpretation. The narrative is enhanced with the use of representative photographs, slides, or demonstrations of various types of bloodstain patterns.

Experts should be prepared to defend their conclusions during cross examination by opposing counsel. Possible cross-examination questions should be posed to the witness prior to trial. It is also helpful to provide questions for cross examination of opposing experts. Credible witnesses are dedicated to accurate and detailed work and do not overstate the facts. Experts testifying concerning bloodstain pattern interpretation should be cautious and conservative with their conclusions, especially when there are a limited number of bloodstains for interpretation. Other activities or events that could produce similar bloodstains should be acknowledged during the direct examination.

Bloodstain Interpretation Questions for Trial

Blunt Force Trauma

1. Have you read any texts or scientific publications pertaining to bloodstain interpretation? Name the publications and authors.
2. Describe the training courses that you have completed in bloodstain interpretation, giving dates of courses and names of instructors.

3. Have you ever conducted any experiments to recreate bloodstain patterns to verify those present at crime scenes?
4. Would you describe courses which you have taught in bloodstain interpretation?
5. Have you authored any scientific articles or books on the subject of bloodstain pattern interpretation?
6. Are you a member of the International Association of Bloodstain Pattern Analysts?
7. Would you state the criteria for membership in that organization?
8. Have you ever qualified as an expert in the area of bloodstain pattern interpretation?
9. How many times and in what jurisdictions?
10. Do you testify only for the defense or prosecution?
11. Is bloodstain pattern interpretation considered a science?
12. How many times have you reconstructed a crime scene utilizing bloodstain patterns?
13. How is this type of reconstruction accomplished and what types of equipment and materials are used?
14. Did you examine the scene in this case?
15. Describe the types of activity that may be verified by bloodstain pattern interpretation at a crime scene.
16. Would you agree that crime scene reconstruction using bloodstain pattern recognition and interpretation should be accomplished by individuals well trained and experienced in that field of expertise?
17. Would you differentiate between the point of convergence and the point of origin of bloodstains?
18. How is the point of convergence determined?
19. How is the point of origin determined?
20. How is the angle of impact of a bloodstain measured?
21. What is a formula for determining the angle of impact?
22. Would you distinguish among low, medium, and high-velocity impact blood spatter?
23. What types of events are commonly associated with each?
24. What other mechanisms can produce bloodstains in the size range of medium to high-velocity that are not related to impact?
25. How often have you observed high-velocity impact blood spatter associated with blunt force beating injuries?
26. Is it possible to estimate accurately the number of blows struck to a victim in one location by observation of medium-velocity impact blood spatter?
27. What type of bloodstain patterns are utilized for estimation of the number of blows struck to a victim in a location?

Figure 10.22 Area of carpet prior to spraying with Luminol.

Figure 10.23 Same area of carpet following application of Luminol shows clear evidence of bloodstains. Note partial handprint at left bloodstain.

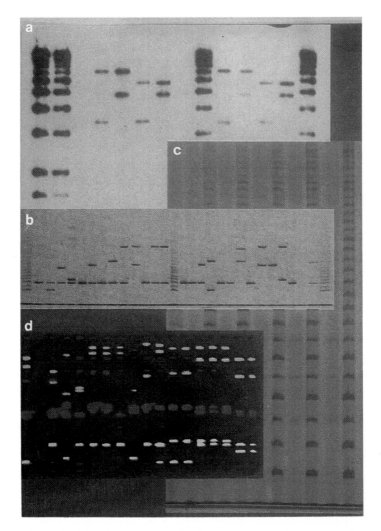

Figure 11.14 The evolution of DNA typing in North America. This montage represents the evolution of DNA typing in North America from the (a) initial single-locus DNA typing profile (D1S7) followed by PCR based methods including (b) AMP-Flaps (D1S80), (c) mini-satellite variant repeats ([MVRs] D1S8) and (d) fluorescent-tagged short-tandem repeats (HumCD4, yellow; HumFABP, blue; HumACTBP2, green; ABI Genescan™ 2500 marker, red). Contributed by the Biology Research and Development Support Unit and Richard Musgrave of the Forensic Photo Unit, Royal Canadian Mounted Police. (Figure courtesy of Eaton Publishing Company.)

28. How are these bloodstain patterns produced and where are they generally located?
29. What is the difference between a cast-off and a wave cast-off bloodstain?
30. Did you examine and photograph the scene for bloodstain evidence before the body was moved?
31. What types of bloodstains did you observe at the scene of the death of this victim?
32. Where was the medium-velocity impact blood spatter located at the scene of this beating death?
33. Was there any evidence of dripping of blood or flow patterns on any surfaces?
34. Did you examine the ceiling, walls, or other objects for evidence of cast-off bloodstains on these surfaces?
35. Did you measure and photograph these bloodstains?
36. Did you reconstruct a point of convergence or point of origin of any of the bloodstain patterns?
37. Were you able to determine where in the residence the altercation may have started?
38. Were you able to determine the relative position of the victim and assailant at the time of initial bloodshed?
39. Did you examine the suspect's person or clothing for bloodstain evidence?
40. How would this examination help to verify conclusions drawn from bloodstains at the scene?
41. Did you examine any weapon associated with the investigation of this death?
42. What kind of bloodstains, if any, did you observe?
43. Were you able to associate any particular type of weapon with the bloodstains you observed at the scene?
44. What type of bloodstains may be present to assist with this determination?
45. What additional information did you utilize to form your conclusions?
46. What other activities may produce similar bloodstains?
47. Which bloodstains, if any, tell you that this defendant struck the victim?
48. How many of the stains utilized in forming your conclusion were tested for human blood?
49. How many of these stains were typed or further classified?
50. If the victim were struck in the position which you describe, what quantity of blood would you expect to find on the clothing of the assailant?

Conclusion

Bloodstain pattern evidence has been generally accepted by the courts as an area of expert testimony. Appellate courts have upheld the validity of such testimony during the appeal process as contained in the following citations.

Supreme Court Decisions Relating to Bloodstain Interpretation

Alabama	Leonard v. State, 551 So. 2nd 1146 1989 Robinson v. State 574 So. 2nd 910 1990
California	State v. Carter 48C, 2nd 737, 312 P. 2nd 665 1957
Florida	Chesire v. State 568 So, 2nd 646 1990
Idaho	State v. Rodgers 812 P. 2nd 1208 1991
Illinois	State v. Erickson No. 79-186, App. 411 NE 2nd 44 1980
Indiana	Hampton v. State 588 N.E. 2nd 1992
Iowa	State v. Hall 2nd 80, No. 62176 1980
Louisiana	State v. Graham, Jr. 422 So. 2nd, 123 1983
Louisiana	State v. Powell 598 So. 2nd 454 1992
Maine	State v. Hilton 431 A, 2nd, 1296 1981
Maine	State v. Philbrick 436 A, 2nd, 844 1981
Michigan	U.S.A. v. Price U.S. Court of Appeals, Sixth Circuit 728 F, 2nd 365
Mississippi	State v. Jordan 464 So. 2nd, 475 1985

Supreme Court Decisions Relating to
Bloodstain Interpretation (continued)

New York	State v. Comfort
	113 AD 2nd. 420
	1985
Oklahoma	State v. Farris
	670 P. 2nd, 995
	1983
Oregon	State v. Bishop
	1978
Rhode Island	State v. Chiellini
	557 A, 2nd 1195
	1989

SUGGESTED READING

1. DeForest, P.R., Gaensslen, R.E., and Lee, H.C. 1983. Forensic Science — An introduction to Criminalistics. New York: McGraw-Hill.

2. Eckert, W.G. and James, S.H. 1989. Interpretation of Bloodstain Evidence at Crime Scenes. New York: Elsevier/CRC Press.

3. Kirk, P.L. 1974. Crime Investigation, 2nd Edition. New York: John Wiley & Sons.

4. MacDonell, H.L. 1971. Interpretation of Bloodstains — Physical Considerations. Legal Medicine Annual, Cyril Wecht, Ed. New York: Appleton-Century-Crofts.

5. MacDonell, H.L. 1981. Criminalistics — Bloodstain Examination. Forensic Sciences, Vol. 3, Cyril Wecht, Ed. New York: Matthew Bender.

6. MacDonell, H.L. 1982. Bloodstain Pattern Interpretation. Corning, NY: Laboratory of Forensic Science.

7. MacDonell, H.L. 1973. Laboratory Manual on the Geometric Interpretation of Human Bloodstain Evidence. Corning, NY: Laboratory of Forensic Science.

8. MacDonell, H.L. 1993. Bloodstain Patterns. Corning, NY: Laboratory of Forensic Science.

9. Redsicker, D. R. 1991. The Practical Methodology of Forensic Photography. New York: Elsevier/CRC Press.

Serology and DNA Typing

11

GEORGE T. DUNCAN
MARTIN L. TRACEY

Introduction

Forensic serology is based on findings from empirical and theoretical studies in many disciplines of biology. Progress has, for the most part, involved applying technologies and concepts from immunology and blood group serology to forensic serology. Recently, however, molecular biology and population genetics have played developmental and supportive roles in new advances utilizing DNA technology.[1,7]

These technologies are used to identify aged, often degraded, and frequently environmentally insulted samples. Often a crime scene is not discovered until many days or months after the crime has occurred. A body buried in a field or a semen sample in the vagina of a victim of a rape homicide are examples of samples environmentally insulted by light, heat, and bacterial degradation.

A True Case Scenario Where Serological Evidence Might Play an Important Role

Let us set up a typical case based on a true incident in which there are several types of evidence. Three armed men break into a home. There are four people, two males and two females at home. All are related to each other. Both females are sexually assaulted and the males are beaten with a pistol. One male who lives in the home forcibly obtains a weapon from an assailant and fires. The robbers flee the scene, and two are later apprehended at another location. The evidence collected from the crime scene consists of: (1) blood stains on the carpet, (2) a leather handbag, (3) several articles of clothing, and (4) cigarette butts and a baseball cap left by an assailant. Both female victims are wearing blue jeans at the time of the attack. Item (5): the women are taken to the sexual assault treatment center and suspect semen samples

0-8493-8101-0/97/$0.00+$.50
© 1997 by CRC Press, Inc.

are collected on swabs from the vaginal vault and perineal area. Item (6): there are also six blood stains on the clothing of the two suspects in custody. Item (7): underwear from both suspects contain what appear to be body fluid stains outside and inside the garment. Item (8): the two suspects are taken to the hospital, where penile swabs are collected and placed into evidence. Item (9): there also are hairs on all of the clothing of both victims and defendants.

There are seven individuals who may have left blood at the scene, three robbers and four victims. Conventional serological testing — that is, tests without DNA analysis — may be able to distinguish between the stains from the seven individuals. If some of them are related, however, conventional serological testing may not distinguish among them. The circumstances of this case are real and point to the power of DNA-based identification technology, which will be discussed later in the chapter. The power of DNA lies in its level of variation among individuals and greater potential to identify them.

There Are Basic Serological Questions a Forensic Serologist Poses When Approaching a Case

What does a forensic serologist do? A serologist asks the following questions when a sample is submitted to a laboratory:

1. What is the biological substance that will be analyzed, i.e., is the stain blood, semen, or another body fluid?
2. Is it of human or animal origin; if it is of animal origin, to what animal or animal group does the sample belong?
3. What physical state is it in: liquid, dry, degraded, putrefied, or fresh?
4. What surface or object was the sample found on and what is the best way to collect and preserve it?
5. Can the stain be linked to an individual source? More specifically, what and how many genetic markers may be used to analyze the stain and give an appropriate answer to the investigator or to a court of law?

Serological Forensic Evidence Comes in Many Forms

Most samples that come into a crime laboratory have dried and degraded, a fact that both aids and hinders the serologist. To be sure, the available genetic markers in liquid blood are quite numerous compared to those in dried blood. The process of drying a sample preserves the genetic markers that allow the forensic serologist to identify, classify, and individualize the stain;

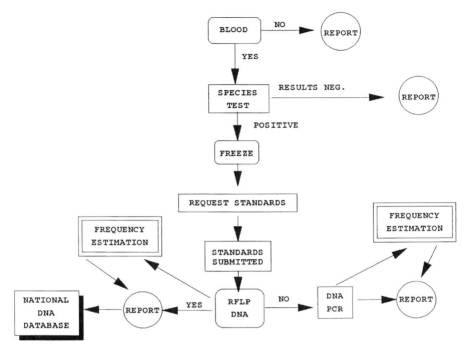

Figure 11.1   Blood analysis flowchart: This represents a typical flowchart of the analysis of bloodstains. Blood is processed by RFLP/VNTR analysis. If the sample is too small or not amenable for RFLP, a DNA/PCR analysis is performed. If RFLP/VNTR analysis gives clear results, the data may be entered into the National DNA Database, maintained by the Federal Bureau of Investigation.

however, when a sample is dried, bacterial contamination decreases since bacteria grow and multiply in a moist warm environment. In addition, chemical degradation is often enhanced in solution.

Since the bulk of evidence is dried material, forensic markers must work on dried samples. In our case scenario, we have a great number of dried stains. The stains on the blue jeans and on the leather handbag present a special problem. Special procedures must be used, as the chemicals in leather and blue jeans may interfere with testing for some genetic markers. The swabs collected at the sexual assault treatment center are immediately placed into a paper envelope so they can air-dry. The only liquid samples collected at the center are vials of blood, preserved to minimize cell membrane breakage and protect the integrity of the DNA molecules. This is usually done by the use of purple or yellow top tubes.

At the scene of a crime, liquid body fluids are sometimes found. Typically they are found where a great amount of blood was shed. Crime scene investigators have the option of soaking up the material on a sterile cotton swatch and allowing it to dry before submission to a laboratory or collecting the material in a tube containing an anticoagulant so the blood cells do not clot,

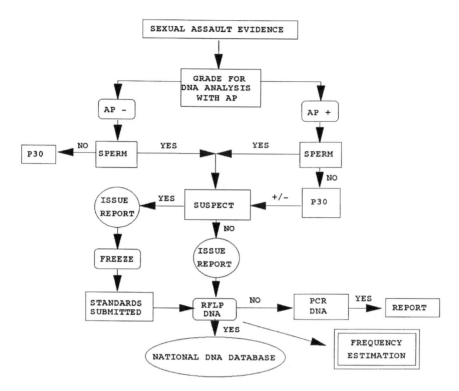

Figure 11.2 Semen analysis flowchart: This is a typical flowchart of the analysis of semen samples from cases involving a sexual assault. Semen is processed by RFLP/VNTR analysis, as in the case of a blood stain. In this example, the amount of semen is graded by use of a presumptive test for the enzyme acid phosphatase, which is found in large quantities in human semen. It could also be graded by the amount of sperm cells detected. If the sample is too small or not amenable to RFLP, a DNA/PCR analysis is performed. If RFLP/VNTR analysis gives clear results, the DNA profile from the suspect and or evidence may be entered into the DNA national database maintained by the Federal Bureau of Investigation.

as mentioned above. The latter method requires that the person processing the scene store the vial in a refrigerated environment until it reaches the laboratory. Collection on a swatch of material is easier and probably used more often by police. Even cellular material from a hit-and-run case can be dried for submission to a laboratory for serological analysis. If it is not dried, the tissue must be frozen in a freezer that does not go through a defrost cycle. The colder the environment the better, with an optimum temperature of –70°C or less.

Biological Analysis Can Be Applied to Many Cell Types in Body Fluids

Blood consists of cellular components plus a liquid phase. The cellular components are red cells (erythrocytes), white cells (leukocytes), and platelets (thrombocytes). Red cells are surrounded by a membrane that contains blood group antigens which can participate in specific antibody-antigen binding reactions.[2] Antigens such as ABO, Mn, Kell, Duffy, and Kidd are found on the red cell membrane and can be used to establish an extensive "blood type" profile.[3] The cytoplasm contains hemoglobin, and protein isoenzymes such as PGM (phosphoglucomutase), Ak (adenylate kinase), and EAP (erythrocyte acid phosphatase).[4] Isoenzymes are defined as multiple forms of a single enzyme. The mature red cells lose their nucleus; almost all circulating red cells have no nucleus and, therefore, have no DNA. On the other hand, white blood cells retain their nucleus throughout their lifetime. There are from 200,000 to over 350,000 red blood cells in a drop of blood, and roughly 4000 white cells are found per microliter (one millionth of a liter) of blood.[5] The white cells are the primary source of DNA in liquid and dried blood. In our case scenario, blood samples are taken from the victims and suspects. These blood samples will be analyzed and the results compared to analyses performed on the evidence.

Blood is not the only biological fluid or tissue shed or left at a crime scene. Body fluids represent a significant contribution to crime scene material. For instance seminal fluid is often part of the evidence in sexual assaults. Skin and other tissue are left many times at hit-and-run scenes. Epithelial cells are deposited on licked stamps, cigarette butts, envelopes, and chewing gum. Fetal material such as cord, cord blood, and fetal tissue originates from an aborted fetus. In our case scenario, not only are blood stains collected, but also seminal fluid from the victims' clothing and vaginal vault. Vaginal fluid conceivably remaining on the penises of the suspects and skin cells on the inside of the hat left by one of the suspects at the scene are collected as well.

Cigarette butts, envelopes, chewing gum, and many other objects which may contain saliva are amenable to PCR (polymerase chain reaction)/DNA analysis and ABO typing.[6] ABO typing can be performed on saliva samples in persons who secrete ABO antigens into their body fluids. These people are called secretors,[5] and comprise 80% of the population. The remaining 20% are nonsecretors who secrete very small amounts of antigen into their body fluids. One has to work with relatively large amounts of saliva to obtain an ABO type. Saliva contains cellular material and thus can be typed by DNA analysis. The caveat is that the amount of saliva present on the item may be extremely low. Envelopes, stamps, and chewing gum present the serologist with small amounts of cellular material. The PCR process then becomes the method of choice to determine a genetic type, because only very few cells are required for analysis. Swabs of the oral cavity, especially swabbing of the cheek area inside the mouth, give more than enough cells and DNA for the serologist to perform DNA typing. This can be an alternative to gathering controls by venipuncture.

Hair evidence is one of the most prevalent kinds of evidence. Hairs may be shed by forceful removal or during the normal course of a day, during which each of us sheds roughly one hundred hairs. There has been much controversy as to the value of hair in forensic analysis. Many laboratories have separate sections devoted to the analysis of hair, while others have no facilities for microscopic examination and comparison of hairs. Microscopic comparison has been the test of choice and its value is based on the examiner's estimation of the rarity of comparisons which match.[5] In any case, statistical values cannot be placed on the probability of finding hairs that match.

Sometimes, forcefully removed hairs with tissue tags or roots are found at a scene. The tissue tag is a portion of the hair follicle from which the hair grows. The tag is most times visible to the naked eye or else under a microscope. If the tag is present, the serologist may add several more tests to the microscopic hair examination protocol. Phosphoglucomutase (PGM), adenylate kinase (Ak), glyoxalase (GLO), and several other isoenzymes are detectable in hair samples with tissue tags.[5] In our mock case, hairs were found on most items of the evidence. First, a microscopic comparison of the hairs in our case evidence would be made against standard hairs to ascertain their probable origin. Remember, however, that human hairs cannot be positively associated with any one individual by microscopy. Twenty five to thirty representative standards from at least four areas of the head would be collected from all individuals involved in the case, since most head hair is variable and of different colors. Pubic hair can be used for classification, but body hairs such as those from the arm and leg are not suitable for microscopic examination. Depending on the individual, characteristics exhibited by each hair can be associated with specific individuals in the case. Once that is done, the hair can be processed for genetic markers. RFLP/DNA, the common type of DNA analysis, can be performed if there is sufficient tissue tag present.[7] A hair with a tissue tag may contain as much as 100 to 500 ng of DNA. RFLP/DNA analysis is possible with less than 100 ng of DNA.[7,26] Recently however, several PCR techniques have been used with excellent success with hair roots and small tissue tags.[8] The PCR process is a very powerful technique which allows the analyst to copy or amplify the amount of DNA present in a small or degraded sample. Mitochondrial DNA (mtDNA) is located to some extent in the hair shaft itself. Using this mtDNA to categorize hair has the potential to bring the analysis almost to the point of complete individualization. The PCR process and mtDNA will be described later.

Until quite recently, bone and teeth were traceable to an individual only through the efforts of a forensic anthropologist. On occasion, if the bone was properly preserved, ABO antigen typing was possible. With the use of PCR and mitochondrial DNA analysis, dental pulp and bone marrow can now yield substantial genetic information to the investigator. Bone and dental material can be identified many years after soft body tissue has degraded. The Armed Forces Institute of Pathology (AFIP) has used mtDNA from teeth and bones in the identification of armed forces personnel found in southeast Asia from the Vietnam war 25 years ago.[9] Similar identification and exclusion analyses have been done on remains of Czar Nicholas Romanov and his family who were executed by the Bolsheviks in 1918.[10]

Fecal matter has traditionally been viewed like bone and teeth, as something with little evidential value. This, however, is changing as biological methods are becoming more sensitive. Several investigators have reported recently that DNA analysis can be accomplished on fecal and vomit samples. Although feces and vomit may be unpleasant, cells and cellular debris are located in large quantity in these types of samples.

Fingernails have begun to be investigated as a tissue source for DNA typing. Early results show that use of PCR/DNA analysis is easily accomplished in tissue attached to fingernail scraping and broken fingernails from a crime scene. Fingernails are a tissue just like hair; in fact, they have many of the same substances and share a great many properties.

Perspiration does not have a large cellular component. Its value in forensic typing remains elusive.

A Serologist Uses Many Methods to Detect Biological Fluids

Generally, there are three methods of detecting items of serological evidence: visual, microscopic, and chemical. Body fluid stains are either visible to the eye or invisible because of the quantity of stain or because they are hidden in another body fluid or on material which precludes visual detection. For example, a semen or saliva stain may be masked by a large quantity of blood on a garment. Some stains, such as semen, have a characteristic texture or color which ranges from milky white to light tan when blood cells are present.

Many methods can be used to visualize a stain, such as a special strong light source, an ultraviolet lamp or laser light sources. Semen stains particularly lend themselves to detection by the above methods. Blood stains are found the old-fashioned way, visually and microscopically by searching areas where they are likely to be found, such as inside the pocket of a pair of pants where a defendant may have put his hands after commission of a crime. The colors of blood stains can range from bright red to dark green. Many other stains such as saliva and perspiration do not have a characteristic color and are usually invisible to the eye. Detection is a two-step process involving a presumptive and a confirmatory step. Presumptive tests are used to screen samples, while confirmatory tests confirm the identity of a stain. Several types of tests that are used to detect blood are listed in Table 11.1.

Semen stains are examined by several different methods. The primary technique is by observation of sperm cells in a specimen. This microscopic

Table 11.1   Some of the Commonly Used Presumptive and Confirmatory Tests Used in a Forensic Laboratory

Test or Chemical Name	Basis of Test	Indication of Result	Sensitivity	Note
Benzidine	Peroxidase activity (catalytic)	Blue, purple color	1 part in 10,000–200,000	C, P
Leucomalachite green	Peroxidase activity (catalytic)	Green color	1 part in 1000	Azodye, P
Phenolphthalein	Peroxidase activity (catalytic)	Red color	1 part in 1000	Safe and widely used, P
Takayama test	Heme-porphyrinpyridine crystal formation	Distinctive crystals	1 part in less than 1000	CN
Tetra-methyl benzidine	Peroxidase activity (catalytic)	Blue, purple color	Same as Benzidine	SC, P
Luminol	Modified catalytic	Blue, luminesces in dark	1 part in 5,000,000	Irritant, P
Spectrophotometric	Visible spectrum	Distinctive spectrum	Same as Takayama test	CN

Note: C = carcinogen, P = presumptive test, CN = confirmatory test, SC = suspect carcinogen.

Source: Sourcebook in Forensic Serology, Immunology, and Biochemistry, R.E. Gaensslen, U.S. Department of Justice, National Institute of Justice, Washington, D.C., 1983.

test is conclusive. If spermatozoa are not detected, several other methods are used to distinguish semen from other substances. These tests involve identification of substances specific to semen and are used to confirm the presence of seminal fluid. The substance detected as a confirmatory test and used in most laboratories in the U.S. is the protein P-30, or prostatic specific antigen. It is detected by several different methods including electrophoresis, ELISA, and gel diffusion.[11,12] P-30 is found only in the male prostate gland and is used as a clinical test to identify carcinoma of the prostate gland.

General Classes of Forensic Genetic Markers, or the Serological Arsenal

There are eight categories of genetic markers which a forensic serologist uses routinely: conventional markers — cellular antigens, serum proteins, cellular antigens; and DNA-based markers — RFLPs (restriction fragment length polymorphism), STRs (short tandem repeats), AmpFlps (amplified fragment length polymorphism), ASO (allele specific oligo), and mtDNA (mitochondrial DNA) analysis.[5,7,13] See Figure 11.4 and Table 11.2 for examples of each group. It is from this arsenal that genetic markers are chosen to answer the

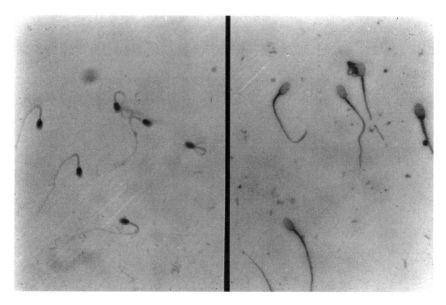

Figure 11.3 Sperm cells stained with christmas tree stain: Sperm cells carry DNA in the nucleus of the cell. Seminal fluid as well as sperm cells carry many other genetic markers. Sperm cells generally are the primary evidence for a serologist to analyze in a sexual assault case. Seminal fluid is amenable to some blood group antigen testing and the examination of a limited number of isoenzymes. Sperm cells are also used in RFLP/DNA testing to characterize stains. Because the PCR/DNA process involves the amplification of parts of the DNA molecule, very few sperm are needed for this process.

questions asked by investigators, attorneys, judges, and eventually the most important individual of them all, the juror.

Group Specific Antigens Form the Basis of Analysis in Conventional (non-DNA) Serological Analysis

Blood group antigens are large molecules that are located both on and off of the surface of a cell. An example is the ABO blood system. Blood group "A" and "B" are antigens and thus contribute to the blood type of an individual. For an in-depth treatment of this system, see reference texts. Classically, this blood group system formed the bulk of serological evidence until the use of other polymorphic blood group systems. "Polymorphic" refers to the existence of two or more genetically different forms of the same protein or DNA type. An example is Rh-positive and Rh-negative blood types. These blood group substances are moderately persistent in dried biological stains and can last for several years in the dried state. Their persistence is, however, not comparable with DNA; DNA lasts in the dried state for much longer periods of time.

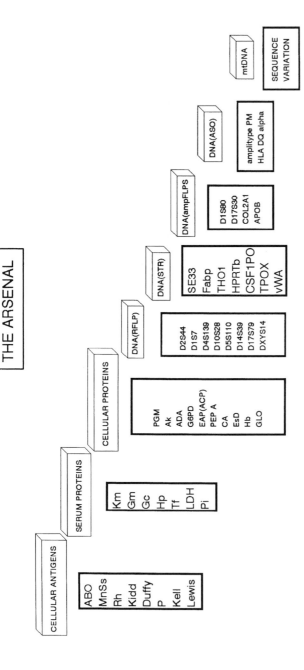

Figure 11.4 There are eight categories of tests in the forensic serologist's arsenal. The forensic serologist's arsenal includes tests based on antigenic and enzyme assays, as well as DNA tests. Antigenic assays couple antibodies which recognize specific forms of the antigen; the familiar ABO blood groups are antigen/antibody assays. Other antigenic tests are listed in the CELLULAR ANTIGENS category. Another set of tests focuses on proteins found in serum or in cells. Some of these use antibodies to recognize specific forms of the protein, while other assays depend on enzymatic activity to visualize the different forms. These are categorized as serum or cellular tests rather than as antigen or enzymatic tests, because both types of assays are used in detecting serum and cellular protein differences. Three of the classes of DNA tests identify length variation at specific human genes. RFLP (restriction fragment length polymorphisms) or, more specifically, VNTR (variable number tandem repeat polymorphisms) are the original DNA tests. STR (simple tandem repeat polymorphisms) and AmpFLPs (amplified fragment length polymorphisms) are tests which can be run with very small samples, because they depend on amplification of DNA. The DNA in ASO (allele specific oligonucleotide) tests is also amplified, but the specificity of these assays is not dependent on length variation; it is dependent on nucleotide sequence differences or short deletions or insertions. Finally, forensic tests may be based on actual sequence data. Mitochondrial DNA (mtDNA) is often used for sequencing, because it is a relatively small and abundant molecule with variable regions.

Table 11.2 Various Methods and Markers Used in DNA Testing Including Analysis Features of Each

Test	Marker	Test Time	Discrimination Power	Cost	Type Of Sample	Sample Size
Immunological	ABO	1–2 Days	Low	Low	BL, S, T, BN[d]	10μL
Electrophoresis	Isoenzyme	1–2 Days	Low	Low	B, S, T, H$_R$	10μL
PCR Dot-Blot[b]	HLA-DQ-ALPHA[a]	1–2 Days	Low–Moderate	Moderate	B, S, T, H$_R$, BN, TH	<5 ng DNA
PCR Dot-Blot[b]	Polymarker[c]	1–2 Days	Low–Moderate	Moderate	B, S, T, H$_R$ BN, TH	<5 ng DNA
PCR	AMPFLP[a]	1–2 Days	Low–Moderate[a]	Low–Moderate	B, S, T, H$_R$, BN, TH	<5 ng DNA
PCR	STR[a]	1–2 Days	Low–Moderate[a]	Low–Moderate	B, S, T, H$_R$, BN, TH	<5 ng DNA
RFLP	VNTR[a]	4–6 Weeks	High	Moderate–High	B, S, T, H$_R$, BN, TH	>50 ng DNA
PCR	MVR	1–2 Days	High	Moderate–High	B, T, H$_R$	>50 ng DNA
Sequencing	mtDNA	1–2 Days	Moderate–High	HIGH	B, S, T, H$_R$, H$_S$, BN, TH	<5 ng DNA

Note: BL = Blood, S = Semen, T = Tissue, BN = Bone, TH = Dental pulp, H$_R$ = Hair root, H$_S$ = Hair shaft.

[a] Several systems usually run in tandem. The 4–6 week timespan is reduced if chemiluminescent probes are used.

[b] ASO (allele specific oligonucleotide), SSO (sequence specific probe).

[c] Assays six systems simultaneously.

[d] Difficult analysis.

Cellular Proteins Then Became the Mainstay of Serological Analysis in the Early 1970's Thanks to Scotland Yard

Cellular proteins are generally referred to as isozymes (also allozymes), as they represent multiple forms of a single protein enzyme. Since there are different forms of one enzyme, these forms can be analyzed by electrophoresis to give a better discrimination value between pieces of cellular evidence. The metropolitan laboratory of Scotland Yard pioneered the use of the many polymorphic proteins for use on dried biological stains in forensic science. Until 1989 these formed the standard protocol in forensic laboratories in the U.S. and all over the world.[4] Cellular proteins, however, are not persistent in dried stains for very long. They are very sensitive to heat, light, and many other environmental factors that play an important role in the degradation of samples in forensic science.

Serum Proteins (Allotyping) Formed a Bridge between Group Specific Antigens and Cellular Proteins to the DNA Technological Advances We Are Experiencing Today

Dr. Moses Shanfeld brought large-scale recognition of the forensic application of serum proteins to the U.S. in the early 1980s. These are characterized by highly polymorphic proteins, which are detected by immunological methods. Their variation and genetics are very complex, but basically their variability is based on amino acid substitutions, which in turn affect the antigenic activity of each type. These types are very persistent in dried cellular materials and remain viable for longer periods of time than cellular proteins.

DNA Technology Represents a Quantum Leap in Discriminatory Power in Forensic Serology

In 1985, Dr. Alec Jeffreys, from the University of Leicester in England, started what can only be described as a revolution in forensic serology. From his early publications sprang what is today the possibility of the individualization of body fluid evidence. In our case scenario, all of the evidence collected at the scene is amenable to DNA typing. See Table 11.3 for a list of applicable DNA methods that could be used in evaluation of crime scene evidence.

Table 11.3   DNA Technology as Applied to the Case Scenario

Evidence	Test 7, 8	State	Compare	Note
Blood from (S) and (V)	DNA(RFLP), PCR(DNA)	Liquid blood or cheek swab	(S), (V) with crime scene samples	a,g,h
Carpet bloodstain	DNA(RFLP)	Dried	Crime scene samples with (S), (V)	b
Leather hand bag with blood	DNA(RFLP)	Dried	Crime scene samples with (S), (V)	
Clothing, (V)	DNA(RFLP)	Dried	Crime scene samples with (S), (V)	c
Cigarette butts from scene	PCR(DNA)	Dried	With (S)	d
Baseball cap from scene	PCR(DNA)	Dried	With (S)	d
Bloodstain on (S) clothing	PCR(DNA), DNA(RFLP)	Dried	With (V)	c
Underwear, (S)	PCR(DNA), DNA(RFLP)	Dried	With (V)	c
Vaginal swabs, (V)	PCR(DNA), DNA(RFLP)	Dried	With (S)	c
Penile swabs, (S)	PCR(DNA), DNA(RFLP)	Dried	With (V)	e
Hair samples, (V) and (S)	DNA(RFLP)	Dried	Crime scene samples with (S)	f

Note: With = compare to, (V) = victim, (S) = suspect.

a   These would be used as standards to compare suspects and victims to crime scene samples. Since four of the individuals are related, a system with high discrimination power is the optimum selection.
b   Used to compare against standards of all seven people.
c   The method of choice here would be dependent on the amount of sample found. In small samples, only PCR(DNA) analysis might be applicable.
d   Usually cigarette butts, stamps, envelopes, and hat bands can only be analyzed by PCR(DNA) analysis.
e   Here we are checking for DNA from contributions from vaginal epithelial cells. DNA(RFLP) can be used in this case but still is dependent on sample size.
f   If hairs are shed and not pulled from the head, there may be little chance for analysis. In the future, mtDNA analysis may be applicable here, because hair is principally dead cells which would contain mitochondria.
g   DNA(RFLP) analysis refers to single-locus DNA VNTR probes.
h   PCR(DNA) analysis refers to dot-blot or gel-based technology.

An Overview of DNA "Fingerprint" Profiling

DNA fingerprint comparisons are based on examination of three to ten highly variable portions of our DNA. Each of us has 6 billion (3 billion pairs) DNA subunits or nucleotides that comprise our DNA code.[13,14] Most of these are identical in all humans, but some regions of the genome, the totality of a cell's DNA, are highly variable in terms of length or sequence.[15,16] These are the parts of the genome used in DNA fingerprinting; we use them because they are variable and we know the frequencies of the variants.[1,17] In order to compare DNA patterns or fingerprints, the variable characteristic of the known and unknown DNA samples must be made visible.

This involves a number of steps (Figure 11.5):

1. DNA extraction
2. Quantity and quality determination; at this stage, a decision is made to proceed with RFLP/DNA analysis or to amplify small quantities of DNA by PCR
3. Restriction enzyme digestion
4. Electrophoretic separation of DNA fragments on an analytical agarose gel
5. Transfer of the separated DNA fragments onto a nylon membrane from the gel, also known as blotting
6. Probing DNA fragments on the nylon membrane with a known, complementary piece of DNA probe
7. Visualization of the different sized fragments by autoradiography
8. Examination of the autoradiogram for exclusions or inclusions
9. Sizing of the DNA fragments declared to match and determination of sized match or nonmatch[18]
10. Calculation of the odds that a match of the type determined would occur between the sample and an unrelated person; these calculations represent the estimation of random error

The Autoradiogram or Autorad Is the Hard Copy of the Forensic DNA Specialist's Analysis of a Series of DNA Samples

Figure 11.6 is an autoradiogram or autorad; it is a photographic image of the pattern of DNA fragments, arranged in vertical columns, produced by known and unknown samples. Larger DNA fragments are at the top of the autorad, because, by convention, the origin or well into which DNA samples were placed for separation by electrophoresis is placed at the top. Since the agarose gel containing the DNA fragments has a sieving effect, the larger pieces do not move as far as the smaller pieces; they stay close to the origin and are at the top of the autorad. Note that only the gel has wells in it; thus, only the gel has real origins. The origins on the nylon membrane and autorad are terminological; they indicate the position of the gel origins. This is legitimate, because the DNA is transferred onto the nylon membrane, and its image is transferred onto the X-ray film.

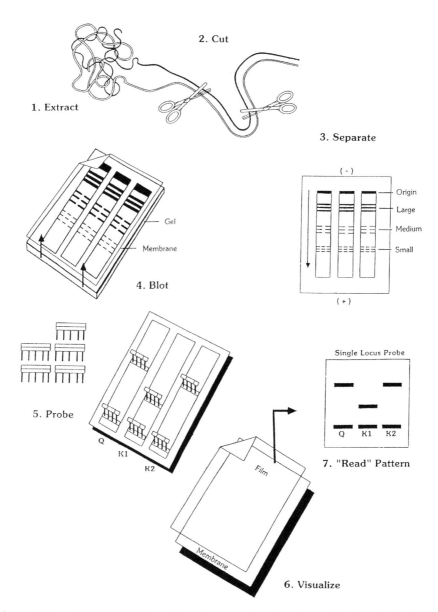

Figure 11.5 A DNA/RFLP (restriction fragment length polymorphism) analysis of variable number of tandem repeats (VNTRs): DNA pattern analysis is a lengthy process which begins by separating cellular DNA from the rest of the cellular material. This is the extraction stage (1). Next, the purified DNA is cut into pieces using a restriction enzyme (2), and the pieces of DNA are separated according to size (3). The size-separated pieces are embedded in a gel, which is not easy to handle and through which DNA does not pass readily. These problems are solved by blotting (4) the DNA out of the gel and onto a nylon membrane. In the probing (5) step, short single-stranded DNAs (the probe) bind to their specific complements or partner strands. The probes bound to their complements have been labeled and may, therefore, be visualized by placing photographic films against the nylon membrane (6). Finally the picture is interpreted (7). (Figures courtesy of FBI Laboratory.)

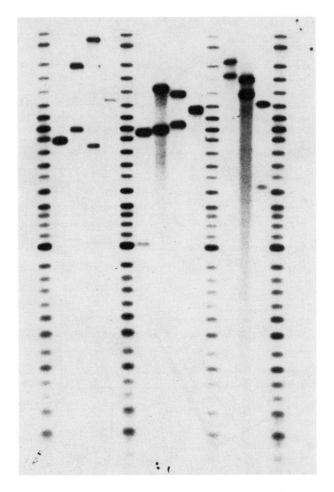

Figure 11.6 An autorad from database sampling has been developed following PH30 (DYS139) probing with ^{32}P (radioactive phosphorous)-label. Molecular size markers or ladders are in lanes 1, 5, 10, and 15. Most people are two-banded phenotypes, but the individuals in lanes 6 and 11 are single-banded phenotypes. Note that none of these samples match.

Figure 11.7 is a pictorial representation of an autoradiogram. There are 14 columns of DNA fragments on this autorad; they are called lanes. Lanes 1, 6, 10, and 14 are easily identified; they have approximately 30 bands or DNA fragments. All the other lanes have one or two fragments or bands. Lanes 1, 6, 10, and 14 are size marker lanes, or ladders. The DNA fragments in these lanes come from known sources such as bacteria, viruses, or chemically synthesized DNA. The important point is that all of these fragments are of precisely known length; thus, they may be used to estimate the sizes of other fragments, just as we use a ruler to measure unknown lengths or a balance to weigh unknown samples.

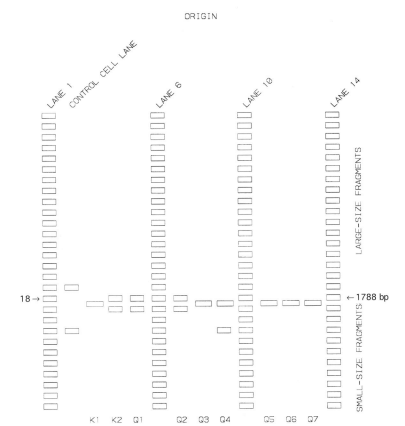

Figure 11.7 Interpretation of an autoradiogram or autorad. Autorads are X-ray films exposed to the nylon membrane onto which the patterns of DNA fragments have been transferred; these sets of bands have been specifically highlighted with labeled probes. When these labeled probes bind to their target sequences which have been fixed to the membrane they are capable of producing an image on a film because they emit beta particles (^{32}P-labeled) or light (chemically labeled). It is this photographic image of the DNA fragments that we are examining. The end of the agarose gel into which the individual DNA samples were placed is called the origin. In order to maintain orientation, we refer to the end of the autoradiogram which corresponds to the origin on the gel as the origin. It is in the figure and is at the top of the page. The origin is, by convention, placed at the top of the autoradiogram. The autoradiogram consists of a series of vertical columns of DNA; these are called lanes and there are fourteen in this figure. Four of the lanes contain ladders or DNA fragments of known size which are used in estimating the sizes of known and questioned or unknown DNA patterns (lanes 1, 6, 10, and 14). Lane 2 is the control or K562 lane. The digested DNA in this lane comes from a commercially available human cell line. Since the DNA fragments for each probe are known for this cell line, it serves as a check on both the process and the sizing of fragments. The evidentiary lanes are divided into K and Q groups. The K lanes are usually DNA from fresh blood samples taken from victims and suspects. These are compared to the Q samples which are from crime scenes and are usually blood or semen stains or tissue samples. Visual matches are seen in this autoradiogram between the Q7, Q6, Q5, and Q3 samples and the K1 sample. This match is the first step in associating victims or suspects with crime scene evidence. A match at this stage at a single probe is certainly not proof that the person who provided the K sample also left the Q samples.

The other 10 lanes on the autorad contain a control, two known samples, and seven unknown samples. Lane 2 is the control lane; DNA from a commercially available cell line K562 was digested and then electrophoresed in this lane. Since the pattern of bands produced for each probe and the band sizes is well known, this lane serves as a control on the processing of samples, the separation of samples and the transfer and imaging of bands.

The two samples marked K1 and K2 are the DNA taken from victim and suspect, usually as fresh blood samples. These are marked K because the source of DNA is known. The Q, or questioned or unknown, DNA samples are usually crime scene evidence and their DNA fragment patterns are compared to those of the K samples to see if they match. A match indicates that the K sample cannot be excluded as the source of the DNA in the Q lane, but it does not prove that the individual from whom the matching K sample was taken was *the* one who left the Q sample at the crime scene. Indeed, further analysis must be done before a visual comparison is declared to be a match.

Visual matches are checked by computer analysis of the fragment sizes. This is done by placing the X-ray film on a light box and taking a computer image of the bands on the autorad. Band-by-band and lane-by-lane, the K562, K, and Q bands are sized by the computer. For example, let's look at K2. The computer image contains two bands which are close together and more or less in between bands 18 and 19 in the ladder lanes. The computer knows that band 18 is a DNA which is 1788 bp long, and that band 19 is 1637 bp long. Since the two bands in lane K2 fall between ladder bands 18 and 19, they must be in the range of 1788 to 1637 bp. The computer finds the center of one of the K2 bands and the centers of ladder bands in lanes 1 and 6, the closest ladder lanes. Using equations which relate the distance of the ladder bands from the origin and their sizes in number of base pairs, the sizes of all K and Q lane bands are estimated by interpolation.

The sizes of the two K562 bands are checked against their known sizes to ensure that the production of this autoradiogram includes no artifacts. If the controls fit, then the sizes of the K lane bands are compared to the Q lane bands to which they previously have been matched visually.

A size match confirmation of the visual match requires that the computer estimate of the Q band size, plus or minus the lab's sizing window, include the computer estimate of the corresponding K band.

Let's look at the comparison between the Q3 and K1 bands. They match on visual inspection, but they are close together. The Q3 band was sized by the computer at 1750 base pairs; the corresponding K1 band was sized at 1755 base pairs. Numerically speaking, they do not match, but common sense tells us that we must account for the variability in the system. To do this, each lab runs and sizes the same DNAs repeatedly. Then they calculate averages for estimated sizes of bands known to be identical. The spread of sizes around this average which includes 95% of the estimated sizes is the match window used in declaring a size match. In other words, each lab knows that the DNA pattern technology in their hands has a particular rate of variation in estimating sizes of knowns. They use this rate to declare matches between unknowns and knowns by producing a window around the estimated size of the Q band.

In our example the Q3 band was sized at 1750. Assume that the lab rate of sizing error is 2½% — that is, for known bands the average size ± 2½% constituted 99% of the labs measurements. Placing a 2.5% window around the 1750 size estimate, we get a range from 1711 (1750 − [.025 × 1750]) to 1799 (1750 + [.025 × 1750]). Any band falling in this 1711 to 1799 range falls into the range where the lab knows that an identical band would fall. The K1 band is 1755; it clearly falls into the match window and the visual match is confirmed.

If the K1 band had fallen outside of the 1711 to 1799 window, the visual match would not have been confirmed. If labs are using a 99% match criterion, they expect that 1% of all real matches will be declared nonconfirmations. Clearly, the decision to conclude that a DNA sample did not originate from a known individual must be based on a number of nonconfirmations. Usually these are visually detectable, and a nonmatch is declared before sizing.

The risk of erroneously declaring a nonmatch is greatly reduced by doing multiple tests. Considering only the 1% sampling error, false exclusion possibility, the overall risk of false exclusion for a four-probe analysis is $(0.01)^4$ or 1 in 100 million.

DNA Can be Isolated from the Nucleus of Any Cell in the Human Body

Since the DNA molecule is housed within the nucleus of all types of cells in the human body, except mature red blood cells, scientists can rely on different tissue sources for collection. Nucleic acid can be extracted from bone, hair, or dried skin; these are the sources for most DNA isolation from older material such as mummies. If we are dealing with a maternity or paternity case in which the putative parent is alive, blood will be the tissue chosen for DNA isolation because it is relatively noninvasive and allows almost painless access. Buccal (mouth) swabbing of epithelial cells contained in the cheek area is another tissue of choice.

DNA is a very long polymer (see Figure 11.8 and Table 11.4). Human cells contain 46 nuclear DNA molecules; each is composed of millions of

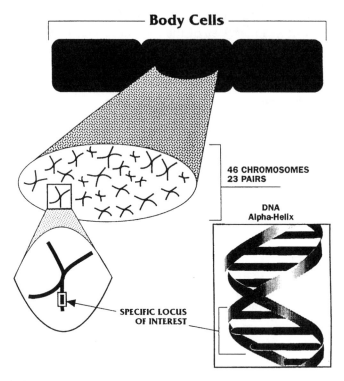

Figure 11.8(A) DNA (deoxyribonucleic acid) is the basic molecule of heredity. DNA patterns are often identified as the "real thing"; that is, people look at the picture containing DNA patterns and think that this band or fragment is the real size of the DNA. This confusion is based on a lack of size references for cells and molecules. The average red blood cell is 2.8 μm in diameter. Assuming that the average head of a pin is 1/16 of an inch or 2 mm in diameter, we will be able to put 40,000 average red cells on this pin head. At the molecular level, we will be able to line up approximately 2 million DNA molecules side-by-side across the top of this pin. The major point is that DNA and other forensic tests do not visualize molecules directly. (Figure courtesy of FBI Laboratory.)

nucleotide pairs. These long DNA chains are susceptible to degradation. Breakdown of DNA into 50,000-bp fragments during regular isolation procedures is almost inevitable. Yet, excessive breakdown of DNA during isolation can produce very small DNA pieces with limited use in DNA fingerprinting. This can be avoided if the protocols are performed gently, carefully preventing contamination by agents that destroy DNA. Several factors are known to contribute to DNA breakdown. Ideally, tissue samples that are dried as soon as possible are most suitable for DNA profiling. The reason is simple: many of the degradative processes require the DNA to be hydrated (surrounded by water); if the DNA is not in solution, it will retain its integrity longer. When samples arrive in the lab, it must be decided whether the DNA isolation will begin immediately. If circumstances do not permit DNA purification, dried samples are stored frozen in a dry environment while wet samples should be just frozen.

46 CHROMOSOMES FOR NORMAL HUMAN BEINGS

23 PAIRS (22 PAIRS OF CHROMOSOMES + 1 PAIR SEX CHROMOSOMES)

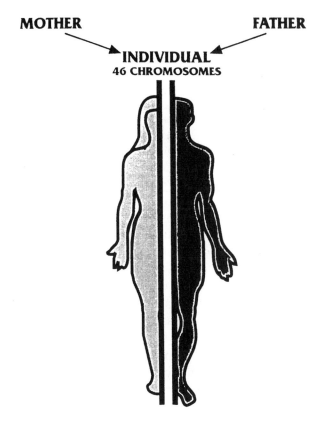

Figure 11.8(B) Normal humans have 46 chromosomes. Each of us is made up of 46 chromosomes, 23 from our father and 23 from our mother. Males have 45 chromosomes plus one Y chromosome. Females have 45 chromosomes plus an additional X chromosome. (Figure courtesy of FBI Laboratory.)

DNA Is Extracted from Cellular Material in a Simple, Straightforward Procedure

There is no single best technique of DNA isolation, and often the method of choice is dictated by the tissue type to be analyzed. For example, blood may be mixed with a solution containing salt, detergent, and an enzyme that breaks down protein. Enzymes that digest proteins are referred to as proteinases. Although there are many proteinases, one that is routinely used is proteinase K because of its efficiency. By digesting proteins into smaller subunits, DNA is released from its cellular compartments. Protein digestion destroys the plasma membrane (the outermost boundary of the cell) as well

Table 11.4   Some Pertinent Human Genome Statistics

Number of chromosomes	22 pairs of autosomes; 1 pair of sex chromosomes, X and Y
Number of base units (nucleotide)	4 (A = Adenine, G = Guanine, C = Cytosine, T = Thymine)
Size of genome in base pairs	3×10^9 (3 billion) bp (base pairs)
Number of genes	50,000 to 100,000
Average size of gene	1000 bp
Size of repetitive sequences	100 to 25,000 bp
Number of cells in human body	1×10^{14} (100 trillion)
Number of mitochondria per cell	70 to 10,000
Number of mitochondrial DNA (mtDNA) per mitochondrion	0 to 10
Base pairs per mitochondrial DNA	16,569

as the nuclear membranae which surrounds the DNA. This, in effect, allows the DNA to go freely into the reaction solution. Salt (NaCl) is added to stabilize the DNA, while the detergent helps in the purification by breaking up lipids or fats. This mixture is then incubated at high temperatures (50 to 60°C) while being shaken to facilitate the DNA purification. Following tissue destruction, the DNA in solution must be separated from other cellular components. Organic solvents such as phenol and chloroform are used for this purpose. Usually phenol is added to the proteinase K reaction mixture in equal volume, and the preparation is gently mixed. Since the proteinase reaction mixture is an aqueous solution, when organic solvents such as phenol and chloroform are added, the less dense aqueous phase separates above the organic solvent, the same way that aqueous vinegar separates from denser oil in salad dressing. This step provides for the segregation of most of the nucleic acid in the form of DNA and RNA in the upper aqueous phase. The rest of the cellular, macromolecular components and protein debris are retained in the lower organic phenol layer.

After a series of phenol/aqueous extractions, the DNA is ready for separation from many of the cellular and noncellular components in the aqueous phase. This is routinely accomplished by alcohol precipitation of the DNA. Before the alcohol is added, salt must be added to increase the aqueous solubility of the nucleic acid component. Following the mixing of the salt with the nucleic acid solution, cold ethanol is added. The precipitated DNA is concentrated by centrifuging and the supernatant is poured off. The nucleic acid precipitated at the bottom of the centrifuge tube is then solubilized by adding water or an aqueous buffer and dissolving it with gentle mixing and heat. The resulting solution is highly enriched in nucleic acids, both DNA and RNA. At this point, the DNA solution is ready for the next step in the analysis process — cutting the DNA into discrete pieces. If it is logistically not desirable to continue with the protocol, then samples can be stored frozen until needed.

Restriction Enzymes Act as Molecular Scissors to Cut Up or Digest DNA Molecules

One of the most important developments in the field of molecular biology was the discovery of restriction enzymes. These are endonucleases which work by identifying and cutting the DNA at short, specific, internal nucleotide sequences such as GGCC, four to six nucleotides in length. Since any given sequence of four nucleotides is found by chance more often than sequences made up of six (4^4 vs. 4^6), the number of enzymatic cuts will be greater when a restriction enzyme that recognizes four rather than six nucleotide pairs is used. DNA that is cut by restriction enzymes that identify shorter sequences will yield more and smaller DNA fragments as compared to enzymes that recognize longer sequences, which produce fewer larger pieces of DNA. For the forensic scientist, restriction enzymes provide a way to cut the long DNA molecules isolated. By cutting long DNA molecules into smaller discrete fragments, they can be characterized according to size. Given the specificity of restriction enzymes, a person's DNA is cut in exactly the same places, yielding identically sized fragments with each restriction digestion. In a typical restriction enzyme reaction, DNA is diluted in a volume of buffer in a small test tube to optimal concentration. In forensic cases, the concentration of crime-scene DNA is usually small due to the meager amount of cellular debris in many evidentiary samples.[19,20] When samples are collected from one or a few drops of blood or semen, forensic scientists routinely work with nanogram and picogram quantities of DNA (one billionth and one trillionth of a gram). The third component added to the digestion mixture is the reaction buffer. After all ingredients are included, they are thoroughly mixed and incubated usually at 37°C for 1 to 16 hours. If enough DNA is available, a small sample of the restriction reaction should be tested for completeness of digestion. This is easily done by electrophoresis in a minigel and by comparing the size of the DNA in the test and completely digested control samples. It is important to digest the DNA to completion; otherwise, artefactual banding patterns, consisting of extra bands,[1] are present and are called partial digests.

Separation of Cut DNA Fragments Is Called Electrophoresis

DNA fingerprinting analysis compares the sizes of DNA fragments containing specific, core sequences. After restriction enzyme digestion, we have a heterogeneous mixture of different-sized DNA fragments. Electrophoresis exploits differences in the size, shape, and net charge of molecules to spread them out in an electric field. This temporal and spatial separation is achieved in DNA fragments in a semi-solid, agarose gel. The basis of DNA fingerprinting is a comparison of DNA fragments after they are separated according to size; thus, a method that holds the DNA fragments in place after separation will facilitate these comparisons. The basis of the DNA fragment separation is simple. A power supply generates a flow of electrons around a closed circuit. The negatively charged DNA molecules migrate towards the positive electrode. Because the cut DNA molecules were loaded into the gel, the negatively charged DNA must move through the agarose gel matrix as they carry the electric flow. Although larger DNA fragments possess proportionally more negative charge (each nucleotide in the chain contributes one negatively charged phosphate group to the DNA), they also will encounter more difficulty migrating through the gelatinous matrix. This is, in fact, the basis for the differential rate of migration of DNA fragments. Larger DNA fragments will encounter more spatial resistance in the gel matrix, and, as a result, their rate of migration will be slower than that of smaller fragments. Due to this differential rate of migration of different size molecules, at the end of the electrophoretic separation, smaller DNA molecules will be closer to the positive electrode in the gel, and the larger DNA molecules will be closer to the origin.

For DNA profiling, many of the systems used (e.g., VNTR and STR) compare the lengths of DNA fragments containing specific core sequences. Electrophoresis is used to sort these fragments by size.

A Process Called Southern Blotting Transfers the DNA to a More Useable Matrix

Agarose is difficult to handle, and the identifiers of specific DNA fragments, the probes, do not diffuse readily into the gel matrix. Fortunately the DNA fragments may be transferred to a better support without altering their positions in the gel. This process is called Southern transfer, after its designer, Ed Southern.[21] A nylon membrane is placed on the gel which sits in a tray full of aqueous buffer, and paper towels are placed on top of the nylon membrane. In this way, the DNA is literally blotted out (by capillary action) of the gel and onto the nylon membrane, which is much easier to handle. Next, the DNA fragments are fixed in position on the membrane as single-stranded DNA fragments.

DNA Fragments Are Visualized by a Specific and Sensitive Process Called Probing

Humans possess approximately 3 billion nucleotides or bases in their genome or full genetic complement. A restriction enzyme which recognizes a four-base sequence will cut the DNA, on average, once every 256 nucleotides (4^4). In humans, such an enzyme will produce approximately 11,718,750 DNA fragments (3,000,000,000/256). Clearly, the pattern of differently sized DNA fragments is too complex to analyze. Try drawing 11 million pencil lines on a sheet of letter-size paper! The solution to this problem is to reduce the number of fragments examined at any one time. This is done by hybridizing a short, single-stranded DNA to the DNA fragments immobilized on the nylon membrane. DNA molecules are double-stranded helices. The nucleotides are held together in each strand of the molecule by covalent phosphodiester bonds, and the two halves of the molecule are held together by hydrogen bonds and other weaker forces formed between specific nucleotides. Bases pair between strands with specific rules: A, adenine, pairs with T, thymine, and G, guanine, pairs with C, cytosine. If a short nine-base fragment has the sequence T-T-G-G-A-C-C-T-A, then its complement will have the sequence A-A-C-C-T-G-G-A-T. Following the rules of base pairing, we expect these two single-stranded molecules to bind together or hybridize under suitable conditions to form a double-stranded helix. This particular sequence, A-A-C-C-T-G-G-A-T of nine bases is expected to be found once every 262,144 bases (4^9). Thus, we can estimate that genomic DNA digested with restriction enzyme which recognizes a four-base sequence and yields approximately 12 million fragments will have approximately 46 fragments which contain the T-T-G-G-A-C-C-T-A sequence. These will, under suitable conditions, hybridize with the complimentary sequence. If this complementary sequence is tagged somehow, the positions of these DNA fragments on the nylon membrane will be visualized. Of course, we do not use base sequences as probes unless they have been tested and shown to be polymorphic.

The probes used in most forensic labs are complements of base sequences in VNTR (variable number tandem repeat) regions of the DNA; each parent contributes one fragment to his or her child. See Table 11.5 for an example of DNA probes used in forensic casework. Visualization of the DNA fragments is achieved by tagging the probes with a radioactive isotope, ^{32}P, or attaching a chemical probe. With ^{32}P-labeled probes, the membrane is placed between two sheets of X-ray film, and the emission of radioactive particles from the probe will produce a pattern on the film. Chemically-tagged probes work in a similar manner.

Table 11.5   Some Common VNTR Probes Used in DNA Fingerprinting and Paternity

Probe Name	Chromosome	Location	Core Repeat
MS1	1	D1S7	9 bp
YNH24	2	D2S44	31 bp
PH30	4	D4S139	31 bp
TBQ7	10	D10S28	33 bp
LH1	5	D5S110	35 bp

Source: J. S. Waye, J. H. Bowen, and R. M. Fourney, Forensic Analysis of Restriction Fragment Length Polymorphism: Theoretical and Practical Considerations for Design and Implementation, in: Proceedings of The International Symposium on Human Identification, Madison, WI (1989).

PCR Technology Represents One of the Most Significant Advances in Molecular Biology since Elucidation of the Structure of DNA

PCR (polymerase chain reaction) is a process in which small fragments of DNA (usually less than 2 to 3 thousand bases long) are repeatedly copied using a semiconservative mechanism.[8,22] The PCR process consists of three major steps: denaturing, annealing, and extension. This process is repeated from 20 to 30 times. Starting with a single copy of a specific nucleotide sequence flanked by primer nucleotide sequences, it is possible to produce millions or even billions of copies of this specific sequence. The number of copies produced depends on the number of replication cycles.

The denaturing step is the separation of the two strands of the DNA molecule. This makes both strands available for further amplification once the strands or templates are primed. This occurs when the DNA double helix is heated to 94 to 96°; at this point, single-stranded DNA sequences of from 6 to over 39 base pairs, the primer sequences, bind to the sequence exterior or flanking sites of the sequence we want to amplify.

Primer binding is called annealing (55 to 72°C). Next, a thermostable DNA polymerase is added to the reaction which adds the bases A, T, G, or C to the single-strand template, thus making a new, complementary single strand. The primer initiates the extension (72 to 75°C) process. Since primer sequences are present in vast excess, the process may be repeated through 2 to 30 cycles creating millions of copies — an exponential chain reaction. Where we started with one double-stranded DNA sequence or two single denatured strands, we now have four single strands. The next cycle will produce eight (4×2) double strands. PCR is applicable to DNA specimens

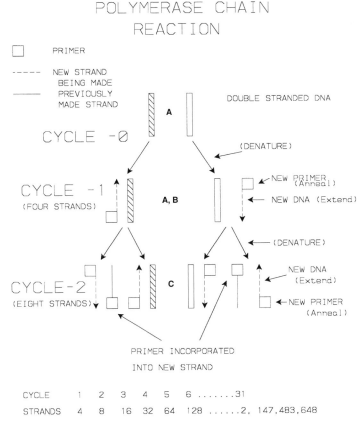

Figure 11.9 The polymerase chain reaction: Multiple copies of specific DNA segments or genes were originally produced by cloning, cutting out the segment wanted and inserting it into a host cell which would, as it reproduced, make copies of the inserted gene along with its own DNA. Now DNA may be copied enzymatically using a temperature-insensitive DNA copying enzyme or polymerase. Starting with double-stranded DNA, the specific site to be amplified is targeted by using primers which flank the target site and act as anchors for the synthesis of a new DNA strand. (A) The first step of a cycle involves melting the DNA to expose the nucleotides of each strand allowing the primers to bind. (B) Next the temperature is lowered and the polymerase enzyme facilitates the synthesis of two new DNA strands using the old strands as templates. (C) These two double-stranded DNA molecules are melted or denatured in cycle 2 to begin the process anew. It is called a chain reaction, because at each cycle the number of previously existing DNA molecules is doubled.

which are degraded or in some way made smaller by actions of physical or environmental agents or age. Because theoretically it is possible to multiply single strands of DNA to essentially millions of copies of that single sequence, PCR is extremely sensitive, and from 1 to 5 ng of DNA can be successfully typed using the process.[23] Figure 11.10 and Table 11.6 compare the differences between conventional RFLP/DNA analysis and PCR/DNA analysis.

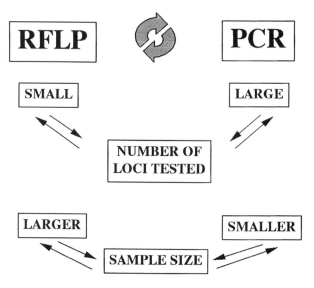

Figure 11.10   Comparison of RFLP (Southern-blot) and PCR (amplified) DNA identification tests: The power of forensic tests depends on their ability to include or exclude individuals as contributors of evidentiary samples, but the application of particular techniques depends on the number of tests required to produce odds of exclusion which suggest that the match means that the evidentiary sample came from the identified individual. Selection of a test or set of tests also depends on the condition of evidence. Fewer RFLP tests than PCR tests are needed to produce a given probability, but larger sample sizes are required for RFLP tests. In the future, PCR-based sequence-like or sequence-based tests may eliminate this difference.

Table 11.6   Comparison of Two Analysis Methods for Forensically Applicable DNA Loci

PCR	VNTR/RFLP
Aged, Degraded, or intact DNA	Intact large sequences
100–3000 bp	500 to 23,000 bp
1–25 ng	Greater than 50 ng
Fewer alleles	Large number of alleles
2- to 3-day analysis time	6- to 8-week isotopic analysis
More loci needed for high discrimination	4 to 5 loci needed for high discrimination
High discrimination	High discrimination
8–22 alleles	250–1,000 alleles

Restriction Fragment Length Polymorphism (RFLPs) of Variable Number of Tandem Repeats (VNTRs) Are the Basis for the Original DNA Profiling

At many locations throughout the human genome, short and long sequences (two to over several hundred base pairs) of DNA bases are repeated over and

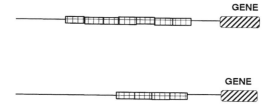

Figure 11.11 Example of a VNTR (variable number of tandem repeat): Genomic DNA, all the DNA in each cell, contains many sections which are repetitive. These often vary from individual to individual, because the number of repeats is different. Because of this, the length of the repeat DNA will vary when this section of DNA is cut out and visualized or amplified and visualized. The "repeat units" can be as small as a single base pair to many hundreds of base pairs making up a repetitive sequence. The sequence may be many thousands or millions of "repeat units". This kind of DNA has been referred to as "junk" DNA in the past, but new evidence may show that it may not be junk after all. Thus, the sequence made up of "repeat units" from our father may differ from the sequence from our mother. When there is a difference between genetically defined multiple forms of a particular character, it is called polymorphism.

over again.[15,24] They are said to repeat in tandem, meaning they repeat continually in a chain-like sequence. The number of these repeating units is highly variable, so that most people have differing amounts of these repeat units inherited from their mother and father (see Figure 11.11). When the length of the repeat units inherited from each parent will be different, this condition is known as heterozygosity. The existence of these repetitive sequences is very important, as they are being used to locate certain genes in our chromosomal structure, and also some have been linked to genetic diseases such as fragile X syndrome and myotonic dystrophy.[25] They are also excellent sites to use in assessing differences among humans.[26] By use of a technique such as RFLP the forensic scientist is able to quantitate the lengths of these VNTRs and use them to identify with high precision and accuracy the identity of an individual. Because there are a limited number of these variations at any one site, different individuals can share similar size VNTRs. It then is not possible to determine the source of a sample from use of one VNTR locus (spot on a chromosome). If, however, many different VNTRs are used, a profile of an individual is created with a very high discrimination power (see Figure 11.12).[27,28] There are several ways to determine the length of the VNTR.

One is by using a restriction enzyme previously described to "cut" the VNTR out of the piece of DNA and then to separate the pieces using electrophoresis. Another way is the use of the PCR process to copy or amplify the VNTR pieces of less than 3000 bp and then separate them by electrophoresis.[29] This does not involve the use of restriction enzymes but the use of PCR primers.

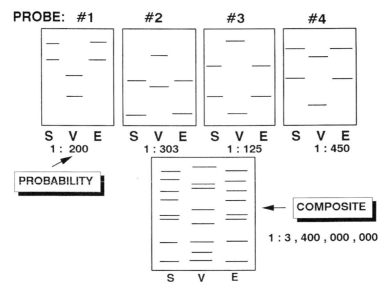

Figure 11.12 Four DNA probe composites of autorads containing samples from suspect, victim, and evidence with a final frequency of occurrence of 1 in 3,400,000,000: The four autoradiograms or autorads in this figure depict matches between the suspect's DNA patterns and those produced by the DNA extracted from the evidence. Since these four pattern matches are first made visually and subsequently by computer sizing, the examiner has estimated the odds of someone other than the suspect also producing a matching DNA pattern for each of the four probes. These are the numbers under each of the four autorad diagrams: 1 in 200, 1 in 303, 1 in 125, and 1 in 450. For the first match, using probe #1, the odds of finding another unrelated person with the same DNA pattern as the evidence are 1 in 200; this means that ¹/₂ of 1% of all humans will produce this pattern. There are, however, approximately 5¹/₂ billion people on this planet; so, we must consider the fact that these odds of 1 in 200 mean that approximately 27 million unrelated people will also produce DNA patterns which match the evidence. DNA pattern matching power depends on the use of three to five different probes to identify independent DNA segments. The independence has been statistically verified and the examiner is, therefore, able to combine the odds for each probe to estimate the odds of finding an unrelated individual, other than the suspect, who would also produce matches on all four autorads. This is done by multiplying 200 × 303 × 125 × 450 to produce composite odds of approximately 1 in 3.4 billion. These odds suggest that slightly more than 1.6 people on the planet who are unrelated to the person who produced the evidentiary pattern will match on all four of the autorads.

Other Types of VNTRs and Sequence Polymorphic Areas of Nuclear and Mitochondrial DNA are Also Used to Profile DNA in Forensic Cases

Small, amplified DNA segments are currently used in sequence-type analysis (mtDNA and MVR), fragment size analysis (STR, AMPFLP), or dot-blot analysis (DQalpha and amplitype PM™).[7,8] In sequence-type analysis, the amplified DNA fragments may be sequenced directly after amplification using any of the sequencing methods, or the amplified fragments may be separated to produce a ladder which resembles a sequencing ladder. Direct sequencing is most frequently done with the highly polymorphic control region or D-loop of mitochondrial DNA, and approximately 400 bp are sequenced.[9] This is a valuable technique for identification, because all maternal relatives are expected to have identical mtDNA; however, it is, for the same reason, less discriminating because maternal relatives are indistinguishable.[30]

Minisatellite Variant Repeats (MVR)

MVR (minisatellite variable repeat sequencing) uses the fact that some VNTR repeats have internal polymorphisms which may be used as terminators in much the same way that Sanger sequencing uses dideoxynucleotides to terminate polynucleotides in synthesis. These are then separated on a gel, and the sequence is read directly off the gel. The minisatellites MS31 and MS32 are currently the only VNTRs being used for identification using MVR methods.[31]

AMPFLP (Amplified Fragment Length Polymorphism) Represents Another Type of VNTR that Is Smaller than the VNTRs Used for RFLP

In AmpFLP analysis (amflip, or amplified fragment length polymorphism), sample DNA is amplified using primers which flank a core repeat of approximately 10 to 20 bp (see Figure 11.13).[7] The fragment length polymorphism, like VNTR polymorphism, is based on the number of core repeats found in a particular allele. Here alleles are defined as DNA segments on homologous chromosomes with different numbers of repeats. For example, the AmpFLP inherited from the mother may have 74 repeats, while that inherited from the father may have 38 repeats. AmpFLP alleles are, however, smaller than VNTR alleles. They range in size from 100 to 1000 bp, while VNTR alleles range from 200 to more than 20,000 bp. Most VNTR alleles are too long at this time to be amplified by PCR, and the ends or termini of VNTR alleles are defined by restriction enzyme cut sites which flank the tandemly repeated core sequences. Long PCR may change this limitation. Long PCR may be able to amplify more than 20,000 base pairs of DNA in the very near future. AmpFLP loci are selected for analysis because the size range of core repeats is efficiently amplified by PCR; consequently, the termini of these AmpFLP alleles are defined by primer sites, not by restriction sites. These differences of size explain, in large part, the fact that VNTR loci have an enormous number of alleles continuously distributed over the size range, while AmpFLP loci have an approximately discrete number of alleles, usually in the range of 5 to 25.

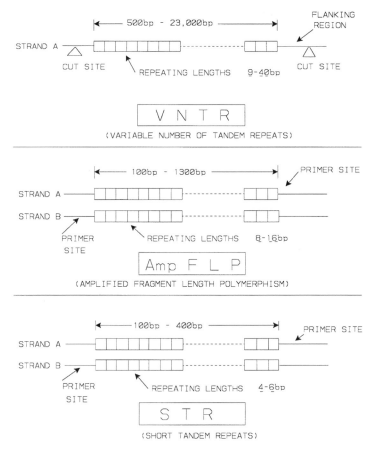

Figure 11.13 Examples of various repeat polymorphisms in the human genome: Genomic DNA, all the DNA in each cell, contains many sections which are repetitive. These often vary from individual to individual, because the number of repeats is different. Since the number of repeats is different, the length of the repeat DNA will vary when this section of DNA is cut out and visualized or amplified and visualized. (A) VNTRs have repeat lengths or cores which range from 9 to 40 bp, depending on which specific gene is being examined. These VNTRs are isolated and visualized for pattern comparisons by restriction enzyme digestion and DNA probing. VNTRs are the genes first used by forensic labs to produce "DNA fingerprints" by combining patterns over four to six genes. Although VNTRs are highly polymorphic, this testing methodology is expensive and time consuming. Two additional repeat length polymorphism tests have been introduced to reduce costs and testing time. Rather than cutting and probing, these tests amplify specific repeats, and the amplified sequences are visualized without probing. (B) AMPFLP (amplified fragment length polymorphisms) have cores which range from 8 to 16 bp. (C) STR (short tandem repeat) cores range from 4 to 6 bp.

Following amplification, the DNA sample is separated on a gel, usually polyacrylamide, and the amplified fragments are visualized with silver stain or fluorescent dyes. As in VNTR analysis, size ladders are included on the analytical gels. In AmpFLP analysis, however, alleles are treated as discrete units which allows visual comparison of alleles with the ladder alleles, unlike VNTR analysis which requires computer sizing.

Short Tandem Repeats (STR) Represent a Very Small VNTR

Another type of amplified repeat analysis is STR, or short tandem repeat analysis. It is very similar to AmpFLP analysis, but the repeat sequences are shorter still (4 to 6 bp). Additionally, a number of STR loci may be amplified and separated simultaneously, a technique known as multiplexing. This increases the discriminatory power of STR analysis, while decreasing the work and time involved in the analysis. There are approximately 4.0×10^8 STR loci dispersed throughout the human genome. STRs consist of small numbers of repeat units, usually three, four, or five repeats, which are from 50 to several hundred base pairs in length.

Much effort is being made at present to shorten the time of analysis of STRs and AmpFLPs, as well as to increase the number of STR and AmpFLP types analyzed. Several types can be analyzed at the same time and on the same gel with sophisticated hardware and novel tags attached to the DNA. One of these attempts has been the use of fluorescent-tagged STRs and AmpFLPs. Dr. Ron Fourney and Dr. C.J. Fregeau of the Royal Canadian Mounted Police have been instrumental in developing this technology (see Figure 11.14).

The First Two PCR Systems to Find Wide Acceptance in the Forensic Community: HLA DQ-Alpha and Polymarker PM

Two discrete allele systems which are not based on repetitive core sequences are currently used with PCR for identification. The first uses a portion of the human major histocompatibility complex (MHC) as a PCR substrate. The MHC is the complex gene or supergene which plays a role in tissue and organ differentiation and is one of the genes which must be matched in organ transplanting. This is the DQalpha locus, which is employed in a dot-blot format.

Probes for the DQalpha alleles are fixed to membranes as dots. The sample DNA is amplified, and allelic identification is achieved by allowing the amplified sample to bind to the appropriate dots on the membrane. The bound sample is then visualized using a conjugated enzyme and dye. Then, the allele is identified as having bound to its complement on the membrane (see Figure 11.15).

The second discrete allele system is amplitype PM™. It consists of certain probes bound to a strip as in the case of HLA DQalpha. The loci or types are as follows: HLA DQ-alpha (separate strip), LDL receptor (LDLR), glyco-phorin A (GyPA), hemoglobin G-gamma globin (HBGG), D7S8, and group specific component (GC). The advantage of this typing system is that one

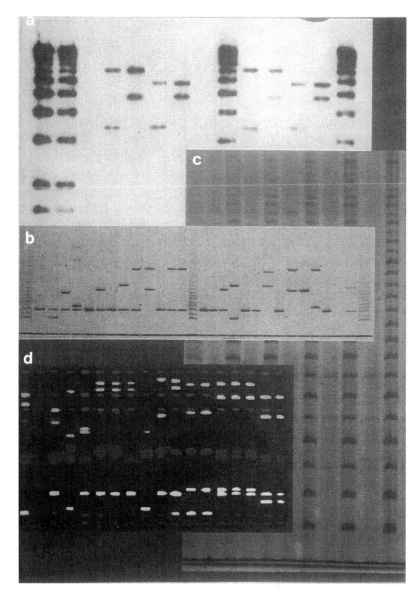

Figure 11.14   The evolution of DNA typing in North America: This montage represents the evolution of DNA typing in North America from the (a) initial single locus DNA typing profile (D1S7) followed by PCR based methods including (b) AMP-Flaps (D1S80), (c) mini-satellite variant repeats ([MVRs] D1S8) and (d) fluorescent-tagged short tandem repeats (STRs, bottom: HumCD4, yellow; HumFABP, blue; HumACTBP2, green; ABI Genescan™ 2500 marker, red). Contributed by the Biology Research and Development Support Unit and Richard Musgrave of the Forensic Photo Unit, Royal Canadian Mounted Police. (Figure courtesy of Eaton Publishing Company.) See color plate following page 228.

works with five loci or types instead of one type as with DQalpha, and the power of discrimination is increased. The average frequency of occurrence can be as low as 1 in 400 or as high as 1 in several million. See Table 11.7 and Table 11.8 for frequency data for HLA-DQalpha and amplitype PM™ markers.

Mitochondrial DNA (mtDNA) Analysis: The New Frontier in DNA Profiling and the Sequencing of Polymorphic Sites of the Nuclear and Mitochondrial Genome

Mitochondrial DNA is located outside the nucleus of the cell in the energy-producing mitochondria. The advantage of this type of DNA is the great number of mitochondria per cell. A single hair root has been successfully typed using mitochondrial analysis. The information in DNA is encoded in the linear array of nucleotides. The genetic code consists of nucleotide triplets which may be converted in transcription and translation to amino acids to form proteins. Ultimately, then, it is reasonable to expect that DNA sequence information will be used by forensic scientists.

Currently the DNA from the mitochondria is being used forensically, because each cell has many mitochondria: the mtDNA is a relatively small molecule, and some regions of the molecule are very polymorphic. When DNA sequences are compared, the scientist looks for identities or differences. In the example below, the sequence in (a) is identical to that in (c), but not to that in (b). Comparing

> (a) ...........TTGCAGCTTAGCCCGATTCGATCGA............
> (b) ...........TTGCAGCTTAGCCCAATTCGATCGA............
> (c) ...........TTGCAGCTTAGCCCGATTCGATCGA............

these sequences we may confidently ascribe (b) as the mutational source of either (a) or (c), and we may estimate the probability that (a) and (c) match by chance (see Figure 11.16).

Variability and Frequency Criteria: The Basis for Frequency Determination in Genetics and Forensic Serology

Human identification depends on two things: (1) characteristics which vary among individuals, and (2) knowledge of character percentages or frequencies. Unless the degree of character variation is known, the characteristic is

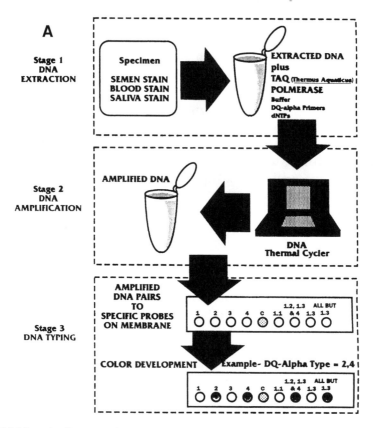

Figure 11.15 The first PCR-based forensic test was DQalpha: In (A), specimen DNA is placed in a tube along with the DNA replication enzyme (TAQ), buffer, primers, and dNTPs (the nucleotides which will be used to copy the DNA). In stage 2, the tube is placed in a thermal cycler which melts the double helix and then lowers the temperature to permit replication; then, the cycle is repeated. Test strips are shown in stage 3; the single-stranded DNA for most of the alleles has been fixed to a nylon membrane which is probed with the amplified specimen DNA. This amplified DNA will bind to its complement, which is visualized (B) by coupling biotin to the amplified DNA. This biotin is detected by streptavidin coupled to a peroxidase which converts a colorless substrate to a dye which is then read as a colored dot. Genotypic determination for DQalpha is done by reading sets of colored dots. (Figure courtesy of FBI Laboratory.)

useless for purposes of identification. Consider hair color: describing a person as having blond hair is very useful identification information in China; it is less useful in Sweden. The reason is that a small percentage of Chinese are blond; thus, this information allows us to eliminate a much larger percentage of Chinese, the nonblonds, than in the Swedish population. The process, however, is dependent on knowing that (1) hair color varies among individuals, and (2) the percentage of people having different hair colors. The percentage of each type may or may not differ across different populations such as Swedes or Chinese. These two qualities — variability and knowledge of frequencies or percentages — are basic to all identification systems.

B

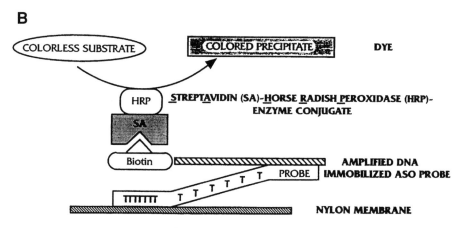

Figure 11.15 (continued)

Table 11.7   Frequencies of the Various
Types of Amplitype PM in Three
Populations

Locus	Allele	Black	Caucasian	Hispanic
LDLR	A	0.25	0.43	0.48
	B	0.75	0.57	0.52
GYPA	A	0.55	0.48	0.61
	B	0.45	0.52	0.39
HBGG	A	0.42	0.53	0.39
	B	0.26	0.45	0.56
	C	0.32	0.02	0.05
D7S8	A	0.66	0.58	0.66
	B	0.34	0.42	0.34
GC	A	0.07	0.33	0.20
	B	0.74	0.15	0.36
	C	0.19	0.52	0.44

Source: Data courtesy of FBI Laboratory.

The Bertillon System of Identification Provides an Analogy to DNA Fingerprinting, Although Its Use Was Discredited Many Decades Ago

An identification system using measurements of a person's head size, right ear size, left foot size, color of the iris of the left eye, and hair color, among other characteristics, was introduced to forensics by the French anthropologist Alphonse Bertillon in the late 1800s.[32] All of the characteristics he used differed among people, and frequencies of the characters were estimated as

Table 11.8   The HLA DQalpha Genotype Frequencies in Three Populations

DQa, Genotype	Caucasian (N = 737)[a]	Black (N = 589)	Hispanic (Composite)
1.1,1.1	0.019[b]	0.020	0.032
1.1,1.2	0.045	0.090	0.057
1.1,1.3	0.024	0.007	0.015
1.1,2	0.031	0.032	0.057
1.1,3	0.039	0.022	0.048
1.1,4	0.085	0.078	0.079
1.2,1.2	0.053	0.065	0.023
1.2,1.3	0.026	0.017	0.034
1.2,2	0.049	0.053	0.034
1.2,3	0.072	0.071	0.073
1.2,4	0.113	0.180	0.107
1.3,1.3	0.008	0.003	0.004
1.3,2	0.014	0.020	0.027
1.3,3	0.016	0.010	0.034
1.3,4	0.054	0.024	0.050
2,2	0.020	0.014	0.031
2,3	0.047	0.024	0.042
2,4	0.064	0.076	0.084
3,3	0.042	0.005	0.040
3,4	0.106	0.090	0.198
4,4	0.072	0.098	0.167

[a] Number of people typed.
[b] Frequency of DQa types.

Source: Data courtesy of FBI Laboratory.

data was collected. The characters of head height and diameter were combined with hair color to produce a composite. The forensic utility of this composite description depended, however, on knowledge of character frequencies, either the individual character frequencies or the composite frequencies. Of course, any system claiming individual identification based on an empirical database would have to measure everyone. For example, head height and diameter measurements of 24 × 22 cm are seen 3% of the time in a database; 35% of the people in this same database have brown hair. If these two characteristics are independent, we may estimate the head size/hair color composite frequency by multiplying the individual frequencies: 3% (24 × 22 cm head) × 35% (brown hair) = 1.05%. If we are correct in assuming character independence, this method of multiplication of frequencies of combinations of characters will quickly and inexpensively produce identifications of individuals. By adding characteristics, an increasingly rare description is produced. This composite description has both qualities required for identification: variability and knowledge of character frequency.

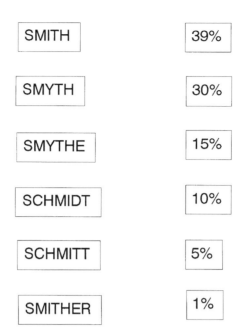

SMITH	39%
SMYTH	30%
SMYTHE	15%
SCHMIDT	10%
SCHMITT	5%
SMITHER	1%

Figure 11.16 Surnames may be analogous with DNA sequences: Picking one sequence as a base sequence, we may describe the changes in the DNA sequence. Suppose that we select SMYTHE as the base sequence. It is related to SMYTH by deletion of the terminal E. It is related to SMITH by deletion of the E and substitution of I for Y. All of the names may be related in this fashion, but the changes required to make these relationships will depend on our selection of a base name or sequence. (Figure courtesy of FBI Laboratory.)

Our knowledge of character frequency, however, is predicated on the assumption that these characteristics are really independent. In other words, our composite descriptions of uniqueness are based on multiplication of character frequencies such as head size and hair color; however, multiplication may not be appropriate. To answer this question, we could construct a database of all composite characters. In this database, all entries will be 1 divided by the number of individuals studied, or 1/N. This empirical method is fine and may be used to support the contention that the Bertillon identification system, for example, provides individual identification or unique descriptions. Once two individuals with the same measurements are found, the whole system must be expanded to include new characteristics or abandoned because the assumption of character independence is only empirically justifiable. It is not based on any underlying principles. This important point will be clearer when we look at characteristics for which the inheritance patterns or the genetics are known. The Bertillon identification system was abandoned in the 1930s, after two individuals were found to have the same measurements.

The Fingerprint System of Identification: the Most Powerful Identifier of an Individual Since the Beginning of the Twentieth Century

Fortunately another identification system, fingerprinting, had been introduced to the U.S. in 1902 by the New York Civil Service Commission as a means of individual identification. The Federal Bureau of Investigation adopted the procedure and by 1933 had an operating latent fingerprint section. In fingerprinting, the variables are classified as arch, loop, and whorl; each of these types exists in a portion of the population (65% loop, 30% whorl, and 5% arch). As in physical description or identification, we have a system based on variable characters of known frequency. The basic principles of identification are the same. Knowing that a fingerprint is a loop or a whorl does not allow us to match another print on file. It does allow us unequivocal elimination of all arch prints from further consideration. Adding features such as ridge characteristics permits further exclusion. For example, if the loop or whorl print also has various ridge characteristics such as dots, bifurcations, and ending ridges, we may eliminate all prints which do not share these features in the same area or position from further consideration. The consideration of multiple characteristics of a fingerprint is the crux of the identification potential of this system. More and more prints are excluded until a unique fingerprint pattern is described. In other words, a fingerprint identification like a physical appearance identification, is a composite where positive identification depends on elimination of more and more classes for each characteristic in the description. In the Bertillon system, we first eliminated all head height and diameter measurements which were not 24×22 cm — some 97% of all individuals were excluded. Only 3% were included.

Fingerprint identification depends on similar exclusion and inclusion logic; if a print is an arch, then all loop and whorl prints (those which are not arch) are excluded. Both physical description and fingerprinting are based on character variability and frequency information. Fingerprinting has the advantage that prints may be left at a crime scene, but it shares the disadvantage that explicit frequency calculations are based on the assumption of character independence which is, of course, statistically tested in forensic labs.

Blood Grouping Offers the Distinct Advantage of Being Firmly Based in Human Genetics

While blood group and serum protein characteristics share the variability and frequency knowledge requirements seen in the use of physical description and fingerprinting, they offer the distinct advantage that the assumption of independence is based in the science of genetics. Patterns of inheritance for physical characteristics such as skull dimensions and for fingerprints are complicated and incompletely understood. On the other hand, the genetics of ABO, MN, Rh, PGM, and other traits used in serological identification are simple and well understood. This important difference between genetically defined polymorphisms (multiple forms of a character) and those polymorphism which are not well known genetically is important in light of our second criteria for polymorphism — knowledge of frequencies of the various forms of each character. We may employ basic principles of the science of genetics to estimate frequencies.

Class vs. Individual Characteristics: The Cornerstones of Identification in Forensics that Brings the Value of Serological Evidence into Perspective when Understood by Laymen

There are three categories of evidence submitted to a crime laboratory: class, individual, and an intermediate category where class evidence approaches individual evidence. Class evidence can be categorized to a specific group or category. Its rarity or uniqueness is derived from the rarity of the group itself. An example of this is a blood stain categorized as belonging to a member of the human race or a higher primate species. Most forensic tests cannot differentiate between higher primates such as chimpanzee and gorilla and humans. Since there are approximately 6 billion or so higher primates, this stain is in the class of higher primates, admittedly a large group but one which eliminates dogs, cats, mice, fish, etc.

Table 11.9 Phosphoglucomutase Types (Phenotypes) Observed in Samples from Three Countries

Country	PGM 1	PGM 2-1	PGM 2
Ireland	74.51%	23.62%	1.87%
U.S.	56.55%	37.30%	6.15%
Turkey	45.83%	43.72%	10.43%

Source: A.K. Roychoudhury, Nei, M., Human Polymorphic Genes, Worldwide Distribution, Oxford University Press, Oxford, 1988.

Intermediate evidence is class evidence that has characteristics approaching the uniqueness of individual evidence. In terms of serological evidence, the intermediate category encompasses a broad spectrum of tests and procedures.

A

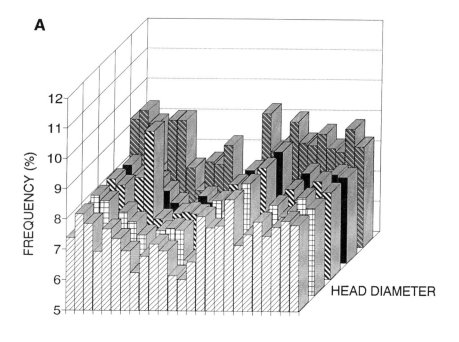

HEAD HEIGHT

Figure 11.17 Various identification systems rely on character variability and knowledge of character frequencies: Characters which do not vary are useless for identification. For example, in searching for a particular person, the information that this person has a head and a chest is not useful, because all humans have heads and chests. These are monomorphic (one form) characters. If, on the other hand, we are told that the person we seek is a male, this is very useful information. It allows us to exclude all females from our search, reducing the search effort by approximately 50%, because females constitute approximately 50% of all humans. (A) In an external physical characteristics description system such as that devised by the anthropologist Alphonse Bertillon, character forms are specified and their frequencies are combined (multiplied if independent) to produce a composite description of known frequency. In this example, measurements of head height and diameter are taken separately. The frequencies of the combined measure are plotted on X,Y,Z coordinates. As in the head and chest vs. male example, identification is achieved by successive exclusion. Individuals with the smallest head height and diameter frequency are plotted in the lower left closest to the origin. Identifying a person as a member of this class does not identify the individual; it does eliminate all individuals in all the other classes. (B), (C), and (D) are hair color, fingerprint, and DNA fragment identification systems; they are similarly used for identification. They differ in their powers of identification, because the number of character states and associated frequencies differ.

The resultant characteristic of an ABO antigen test is technically a genetic phenotype. This characteristic allows the examiner to narrow down the stain class even further than a general category of human or animal stain. Compare the ABO locus (position) on chromosome 9 and the VNTR (variable number of tandem repeats) YNH24 probe at the D2S44 locus on chromosome 2. The ABO locus has four classes or phenotypes, A, B, AB, and O and some that are rare. There are four common alleles at this locus: A_1, B, A_2, and O.[3] The

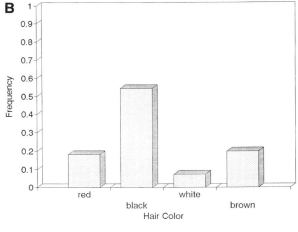

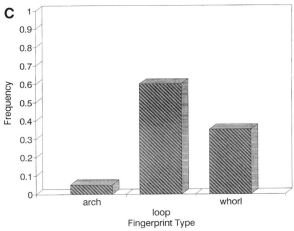

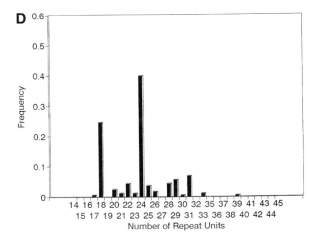

Figure 11.17 (continued)

most an examiner can hope for is to find the rarest type, AB, in this system. This type coincides with roughly 4% of the Caucasian population of the U.S. The VNTR D2S44 genetic locus has over 400 phenotypic classes, the most common present in approximately 15% of some populations; other phenotypes are considerably less frequent. Using this D2S44 locus significantly increases the informative value of the stain. The odds of finding a person with the same phenotype can range from 1 in 6 to 1 in several thousand. Genes like these clearly fill the requirements of an efficient system for identification. They are highly polymorphic and the frequencies are rather low.

Individual evidence is at the opposite pole from class evidence. Individual evidence itself is in such a rare class, or its individual characteristics are so uncommon, as to make it unique. A good example of this is a fracture pattern of a broken piece of glass. Every piece of glass that is broken produces a unique and individual fracture pattern. If you were to break a glass an infinite number of times, a particular fracture pattern would never be reproduced.[5,7,11] Another example would be the arrangement of the nucleotides or bases in a person's DNA molecules. Because of the laws of genetics, your DNA will never be duplicated again, except in an identical twin. Using tests for different loci such as 4 VNTR loci and 8 to 12 STR loci, the odds of finding the same type in a random population can be as little as 1 in several hundred million or even billions or trillions.

Elimination or Inclusion Is the End of the Journey in the Forensic Scientists' Quest for Information

Often the question asked is "How can I eliminate or include person A as the source of items of crime scene evidence?" This is the issue in most cases involving suspects being held or charged with a crime. The most important factor then becomes selection of the appropriate genetic marker system, which should be chosen to include or exclude the victim or defendant. Forensic serologists have a growing arsenal of genetic markers ranging from ABO antigen typing to DNA/RFLP analysis at their disposal. Some genetic markers are relatively weak discriminators, whereas others provide extremely high discriminatory power and can approach individualization.

A serologist uses a simple statistical test to measure the value of genetic markers for individualization. This is the power of discrimination (P_D) test.[11] Two premises must be established. The frequency distribution of the types in the system must be known from population surveys; it is hoped that the distribution is known in many different populations. Next, the genetic marker must not be statistically associated with the other genetic markers that the serologist will use. First, let us take as an example the isoenzyme phosphoglucomutase (PGM). Let us see how its discriminatory power can be calculated, and how it can be useful in our case scenario. There are three PGM types of individuals found in a random sampling of populations: type 1, type 2-1, and type 2. (See Table 11.9.) These types are unevenly distributed in the population.[2] As an analogy, let's flip a coin. What is the probability that, in flipping a coin, it will turn up heads two consecutive times? Since there are two possible outcomes, one heads and one tails, or 50% heads and 50% tails, the answer becomes 1/2 × 1/2, or 1/4 or 0.25. There is a 25% chance that it will be heads both times. In PGM frequencies, the serologist would ask, what are the chances of selecting two type 1 individuals from a random population? The answer, just as in the case of the two coins, is 0.57 × 0.57, or 0.32 or 32%. There is a 32% chance of drawing two type 1 individuals from a random population. Now do the calculations for the other types, 2-1 and 2. The chance of drawing two type 2-1 or type 2 individuals is $(0.3730)^2 = 0.14$ (14%) and $(0.0615)^2 = 0.0038$ (0.38%), respectively. The total of the joint frequencies of all of the PGM types is represented by the following equation:

$$(f[PGM\ 1] + f[PGM\ 2\text{-}1] + f[PGM\ 2])^2 = 1$$

Here, f(PGM 1) is the frequency of PGM 1 in the population and f(PGM 1) × f(PGM 1) is the frequency with which two PGM 1 individuals are selected. Similarly, 2 × f(PGM 1) × f(PGM 2-1) is the frequency at which we expect to pick one PGM 1 and one PGM 2-1 individual. Note that the order does not matter, and the coefficient 2 indicates that this can occur in two ways. We are, however, interested in only those situations involving two similar or matching phenotypes: PGM 1 and PGM 1, PGM 2-1 and PGM 2-1, or PGM 2 and PGM 2. This is called the probability of identity, P_I. This is the probability that you would choose two individuals of the same type in a random population draw. It is equivalent to the probability you would flip a coin and have it turn up heads or tails twice in a row. Of course, the probabilities may differ. In this example:

$$P_I = (PGM\ 1)^2 + (PGM\ 2\text{-}1)^2 + (PGM\ 2)^2$$

If the average P_I is large, the probability of drawing two identical genetic types in a particular system from a random population is high. This means that by increasing P_I the system encompasses more individuals, until the number approaches 1 where every individual you draw will be the same type.

This occurs in monomorphic systems. In other words, P_I indicates that this is a test system which identifies a class. Conversely, the smaller this probability, the greater the chance you have of discriminating between two people picked at random. At the extreme, we would have a test system capable of individualization.

Often it's more convenient to think in terms of discriminating between individuals rather than including individuals so the statistic P_D is used. This is called the power of discrimination, represented by the following equation:

$$PD = 1 - P_I$$

$$PD = 2\ f(PGM\ 1) \times f(PGM\ 2–1) + 2f(PGM\ 1) \times f(PGM\ 2) \\ + 2f(PGM\ 2) \times f(PGM\ 2\text{-}1)$$

Note that this P_D equation plus the P_I equation will equal 1 as shown in the equation. In other words, all possible outcomes have been accounted for if we have phenotypes for both samples. Either they match, P_I, or they do not match, P_D. In the PGM isoenzyme system, the chances of discriminating between two individuals drawn at random from the U.S. population is 0.54, or 54%. The power of discrimination is equal to 1 minus the sum of all probabilities of identity:

$$P_D = 1 - \text{sum } P_I$$

$$= 1 - (0.5655^2 + 0.373^2 + 0.0615^2)$$

So, a serologist has a 54% chance of discriminating between two stains of different individuals. It really does not matter how you want to think about it; both numbers guide the serologist toward the choice of a genetic marker. Note one thing: if a genetic marker is represented, not by 3 equally frequent types, but by 10 or 20 equally frequent types, the power of inclusion goes down rapidly and the power of discrimination increases rapidly. This means that if you have a genetic marker with more types than another with even frequency distributions, this marker becomes much more discriminatory. This approaches that point that all serologists seek, individualization. But using one genetic marker is far from individualizing a sample of biological evidence. If you perform one more test using a different genetic marker that is not linked in any way with the other marker, one multiplies the new markers' P_I times the first P_I. For example, if we choose another marker that has a $P_I = 0.20$, the final probability of identity becomes $0.46 \times 0.20 = 0.092$, or a power of discrimination of:

$$P_D = 1 - 0.092 = 0.908$$

With these two genetic marker systems in hand, the serologist has the power to discriminate between two blood stains from a different source 90% of the time.

In all cases which yield results, a simple PGM test plus another genetic test may eliminate a suspect in an investigation if the evidentiary samples are pure. PGM blood grouping along with other genetic markers provide the serologist with good tools for eliminating individuals. On the other hand, PGM is a poor system to individualize a stain. At best, using the U.S. population data, 2% share the PGM 2 allele. In a population of 1 million individuals, there are approximately 20,000 that are PGM type 2. In addition to P_I considerations, the sample amount and its state of degradation must be factored into the critical choice of which genetic marker to use for analysis. In some cases, for example, amount and state of degradation may dictate the use of a test with a lower P_D.

Errors in Forensic Exclusion/Inclusion

All of the DNA-based systems described, like all other measurement activities, are subject to measurement variation. Rigorous validation of techniques, as well as stringent quality control and assurance, will minimize, but never entirely eliminate, measurement variation. In the final analysis, measurement variation is part of the system.

The goals of the forensic scientist in regard to error are to minimize its occurrence and to limit its effects when it does occur. In comparisons of evidence characteristics, and suspect characteristics the general question is "Do they or do not they match?". Are both samples, evidentiary and suspect, likely to have come from the same person, the suspect, or the victim? Errors may occur at this stage of the analysis either by declaring a match when, in fact, the evidentiary and suspect DNA is different. In other words, the evidentiary DNA did not come from the suspect, but the examiner has declared a match suggesting that the origin of both samples could have been the same individual. Alternatively, a nonmatch may be declared in which the DNA characteristics are said not to match when they actually have come from the same individual (see Table 11.10).

Table 11.10   Type I and Type II Errors in Forensic Serology

	Suspect Is Source of Evidence	Suspect Is Not Source of Evidence
Inclusion/Match	Correct	Incorrect/Type II Error
Exclusion/Nonmatch	Incorrect/Type I Error	Correct

In the first scenario, a match is declared. For example, in a VNTR analysis a set of evidentiary and suspect fragments or bands are visually and numerically declared to match within the limits of visual analysis and laboratory measurement error. Each laboratory must estimate measurement error for any new technique before doing case work. In VNTR analysis, estimation of measurement error involves repeated sizing of known fragments. The average fragment sizes and the variation in these size measurements are computed and used as standards in declaring match or nonmatch among samples (see Figure 11.18).

The evidence and suspect bands match visually and the numerical size of the S, or suspect, band in base pairs is within approximately twice the lab measurement error estimate. Thus, a visual and numerical match is declared. It is, however, recognized that uncertainty is associated with fragment size estimation. That is the reason labs estimate measurement variation. The real length, in base pairs, will fall within a range of the estimated size most of the time. Consequently, two bands, are declared to match if they are approximately no more than twice the lab variation apart.

Similar arguments may be made for the second evidentiary DNA fragment and the suspect's fragment or band. Often, for example in sexual battery cases, evidence-victim matches are known and serve as an internal control.

Type I/Type II Errors

Null Hypothesis:

> Evidentiary phenotype = suspect phenotype. The data prediction is that the bands are visually in the same position and within the match-window after sizing of the DNA fragments.

Alternative Hypothesis:

> Evidentiary phenotype/suspect phenotype. The data prediction is that the bands do not match visually.

The presumption of innocence is not violated by formulating the null hypothesis in this way, and we may attach an error probability to the test of type I, i.e., false exclusion.

In this case, we accept the hypothesis match, because the bands are the same, suggesting that the samples came from the suspect (see Figure 11.18b).

Genetic Basis of Character Form (ALLELE) Frequency Knowledge

The laws of genetics which underlie the inheritance and frequency distributions of characteristics used in forensics are few and relatively straightforward. First,

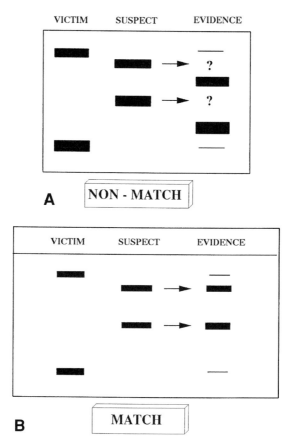

Figure 11.18 Comparison of DNA fragment patterns produced by probing with a single locus probe: Although DNA isolated from evidence, suspect, or victim samples contains millions of fragments separated during the electrophoretic process and transferred to a nylon membrane, the VNTR process identifies one or two fragments at a time by using probes which single out these one or two fragments from all the others. Although each of us has only one or two fragments, the human population has hundreds of different fragments, and it is this large number of differently sized DNA fragments which makes the technique so powerful. Technically, the power of VNTR analysis is attributable to the high level of polymorphism, but this means that there are many forms or sizes of the fragments. In analyzing these three patterns, the examiner looks horizontally across from the victim's upper band to see if it is in the same position as the suspect or evidence bands. In (A, nonmatch), the upper band is clearly higher than any other bands, so a nonmatch is declared. Next, the upper band in the suspect's lane is compared to the evidence lane; again, it does not match. It is not in the same position. Since there are no fragment pattern matches, we can confidently conclude that none of the three DNA sample came from the same person. In (B, match), the upper band in the suspect lane is, by visual inspection, in the same position as the upper band in the evidence lane; this is also true for the lower band. We may conclude that the DNA samples may have come from the same individual, because the patterns match. This conclusion, however, is not as firm as the nonmatch conclusion, because other humans will also have DNA bands or fragments in the same positions as those in the evidence lane. Thus, match determinations are checked by computer sizing against the size ladders and, if confirmed, these matches are weighted by the odds of finding another human who would also match.

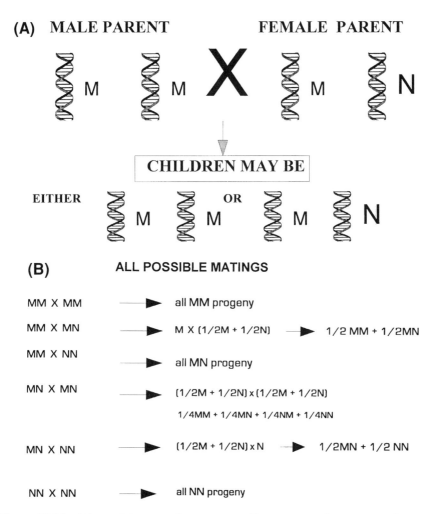

Figure 11.19 (A) Mendel's Law of Segregation allows progeny-frequency predictions: if the allelic constitution, the genotype, of the parents is known, progeny frequencies are predicted as algebraic products of gamete frequencies for a homozygote (an individual who has inherited the same allele at one or more loci) by heterozygote (an individual who has inherited different alleles at one or more loci) matings (A) or all possible matings (B). Here, in considering the probabilities associated with reproduction involving one set of parents, the probabilities that a child will get an allele, say M or N, depends on the number of copies of that allele carried by the parent. An MM parent has a 100% chance of giving the child an M and a 0% chance of giving the child an N. An MN parent has a 50:50, 1:1, or 1/2:1/2 chance of giving M or N to the child. Locus refers to a position that a gene or segment of DNA occupies in or within a portion of genomic DNA. (B) The frequencies of children's genotypes are easily predicted when the parent's genotypes are known. (A) depicts a man who has the genotype MM and can, therefore, produce only M sperm. The female, however, can produce either M or N eggs, because she is an MN heterozygote. Mendel's Law of Segregation, which is based on meiotic disjunction, predicts that she will produce M and N eggs in a 1:1 ratio. (B) enumerating all possibilities, the algebra of Mendelian Segregation becomes clear. In the mating of two MN individuals, each is producing gametes in a 1M:1N ratio; as gametes unite at random, we may multiply (1/2M + 1/2N) × (1/2M +1/2N) to get the 1MM: 2MN: 1NN genotype ratio among the children. This is the same process used in (A) where we multiplied the mothers (1/2M + 1/2N) by the fathers (1 M).

Mendel's Law of Segregation says that the portion of a DNA molecule which represents one form of a gene (an allele) is inherited from one parent and one copy of the gene is passed to a child. Since we all receive one copy of each gene from each parent, we have at fertilization and the rest of our lives two copies of each gene or two alleles (gene variants). These alleles may be identical, in which case the individual is said to be a homozygote, or the alleles may be different in which case the person is a heterozygote. The first law of genetics, the law of allele segregation, allows us to predict progeny frequencies from couples because homozygotes, having only one form of the gene-allele, produce 100% of one gametic type, while heterozygotes produce 1:1 ratios of the two alleles they carry (see Figure 11.19).

Genetics of Paternity

The inference involved in using genetic loci or characters known to be inherited in a simple Mendelian fashion to test for the possibility of parentage is the reverse of the reasoning involved in predicting offspring frequencies when parental genotypes are both known. Consider the child whose mother is known to be homozygous MM, as is the child (see Figure 11.20). The father of this child must have produced a sperm cell carrying the M allele; only homozygous MM or heterozygous MN men can do this. Thus, we know that all NN men are excluded. If the alleged father is NN, his case for not being the father is only as weak as the possibility of mutation, which is usually 1 in a million or less but may be higher for VNTR/STR loci. MM and MN men could be the father. Given an alleged father who is either MM or MN, we may wish to estimate the likelihood that someone else is the father. One way of phrasing the answer to this question is to ask, "What percentage of all men carry an M allele and could be the father ?". The answer is simply the frequency of M in the population. In this case, 45% of all men are excluded, because they are NN and do not carry an M allele; 55% of all men, however, could have fathered this MM child. What we have just done for paternity determination or, more properly, paternity estimation may be formalized in terms of another law of genetics. In this case, we are working in the subdiscipline of population genetics rather than Mendelian genetics. In part B of Figure 11.19 we were able to list the frequencies of offspring genotypes if we knew the parental genotypes. In Mendelian genetics, we examine one mating at a time and predict progeny frequencies. In parentage determination, we work backwards to infer the genotype(s) of possible parents. In population genetics, we consider all possible matings, predict progeny frequencies of all matings, and add these progeny frequencies together to permit specification of genotype frequencies for all the progeny in a population. Referring back to Figure 11.19, we see that there are three possible genotypes — MM, MN, and NN for both males and females. The rules of Mendelian genetics allow

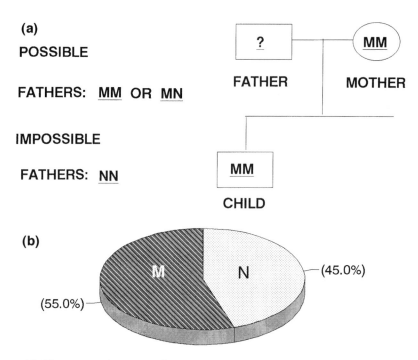

Figure 11.20 Disputed paternity (or maternity): The inference involved in disputed parentage inverts the logic of progeny ratio predictions. Instead of working with the ratios of gametes produced by the parents and multiplying them to predict progeny genotypes, we know the child's genotype and we infer the genotype(s) of unknown parents. The strength of any argument for a particular individuals parentage will depend on the number of genetic tests done and the frequencies of the alleles shared by the child and the disputed parent. In (a), an MM mother and an MM child allow us to confidently conclude that the father of this child must have been capable of producing M sperm. Thus, any MM or MN male could be the father; and all NN males are excluded. The allelic frequencies are presented as a pie diagram and histogram in (b). Since 45% of all the alleles are N, this test eliminates 45% of all males.

us to predict the progeny ratios for each possible mating, and we may predict the frequency of each of the possible matings if we assume that selection of a mate does not depend on our M-N genotype. That is, we are assuming that mate selection occurs at random with respect to this gene. The frequencies of the various matings are given by multiplying the male genotypic array by the female genotypic array:

$$(xMM + yMN + zNN) \text{ males} \times (xMM + yMN + zNN) \text{ females}$$

The predicted progeny ratios for the entire population may be obtained by multiplying the frequency of each type of mating times the expected frequency of progeny for that mating and then adding all the progeny together. When this is done, we see that the allele and genotype frequencies

PARENTAGE TESTING

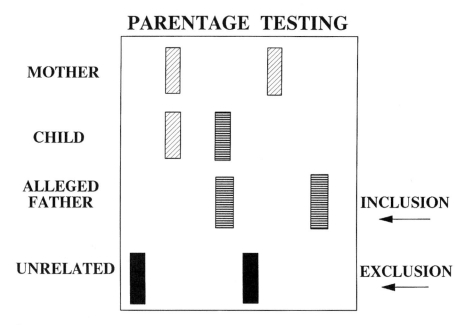

MOTHER

CHILD

**ALLEGED
FATHER**   INCLUSION

UNRELATED   EXCLUSION

Figure 11.21   Parentage testing using DNA: Note that the mother and child share a DNA fragment or band; this was present in the egg at fertilization. The other fragment or band must have come from the father. In other words, the child shares one band with the mother and one band with the father. We may use this basic genetic knowledge together with knowledge of the band frequencies to include or exclude alleged parents. The alleged father is not necessarily the father of this child, but he cannot be excluded. All men who do not carry the nonmaternal allele seen in the child may be excluded. The argument is exactly analogous to that for MM, MN, and NN testing.

of the offspring or progeny are identical to the frequencies of their parents. This is the Hardy-Weinberg Law or the application of the multinomial distribution to genetics. RFLP/DNA presents the same scenario as above and is very simple to see (see Figure 11.21).

Hardy-Weinberg Law and the Multiplication Rule

Applying the Hardy-Weinberg Law to real situations, using real data, often involves the calculation of genotype frequencies from allele frequency data. This is referred to as the application of the product rule, and use of the product rule involves the assumption that alleles combine at random. In other words, we are multiplying allele or gamete frequencies to predict genotype or offspring frequencies. This will be a valid procedure only if we can show to a reasonable approximation that some alleles are not found together in offspring more or less frequently than they would be if drawn at random. The situation is analogous to coin tossing or die rolling. Two fair, two-sided coins may be tossed and the percentage of times in which they both come up heads (H,H), they come up head and tail (H,T or T,H), or they both come up tails (T,T) is predicted by squaring the sum of head-plus-tail probabilities:

$$(H + T)^2 = (0.5 + 0.5)^2 = 0.25 \text{ H,H} + 0.50 \text{ H,T} + 0.25 \text{ T,T}$$

This expression is a convenient method for combining single events into double events. A number of points are worth noting. The possible outcomes, head or tail, must all be included within the parentheses, because we are expressing the combinations of all single events. In genetics, this means all the alleles in a population must be included. If there were six alleles, rather than two, dice would be a more appropriate analogy: $(p+q+r+s+t+u)^2 = p^2 + 2pq + \ldots + u^2$. Also, all possible outcomes must add to one. If this is not true, all possibilities have not been accounted for. In genetics, this means that all of the alleles must be represented. For example, we cannot predict ABO genotypes with an allelic expression which excludes the frequency of an allele.

The probabilities or frequencies within the parentheses are haploid or allele frequencies; those on the right-hand side of the expression are combinations of alleles — one from each of the parents — or genotypes. Thus, multiplying the two expressions is the mathematical equivalent of fertilization or the random union of two gametes.

The power of these expressions is always 2, no matter how many alleles are present, because we always have just two biological parents. In some cases involving relatively few alleles, it is relatively easy to test the assumption of allelic independence before multiplying allele frequencies to predict genotype percentages. Sample sizes must be fairly large, however, and the test will not detect small departures from allelic independence. If large numbers of alleles are involved, independence must still be tested, but the tests are not quite so simple. The value of the Hardy-Weinberg Equilibrium Law in forensic identifications is chiefly found in genetic systems with a great many alleles. Similar arguments hold for the use of many loci or genes with fewer alleles. Here, the independence of alleles across the relevant loci is the issue. As the arguments are similar, although somewhat more complicated, they will not be considered here. The relationship between the number of alleles, n, and number of genotypes, G, is:

$$G = n(n+1)/2$$

Loci such as the MN locus with two alleles will have two homozygous genotypes, MM and NN; there is one for each allele. There is only one heterozygous genotype in this two allele case, MN. Other loci may have far more alleles, for example the DQ alpha locus as used in forensic labs has six alleles and $(6 \times 7) \div 2$, or 21 genotypes (see Figure 11.22). Other loci used

**21 POSSIBLE COMBINATIONS OF 6 (SIX) DIFFERENT
ALLELES**

(1.1, 1.2 , 1.3,   2,   3,   4)

1. 1.1, 1.1   12. 1.3, 1.3

2. 1.1, 1.2   13. 1.3, 2

3. 1.1, 1.3   14. 1.3, 3

4. 1.1, 2   15. 1.3, 4

5. 1.1, 3   16. 2, 2

6. 1.1, 4   17. 2, 3

7. 1.2, 1.2   18. 2, 4

8. 1.2, 1.3   19. 3, 3

9. 1.2, 2   20. 3, 4

10. 1.2, 3   21. 4, 4

11. 1.2, 4

Figure 11.22   The number of genotypes is predictable from the number of alleles, $G = n(n+1)/2$: Since the number of genotypes is related to the number of alleles as a product, $n(n+1)$, an increase in the number of alleles produces a very rapid increase in the number of genotypes. The familiar ABO blood group locus has three alleles A,B, and O; this means that there are six, $(3 \times 4) \div 2$ genotypes. There are six alleles at the DQalpha locus, 1.1, 1.2, 1.3, 2, 3, and 4. This locus produces 21 genotypes, $(6 \times 7) \div 2$. Note that the number of alleles has doubled from three ABO to six DQalpha, but the number of genotypes has more than tripled. The 21 DQalpha genotypes and estimates of their frequencies in three commonly identified groups of humans are tabulated. (Figure courtesy of FBI Laboratory.)

in forensic labs may have 30 or more alleles with in excess of $(30 \times 31) \div 2$, or 465 genotypes. Why is the Hardy-Weinberg Law important? In the section on Elimination or Inclusion, we used the three genotypes of the phospho-glucomutase locus to illustrate probability of identity, P_I, and power of discrimination, P_D, calculations. Three points are obvious when we begin to consider P_I and P_D in the light of allele and genotype numbers:

1.   Because all the alleles add up to 100% and all the genotypes add up to 100%, loci with more alleles or genotypes are more useful in identifying or discriminating among individuals. Two equally frequent alleles will be present at frequencies of 50%, and genotype frequencies will be equal to or less than 50%. Ten equally frequent alleles, however, will be present at frequencies of 10%. The most common of the 55 genotypes will be found at frequencies of only 2% (that is, $2 \times .1 \times .1$).

2.   Since the number of genotypes increases exponentially with the number of alleles, genotypes will be more useful in identification and discrimination.
3.   The use of the Hardy-Weinberg Law allows labs to build databases of reasonable size — a few hundred individuals.

These may be used to predict genotype frequencies if the assumption of independence is tested. How does this genetic information relate to P_I, P_D, fingerprinting, and identification by physical description? Identification is based on two elements: character variability and variant frequencies. Identification techniques which use more variants of lower frequency are more powerful discriminators and identifiers. For example, the accuracy of the Bertillon system will increase if we increase the number of foot-size classes used to classify people. Similar arguments may be made for all other identification systems, but the increased powers of discrimination or inclusion are easier to document and quantify for genetically based systems. This is because of the simple, exponential relationship between the number of alleles and the number of genotypes, as well as the ability to estimate Hardy-Weinberg genotype frequencies from databases containing adequate data on allele frequencies.

This principle (use characters with the maximum number of forms of known frequency) has been used in forensic serology for many years in analyzing serum proteins. Most serum proteins, however, have relatively few alleles. This means that comparisons of evidentiary samples with a suspect's samples allows only two conclusions: one, firm exclusion, and the other, probabilistic inclusion.

1.   The evidentiary sample and the suspect's sample do not match. For example, an evidentiary PGM-1 does not match an evidentiary PGM-2. Thus, the evidentiary material could not have come from the suspect.
2.   The evidentiary and suspect's sample match. For example, an evidentiary PGM-1 matches a suspect's PGM-1. Thus, this evidentiary material *could* have originated from the suspect's body. The judicial weight of this inclusion will, of course, depend on the commonness or rarity of PGM-1 individuals.

Statement one, given an accurate chain of custody and an accurate PGM test, is an absolute. The two enzyme phenotypes could not have come from the same individual. The suspect is excluded unambiguously as the source of the evidentiary material. Statement two includes the suspect as a possible source of the evidence, but the power of this inclusion — the weight of this evidence — depends on the frequency of PGM-1 in the population. If PGM-1 phenotypes are found in the population at a frequency of 25%, we may make a number of interpretive statements about this match. None of these statements is an absolute, and the size of the inclusion percentage prohibits the serologist from saying that the suspect is, within the limits of scientific accuracy, the source of the evidentiary material. The serologist can say:

1. If the suspect was not the person from whom the evidentiary material originated, he/she had a 3:1 chance (75%:25%) of being excluded by this test. The chance that individuals who were not the source of the evidence will be included is 25%.
2. Although one person is the source of the evidence, 25% of the population has a PGM-1 phenotype. They will all match. In a population of 1 million, 250,000 will be PGM-1 matches.

In order to use matches for identification, inclusion probabilities must exceed the population size.

Certainly, standing alone, these PGM-1 numbers are not very convincing. To increase the power of discrimination, P_D, results from a number of serological tests of inherited and variable characteristics are combined to produce multi-locus or multi-gene matches. It is well worth noting that this is not necessary for nonmatches; a single nonmatch on a valid test is an exclusion. The probabilities or inclusion odds calculated for combined tests use the product rule; that is, phenotype frequencies for each test match are multiplied to estimate the frequency of the multi-locus phenotype. For matches involving five or six tests, odds in the range of 1:1000 are often generated. By doing more and more tests, the odds could theoretically be extended into ranges of 1 in a million or 1 in a billion. Two limitations of serological protein assay have prevented this extension to more tests: (1) an insufficient number of forensically useful assays is available, and (2) most cases do not involve sufficient evidentiary material to run 20 to 40 tests. These limitations confined serologists to match conclusions phrased in "failure to exclude" terms until the mid 1980s. In 1985, Alec Jeffreys introduced the use of DNA for the identification and exclusion of humans; he dubbed the multilocus technique he used "DNA fingerprinting".[26,33,34,35] As we have emphasized, both classic fingerprinting introduced by Francis Galton in the last century and DNA typing depend on variability and knowledge of the frequencies of the different variables. In fingerprinting, the variables are classified as arch, loop, and whorl; each of these types exists in a certain percentage of the population. Knowing that a fingerprint is an arch does not allow matching to another fingerprint on file. It does allow us to eliminate all loop and whorl prints from further consideration, just as PGM nonmatches permit exclusion. Adding additional characteristics such as core or delta focal point permits further exclusion until a unique fingerprint identification is achieved. In DNA fingerprinting, a similar process is followed. A specific and highly variable portion of human DNA is used to highlight DNA from known individuals, say suspects, and the sizes obtained are compared to unknowns, say crime scene evidence. Here the character examined is the size of a specific piece of DNA. This is a particularly useful character, because some sections of our DNA exhibit tremendous variability. Instead of having six to seven hair colors or arch, loop, or whorl fingerprints, a partial DNA typing may involve a character with hundreds of classes or phenotypes, and each of these may be present in only a few percent of all people. Thus, DNA typing identification of an individual depends on exclusion of others, as does the theoretical possibility of protein serological typing. The difference is that DNA is by far the most powerful exclusionary technique available to the forensic scientist, because the vast number of DNA fragment sizes or alleles and the limited amount of evidentiary material required to perform a number of tests makes these tests a reality, not just a possibility.

The National DNA Identification Index (CODIS) Is being Applied to Solve Cases, Especially Violent Crime Investigations

To take full advantage of the power of a technology such as DNA, the FBI is developing a national DNA identification index. It consists of a population file, a forensic index, a convicted offender index, and a missing person index. The population file consists of anonymous DNA profiles and assist local laboratories in the statistical interpretation of DNA profiles that are generated from casework. The forensic index consists of profiles derived from forensic crime-scene body fluid stains, such as blood and semen. When a DNA profile is obtained from a crime-scene body fluid stain, for example, in which no suspect has been identified, the convicted offender index and the forensic index would be queried. The DNA laboratory will search against the forensic index to associate the case under investigation with any other case, nationwide. The result can be the detection of association with other cases without suspects or associations with cases in which a suspect has been identified. The leads generated from these searches would allow police officers in multiple jurisdictions to coordinate their respective investigations.

The convicted offender index contains DNA profiles derived from blood samples collected from individuals convicted of crimes or otherwise eligible for inclusion according to state statute. At this time, 24 states have enacted legislation requiring individuals convicted of certain crimes to provide blood samples for DNA profiling. There are currently over 80,000 DNA records of convicted offenders in eight states that have been running RFLP/VNTR profiles of these individuals.

The first case solved in the U.S. by searching convicted offender DNA records was a rape/murder in Minnesota in 1991. The DNA profile from the crime scene semen was searched against the approximately 1200 convicted offender DNA records on file at the Minnesota Bureau of Criminal Apprehension (MBCA). A suspect was identified, arrested, and convicted. Another case, from the Metro-Dade County Police Department, Miami, Florida, was solved by linking DNA crime-scene evidence with an unknown suspect to evidence from another rape case already solved by police; the suspect plead guilty to both crimes. These are merely the first examples of the power of this type of database.

Another powerful use of this system will be assisting investigators in the identification of an unidentified person. In the case of small children recovered alive or dead, or an unidentified murder victim, the identity of the victim will be established and the investigation would then proceed.

Quality Control and Quality Assurance have the Greatest Impact on the Forensic Serologist as the Presentation of this Evidence in Court has such a Powerful Impact on the Jury's Decision of Guilt or Innocence of a Suspect

The following question may be the most appropriate from a scientific and legal standpoint. Have quality control and quality assurance controls been worked out for the procedures you are using? Quality control allows the serologist to be sure that the result he or she obtains is precise and accurate. In recent years, forensic science has been under scrutiny by the press, the courts, and the scientific community through several processes such as proficiency testing and certification of examiners. The most important kind of quality control is the individual analyst. The following represents the best personal quality control that a scientist can have. When you form a conclusion, ask yourself the following:

Have I tried to prove the opposite?
Have I worked as hard to find dissimilarities as similarities?
Have I made notes of my observations and not just my conclusions?
Can I demonstrate my findings to others?
Do the elements in the questioned material stand on their own?
Have I obtained an independent verification of my results?[36]

Acknowledgments

The authors wish to thank Maria Aloya, Dr. Roger Kahn of the Metro Dade Police Crime Laboratory and Dr. Dan Garner, President of Cellmark Diagnostics, U.S.A., for reviewing this chapter and providing extremely valuable suggestions and comments. We would also like to thank Sgt. Bob Haarer of the Broward Sheriff's Office Crime Scene Section and Sandra Sovinski of the Indianapolis-Marion County Forensic Services Agency for their artistic craftsmanship on many of the figures.

References

1. M. Farley and J. Harrington, Eds., *Forensic DNA Technology* (Lewis Publishers, New York, 1991).

2. K. E. Boorman and B. E. Dodd, *An Introduction to Blood Group Serology* (Churchill Livingstone, Edinburgh, 4th ed. 1970).

3. O. Prokop and G. Uhlenbruck, *Human Blood and Serum Groups* (Wiley Interscience, New York, 1969).

4. B. J. Culliford, *The Examination and Typing of Bloodstains in the Crime Laboratory* (U.S. Department of Justice, Washington, D.C., 1971).

5. R. Saferstein, Ed., *Forensic Science Handbook*, vol. I (Prentice Hall, Englewood Cliffs, NJ, 1982).

6. L. Presley, personal communication, FBI Laboratory (1994).

7. R. Saferstein, Ed., *Forensic Science Handbook*, vol. III (Regents/Prentice Hall, Englewood Cliffs, NJ, 1993).

8. K. B. Mullis, F. Ferre, R. A. Gibbs, Eds., *The Polymerase Chain Reaction* (Birkhauser, Boston, 1994).

9. M. M. Holland et al., *J. Forensic Sci.*, 38, 542 (1993).

10. M. Stoneking et al., *Nature Genetics*, 9, 9 (1995).

11. R. E. Gaensslen, *Sourcebook in Forensic Serology, Immunology, and Biochemistry* (U.S. Department of Justice, National Institute of Justice, Washington, D.C., 1983).

12. R. Saferstein, Ed., *Forensic Science Handbook*, vol. II (Prentice Hall, Englewood Cliffs, NJ, 1988).

13. C. A. Villee et al., *Biology* (Saunders College Publishing, Philadelphia, 2nd ed., 1989).

14. J. D. Watson et al., *Molecular Biology of the Gene* (Benjamin/Cummings Publishing Company, Menlo Park, CA, 4th ed., 1987).

15. R. J. MacIntyre, Ed., *Molecular Evolutionary Genetics* (Plenum Press, New York, 1985).

16. M. Singer and P. Berg, *Genes and Genomes* (University Science Books, Mill Valley, CA, 1991).

17. B. Budowle et al., *Crime Lab. Dig.,* 18, 9 (1991).

18. Cellmark Diagnostics, DNA Fingerprinting, The Ultimate Identification Test, Germantown, MD (1992).

19. E. Kanter et al., *J. Forensic Sci.,* 31, 403 (1986).

20. A. Giusti et al., *J. Forensic Sci.,* 31, 409 (1986).

21. E. Southern, *J. Mol. Biol.,* 98, 503 (1975).

22. R. K. Saiki et al., *Science,* 260, 1350 (1985).

23. H. Erlich, *Principles and Applications for Forensic Amplification* (Stockton Press, Stockton, 1989).

24. J. C. S. Fowler et al., *J. Forensic Sci.,* 33, 1111 (1988).

25. H. G. Brunner et al., *Am. J. Hum. Genet.,* 52, 1032 (1993).

26. A. J. Jeffreys, V. Wilson, S. L. Thein, *Nature,* 314, 67 (1985).

27. L. T. Kirby, *DNA Fingerprinting, An Introduction* (Stockton Press, New York, 1990).

28. B. Budowle et al., *J. Forensic Sci.,* 35, 530 (1990).

29. D. Botstein et al., *Am. J. Hum. Genet.* 32, 314 (1980).

30. J. C. Avise, in *Ann. Rev. Genet.,* 25, 45 (1991).

31. A. J. Jeffreys and R. Neumann, V. Wilson, *Cell,* 60, 473 (1990).

32. J. Zonderman, *Beyond the Crime Lab* (John Wiley & Sons, New York, 1990).

33. A. J. Jeffreys and J. F. Y. Brookfield, R. Semeonoff, *Nature,* 317, 818 (1985).

34. J. Wambaugh, *The Blooding,* Bantam Books, New York (1989).

35. A. J. Jeffreys and J. F. Y. Brookfield, R. Semeonoff, *Nature,* 322, 290 (1986).

36. W. C. Smith, *Am. Assoc. Firearm Toolmark Examiners J.,* 25, 260 (1993).

Forensic Odontology

12

MARK BERNSTEIN

Introduction

Forensic odontology can be defined as the application of dental expertise to the legal system. The term *forensic dentistry* is used synonymously. The scope of forensic odontology includes:

1. Identification of unknown decedents by the teeth, jaws, and cranio-facial bones
2. Bite-mark investigation
3. Analysis of oro-facial trauma associated with person abuse
4. Dental jurisprudence, including expert witness testimony

Forensic dental services are of value both in death investigations and in clinical forensic medicine for evaluation of living victims of sexual assault, child abuse, and other domestic violence.

Historic Milestones in Forensic Dentistry

The sovereign science of forensic odontology is descended from rather inauspicious beginnings in antiquity. It is said that the first dental identification was made between 49 and 66 A.D. when Agrippina, the jealous wife of Roman Emperor Claudius, demanded the disembodied head of her husband's mistress, Lollia Paulina. A discolored anterior tooth or malocclusion served to confirm her identity.[1,2] An alternative story credits Sabina, Nero's mistress, as the victorious forensic odontologist who examined the severed head of her rival.[3] In any event, neither of the two women is likely to be remembered as the mother of forensic odontology. Folklore also ascribes the first use of bite-mark identification to King William the Conqueror, circa 1066 A.D., whose habit it was to secure his mail with sealing wax imprinted with his bite. His anterior teeth were malaligned, thus allowing verification of authenticity of his documents.[2]

0-8493-8101-0/97/$0.00+$.50
© 1997 by CRC Press, Inc.

Sporadic notations of forensic dental triumphs dot the pages of recorded history. The following provides an incomplete list of famous moments in forensic dentistry.

1453 — First formally reported dental identification. Fallen soldier, John Talbot (Earl of Shrewsbury), was identified following the battle of Castillon.[4]

1692 — First bitemark case in a criminal trial. Reverend George Burroughs was accused of witchcraft in Salem, Massachusetts. Bitemarks on the wrists of a female acquaintance were claimed to be his. The fact that Burroughs was imprisoned when the bitemarks appeared was not an adequate defense (for a witch) and Burroughs was hanged.[5] The case did little to advance bite-mark science.

1776 — First dental identification by the dental profession.[6] Dentist-patriot, Paul Revere, identified his friend and patient, Dr. Joseph Warren, who was killed in the battle of Bunker Hill and interred in an unmarked grave. The exhumed body was identified by a prosthesis recognized by Revere.[7]

1914 — First dental identification in a criminal case.[6] Mrs. McAlister's body was robbed from the grave. This common practice in 19th century Scotland supplied corpses for medical school anatomy class. The identification was confirmed by Mrs. McAlister's dentist, who fit her newly constructed denture on the maxillary ridge of the corpse. Subsequently, his conclusion was proven incorrect.

1837 — Dr. Edwin Saunders established the eruption sequence of teeth as the criteria to determine the legal age of children for England's child labor laws.[8]

1849 — First dental evidence admitted into a U.S. court.[7] Identification of the incinerated remains of Dr. George Parkman was made by Dr. Nathan Cooley Keep, (later appointed first Dean of Harvard Dental School). Dr. Keep recognized a partial denture fabricated for his patient and fit the prosthesis onto Dr. Parkman's cast. This resulted in the conviction and execution of Dr. J. W. Webster for murder.[7]

1878 — First mass disaster in which dental evidence was used to make identifications: fire at the Vienna Opera House.[9]

1897 — Fire at the Bazar de La Charite in Paris; 126 perished, some of whom were identified by dental means. This resulted in the first textbook of forensic dentistry (*L'Art Dentaire en Medecine Legale*) by Dr. Oscar Amoedo, considered the father of forensic odontology.

1952 — First U.S. bite-mark case resulting in a conviction: Doyle vs. Texas. Doyle was convicted of burglary based on his bitemark in partly eaten cheese found at the scene.

1950s — Increasing use of dental identification as a result of World War II, the Korean War, and mass disasters.

1970s — Formal international and American organizations in forensic dentistry were established. Judicial acceptance of bite-mark evidence burgeoned in American courts.

1980s — Computer programs were designed for forensic dentistry, particularly for mass disasters, war casualties and national tracking of missing persons and unidentified dead.

1990s — Organized forensic dentistry develops and formalizes guidelines and standards for identification, bite-mark management and mass disasters. There is increasing emphasis and awareness of dentistry's role in domestic violence (child, spouse and elder abuse).

Famous and notorious figures identified through forensic dentistry: John Wilkes Booth, Adolf Hitler, Martin Bormann, Eva Braun, Joseph Mengele, Lee Harvey Oswald, Czar Nicholas II and family.

Current Forensic Dentistry

Today, forensic dentistry enjoys an active role in the forensic sciences. Organizations in forensic dentistry have promoted education and research and have set guidelines in the discipline. These organizations also award credentials which recognize various levels of achievement and competence among forensic odontologists. The American Society of Forensic Dentistry was founded in 1970. It accepts as members anyone interested in forensic dentistry. The society holds its organizational and educational meeting each February to coincide with the annual meeting of the American Academy of Forensic Sciences (AAFS). The society also publishes a quarterly newsletter.

The AAFS is comprised of all of the disciplines of the forensic sciences. Various levels of affiliation include provisional member, member, and fellow. To be considered for membership in the Odontology section, a dental degree is required. Five years of membership and participation in the Academy are prerequisites for fellowship status. Similar organizations exist in Canada, England, and Scandinavia, as does the International Society for Forensic Odonto-stomatology.[1]

The American Board of Forensic Odontology was established in 1976 and is sponsored by the AAFS. The Board functions to advance the science of forensic dentistry and certify qualified experts, designated as Diplomates. In order to be eligible to take the Board examination, dentists must have completed a prescribed 5-year apprenticeship in forensic dentistry including educational requirements, a formal affiliation with a medicolegal agency, and active membership in an acceptable forensic dental organization.

Forensic Dentistry in the Medicolegal System

A medicolegal agency should anticipate the need for forensic dental services and should secure a consultant before the need arises. While it is true that many general dentists potentially have the requisite skills to render an opinion in a simple identification case, reliance on such a dentist can create problems. Many dentists are unwilling to become involved in death investigations due to the unpleasant nature of these cases or the stresses and obligations of the legal system. Others may not be able to accommodate unscheduled requests for services during office hours. More significantly, an untrained dentist cannot be expected to analyze a difficult identification or bite-mark case. Gustafson cites multiple instances of mistaken identities concluded by dentists untrained in forensic dentistry.[9] The forensic dentist must have an understanding of forensic pathology, anthropology, forensic medical and legal protocol, evidence photography, and management. Final reports must reflect this knowledge and must be complete and accurate so as to reconstruct cases and withstand legal scrutiny. Lastly, the forensic dentist must appreciate his or her ethical role as an objective and unbiased analyst.

In selecting a dentist with interest and skills in forensic odontology, a medicolegal administrator may contact any of the above-listed organizations for a membership roster. A dental school or local dental society can provide names of interested individuals. Most forensic dentists serve as sporadic consultants on a fee-for-service basis. Some large jurisdictions have created salaried staff positions for an odontologist.

Human Dentition

The adult human dentition consists of 32 teeth arranged in two arches, one arch in the upper or maxillary jaw and one in the lower or mandibular jaw. Since the arches are symmetrical, each quadrant contains the same number and type of teeth, as follows: 2 incisors, 1 cuspid, 2 premolars, and 3 molars. Incisors are the wide, front teeth with flat, thin biting edges. The cuspid or "eye tooth" is at the corner of the arch and has a pointed cusp. Each premolar typically has two cusps. The molars have 3 to 5 cusps and a wide biting

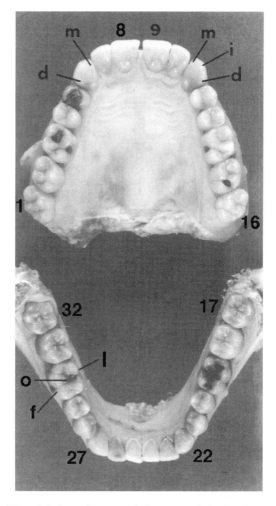

Figure 12.1 Resected jaws showing a complete dentition, #1-32 by the Universal System. Surfaces shown: m-mesial, d-distal, o-occlusal, i-incisal, l-lingual, f-facial. Note fillings in teeth #3, 5, 14, 15, 19, and 30.

surface to chew and crush food. The third molar or wisdom tooth is the last tooth in the arch (Figure 12.1).

Each tooth has a crown and a root. The crown is the visible portion that protrudes above the gum. The root is embedded into a socket in the jaw (Figure 12.2). Incisors and cuspids each have a single root. Premolars have 1 or 2 roots and molars usually have 2 or 3 roots.

The crown of the tooth is capped by enamel, the hardest tissue of the human body. Under the enamel is dentin, which comprises the bulk of the crown and root. Unlike enamel, dentin is alive and capable of transmitting pain. In the center of the tooth is a cylindrical canal of soft tissue called the pulp. It functions to sense pain and, throughout life, slowly produces dentin which narrows the diameter of the pulp canal as the individual ages. The root is surrounded by a thin layer of bone-like tissue called cementum.

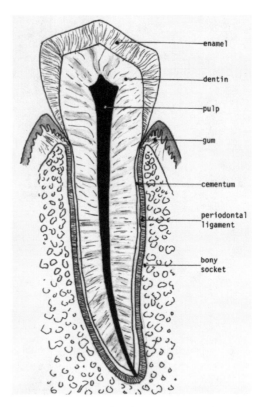

enamel

dentin

pulp

gum

cementum

periodontal ligament

bony socket

Figure 12.2   A tooth within its bony socket.

Fibrous tissue called the periodontal ligament holds the tooth in the jaws because it is embedded into both the cementum and the bony socket wall (Figure 12.1).

By convention in the U.S., dentists identify individual teeth by the Universal System which numbers the teeth from 1 to 32 starting at the upper right third molar across to the upper left third molar and then continuing with the lower left third molar and concluding with the lower right third molar (Figure 12.1). Each number refers to a specific tooth bearing its own specific anatomy. Even though some teeth look alike, a dentist can examine an isolated, extracted tooth and determine its correct number in most cases. Other countries use different tooth numbering systems.

Children have 20 teeth called deciduous or primary teeth. They have no premolars and no third molars. These teeth begin to erupt at the age of 6 months and are completely erupted by 2½ years. Primary teeth are lost and replaced by the permanent teeth starting at age 6 or 7. In the Universal System, primary teeth are designated by letters A through T.

The surfaces of teeth are named as follows: the surface which faces outward toward the face, lips, and cheeks is called facial, labial, or buccal. The surface facing inward toward the tongue is termed lingual. The biting surface is called incisal when referring to the front teeth and occlusal when applied to premolars or molars. The side of the tooth facing the midline is called mesial, and the side away from the midline is distal (see Figure 12.1). Familiarity with these terms and the tooth numbering system will facilitate understanding of the text to follow.

Dental Identification

The Need to Identify

The identity of most decedents in an organized and stable society can be accounted for. This is particularly true for victims of natural disease where death occurs in a hospital, institution, or home. In these cases, identity is known beforehand and can be visually verified by friends and relatives. However, in unexpected or unnatural deaths and in deaths away from home, these proximal linkages might be lost. Physically destructive forces and delayed recovery of corpses can obviate visual identification. This is magnified in war and mass disasters. Even a viewable body is not visually identifiable if there are no suspects or no one who recognizes the body.

The identification of the dead is imperative in society. The reasons are both humanitarian and legal. Humanity demands the dignity of identification of its dead and proper interment according to religion and family wishes. More compelling is the anguish shared by the living relatives and friends of missing persons that remain unidentified after being found dead. Legal problems exist for these families. A death certificate is not issued on a missing person for a period of up to 7 years or longer.[2,10] This time must elapse before wills are probated, life insurance benefits are paid, business matters and law suits are settled, and remarriages are sanctioned. Before a coroner or medical examiner disposes of an unidentified remains, it should be remembered that failure to record the dental findings might permanently prevent an identification and remove all hope for a family to learn the disposition of a vanished loved one. Lastly, in a homicide, identification of the corpse helps direct the investigation and is usually necessary for charging a suspect with the crime.

Methods of Identification

Visual recognition by acquaintances and reliance on personal effects are the common, practical means of identifying the dead. However, these methods are subject to error. Facial alterations seen with rigor mortis, early decomposition, or animal predation can obscure visual appearance. Deliberate misidentification can be fraudulent and associated with homicide and financial gain. Borrowed or stolen possessions can result in erroneous identifications if personal effects are used. Scientific methods of identification such as fingerprint, dental, and DNA techniques eliminate concerns of criminal or accidental misidentification since they are objective, valid, and reliable. Thus, any competent investigator, applying the techniques will reach the same correct conclusion.

Scientific Basis for Dental Identification

In order for bodily features to qualify as scientific identifiers, they must fulfil three requirements: they must confer uniqueness, they must be stable, and they must be prerecorded as belonging to a known individual. The identification can then be made by comparing the features to the known record. The teeth easily fulfil the requirement of uniqueness. Each of the 32 teeth has five surfaces that accommodate decay or various types of fillings. Any number of these teeth may also be missing. The combinations and permutations of missing, decayed, and filled teeth are effectively limitless. Persons without fillings or extractions still show characterization in the anatomy of their teeth and jaws. Additionally, the soft tissue elevations on the anterior palate (rugae), the furrow patterns of the lip mucosa, and radiographic morphology of the frontal sinuses are sufficiently characteristic to establish identity (Figures 12.3 and 12.4). Even edentulous individuals show distinctive radiographic anatomy of the jaw bone, while denture teeth can be distinguished by shade, size, pattern, manufacturer, and composition. These characteristics can be detected by the forensic dentist and matched to dental records.

The stability of the dento-facial structure is well known. Teeth are among the most durable human tissues after death, surviving decomposition, mutilation, and the most intense fires. Even prehistoric human remains retain the dentition.

The last requirement for a scientific method is a source of antemortem information. Most Americans have been seen by a dentist and have a record of their dentition. This may be in the form of written records, X-rays, dental models, and, occasionally, close-up photographs.

Through the National Crime Information Center (NCIC) computer, dental data can be entered on missing persons and unidentified dead. In this way, a John or Jane Doe inquiry can spark a "cold hit" on a missing person entered elsewhere. This establishes the potential for dental identification even when there is no known putative victim for comparison. Systems similar to NCIC operate at the state level in some jurisdictions.

Comparison of Dental Identification to other Scientific Methods

Each scientific method has its own advantages, disadvantages, and applicability. No one technique is "best", and each, in its proper setting, can ensure unconditional proof of identity.

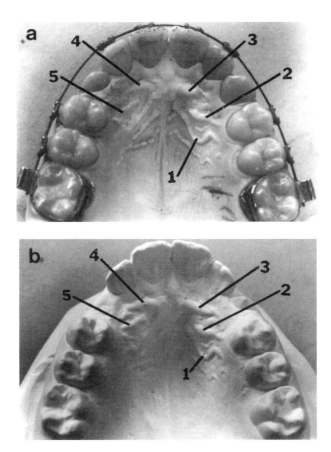

Figure 12.3 Postmortem jaw specimen (a) showing five rugal ridges that correspond to the five ridges seen in an antemortem dental mold (b).

Fingerprint identification (dactyloscopy) has been used for over 100 years. The human friction ridges are unchanging throughout life, and there has not been duplication of any two sets of prints. The FBI stores prints in a central clearinghouse where they are coded and catalogued for easy retrieval and comparison to a suspect. A "cold hit" (identifying an unknown individual) via fingerprint files is possible but can be a laborious procedure.

There are two distinct disadvantages of fingerprints. Less than 25% of the U.S. population has fingerprint records on file.[11] These are mainly individuals who have taken a military physical examination, work in a security position, or have been arrested for felony offenses. Effectively, about 80% of U.S. population is excluded for possible fingerprint identification. This represents a change from two decades ago when 80% of American men over the age of 18 and 50% of women had fingerprint records.[12] Dactyloscopy is also precluded if the palmar skin is destroyed by fire, decomposition, or mutilation.

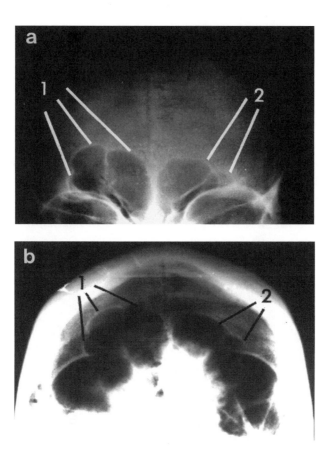

Figure 12.4   Postmortem X-ray (a) showing a series of humps in the right and left frontal sinuses that correspond to the humps in an antemortem X-ray (b).

The dental method is not without disadvantages. Dental records are dispersed throughout dental offices across the country and can be more difficult to locate than fingerprint records stored in a central repository. Additionally, there is no standardization of dental records. Records may be inadequate and written entries are subject to error. Another shortcoming of teeth is that they can be altered (decayed, filled, or extracted) after the last antemortem entry.

Practically speaking, in today's society there is greater opportunity to make a dental match than a fingerprint identification. This is because of the superior resistance of dental structures to destruction and the greater bank of antemortem dental records.

DNA comparisons may well prove to be the most reliable and useful method of identification in the future. DNA is a stable molecule and can survive decomposition when contained within bones and teeth. There must be a sample for comparison, such as a retained antemortem blood smear or tissue from known relatives. Of particular use is mitochondrial DNA which is practically identical in all siblings and maternal relatives. At present, DNA analysis is expensive.

When a Dental Identification Is Needed

Currently, dental identification represents the most useful of the scientific methods under the following conditions:

1. Decomposing remains
2. Skeletonized remains
3. Charred remains
4. Intact remains in which there is no putative victim (Doe identification)
5. When the need for scientific verification of identity is anticipated (homicide, large insurance settlement)
6. Whenever multiple bodies are recovered from a common location to assure correct sorting
7. Mass disasters

From the perspective of the medicolegal authority, dental identifications can be divided into those in which there is an initial presumption of identity based on personal effects or a locally missing person and those offering no clue of identity.

Examples of the former situation might be burned remains in a house or car fire, a clothed skeleton with a wallet, or a drowned body found after a report of a recently missing swimmer. In such cases, a confirmatory identification is needed. The process is expedited because a search for dental records can be directed at the named suspect and instituted immediately. In my experience, there are rarely surprises in confirmatory identifications; the presumed victim is generally the decedent. This fact should not lull the investigator into dispensing with a scientific verification of identity. Reliance on personal effects and circumstantial assumptions may be a statistically good bet but it is a gamble nevertheless and the stakes are too high to court a negligent decision.

At the other end of the spectrum are the human remains found with no clue to identity and in the absence of any missing local people. Such a body may represent any of 200,000 missing persons reported annually or may be the residue of unresolved cases from past years. Also included are illegal aliens, drifters, runaways, prostitutes, or fugitives who have not been reported missing. In such John or Jane Doe cases, a reconstructive dental examination is performed initially which seeks to gain clues about the decedent that, along with other physical features, help profile the victim for a press release or NCIC computer entry. If this step helps to locate a record, a comparison can be attempted.

Reconstructive Dental Determinations

When there is no suspect for a comparison, the teeth can help to determine a person's age, gender, race, occupation, habits, and socio-economic status. This may help narrow the search for a victim or corroborate a proposed victim.

Age Determination

The teeth develop in a regular and sequential manner until the age of 15 years, permitting an age estimation within 1 year. The dentition offers better precision than any other anthropologic measurement during this period of development. The deciduous dentition begins to develop during the 6th week of intra-uterine life. Mineralization of these teeth begins at 14 ± 2 weeks and continues after birth.[3] The trauma of childbirth induces metabolic stress on the tooth-forming cells. This cellular disruption results in a thin band of altered enamel and dentin called the neonatal line. The neonatal line indelibly inscribes the event of birth into any tooth under-going enamel and dentin apposition at the time. When detected in the remains of an infant, it proves that the child was born alive. Since enamel and dentin form at a relatively fixed daily rate, crude age assessment is theoretically possible in deceased children by measuring the thickness of tooth structure beyond the neonatal line. The permanent dentition begins to calcify at birth, starting with the first molar and continuing until the root of the second molar is complete by age 15 ±1 year. A number of standard references enable age determination based on the clinical or radio-graphic stage of tooth development (see Figure 12.5).[9,14-16] Determination of ages between 15 and 22 years depends on the development of third molars (wisdom teeth) which are the most variable in the dentition. The margin of error falls to ±2 years during this time.[17] After age 22, poster-uptive, degenerative changes are used for aging.[9] These changes are influ-enced by slowly acting pathologic processes and are too variable for most forensic applications. The only posteruptive method that holds promise of precise aging (±1 year) is the quantification of D-aspartic acid.[18] This technique relies on a linear and stable time-related conversion of L-aspartic acid into its D-isomer, which accumulates in metabolically inactive den-tin.[19] Few centers have experience with this fastidious gas chromatographic technique needed to make the determination.

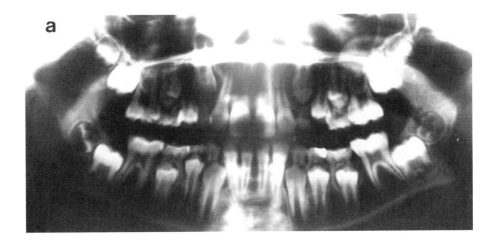

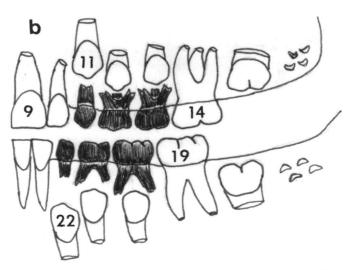

Figure 12.5 Panographic X-ray of a child (a) showing a pattern of tooth eruption and development suggesting an age of 9 years (6-year molars are erupted but root is not fully developed; 12-year molars are unerupted with crown and root trunk formed; all incisors are erupted; deciduous cuspids and molars are not yet lost). Compare to the diagram adapted from Schour and Massler[14] (b) showing the dentition of a 9-year-old.

Gender Determination

The size and shape of teeth are too similar between males and females to allow reliable gender determination. The tooth showing the greatest sexual dimorphism is the mandibular cuspid. Anderson noted that a mesio-distal diameter less than 6.7 mm = female, whereas a measurement greater than 7 mm = male in 74% of cases evaluated.[20] The maxillary cuspids also show

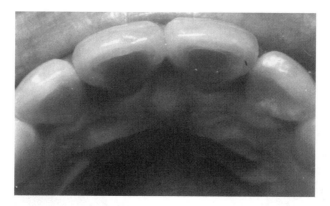

Figure 12.6 Shovel-shaped incisors of a Chinese woman.

sexual differences with root lengths being, on the average, 3 mm longer in males.[21] These measurements are valid only on fully-formed, nonabraded teeth. Dorion has shown that gender could be determined from the mandible by multiplying the distance in centimeters between the tips of the coronoid processes by the external distance between the angles of the jaw.[22] A product over 90 cm is almost invariably male while a product below 78 mm is almost always female. Sex can also be determined from pulp tissue. The long arm of the Y-chromosome shows preferential ultraviolet fluorescence when stained with 0.5% quinacrine dihydrochloride. Unfortunately, the test is neither sensitive nor specific, with incorrect sexing ranging up to 30% in one study.[23] Most recently, DNA probes of the dental pulp have been used to determine gender.

Racial Determination

Racial determination is not reliable on the basis of teeth and jaws, although certain morphologic attributes show statistical differences in frequency between races. No single trait is diagnostic and a cluster of traits more safely predicts race. Table 12.1 lists traits that assist in racial determination.

Table 12.1   Dentognathic Attributes of Race

Mongoloid Features

1. Shovel-shaped incisors — maxillary incisors show a distinct shovel shape in 85 to 99% of Mongoloids.[24] This is attributable to prominent lingual marginal ridges that render a scooped appearance to the lingual contour of the tooth (Figure 12.6). Two to nine percent of Caucasoids and 12% of Negroids show shoveling, although it is less distinct.[24]

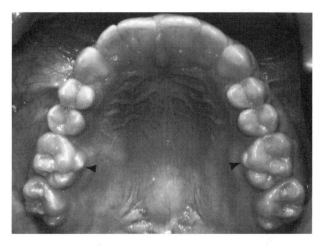

Figure 12.7 Mesiolingual cusps of Carabelli on upper first molars of a Caucasoid individual. Note lack of shovel-shaped incisors.

Table 12.1 (continued) Dentognathic Attributes of Race

2. Protostylid — this accessory cusp appears on the mesio-buccal surface of mandibular first molars and is seen almost exclusively in Pima Indians. Its residua appears as a deep pit common in other Amerindians, Eskimoes, or those with Native American ancestry.[25,26]
3. Dens evaginatus — this accessory tubercle is seen on the occlusal surface of lower premolars in 1 to 4% of Mongoloids.[27]
4. Enamel pearls — these displaced nodules of enamel on the root trunks of molars are more commonly seen in Native Americans and Eskimoes but can be seen in any group.[27]
5. Extra distal roots on mandibular first molars — found in 20% of Mongoloids but in only 1% of Caucasoids.[27]
6. Elliptical maxillary arch with flattened palatal vault.
7. Vertical, wide ascending ramus — blacks and whites have a slanted, pinched ramus.[24]
8. Straight lower border of mandible — blacks and whites have an undulating border.

Caucasoids Features

1. Cusp of Carabelli — this mesio-lingual accessory cusp is found almost exclusively on the maxillary first permanent molar and its deciduous second molar counterpart (Figure 12.7). It may be prominent or reduced to a dimple. Its reported incidence in Caucasoids (35 to 50%) reflects nonuniformity in anatomic criteria used by various investigators. Uncontested is the fact that it is much less frequent in non-Caucasoids, particularly Mongoloids.[28]

Table 12.1 (continued)   Dentognathic Attributes of Race

2. Bucco-lingual flattening of the mandibular second premolars[6]
3. Class II malocclusion with crowded anterior teeth
4. Narrow, elongated, parabolic arch with high-vaulted palate
5. Prominent and bilobate chin — blacks and Mongoloids have a blunt, vertical chin.[24]

Negroid Features

1. 2 to 3 lingual cusps on mandibular first premolar[29]
2. Class III malocclusion more common
3. Open bite more common
4. Wide, hyperbolic arches with narrow palatal vault
5. Bimaxillary protrusion — both the maxillary and mandibular alveolar bone are protruded with incisors slanted labially. Mongoloids and non-Anglo Caucasoids may show this trait but it is more pronounced in the black population.[24] Twenty percent of blacks do not show the trait due to racial interbreeding.[24]
6. Tuberculum intermedium — auxillary lingual cusp between the disto-lingual and mesio-lingual on mandibular first molar.[28]

Essentials of Dental Identification

The sequential steps in the process of dental identification include:

1. Preparation
2. Postmortem examination (oral autopsy)
3. Locating and securing antemortem dental records
4. Comparison of antemortem to postmortem information
5. Conclusion
6. Final report

Preparation

When the dentist is summoned to perform an identification, he or she should be informed as to the nature of the case. Various situations dictate equipment needs and time expenditure. Cases are managed differently at scenes than they are in a morgue or funeral home. Skeletonized, decomposed, and intact remains all call for different protocol. It should be noted that a dentist can perform an identification on a decedent without a license to practice dentistry and is legally protected as long as he or she operates under the umbrella of the authorized agency.[30]

Postmortem Examination

The dentist examines and charts as if on a patient, noting present, missing, filled, and replaced teeth. Characteristics of the gum tissue and jaw relations are recorded and unusual findings and pathologic conditions are documented. Photographs and X-rays will probably be made.

The condition of the head area determines the most feasible way in which to access this data. Luntz and Luntz describe five situations, each presenting special challenges in interpretation and management:[7]

1. Skeletonized remains
2. Decomposing remains
3. Charred remains
4. Mutilated remains
5. Viewable bodies

Skeletonized Remains

Fully skeletonized remains are the easiest to examine, photograph, and X-ray as they are dry, nonodoriferous, portable, and detached from constraining soft tissue. Certain precautions are necessary with skeletonized remains. Dry teeth become brittle and can easily shatter and chip.[7] They should be cushioned in transport. Single-rooted front teeth can fall out of their sockets and be lost (Figure 12.8). In fact, careless recovery of skeletonized remains at the scene often overlooks teeth which have fallen out or jaw fragments dispersed by animals. The head area should always be searched if the jaws are seen to contain empty sockets.[7] If recovered, such teeth should be individually labeled rather than replaced in the sockets.[30,31] The forensic dentist can distinguish postmortem loss and fracture from agonal trauma.

Decomposing Remains

Decomposing remains are difficult to examine *in situ*. The mouth cannot be illuminated and the teeth are covered with debris. It is easy to overlook small or cosmetic fillings under these circumstances. Access is poor for photography and radiography. Since the dentist has but one opportunity to record findings accurately, it is generally agreed that the removal of the jaws is the best way to ensure a complete and accurate examination.[5,7,30,31] Since such bodies are not viewable, this procedure cannot be considered a mutilating process.

The jaws are removed by cutting through the lips and cheeks, thereby exposing the mandible and maxilla for resection with a saw or pruning shears. The resected specimens can now be examined, then placed in 10% formalin or 70% alcohol for fixation, sterilization, and preservation. Later, they can be cleaned and deodorized, articulated, charted, photographed, and X-rayed as easily as skeletal remains.

In examining decomposed remains, one occasionally notes pink teeth (Figure 12.9). This phenomenon represents hemolysis within the pulp with leeching of heme pigment into the porous dentin. It tends to be intensified

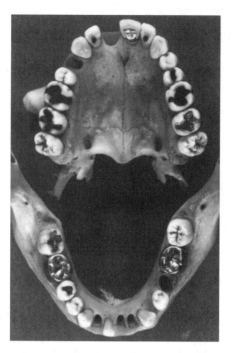

Figure 12.8   Skeletonized jaw specimens showing postmortem loss of teeth #5, 8, 20, 23, 24, 26 as indicated by distinct bony sockets. Note that teeth #17 and 32 were extracted a long time ago and their sockets are healed.

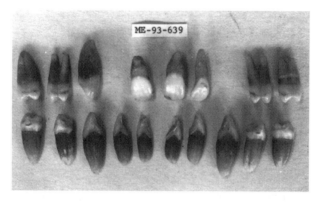

Figure 12.9   Red-pink darkening of the roots of upper and lower premolars, cuspids, and incisors in a victim of strangulation followed by decomposition in a moist environment.

in young people (larger pulp, more porous dentin) and might be accentuated by agonal chronic passive congestion and dependent lividity of the head area, as well as fluidity of cadaveric blood. The pink color is best formed and retained in a moist, dark environment and dissipates in air and sun. Some authors have associated these physiologic changes with cause and manner of death, particularly those related to perimortem head congestion or inhibition of clotting. Accordingly, pink teeth have been ascribed to sudden death, hanging, drowning, asphyxiation, and carbon monoxide poisoning. At this juncture, it is speculative to attribute pink teeth to a particular cause and manner of death.

Charred Remains

Charred remains are the most difficult to examine.[7] Thermally damaged skin and soft tissue becomes hard, dry, contracted, and friable, making access to the dentition difficult. Heat also affects teeth and bone, particularly in the anterior jaws. Rapid exposure to flames causes enamel to exfoliate, leaving rounded cores of dentin, while gradual buildup of heat results in a clean separation of the entire crown at the gumline.[30] Usually, the tongue and cheeks protect the posterior teeth from total destruction even in the most intense fires.

As bone burns it carbonizes, turns black, and brittle, and is easily fractured. Continued combustion oxidizes the carbon until only grey-white inorganic calcium and phosphate, known as calcined bone remains (Figure 12.10a). Burned bone is fragile, but, if handled carefully, its anatomy is preserved and can yield useful X-rays (Figure 12.10b). Teeth are easily lost from sockets of burned bone due to destruction of the periodontal ligament. At the scene, the head area should be searched for dental roots. If recovered, they should be kept separate rather than replaced in the sockets.

Charring of teeth complicates identification. Information is lost or obscured. There is shrinkage of from 2 to 20%.[5] The destructive effects are temperature related. At 500°C (932°F), enamel exfoliates away from dentin and turns opaque and white. At 540 to 650°C (1000 to 1200°F), dentin carbonizes.[5,30] At 900°C (1600°F), silver amalgam fillings become dull as the mercury evaporates and the solid metal returns to powder. Drops of mercury may be seen in the surrounding area. Dental gold melts between 843 and 1099°C (1550 to 2010°F), and some porcelains may withstand temperatures of over 2400°F. Considering that the usual household fire reaches 1200°F and that the heat of cremation is between 1500 and 1600°F, preservation of dental evidence is the rule rather than the exception after most fires.

The dentition should be charted and photographed *in situ* before the jaws are removed in severely burned corpses because ashed teeth and bone shatter during resection.[2,6] Following resection, findings related to cause and manner of death (e.g., soot in the airways, red color of carbon monoxide) should be noted before they are obliterated by washing or fixation. Char fractures should be differentiated from perimortem trauma if possible, particularly in motor vehicle accidents, air crashes, and arson. After prolonged burning in intense fires, bodies can be almost completely consumed, leaving

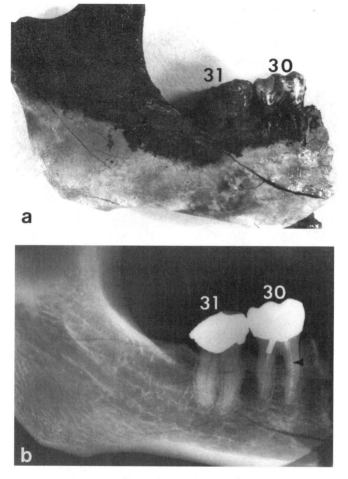

Figure 12.10 (a) Charred and calcined jaw fragment showing soot-covered gold caps on molars. (b) X-ray of specimen in (a) showing normal bony and dental anatomy, including gold crowns and a root canal filling in tooth #30 (arrow).

a disorganized rubble of bone and tooth fragments comingled with metal, wood, and other nonhuman materials. Teeth can then be located radiographically by using a grid (Figure 12.11).

Viewable Remains

When the face is potentially viewable (as in a Doe case) removal of the jaws may be contraindicated, necessitating *in situ* intraoral examination. Rigor mortis or cold temperatures may complicate this procedure. The internal pterygoid and masseter muscles can be severed to facilitate jaw opening without perforating the skin.[5] A mouth prop can be used to keep the jaws open.[30] Under the best of circumstances, poor accessibility compromises the

Figure 12.11 X-ray of scattered debris following a house fire. Note multirooted human tooth fragment (top center).

dentist's ability to chart findings and make photographs and radiographs. Keiser-Nielsen has described a technique for jaw resection that avoids facial cuts, after which the skin can be flapped over the replaced specimens and facial appearance can be reconstituted.[31] The jaws can also be delivered through an intact mouth by using pruning shears.

Mutilated Remains

In mutilated bodies, agonal oral trauma such as broken and avulsed teeth and jaw fractures should be recorded before the jaws are removed. It is of particular importance to record the presence of jaw fractures, as resection cuts can obliterate the pathology.

Securing Antemortem Records

In order to locate antemortem dental records, the name of a putative victim must be in hand. Then, family and friends of the suspect can proffer the name of a dentist who can supply a record. Official requests for dental records must be considerate of the family dentist. A policeman who suddenly and unexpectedly demands a patient's file can intimidate and irritate the dentist. The practitioner may be reluctant to release records, believing that he or she is under investigation or that the patient's privacy will be violated. If the dentist refuses to cooperate, the investigation will be delayed until the records are subpoenaed. It is much simpler to courteously ask for the records after explaining why they are needed. No reasonable dentist would knowingly impede a death investigation on a patient. The forensic odontologist, as a colleague, can help facilitate this process by allaying the concerns of the dentist.

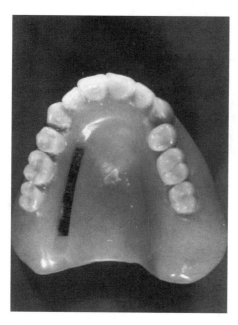

Figure 12.12   Removable denture labeled with patient name. (Courtesy of Dr. James Woodward.)

If a dentist of record cannot be located, other resources are available. Dental data can exist on individuals who have never had dental work or never visited a family dentist. Anyone who has had a military physical examination has a dental record which is maintained at Military Records Depository, 900 Paige Boulevard, St. Louis, Missouri. Many individuals institutionalized in hospitals, prisons, mental facilities, and orphanages have been checked by a dentist and have a dental file. Other sources of information include insurance carriers through employers. Computerized pharmacies list patients, their prescriptions, and the names of dentists or physicians who have prescribed medication. Even indigent people, upon whom hope of finding a dentist seems slim, may have a file at a neighborhood clinic or dental school visited for emergency treatment. In decedents found to be wearing removable dentures, the prostheses should be checked for engraved identification information (Figure 12.12). At least ten states require the marking of all removable prostheses. Some denture wearers may retain old dentures at home. An identification can be established if a denture in a suspect's home fits in the victim's mouth. Even nondental records may fortuitously reveal dental information; medical or chiropractic skull X-rays usually show teeth. If the suspect had visited an emergency room following head trauma, such X-rays are bound to exist. Lastly, family pictures such as wedding or graduation photographs that show the victim smiling can serve as an antemortem "dental record" (Figure 12.13).

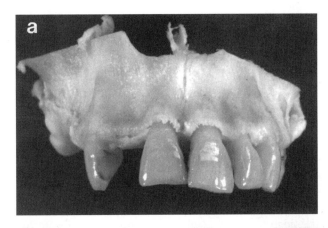

Figure 12.13 Upper jaw specimen (a) of a decomposed homicide victim showing missing #7 and a downward-sloped incisal edge on #9. An antemortem "smile" photograph (b) of the putative victim showed correspondence of those attributes.

Original and complete antemortem records should be requested, including written records, X-rays, study models, etc. Photocopies, duplicates, and faxes show altered contrast, loss of detail, and/or loss of color discrimination. Duplicated X-rays lose left/right orientation. Antemortem dental evidence that has been retrieved and transported should follow protocol for chain of custody and should include the dentist's name and address which is often missing from the file. As already mentioned, if no records are forthcoming, as in a Doe case, a reconstructive dental exam followed by an NCIC inquiry should be initiated.

Comparison

Unlike the fingerprint examiner, the dentist must expect discrepancies when comparing antemortem and postmortem data. A discrepancy or inconsistency may be defined as a contradiction in a recorded finding between antemortem and postmortem data. Discrepancies are common and may be of several types. Temporal discrepancies reflect changes that occur over time. Teeth may be filled or removed after the last recorded dental visit. Such discrepancies can be explained logically. Spatial discrepancies may occur when antemortem and postmortem X-rays appear to differ because they were made at different angulations. This can be resolved by re-taking postmortem X-rays with the same orientation as the antemortem films. Human error constitutes another form of discrepancy and appears as omissions or incorrectly transcribed tooth numbers or filled surfaces in written records. These can be difficult to resolve, although experienced forensic dentists are familiar with common patterns of errors. Finally, there are certain discrepancies that are irreconcilable, such as the postmortem presence of a tooth that is absent on antemortem X-rays or an unfilled tooth noted postmortem that shows a filling antemortem. When making conclusions, a few explainable inconsistencies are acceptable as long as they are accompanied by multiple or specific concordant features. However, even one incompatible discrepancy would exclude the suspect.

There is no requisite number of match points needed to make a dental identification as there is in fingerprints. An X-ray of a single dental filling may show enough characterization in its radiographic silhouette to confer uniqueness. Because of its ability to record a myriad of details in a single image as well as its objectivity for visual verification, the X-ray is preferred to the written record (Figure 12.14). Although medical examiners and coroners may be able to note teeth and fillings, read a dental chart, and recognize concordant points, only a dentist would be expected to evaluate the discriminating potential of these match points and render a meaningful interpretation.

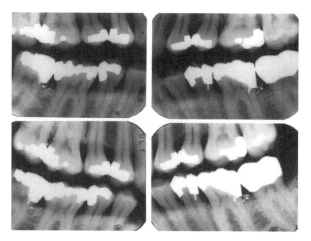

Figure 12.14   Antemortem bitewing X-rays (top) compared to postmortem films (bottom) show precise and specific morphologic concordance between teeth, bone, and the 16 fillings (noted as white areas).

Conclusion

The forensic dentist should state his or her degree of confidence in the identification. A positive dental identification is *established* when the concordance between antemortem and postmortem data confers uniqueness and there are no incompatible inconsistencies. A positive identification is *confirmed* when the dental data alone is compelling but insufficient to unconditionally assure identity, yet authorities are reasonably certain of identity based on circumstantial evidence. In such a case, the combination of all the data elevates the level of confidence in the identification to positive. Sometimes there are merely superficial similarities between antemortem and postmortem dental data, but they are too few or too nonspecific upon which to base an identification. In such a case, the dental findings are noncommittal and can only be supportive to the extent that the suspect is not ruled out by the dental evidence. Occasionally, a case is evaluated in which the antemortem material is of no comparative value because it is too old or shows teeth not recovered in the postmortem material. In this case, no meaningful assessment of identity can be made and dentistry is noncontributory to the identification effort. Lastly, if there are multiple or irreconcilable inconsistencies in the absence of meaningful consistencies, the putative victim can be *excluded* as the decedent.

The Final Report

The forensic dentist should report an identification as soon as it is established so that the body can be released and relatives notified. A final written report should follow. It should be complete and thorough and should contain all the antemortem and postmortem facts that support the conclusion.[5] Months or years after its submission, the report may be needed in court. It should not read as a cryptic, disorganized document but should allow the court to reconstruct the case and document an unbroken chain of custody for all specimens and records.

Bitemarks

Definition of a Bitemark

Cutaneous bitemarks represent patterned injuries in skin produced by teeth. Those of forensic significance most often accompany violent crimes such as homicide, sexual assault, child abuse, domestic violence, and battery. Bitemarks can also be inflicted by animals, most notably dogs and cats.

Significance

Each human dentition is unique, differing even in identical twins.[32] Its imprint in skin can show this individualization. Accordingly, perpetrator identification is possible. For this reason, bitemarks have been referred to as "dental fingerprints". The analogy is superfluous. Bitemarks seldom mark with the rubber stamp accuracy expected with fingerprints. Yet, in some ways bitemarks are more valuable. Fingerprints found at a scene indicate only that a suspect was there. They do not imply criminal activity or a time relationship to the crime. Bitemarks suggest an altercation between the victim and perpetrator, and their temporal coincidence to a crime can be determined. Even in cases where a biter cannot be identified, the mere presence of a bitemark supports the allegation that sexual assault or child abuse has occurred. When a suspect claims that intercourse was consensual or when the sole caretaker of a child alleges that the fall was accidental, the presence of a bitemark suggests otherwise.

Judicial Acceptance

In America, bite-mark evidence has been upheld in appellate courts since 1954.[33] In 1975, it survived the scrutiny of the Frye standard, which requires that scientific evidence be generally accepted by the scientific community.[6] In the future, it is likely that bite-mark evidence will be admissible on a case-to-case basis as Federal Rules of Evidence replace Frye.[34] In 1993, the U.S. Supreme Court announced that Federal Rules superseded Frye in the landmark Daubert decision.[35] To date, 226 citations at the appellate level have been reported as related to bitemarks.[33]

Objectives

The objectives of a bite-mark investigation are threefold: first, to recognize the bitemark; second, to ensure that it is accurately documented; and third, to compare it to the teeth of an alleged perpetrator. If a patterned injury is undetected or unrecognized as a bitemark, the entire investigation is preempted because the forensic dentist will not be notified and the opportunity to correctly collect evidence will be lost. The collection of bite-mark evidence requires knowledge and experience. It calls for time-consuming and fastidious technical handling aimed at recording the patterned injury in a way that it can be reproduced at correct size and shape for later comparison to gypsum replicas (study models) of a suspect's teeth.

Description of the Prototypical Bitemark

A paradigmatic bitemark appears as a circular or oval patterned injury measuring from 3 to 5 cm in widest diameter (Figure 12.15). It is composed of two separate, curved arches facing one another. Each arch is composed of a row of contusions, abrasions, lacerations or depressions approximating the size and shape of the biting surfaces of human front teeth. There may be as

Figure 12.15 A well inflicted, nondistorted adult human bitemark showing two distinct arches (larger upper, smaller lower) defined by a series of individual tooth marks. Note the presence of markings of lingual anatomy from upper and lower incisor teeth.

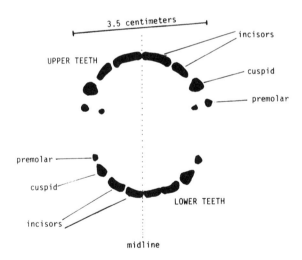

Figure 12.16 Diagrammatic depiction of the adult human bitemark reflecting the typical pattern of the contacting surfaces of the teeth.

many as 16 individual tooth marks (8 in each arch), although between 6 and 12 is more often the case.

In well inflicted bites, the so-called class characteristics of human teeth can be seen (Figure 12.16). These represent the basic features shared by human dentitions. Incisor teeth record as linear or rectangular markings and cuspids as circles or triangles. In clear, nondistorted bites, the upper arch can

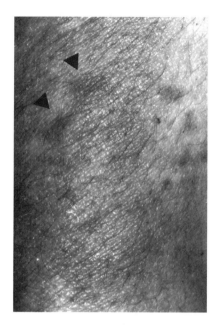

Figure 12.17 Typical bite pattern left by a child. Note spacing between teeth and note relatively small upper central incisors (arrows).

often be distinguished from the lower. The upper arch is larger but is usually less defined than the lower arch because the lower teeth hold the skin more securely. The upper central incisor markings also distinguish the upper arch because they are larger than the adjacent lateral incisors, whereas the four lower incisors are about the same size. Bitemarks made by children can be distinguished by their size <3.5 cm and their small, spaced tooth marks (Figure 12.17).

Any portion of the external anatomy can and has been bitten, but the extremities and breasts are frequent targets in heterosexual assaults, while the back and shoulders are common in male homosexual assaults.[36,37] In child abuse cases, the pattern is random.[36]

Variations

Bitemarks are not simply mechanical tool marks. The act of biting with the ensuing struggle causes unpredictable distortion. Factors that influence the appearance of the mark include the anatomic location and composition of the skin, the position during biting, the direction and force of biting, as well as age, gender, and systemic health of the victim. These variables allow bitemarks to display a variety of forms and deviant patterns, the most common of which are described next.

Central Contusion

An area of petechiae or ecchymosis in the center of the bitemark (Figure 12.18) has long been attributed to suction and/or tongue thrusting.[6] While this is true of some cases, central contusion can also result from the

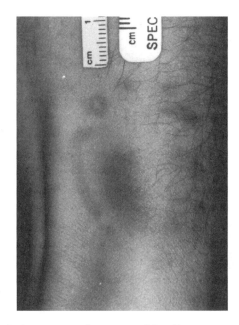

Figure 12.18 Area of contusion centrally located between the arches in a bitemark.

pinching of skin between teeth. This is important because older literature equates central "suck marks" with protracted bites of a sexual, sadistic nature.[36] This simply is not necessarily true.

Sunburst Pattern

Radiating abrasions or contusions are often seen near the periphery of the mark oriented perpendicularly and radiating outward or toward the center. Some of these represent "drag marks" indicating where teeth scraped along the skin before or after they took hold. They appear as a series of linear red streaks (Figure 12.19). A sunburst pattern may also be made by the lingual surfaces of the teeth pressed against the skin.[38] These contusions are directed inward and show the tapered anatomy of the lingual surfaces (Figures 12.16 and 12.20).

Avulsive Bites

Particularly vicious bites may tear out a section of tissue, leaving an ovoid gaping laceration with torn, scalloped edges (Figure 12.21).

Multiple Bites

Bitemarks can be multiple and superimposed. These are often seen in non-felonious assaults between children at play (Figure 12.22).

Single-Arched Bites/One-Sided Bites

There are occasional reports of bitemarks showing only one arch. In such cases, the dynamics of biting, superimposed clothing, and other factors can

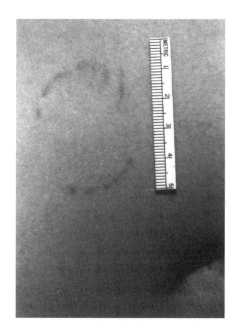

Figure 12.19 Well-inflicted bitemark showing linear streaks on the upper right where those teeth scraped the skin surface during the act of biting.

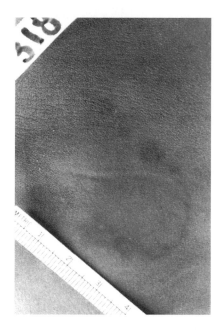

Figure 12.20 Bitemark in child abuse/homicide showing an indistinct upper arch but a defined lower arch in which up to nine teeth appear. Four front teeth demonstrate their lingual anatomy.

explain this phenomenon. A bite can also show only the right or left side of both arches due to such factors as uneven biting force, skin curvature, absence of teeth or tooth placement during biting.

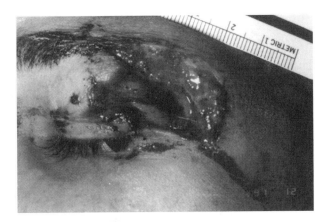

Figure 12.21   Avulsive, lacerated human bite above the eye. (Courtesy of Dr. William Smock.)

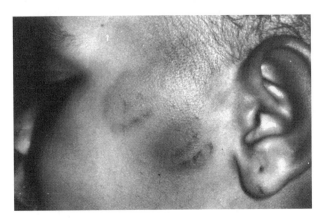

Figure 12.22   Two facial bitemarks inflicted by an unsupervised child at day care.

"Toothless" Bitemarks

A simple ring of homogeneous contusions approximating the size and shape of human arches but not showing individual tooth marks should be recognized as a possible bitemark (Figure 12.23). Sometimes, tooth marks are present but indistinct, appearing as fused, scalloped areas within a continuous curvilinear contusion. Occasionally, tooth marks or arch configurations are obscured by massive contusion around the bitemark. There are several explanations for toothless marks. Soft skin or skin overlying fat is resilient and resists individual tooth pressure even though the collective pressure causes diffuse hemorrhage. Wide-surfaced teeth may be too dull to leave individual markings. Superimposed clothing can cushion skin, protecting it

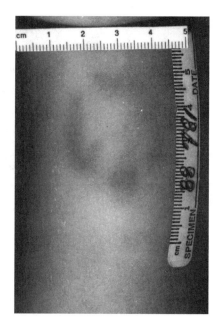

Figure 12.23 Diffuse bitemark on the leg of a child homicide victim. Scalloped, fused contusions indicate tooth contact but fail to show individual incisal anatomy.

from tooth imprints. Lastly, in healing bitemarks, the tooth marks often fade before the background contusion does.

"Solid" Bitemarks

A solid red circle or oval may be seen instead of the typical ringed shape, especially in acute bitemarks where early inflammation causes diffuse superficial erythema or where central contusion is extensive.

Healed Bitemarks

Scars and subtle areas of pigmentation or depigmentation may remain after a lacerated bite and may persist for many months or years.

Differential Diagnosis

Other patterned injuries bear a superficial resemblance to bites, particularly bitemarks which are distorted or indistinct. Heel marks leave a "one-arched" mark of compatible size and shape (Figure 12.24). Ridges or nails in the heel may even create individual marks that could simulate teeth.[6] Hoof marks from farm animals can mimic one-arched bitemarks by virtue of their curvature. Burns caused by paddles during cardioversion simulate "toothless" bitemarks, creating a red-brown circular injury. They are larger than typical bitemarks, are invariably located on the chest, and can be diagnosed by history. Ringworm can mimic a bitemark. Inspection will show slightly raised, scaly skin without class characteristics of human teeth (Figure 12.25). Dogs

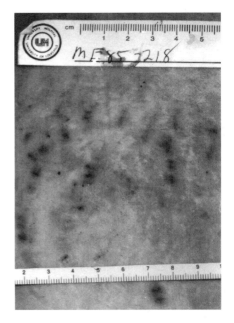

Figure 12.24 Homicide victim showing a curved patterned injury composed of individual abrasions caused by stomping with a shoe heel.

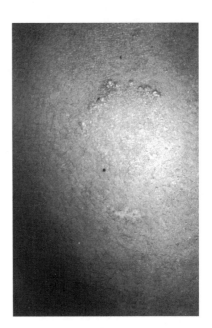

Figure 12.25 Oval-shaped fungal infection of skin showing similar size and shape of a bitemark.

and cats cause most of the animal bites. Their fang-like cuspids and posterior teeth produce multiple, deep, streaked lacerations (Figure 12.26). The diminutive incisors may or may not mark. Cat bites are small and usually accompanied by scratches.

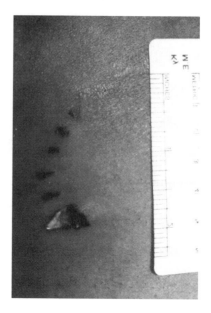

Figure 12.26 Dog bite showing streaked abrasions left by incisors and a deep laceration made by a cuspid tooth. (Courtesy of Dr. William Smock.)

Evidence Collection on Victims

The detection of a bitemark constitutes the only forensic dental emergency. Bitemarks fade in decedents and heal in living victims. The pattern can be effaced in a day, making immediate documentation imperative.

It would be ideal to preserve every aspect of the bitemark (size, color, morphology, three-dimensional contour, texture, and consistency), but no single medium is suitable for all these objectives. Fortunately, correctly made photographs can, alone, provide sufficient information. Dental impressions can add auxiliary data in certain cases. A step-wise protocol has been developed for bite-mark evidence collection.[39] As with all patterned injuries, the bitemark should be described, measured, and, if possible, documented with a labeled sketch.

Initial Orientation Photographs

Before any "touching" alters the evidence, photographs of the bitemark are made. Initial photographs omit rulers, case numbers, or anything else that might be construed as modifying or concealing evidence. The first images are not intended for close-up comparative work but only to orient the position of the mark(s) on the body (Figure 12.27). Color slide or print film is used. Following saliva trace evidence collection, the area should be rephotographed with a case number in place.

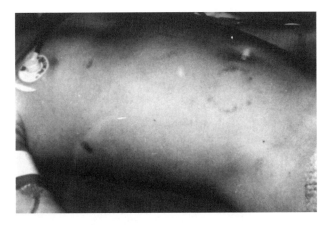

Figure 12.27 Orientation photograph showing the anatomic position of two bitemarks in the abdomen of a victim of child homicide.

Trace Evidence Collection

If the body has not been washed, saliva stains can be collected for ABO typing of secretors. In a questionable bite, its origin from human teeth is supported by amylase determination, which indicates the presence of saliva. In the future, actual perpetrator identification may be possible from DNA sequences recovered from cells in saliva.

Close-Up (Working) Photographs

The forensic dentist is the most appropriate person to make the photographs needed for comparison to a suspect's teeth. If the dentist is unavailable, an evidence technician, medical examiner, or coroner familiar with the basic tenets of bite-mark evidence photography is the best alternative. Working photographs are the critical images that will be used for size-controlled comparison to the suspect's teeth. Size and shape must be retained. The bitemark should be washed of debris and blood, and hair should be carefully clipped. A case number and an accurate, rigid ruler is placed alongside but not obscuring any portion of the bitemark. For accurate recording of size, the ruler must be parallel to and on the same vertical plane as the bitemark. A circular scale, such as a quarter, is desirable to maintain perspective. The ABFO #2 ruler provides both linear and circular scales and is excellent for this purpose[5] (Figure 12.28). The camera lens is oriented directly over and perpendicular to the bitemark with the film plane parallel to the plane of the bite-mark/ruler assembly. Fine-grain print film, either black-and-white or color, is used in a camera that allows close-up views, typically a $1/3$ to $1/5$ life-sized reproduction (3×5 to 5×7 in. field). Illumination is typically supplied by ring or point-source electronic flash used at various angles. Severely obtuse

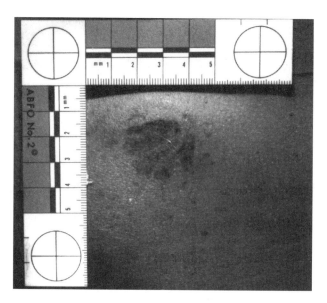

Figure 12.28   The ABFO #2 ruler includes accurate linear and circular scales. Black and white centimeter rectangles are included in case improper exposure obliterates fine detail in the linear scale. The bitemark shows prominent central contusion but little tooth detail. Ruler available from Lightning Powder Co., Inc., 1230 Hoyt S.E.; Salem, Oregon 97302-2121.

lighting angles are used to bring out subtle indentations made by shadow detail. Unpredictable reflection occurring with flash can be controlled with a diffuser or by substituting ambient light. Apertures of F8 or smaller are recommended for proper depth of field in close-up views.

The bitemark should be photographed with the skin in the position it was bitten. In live adults, this might be ascertained by history. In decedents and young children, the skin should be photographed in its range of positional possibilities.[39]

The bite injury pattern usually begins to degrade within a day or two of infliction but may improve. The bitemark should be examined over several days and rephotographed if new information is seen.

Life-sized photographic prints are achieved by enlarging the ruler in the picture to actual size. The circular scale indicates undistorted perspective if it retains its circular shape. If it acquires an elliptical shape, the image can be rectified by tilting the enlarger easel.

Diagnostic Imaging

Optional infrared (IR) or ultraviolet (UV) images can be made if the special expertise and equipment are available. These techniques complement but do not replace conventional photography. Ultraviolet imaging has two goals. UV radiation does not penetrate skin, and it renders extremely sharp surface detail, an advantage in delineating subtle abrasions and indentations. Secondly, UV is absorbed by melanin and reveals subtle pigmentary changes not seen visually.[5] Invisible, healed bitemarks months old can suddenly reappear with UV photography.

Infrared radiation has an opposite effect. IR penetrates 3 mm into skin and effectively renders skin translucent by "looking through" superficial abrasions and surface melanin in blacks, thereby de-emphasizing surface detail and accentuating underlying collections of blood. IR imaging can detect unseen volumes of blood below the surface.[41] Invisible contusions and superficial veins are revealed, giving new information on patterns of injuries.

Impressions

The forensic dentist may make impressions of the bitemark which will record three-dimensional indentations and surface contour. Such impressions are extremely accurate and can serve for scanning electron microscopic studies to detect nuances in surface injuries that might correspond to tiny chips or sharp edges in a perpetrator's teeth.

Dental impressions of the victim's teeth may also be needed if the bitemarks are accessible to the victim's mouth. Self-biting has been reported in natural and combative situations.

Resection

A bitemark on a decedent can be excised and placed in formalin. Simple excision will cause immediate shrinkage as tissue tension is relieved, followed by additional shrinkage, distortion, hardening, and color alterations from fixation. Dimensional stability can be retained by affixing the skin to an acrylic polymer ring with cyanoacrylate glue before excision.[42] The specimen can be transilluminated to see the extent of contusion. Fixed tissue can also be examined histologically to "age" the injury relative to time of death. These techniques are destructive and, if performed, are done last.

Testimonial Evidence on Live Victims

Assaulted adults can answer questions that assist in bite-mark analysis and help to determine the veracity of the victim. Table 12.2 lists important historical data to obtain from the victim. The victim should be educated as to the possibilities of bitemark matching to effect cooperation in evidence collection. After evidence collection, the bitemark should be treated if necessary and the patient should be counseled regarding any concerns such as HIV transmission.

Table 12.2   Questions for the Bite Victim

1. How long ago were the bites inflicted?
2. Were the bites made through clothing?
3. Were the bites washed or treated?
4. What was the assailant's head position during biting?
5. What was the victim's position during biting?
6. Was there struggling during biting?
7. What, if anything, provoked the biting?
8. Was the bite painful?
9. Did the victim bite the assailant?

Evidence Collection on Suspects

When a suspect materializes, the dentist will, after proper informed consent or a court order, perform an examination and make photographs, bite registrations, and dental impressions for study models.

Comparison

The suspect's teeth are compared to the bitemark by various techniques, including direct and indirect superimposition, bite exemplars, and measurements (Figures 12.29 and 12.30).

Concluding Concordance

The concept of comparing two sets of data as a means to assess the likelihood of a common origin is the same for bitemarks as it is for dental identification on decedents. In practice, proportionally fewer bitemark cases yield unconditionally positive identifications. It is true that a person's teeth are unique, but that uniqueness does not reflect in bitemarks as often as it does in antemortem dental X-rays. Skin is not a good impression material and cannot be expected to faithfully record minute details in a way that can be accurately and reliably measured. Bleeding or abrasion under areas of tooth pressure is not obliged to duplicate the anatomy of the teeth. Some skin under pressure may not be disrupted while, elsewhere, bleeding may extend beyond the bitten skin. In fact, it is remarkable that so many bitemarks do show fairly accurate size and pattern duplication of the assailant's teeth.

Based on similarities shared by all human dentitions and the opportunity for distortion or illegibility in a bitemark, the forensic dentist must be cognizant about what constitutes a match or a mismatch. Concordance or lack of concordance in the size of the arches, for instance, is mostly fortuitous.[40] Human arches are fairly similar in size and the potential for distortion due to skin elasticity obliterates one's ability to match or discount the suspect on the basis of arch size unless the differences are large. Similarly, arch shape is

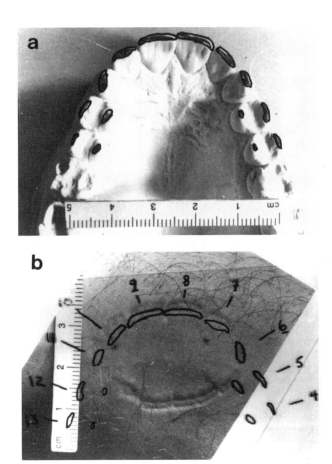

Figure 12.29 Transparent tracing of a suspect's upper dental model (a) overlaid onto an equally sized photograph of a bitemark (b) to show similarity of features. Exact superimposition is avoided to allow reader to compare the tracing and skin markings side by side.

irrelevant unless it is unusual because many people share U-shaped arches which can record with distortion in a bitemark. Even a similarity between individual tooth marks in a bitemark and a suspect's teeth do not assure common origin. Many people share common tooth size and alignment. A "match" may simply reflect the class characteristics that people have in common. The forensic dentist must show restraint in concluding that a suspect made a given bitemark when the match lacks specific characterization. Ultimately, it is the concordance of unusual characteristics which allows the conclusion that a particular suspect made the mark. Such features as tooth rotations, malalignment, spacing, chips, sharp edges, etc. make a convincing argument for a confident identification of a perpetrator. It is important for crime investigators and prosecutors to understand the basis for a bite-mark conclusion because an overzealous dental opinion can discredit an investigation.

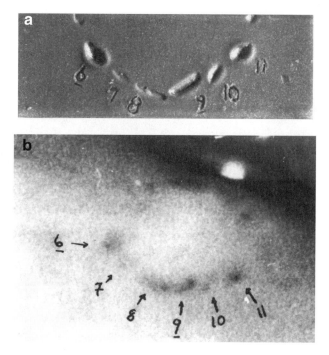

Figure 12.30 Wax bite imprinted by suspect's upper teeth (a) duplicates the size, pattern, and individual tooth characteristics of the bitemark (b). Compare to the orientation image of the same bitemark in Figure 12.27.

The forensic dentist should be able to convince an investigator of his or her conclusion through illustration and supported fact rather than on blind faith.

In stating a conclusion, the forensic dentist should use language that accurately reflects his or her confidence in the likelihood that the suspect made the bitemark. Conclusions such as "its a match" or "bitemark is consistent with suspect's teeth" are subject to misinterpretation and should be avoided. These terms do not specify the strength of the relationship of bitemark to suspect teeth which might range from a fortuitous similarity of nonspecific features to a perpetrator identification based on distinctive attributes. The terms "match" and "consistent with" are not used in a standardized manner by odontologists and jurors tend to equate them with a positive identification which can persuade them to convict. It is more acceptable to use terms like "possible biter", "probable biter" and "reasonable medical certainty" to indicate increasing degrees of likelihood that a specific suspect made a bitemark. Although not precise, these terms more accurately communicate the dentist's opinion to lawyers and jurors.

In summary, it is not necessarily the number of teeth in a bitemark nor the fact that it conforms to the suspect's teeth — but the recognition of

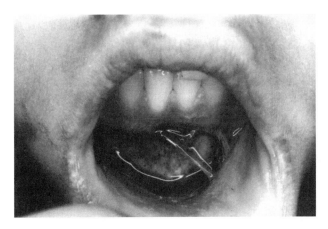

Figure 12.31 Laceration of the lower vestibular fold due to forcible displacement of the lip.

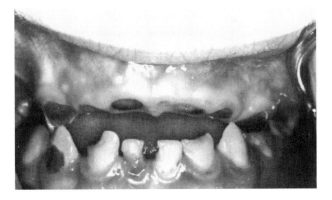

Figure 12.32 Rampant tooth decay in nursing-bottle mouth syndrome. (Photograph courtesy of Dr. Thomas O'Toole.)

an unusual pattern reflected in a suspect's dentition that determines its value. Since this determination is not apparent until the comparison stage, any bitemark regardless of quantity or quality, should be worked up. Its usefulness is not known until all the facts have been gathered.

Dental Findings in Child Maltreatment and Other Person Abuse

In 1962, Kempe et al.[43] described the "battered child syndrome" and summarized the physical findings that, when seen in the proper setting, were suspicious of child abuse. With increased awareness and changing definitions of child abuse and neglect, the medical profession has recognized additional

Table 12.3   Oral Findings of Child Maltreatment

Findings	Cause
Multiple broken, discolored, missing, or avulsed front teeth	Repeated episodes of mouth trauma
Peculiar malocclusions and nonoccluding jaw segments	Healed jaw fractures which were displaced and not reduced
Laceration of labial or lingual frena (Figure 12.31)	Forceful lip pulling or slapping
Isolated laceration of soft palate	Insertion of a utensil during forced feeding
Horizontal abrasions or contusions extending from lip commissures	Application of a gag
Tooth marks in labial mucosa corresponding to child's teeth	Pressure from smothering
Bitemarks on skin	Child bite (unsupervised children); adult bite (anger biting)
Rampant caries (decay) (Figure 12.32)	"Nursing-bottle mouth syndrome" — child is continually allowed to fall asleep with bottle in mouth, containing sugar from milk, juice, etc. (possible child neglect)
Venereal disease	Venereal warts, gonococcal stomatitis and pharyngitis, syphilitic lesions (indicates sexual abuse)

physical findings and syndromes suggestive of nonaccidental injuries. Among these are shaken infant syndrome, Munchausen's syndrome by proxy, and specific oral lesions. It is not surprising that the dental profession has played an active role in the detection of physical child abuse, considering that head and neck injuries occur in 50% of cases.[5] The oral cavity and perioral region of suspected victims of child maltreatment should be examined. Table 12.3 lists oral findings of child abuse and neglect and their causes.

Not every traumatic injury in a child is suspicious, and some judgment is needed. Single-event injuries, showing facial abrasion and laceration with or without tooth fracture are not necessarily deliberate injuries and do occur as simple accidents in ambulatory, active children. Bitemarks are frequently exchanged between children at play. Nursing-bottle mouth syndrome does not always constitute willful neglect and may reflect poor parenting skills. Of course, if it reoccurs or remains untreated after counseling, the caregiver should be considered neglectful.

Spouse and elder abuse reports are increasing as society is becoming more aware of these pervasive crimes. Head and neck trauma is seen in most cases[44] and includes fractured teeth and jaws, oral and facial abrasions, contusions, and lacerations. Up to 30% of female emergency room patients present with injuries sustained during domestic violence.[45]

Forensic Dentistry in Mass Disasters

When a jurisdiction is suddenly overwhelmed with a large number of fatal casualties, a mass disaster situation exists. Airplane crashes, building fires, shipwrecks, explosions, and wars comprise the bulk of manmade disasters. Natural disasters such as earthquakes, volcanos, floods and hurricanes also exact a large toll of human lives. These disasters leave bodies burned, mutilated, and decomposed beyond recognition. Often, it is difficult to determine who was involved in the disaster. Identification of victims in such circumstances is a challenge and is most often made through dental means. A survey of 22 aircraft accidents from 1951 to 1972 involving 1080 fatalities showed that 40% of the identifications were made or assisted through dentistry.[30] Since that time, the success rate of dental identifications either alone or assisted has risen to approximately 75%.

The Dental Identification Team

Although manpower needs and operations vary based on the nature of the catastrophe, some basic maxims apply in the organization and implementation of the dental team. The essence of expedient and accurate functioning is preparation, teamwork, and communication.[46] Preplanning involves the preparation of an operations manual, selection of responsible and knowledgeable dentists, access to needed supplies and equipment, and mock disaster drills. A team leader must be on ready alert and able to effect instant mobilization of the team. Each member should have an identification card or badge to permit access into secured areas.

The mass disaster team consists of three sections and a team chief. The role of the postmortem section is to record dental findings on decedents. The antemortem section functions to locate dental records of proposed victims and to make the dental findings interpretable. The comparison section serves to compare and match sets of records and finalize identifications.

Making dental identifications in mass disasters is no different from individual cases except for the risk of loss and mixups incurred by having multiple bodies and multiple dentists. The dental team chief oversees the entire dental operation and acts as a liaison between other sections and the medical examiner or coroner in charge. The team chief functions as manager, spokesperson, coordinator and facilitator.[46]

Operations at the Scene

After the search for and triage of living victims is made and the area is safe and secure, the recovery of the dead begins. No matter how chaotic the scene appears, it is the most organized it will be. As it is dismantled, it will become increasingly difficult to reconstruct the circumstances of the disaster. The scene should be subdivided into a grid of numbered squares. If possible, aerial photographs are made to show a panoramic orientation of the disaster scene. Each square is searched, photographed with a still or video camera, sketched, and labeled. Sketching and photography are integral parts of the mass disaster protocol. Even if bodies are correctly identified, their positions and locations are of critical importance in accident reconstruction and the litigation to follow (Figure 12.33). Any personal effects or body parts are tagged and identified as to grid section location. Prewritten tags are used to avoid duplication. Dentists from the postmortem section should be utilized to help identify jaw or tooth fragments. Any fragments found should be individually labeled, especially if there are comingled remains. Burned or skeletonized heads should be bagged in plastic during transport to avoid loss or breakage. Bodies are placed on a gurney for transport to and from the various processing areas.[46]

Postmortem Section

In the schema of the processing line, dental examination is sequenced after in-processing, photography, collection of personal effects, fingerprinting, and full-body radiography. Anthropologic triage and autopsy may also precede the dental exam. The jaws are exposed and/or removed, radiographed, and cleaned.[46] One dentist performs the exam while another dentist or auxiliary records. The examiner and recorder then switch and repeat the process for verification. Charts, X-rays, and specimens are labeled, initialed, and kept together, then delivered to the comparison section.

Antemortem Section

The antemortem section is out of the body-processing loop and is primed by incoming names of putative victims derived from a manifest, reported missing persons, or people who believe an acquaintance might be a victim. Once the names are in hand, relatives must be located, family dentists sought, and dental records received and logged in. Data from these records are condensed onto a composite, standard form that can be compared with the postmortem form. The completed form along with the original records are delivered to the comparison section.

Comparison Section

The comparison section receives the antemortem and postmortem dental data, as well as any personal effects and clothing information and physical, anthropologic, and medical descriptions derived from other sections. If manual sorting is used, the postmortem files are divided into mutually exclusive

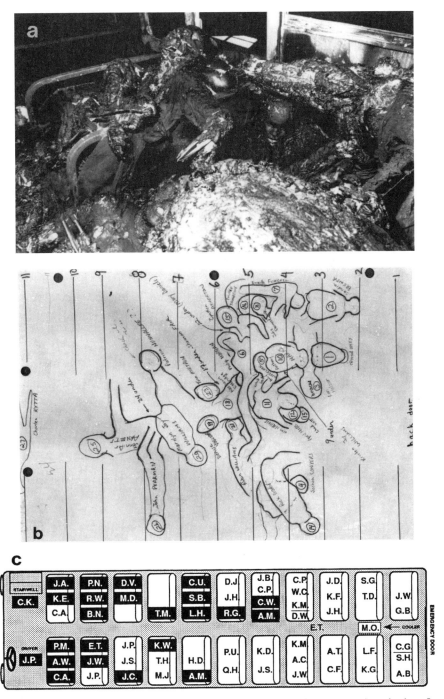

Figure 12.33 *In situ* scene photograph of burned victims in seats 4 and 5 of a bus fire (a) and shown diagrammatically (b). Although the photograph is more detailed and accurate, the sketch is more complete and permits labeling. This evidence was compared to the seating plan recollected by survivors (c) to allow accident reconstruction.

groups (e.g., race, gender).[46] Then, those antemortem records with a characteristic dental finding are selected and the proper group of postmortem files is scanned for that finding in search of a tentative match.[46] The more difficult cases are performed last. This process is time consuming in large disasters. Computer matching is valuable when the number of cases exceeds 100. The military CAPMI program has proven useful in mass disasters. Time lost entering antemortem and postmortem data is easily recovered, as the computer performs the initial sorting in seconds. The computer does not make matches; it only prioritizes the order of likely matches. After initial sorting, final matching is performed by dentists who compare the most objective data, usually radiographs, accessing uniqueness and explaining all inconsistencies.

After records are matched, it is the chief who is responsible for verifying the identifications and delivering the results to the head of disaster operations.

Following the identification report, the comparison section photographs, copies, and duplicates materials to be returned and prepares a packet on each person consisting of the antemortem and postmortem record (including all duplicates) and photographs of specimens. Also submitted is a summary document which lists all body numbers with their grid locations and their determined identities.

References

1. Luntz, L. L., History of forensic dentistry, *Dent. Clin. N. Am.*, 21, 7, 1977.

2. Cottone, J. A. and Standish, S. M., *Outline of Forensic Dentistry*, Yearbook Medical Publishers, Chicago, 1982.

3. Vale, G. L., The dentist's expanding responsibilities: forensic odontology, *J. S. Calif. Dent. Assoc.*, 37, 249, 1969.

4. Swanson, H. A., Forensic dentistry, *J. Am. Coll. Dent.*, 34, 174, 1967.

5. Averill, D. C., *Manual of Forensic Odontology*, ed. 2, American Society of Forensic Odontology, Colorado Springs, Colorado, 1991.

6. Harvey, W., *Dental Identification and Forensic Odontology*, Henry Kimpton Publishers, London, 1976.

7. Luntz, L. L. and Luntz, P., *Handbook for Dental Identification: Techniques in Forensic Dentistry*, J. B. Lippincott, Philadelphia, 1973.

8. Miles, A. E. W., Dentition in the estimation of age, *J. Dent. Res.* (Suppl. #1), 42, 255, 1963.

9. Gustafson, G., *Forensic Odontology*, American Elsevier, Inc., New York, 1966.

10. Woolridge, E., Legal concerns of the forensic odontologist, *New Dentist*, 11, 20, 1980.

11. Bernstein, M. L., The identification of a "John Doe", *J. Am. Dental Assoc.*, 110, 918, 1985.

12. Stimson, P. G., Forensic odontology, *Dent. Asst.*, 40, 100, 1971.

13. Kraus, B. S., Calcification of the human deciduous teeth, *J. Am. Dental Assoc.*, 59, 1128, 1959.

14. Schour, I. and Massler, M., The development of the human dentition, *J. Am. Dental Assoc.*, 28, 1153, 1941.

15. Moorrees, C. F. A., Fanning, E. A., and Hunt, E. E., Age variation of formation stages for ten permanent teeth, *J. Dent. Res.*, 42, 1450, 1963.

16. Harris, E. F. and McKee, J. H., Tooth mineralization standards for blacks and whites from the middle southern United States, *J. Foren. Sci.*, 35, 859, 1990.

17. Mincer, H. H., Harris, E. F., and Berryman, H. E., The ABFO study of third molar development and its use as an estimation of chronological age, *J. Forensic Sci.*, 38, 379, 1993.

18. Ogino, T. and Ogino, H., Application to forensic odontology of aspartic acid racemization in unerupted and supernumerary teeth, *J. Dent. Res.*, 67, 1319, 1988.

19. Ohtani, S. and Yamamoto, K., Age estimation using the racemization of amino acid in human dentin, *J. Forensic Sci.*, 36, 792, 1991.

20. Anderson, J. L. and Thompson, G. W., Interrelationships and sex differences of dental and skeletal measurements, *J. Dent. Res.*, 52, 431, 1973.

21. Verhoeven, J. W., van Aken, J., and van der Weerdt, G. P., The length of teeth: a statistical analysis of the differences in length of human teeth for radiologic purposes, *Oral Surg.*, 47, 193, 1979.

22. Dorion, R. D. J., Sexual differentiation in the human mandible, *J. Can. Soc. Forensic Sci.*, 15, 99, 1982.

23. Whittaker, D. K., Llewelyn, D. R., and Jones, R. W., Sex determination from necrotic pulpal tissue, *Br. Dent. J.*, 139, 403, 1975.

24. Gill, G. W. and Rhine, S., *Skeletal Attribution of Race: Methods for Forensic Anthropology*, Maxwell Museum of Anthropology: Anthropological papers #4, Albuquerque, NM, 1990.

25. Hanihara, K., Racial characteristics in the dentition, *J. Dent. Res.* (Suppl. to #1), 46, 923, 1967.

26. Dahlberg, A. A., The evolutionary significance of the protostylid, *Am. J. Phys. Anthropol.*, 8, 15, 1950.

27. Pindborg, J. J., *Pathology of the Dental Hard Tissue*, W. B. Saunders, Philadelphia, 1970.

28. Kraus, B. S., Jordan, R. E., and Abrams, L., *Dental Anatomy and Occlusion*, Williams & Wilkins, Baltimore, MD, 1969.

29. Kraus, B. S., The genetics of the human dentition, *J. Forensic Sci.*, 2, 420, 1957.

30. Sopher, I. M., *Forensic Dentistry*, Charles C Thomas, Springfield, IL, 1976.

31. Keiser-Nielsen, S., *Person Identification by Means of the Teeth*, John Wright and Sons, Bristol, England, 1980.

32. Sognnaes, R. F., Rawson, R. D., Gratt, B. M., and Nguyen, N. B. T., Computer comparison of bitemark patterns in identical twins, *J. Am. Dental Assoc.*, 105, 449, 1982.

33. Pitluck, H. M., Bitemark citations, presented at Tom Kraus Memorial Bite-Mark Breakfast, American Academy of Forensic Sciences, 1996, Nashville, TN.

34. Imwinkelried, E. J., The evolution of the American test for the admissability of scientific evidence, *Med. Sci. Law.*, 30, 60, 1990.

35. Imwinkelried, E. J., The Daubert decision: Frye is dead, long live Federal Rules of Evidence, *Trial*, September 1993.

36. Levine, L. J., Bite-mark evidence, *Dent. Clin. N. Amer.*, 21, 145, 1977.

37. Vale, G. L. and Noguchi, T. T., Anatomical distribution of human bitemarks in a series of 67 cases, *J. Forensic Sci.*, 28, 61, 1983.

38. Sperber, N. D., Lingual markings of anterior teeth as seen in human bitemarks, *J. Forensic Sci.*, 35, 838, 1990.

39. American Board of Forensic Odontology, Inc., Guidelines for bite-mark analysis, *J. Am. Dental Assoc.*, 112, 383, 1986.

40. Bernstein, M. L., Two bite-mark cases with inadequate scale references, *J. Forensic Sci.*, 30, 958, 1985.

41. Bernstein, M. L. and Blair, J., Comparison of black and white infrared photography to standard photography for recording abrasion/contusion injuries, presentation at American Academy Forensic Sciences, 1987.

42. Dorion, R. B. J., Preservation and fixation of skin for ulterior scientific evaluation and courtroom preservation, *J. Can. Dent. Assoc.*, 2, 129, 1984.

43. Kempe, C. H., Silverman, F. N., Steel, B. F. et al., Battered child syndrome, *J. Am. Dental Assoc.*, 181, 17, 1962.

44. Raunsaville, B. and Weissman, M. M., Battered women: a medical problem requiring detection, *Intl. J. Psych. Med.*, 8, 191, 1977-1978.

45. McDowell, J. D., Kassebaum, D. K., and Stromboe, S. E., Recognizing and reporting victims of domestic violence, *J. Am. Dental Assoc.*, 123, 44, 1992.

46. Morlang, W. M., Mass disaster management update, *CDA J.*, 14, 49, 1986.

The Scope of Forensic Anthropology

13

MEHMET YAŞAR İŞCAN
SUSAN R. LOTH

Introduction

The medicolegal system has sought the assistance of physical anthropologists for their expertise in skeletal analysis long before the Physical Anthropology Section of the American Academy of Forensic Sciences (AAFS) was formally established in 1972.[1] Forensic anthropologists concentrate on human biological characteristics at the population level, with special attention to uncovering the uniqueness that sets one individual apart from all others. This focus on isolating each human being as a unique entity is the essence of forensic anthropology.

The practice of forensic anthropology centers on the assessment of every aspect of skeletonized human remains in a medicolegal context for the purpose of establishing identity and, where possible, the cause of death and circumstances surrounding this event. It also encompasses facial image analysis, reconstruction, identification, and comparison of both the living and the dead. The forensic anthropologist is most often called upon to assist law enforcement agencies when decomposition, dismemberment, or other grievous injury makes it impossible to recognize a person or use the normal array of techniques such as fingerprints. Beyond murder, war, and mass disaster, these specialists are also consulted by governments and individuals to investigate and authenticate historic and even prehistoric remains and relics.

The purpose of this chapter is to give an overview of the scope and workings of the field of forensic anthropology. Since the first edition of this book was published in 1980, the discipline has expanded dramatically as the result of an almost exponential increase in research and new technologic developments. Old techniques have been modified or discarded, and, more importantly, new ones have been introduced that have greatly increased the accuracy of skeletal analysis. Obviously, it is impossible to cover all aspects in depth, but there are many references available for further information.[1–8]

The following tabulation summarizes the topical scope of forensic anthropology as covered in this chapter:

Identification: Degrees of Certainty	Forensic Taphonomy	Demographic Characteristics	Personal Identification	Cause of Death
Possible	Time since death	Age	Individualization	Disease
Indeterminate	Burned bones	Sex	Facial imaging	Trauma
Positive		Race	Superimposition	
Identification		Stature and build	Photo Comparison	
			Facial Reconstruction	

Identification: Degrees of Certainty

Forensic anthropologists are often called upon as expert witnesses to render an opinion in a court of law about the identification of an individual. Several outcomes are possible for attempts to establish identity. If there is nothing to rule out a potential match, the degree of certainty of an identification depends on the accuracy of the techniques and the presence of indisputable factors of individualization. The following categories have been suggested.[1]

Possible

A match is "possible" if there is no major incompatibility that would exclude an individual from consideration. However, it must be emphasized that, while this assignment prevents immediate exclusion, it does not imply probability. A judgment of "possible" merely makes this individual eligible for further, more rigorous and specialized testing.

Indeterminate or Inconclusive

Numerous prospective matches survive initial screening, but most of these will wind up in the "indeterminate" category. This is due to the fact that a large number of very similar features are shared by the members of any given age, sex, race group, or nationality, and thus cannot be deemed diagnostic of identity. General examples include pattern baldness, squared jaw, brown eyes, pug nose, and ear protrusion. Population-specific features such as alveolar prognathism in blacks, shovel shaped incisors in American Indians, and brachycephaly in whites are also not definitive. If no idiosyncratic characteristics or factors of individualization can be isolated and matched, the comparison can only be considered "indeterminate or inconclusive". The existence of only general, shared similarities means that a definite conclusion cannot be reached one way or the other. Even if there appears to be a strong probability of a match, without a unique feature to set that individual apart, the final classification must be in this category.

Positive Identification

A positive identification can only be declared if there is absolutely no contradiction or doubt. This conclusion can only be reached based on the presence of unique factors of individualization.

Forensic Taphonomy

Taphonomic analysis traces events following the death of an organism to explain the condition of the remains.[9–12] Numerous factors must be considered, including decomposition, animal predation and scattering, weathering and temperature variation, burial, submersion in water, erosion, burning, etc. It is essential to be familiar with the manifestations of these factors in order to establish vital information such as time since death and distinguish the effects of environmental events from antemortem or perimortem disease or trauma.

Time Since Death

Establishing when death occurred is one of the key determinations for law enforcement personnel to make. It is rarely easy to estimate time since death precisely, and this determination gets more difficult with each passing hour. The forensic anthropologist is not usually called in on a case until decomposition or mutilation renders a victim unrecognizable and obliterates other identifying features. The degree of decomposition and sequence of insect infestation yield important clues but can only be interpreted properly if the examiner is familiar with how factors such as temperature and burial conditions affect the rate of these processes. For example, cold, coverings, and burial retard deterioration; heat, humidity, and exposure accelerate it. Even wily criminals on television are imbued with a smattering of this knowledge and attempt to mislead authorities by storing a body in a freezer to alter the apparent time of death.

Often, forensic anthropologists are presented with completely skeletonized remains. In this situation, the investigator must look for more subtle clues. Is hair present? Are the bones still greasy? Is there any odor? Has bleaching occurred? Are they buried with artifacts from another era — such as a musket ball embedded in a bone? If personal effects are found, they too can help narrow the time period. In general, it is only possible to assign a lower limit, e.g., the victim has been dead for at least 6 months.

Burned Bones

Biological anthropologists have conducted studies to determine the effects of burning on bone.[3,13] There are many forensic situations where this is vital, ranging from fatal building fires to car or plane crashes to attempts to destroy the body of a murder victim. The color and texture of a bone gives important clues to the heat and intensity of the blaze, as well as the approximate duration of exposure. Limited or indirect exposure to the heat source may produce only streaks of soot or yellow/brown discoloration, while direct, intense exposure will cause cracking and char or blacken the bones. If burning is direct and prolonged, only white ash may remain. A skeleton or even a single bone may show various levels of destruction based on position relative to the fire. The burning process also causes drying and shrinkage, thus distorting the size, weight, and shape of the bone.

Experts can detect if cremated remains, even in very fragmented condition, are human or nonhuman by the size and configuration of both their macro- and microstructure. Often immolation is incomplete and enough is left to determine if the victim was immature or adult. If the end of a long bone is intact, the presence or absence of epiphyseal fusion will indicate maturity. Moreover, if tiny bone fragments are found with fused ends, this points to a small adult animal rather than a human infant.

Demographic Characteristics of the Skeleton

Most people would have little difficulty separating a group of normal, unclothed humans by age, sex, and race because they have learned to recognize the morphological manifestations of these categories. However, these seemingly simple determinations become much more difficult if one is dealing with a group of defleshed skeletons (Figure 13.1). For this, special training and experience are needed (the figure also shows the sequence and direction of bone removal at the time of excavation of a skeleton in order to avoid possible damage).

All skeletal assessments begin with what Krogman[3] referred to as the "big four" — age, sex, race, and stature. Each characteristic narrows the pool of possible "matches" considerably — sex alone cuts it by half. If a skeleton is complete and undamaged, these attributes can be assessed with great accuracy. Using the latest techniques, sex can be determined with certainty, age estimated to within about 5 years, and stature approximated with a standard deviation of about 1.5" (3.5 cm). Assignment to the Caucasoid, Mongoloid, or Negroid race group can be accomplished with a high degree of certainty in the absence of admixture. However, forensic anthropologists are more

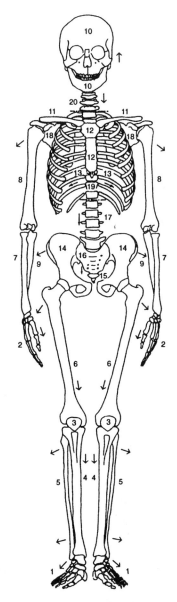

Figure 13.1 The human skeleton. Arrows show the sequence and direction of bone removal: 1. foot bones, 2. hand bones, 3. patella, 4. tibia, 5. fibula, 6. femur, 7. forearm (radius and ulna), 8. humerus, 9. iliac epiphysis, 10. skull and mandible, 11. clavicles, 12. sternum, 13. ribs, 14. coxa, 15. coccyx, 16. sacrum, 17. lumbar vertebrae, 18. scapula, 19. thoracic vertebrae, 20. cervical vertebrae. (Modified from Georg Neumann, personal communication.)

likely to be dealing with partial, fragmented specimens so they must be prepared to glean as much information as possible from every bone.

Age

During the early years of growth and development, the skeleton undergoes an orderly sequence of changes beginning with the formation and eruption of deciduous teeth and their replacement with permanent dentition by about the age of 12 years (excluding third molars). Although the timing of this process varies somewhat by sex, race, and health factors, age at death can be estimated to within 1 year in a normal subadult if the appropriate standards are used (see Figure 13.2).[14–15]

Once the second molars are fully erupted, attention is focused on the skeleton.[16] The bony skeletal system is not complete at birth, but rather begins with the formation and growth of centers of ossification. With a few exceptions, bones are endochondral in nature, that is, first formed in cartilage which is gradually replaced by bone. Until the beginning of adolescence, long bones, for example, consist of a diaphysis (shaft) and epiphyses at both ends. These are connected by cartilaginous metaphyses or growing regions that are replaced with bone when growth is complete. Because growth at each bony joint is completed at different ages and in a set order, tracing the progression of epiphyseal union will allow age estimates to within 1 year from about 13 through 18 years. Figure 13.3 shows the order of progression starting with the elbow and ending with the shoulder. Thus, if a humerus has the distal (lower) epiphysis fused and the proximal (upper) epiphysis open, this indicates an adolescent between 13 and 18. Age is then pinpointed by determining which joints in the rest of the body have fused, where union is beginning, and where all epiphyses remain completely open. As with dentition, there can be variation by sex, population, and health status.

Once growth is complete, age estimation becomes much more difficult because postmaturity age changes are subtle, irregular, and often highly variable from one individual to the next because remodeling rates and patterns are sensitive to a myriad of internal and external factors. Thus, there is a great deal of variation in the aging process itself, as well as in how it is reflected in the body. Even among the living there are always individuals who "look" much older or younger than their chronological age. It is the same, if not worse, in the skeleton.

Since the early 1980s, there has been a surge of interest in research on adult age assessment. Although age cannot be determined with absolute precision (even from fleshed remains), modifications of existing techniques and, more importantly, the introduction of methods from new skeletal sites have greatly improved accuracy. Of these, the phase technique from the sternal end of the rib is proving to be the most reliable,[17] and has withstood intensive external testing.[18,19] Introduced by the authors,[20–22] these standards divide the range of observed morphologic progression from the teens to over 70 years into nine phases (0 to 8) (Figure 13.4). The narrow 95% confidence intervals of the mean yield ranges of about ±1.5 years to age 30 and ±5 years thereafter until the open ended "over 70" terminal phase. It is important to bear in mind that the methods used were designed to yield a high probability age range; point estimates are neither realistic nor statistically sound. Blind

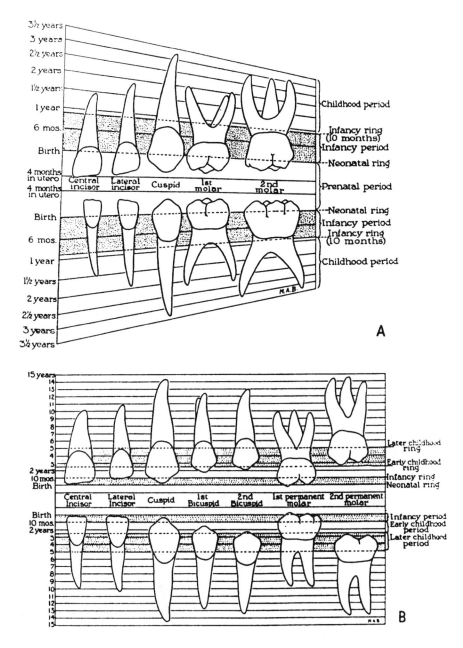

Figure 13.2 Development and eruption of deciduous teeth (A) and permanent dentition (B) with corresponding ages (modified from Reference 14).

studies have revealed that the rib system is easy to apply with little intraobserver error. Further research concluded that even though standards were based on the fourth rib, adjoining ribs 3 and 5 were almost always in the

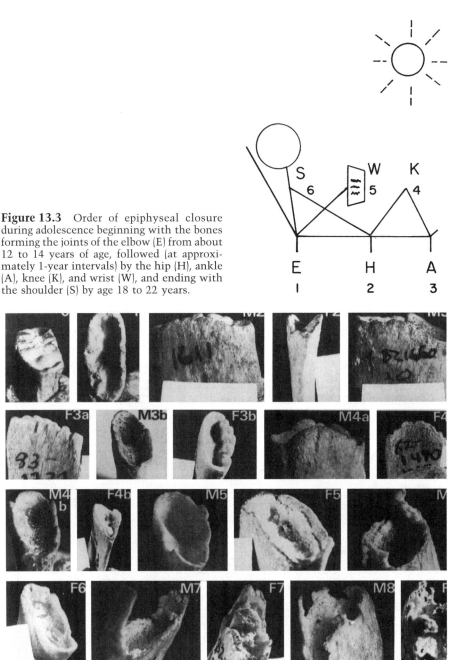

Figure 13.3 Order of epiphyseal closure during adolescence beginning with the bones forming the joints of the elbow (E) from about 12 to 14 years of age, followed (at approximately 1-year intervals) by the hip (H), ankle (A), knee (K), and wrist (W), and ending with the shoulder (S) by age 18 to 22 years.

Figure 13.4 Progression of age changes at the sternal end of the rib in males (M) and females (F) beginning with a smooth, firm bone with flat or billowy ends with rounded edges and epiphyseal lines in the immature rib (Phase 0) and proceeding through a series of changes characterized by the formation and deepening of a pit at the costochondral junction, accompanied by thinning and sharpening of the edges of the bone throughout life to Phase 8 in extreme old age (over 70 years) (also see Table 13.1) (Modified from Reference 23).

same phase.[24] Comparisons of pubic symphyses (the most often used site since the 1920s) and ribs from the same individuals indicated that the rib was twice as likely to reflect age accurately.[17] Photographic rib phase standards can be found in many sources,[3,25–28] and rib casts were introduced in 1993.[29]

Unfortunately, skeletonized forensic cases are not usually complete and undamaged, so the forensic anthropologist must be able to determine age at death in as many ways as possible because the bone of choice is not always found. For over 60 years, the pubic symphysis was most often depended upon for age estimation, but by the mid-1980s it became apparent that there were problems with existing standards, and several modifications of Todd's[30] original 10 phases were offered. Some of these were designed for seriation-dependent analysis of paleodemographic assemblages,[31,32] while others, including symphyseal casts, were specifically created for use on individual forensic cases.[33] Yet, while it is not too difficult to match the bones to the casts, the extremely wide 95% confidence ranges reach an almost meaningless 50+ years.[34] Suchey (personal communication) considers the pubic symphysis reliable for individuals under 40, but notes that the utility of this indicator diminishes after age 30 or following completion of the ventral rampart. For cases over 40 years of age, Suchey states that sternal rib end morphology is the only reliable age indicator. Table 13.1 contrasts the unwieldy symphyseal phases with the narrow, manageable ranges for the rib phases. Moreover, independent tests of these symphyseal casts along with those from earlier studies concluded that all of these techniques proved disappointing in their accuracy.[35]

Often, only a skull is found, and, while there are many clues to age, none of them are precise or reliable.[36] The bones of the cranium articulate at jagged lines called sutures that close and may become obliterated with age. However, the progression of cranial suture closure is so variable that few practitioners consider them accurate to within 20 years in either direction (see İşcan and Loth[37]). Although this site was the first chosen for a systematic quantification of aging in the 1920s, it has never been considered reliable. Even the authors of the most recent modifications do not advocate their use alone.[38] Tooth wear should be considered, but, again, not as a sole indicator in modern populations.[39]

Age changes can also be detected in long bones, but only radiographically or histologically. X-rays can reveal alterations in bone density that reflect the thinning that occurs with advancing age, but not with any degree of exactitude.[40] Changes can also be observed at the cellular level based on histomorphometric analysis of a cross-section of long bone or rib.[41–42] Age is calculated from osteon counts converted in regression equations. The major drawbacks to this technique include destruction of the bone, time-consuming preparation that must be very precise, specialized equipment, and interpretation by

Table 13.1   Comparison of Mean Ages and 95% Intervals from Phase Methods for the Rib[20-21] and Pubic Symphysis[34]

Phase	Rib		Pubic Symphysis	
	Mean	95% Range	Mean	95% range
		Males		
1	17.3	16.5–18.0	18.5	15–23
2	21.9	20.8–23.1	23.4	19–34
3	25.9	24.1–27.7	28.7	21–46
4	28.2	25.7–30.6	35.2	23–57
5	38.8	34.4–42.3	45.6	27–66
6	50.0	44.3–55.7	61.2	34–86[a]
7	59.2	54.3–64.1		
8	71.5	65.0–78.0[a]		
		Females		
1	14.0	19.4	15–24	
2	17.4	15.5–19.3	25.0	19–40
3	22.6	20.5–24.7	30.7	21–53
4	27.7	24.4–31.0	38.2	26–70
5	40.0	33.7–46.3	48.1	25–83
6	50.7	43.3–58.1	60.0	42–87[a]
7	65.2	59.2–71.2		
8	76.4	70.4–82.3[a]		

[a] Terminal phase age ranges are open ended.

a professional experienced in this method. Finally, there is significant individual variation that can be produced by factors apart from the aging process.

Teeth can also be thin sectioned for age assessment. Several features can be subjected to regression analyses.[43-44] Of these, root transparency was found to be the most important criterion, especially in recent forensic cases. Scanning electron microscopy is used to quantify incremental growth layers in the dental cementum. This approach was originated by wildlife biologists and was only recently attempted on humans.[45] Again, these techniques are time consuming, require removal and destruction of teeth, rely on specialized preparation and equipment, and are subject to considerable variation, especially in the older age ranges.

Sex

In the normal living and still fleshed dead, sex is a discrete variable — one is clearly either male or female. Differences between the sexes are much less distinct in the skeleton where both morphologic and metric manifestations overlap to form a continuum. There is, for example, no absolute size above which all are male and below which all are female. Again, if the adult skeleton is complete or at least has an intact pelvis, sex can usually be determined with 100% accuracy. However, as mentioned earlier, forensic skeletons are rarely complete and the available bones may not be obviously dimorphic. Many publications attest to the complexities of sexual dimorphism.[3,36,46]

Primary sexual characteristics (e.g., external genitalia) are present in the soft tissue even before birth, but no such definitive marker has yet been observed in the skeleton.[3,47] Although sex differences have been quantified in immature skeletons, they remain subtle until secondary sex characteristics begin developing during adolescence. Attempts at sexing prepubescent bones have been made by using measurements of growth-based differences between males and females, but the results are far from definitive.[3,48]

In the adult, the simplest and most accurate determination of sex can be made by morphological assessment of the pelvis. As can be seen in Figure 13.5, the pubic bones and sciatic notch are wider in females, resulting in an obtuse subpubic angle and more open pelvic inlet to facilitate childbirth. The male pelvis is narrower and constructed only for support and locomotion.

A thorough knowledge of cranial morphology can allow experts to approach 90 to 95% accuracy. However, the observer must be familiar with population-specific variants because sex-linked characteristics vary from one group to another. In general, however, males tend to have rougher bones with larger crests and ridges, because these are often sites of muscle attachment (Figure 13.5). New research has led to the discovery that the mandible alone is nearly as sexually dimorphic as a complete pelvis. In adult males, Loth and Henneberg[47] observed that the posterior ramus has a distinct angulation or flexure at the level of the occlusal surface of the molars, while females retain the straight, juvenile configuration (see Figure 13.5).[49]

Quantification of size differentials sometimes allow a reasonable degree of separation of the sexes. Although there are a number of metric techniques from the skull and pelvis, this type of analysis is especially useful in long bones where morphological differences are not obvious. Discriminant function formulae have been calculated from the dimensions of numerous bones and their substructures, but these methods are highly population specific, even within the three major race groups. Asian Indians are, for example, Caucasoid, but they are significantly shorter and more gracile than American or European whites. Thus, most Indian males will be metrically misdiagnosed as females if American standards are used. Interestingly, the overall length of a long bone is usually not as good a discriminator as head diameter, shaft circumference, or distal epiphyseal breadth.[50-51]

For many years, skeletal biologists have attempted to find evidence of childbearing in the pelvis. Angel[52] knew that both pregnancy and parturition are associated with tearing and reattachment of the ligaments on the dorsal

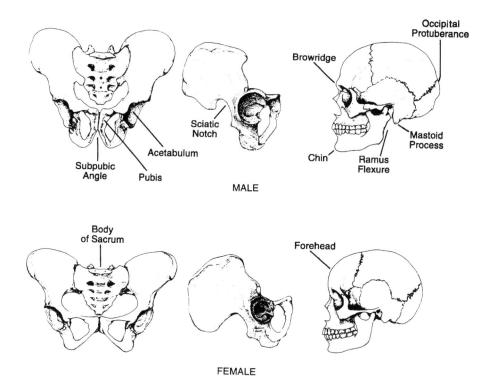

Figure 13.5   The male pelvis is characterized by a narrow subpubic angle, triangular pubic body, and proportionately wide body of the sacrum, in contrast to the wide subpubic angle, square pubic body, and smaller sacral body in the female. Male skulls have a sloping forehead as opposed to a more vertical forehead in females. A prominent browridge, large mastoid processes, and well developed occipital protuberance are also associated with the male skull. The male mandible has a flexed ramus and straight or concave chin; in females, the ramus is straight and chin is round or pointed. (Modified from Reference 27, courtesy of D. France.)

surface of the pubic bone. He reasoned that the degree of scarring thus created may be used to estimate the number of births (Figure 13.6). Houghton[53] and Dunlap[54] supported this concept and applied it to the preauricular sulcus. However, further observations have revealed similar pitting in childless females, leading to the conclusion that other factors may also be responsible for these formations.[55]

Race

Race may be defined as a rough classificatory mechanism for biological characteristics. There are three major race groups to which most people may be assigned: Caucasoid, Mongoloid, and Negroid. However, there will always be equivocal cases because of admixture. Moreover, there is a great deal of variation within each group, and skin color is only one aspect of racial

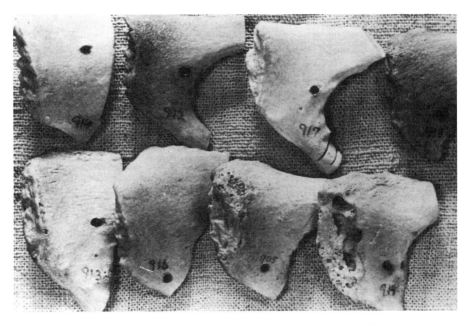

Figure 13.6   Parturition pits on the dorsal aspect of the female pubic bone ranging from nulliparous (no children) (top left) to numerous births (bottom right). (From Angel, J. L., *Am. J. Phys. Anthropol.*, 30, 427, 1969. With permission.)

classification. Swedes, Italians, Egyptians, and Asian Indians look very different, but are all skeletally "white" even though some Indians may have dark brown skin. Finally, even if a skeleton is clearly Caucasoid, there is no skeletal indicator of soft-tissue features such as eye color or hair form.

In the skeleton, cranio-facial morphology is the best indicator of racial phenotype (Figure 13.7). A long, low, narrow skull exhibiting alveolar prognathism (forward protrusion of the jaws) and a wide, flat nose with smooth sills is characteristically black. Whites are typified by a high, round, or square skull, an orthognathic or straight face, and long, narrow, protruding nose with sharp sills. It must be kept in mind that these are archetypal or ideal descriptions and there are many variations within each group and overlap with the others. It also must be emphasized that bones do not give any direct indication of the intensity or shade of skin color within a race. Furthermore, the color of the bones themselves only reflect what the remains were exposed to since death.

Although not as obvious, racial differences can be found morphologically and metrically in many parts of the body.[56] Whites exhibit noticeable anterior curvature of the femur as compared with the straighter femora of blacks.[57] The pelvis is narrower in blacks, but this is better detected through measurements.[58] Size differentials reflect disparities in total body proportions. On the

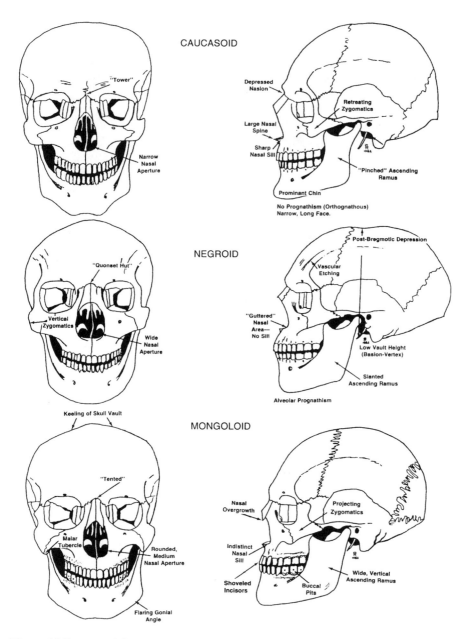

Figure 13.7 Race differences in the skulls of Caucasoids, Mongoloids, and Negroids. (Modified from Reference 27, courtesy of D. France and S. Rhine.)

average, blacks have proportionally longer limbs than whites; the reverse holds true for Mongoloids.

Like sexual dimorphism, the existence of racial dimorphism has led to the development of discriminant function formulae from measurements of many parts of the skeleton, but these methods are both sex and subpopulation specific.[46] In the final analysis, multiracial admixtures can confound even the best practitioners and not be unequivocally classified by the most modern techniques simply because the range of normal variation is so great that all possible variants cannot be anticipated.

Stature and Build

Almost every bone contributes to the overall stature of an individual; however, the relative contribution varies greatly. Singularly and collectively, the femur and tibia are the most important components of height. In contrast, a foot bone has very little input. Therefore, the best assessment of height is obtained from regression formulae derived from femoral and tibial lengths. These equations have been calculated for all of the long bones — even though an arm bone will not be as accurate as one from the leg, it may be the only part found. Attempts have been made to increase accuracy by using the combined contributions of multiple bones.

Because skeletal biologists and forensic anthropologists are often confronted with damaged bones, formulae have been devised to estimate stature from fragmentary remains.[59,60] First, the total length of the bone is extrapolated from the fragment, then that figure is used for the final regression. This extra step adds to the standard error of estimation, but is better than no estimate at all.

Body proportions vary by both race and sex.[46] Blacks, for example, have longer limb bones relative to height than whites. Thus, it is necessary to establish sex and race in order to use the correct regression formulae for the estimation of stature. The most often used standards are by Trotter[61] for whites and blacks.

Some clues to body build can also be found in the bones since they act as sites of muscle attachment. Prominent crests and ridges and roughness of the bones indicate that a person was muscular at some point during life. Smooth bony surfaces and small muscle origins are characteristic of a gracile or sedentary individual. It is important to keep in mind that although males inherently have more muscle mass than females, so-called "wimpy"-looking males will not have as well developed attachment sites as female body builders.

Robustness can be approximated by assessing the diameters or thickness of the bones and their substructures relative to the total length of the bone. All short people do not necessarily have slim builds; conversely, great height is not always linked to massiveness. Although average weight can be approximated for a given height, there is no way to ascertain obesity from the skeleton.[62]

Personal Identification

Once remains have been limited to a specific age, sex, and race group, an attempt must be made to establish the identity of the victim by searching for factors of individualization — traits that set one 5'7" to 5'9" white male in his 40s apart from all the others that meet this description. If this assessment fails to pinpoint a specific person, facial imaging is then attempted to match or recreate appearance.

Factors of Individualization

Even after general group affinities and demographic characteristics have been determined, the forensic anthropologist must then attempt to find traits that are peculiar to one particular individual. In the living, one may observe distinctive features such as fingerprints, scars, tattoos, an unusually large nose, protruding ears, a limp, lost limbs, missing or broken teeth, etc. In the skeleton, individual anomalies can range from evidence of surgical intervention such as a steel pin to repair a broken bone or wire sutures in the sternum resulting from heart surgery. The degree of healing can reveal if days, weeks, or years have passed since the operation. The presence of dental work is very helpful. If a person was treated by a dentist, comparisons can be made with the dental records of missing persons. It is also possible to match distinctive features on antemortem and postmortem X-rays.

A number of diseases leave their traces in the skeleton.[63] Primary bone cancers and advanced metastatic tumors (e.g., osteosarcoma, multiple myeloma) form characteristic lesions, as may infectious diseases (e.g., osteomyelitis, meningitis, tertiary syphilis, leprosy, and tuberculosis). Disorders such as Paget's disease, rickets, achondroplasia, anemia, and arthritis can cause mild to severe deformations. Trauma can also be identified — a broken nose that healed asymmetrically, a nonfatal bullet lodged in the skull, callous formation following a fracture.[64] A relative might remember a certain injury and a doctor or hospital may have X-rays to compare with the remains.

Bones can be marked with recognizable use patterns that may indicate handedness and occupational stress.[65] A right-handed professional pitcher or tennis player would exhibit a greater degree of differential wear along with evidence of disproportionate muscle development on that side. Baseball pitching has also been associated with the presence of bony spicules on the ulnar notch. Distinctive formations have been linked to numerous occupations and activities for which they were named such as milker's neck, cowboy thumb, seamstress's fingers, miner's knee, and weaver's bottom, to name a few.

The ultimate individualizer is DNA — everyone's unique genetic code. In the absence of blood or soft tissue, DNA can sometimes be extracted from bones. However, like fingerprinting, there must be a record of the victim's DNA profile for comparison to make a positive identification. If there is no record, the DNA can be compared with that of a close relative, but this can only rule out the possibility of kinship.

Facial Imaging

If the search is narrowed to a few possible individuals, their photographs may be compared to the remains. This procedure is known as skull to photo superimposition. If no known missing person fits the description, the only option is to attempt facial reconstruction — the difficult task of recreating appearance during life from the features of the skull. Though not an exact science, the resemblance is sometimes close enough to facilitate identification.

Establishing identity is not limited to skeletal remains. It is becoming increasingly important to be able to determine if two or more photographs depict the same individual. Photo-to-photo comparison entails the comparison of photographic images taken at different times under different conditions. This relatively new type of analysis relies on both metric and morphologic assessment and comparison of facial features.

Forensic Analysis of the Skull, edited by İşcan and Helmer,[5] is the only book of its type on this subject and presents state-of-the-art techniques developed by an international array of experts.

Skull-to-Photo Superimposition

This method can be attempted if photographs or X-rays are available of individuals that answer the description derived from a skeleton with the skull and mandible intact. In this procedure, the soft tissue outlines depictable in a photograph are superimposed over the actual skull in question (Figure 13.8).[66–67] If the bony landmarks of the skull align with the size, configuration, and placement of the features in the photograph, a match becomes possible but cannot be considered conclusive. If, however, superimposition reveals an obvious disparity, such as the position of the orbits or length of the nose or size of the chin, that individual can be eliminated as being the victim.

Facial Reconstruction

Attempts to duplicate appearance from the skull have been made since 1895.[68] Over the years, numerous technical refinements have increased the success rate, but facial reconstruction is still far from an exact science. It can be attempted in two ways: as a two-dimensional drawing or three-dimensional sculpture built on the skull itself or an exact replica. The latter was often undertaken to assess skulls thought to belong to famous people, such as the reconstruction of Bach pictured in Figure 13.9.

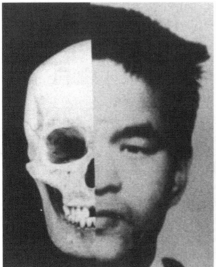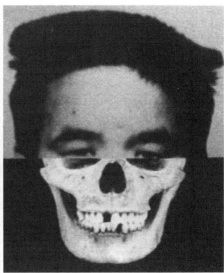

Figure 13.8   Skull-to-photo superimposition showing vertical (left) and horizontal (right) split comparisons of a skull with a photograph of the victim.[67]

The interrelationship of the face and skull has been studied extensively.[5] Some features can be better predicted than others, but in most cases there are few absolute rules. Fedosyutkin and Nainys[69] noted that the size and shape of the nasal spine gives a good indication if the tip of the nose is horizontal, upturned, or prolapsed downward. The temporal lines are a guide to forehead width, the shape of the alveolar arc of the mandible predicts lower lip projection, and the tragus of the ear corresponds to the upper edge of the external auditory meatus. Many other associations are more tentative, such as the correlation of the shape of the mastoid process with attached or free ear lobes and supramastoid crest with ear protrusion.

In any type of facial reconstruction, once the average tissue thicknesses are calculated and bony contours followed, many remaining details are left to conjecture because the skull does not provide all the indicators necessary to predict every soft tissue formation. Even the most skilled practitioner cannot determine such vital features as fatness, hair color or style, exact flesh tones, facial hair, or if a person looked older or younger than his chronological age.

Photographic Comparison

Although most of their work revolves around deceased victims, forensic anthropologists are being called upon with increasing frequency to identify the perpetrator of a crime. This can be directly linked to the skyrocketing use of video surveillance apparatus as a deterrent to crime. This approach has been tried for

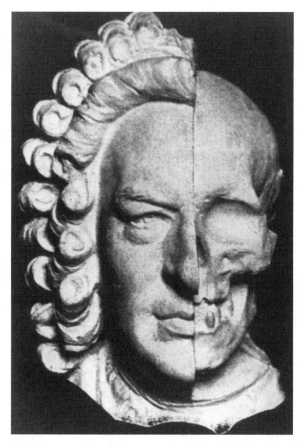

Figure 13.9   Facial reconstruction from the skull of J. S. Bach.[68]

many years, but methodological development in photographic comparison is still in its infancy. Research is now underway to establish standards for anthro-pometric and morphologic analysis of a photographic image based on an in-depth understanding of facial morphology and how it can be quantified from photographs.[70]

One of the most challenging issues is the attempt to match pictures of the same person at various ages. There appear to be two types of morphological features: (1) those that are clearly vulnerable to the effects of age, and (2) those that remain relatively stable throughout adulthood. The manifestations of the aging process and the rates at which they occur vary greatly from one individual to another because there are so many genetic and environmental factors involved. This makes it impossible to predict all but the most general trends. To complicate matters further, changes over time are not all due to aging; some can be linked to alterations in lifestyle and health, such as fluctuations in nutrition, physical activity, smoking, and exposure to

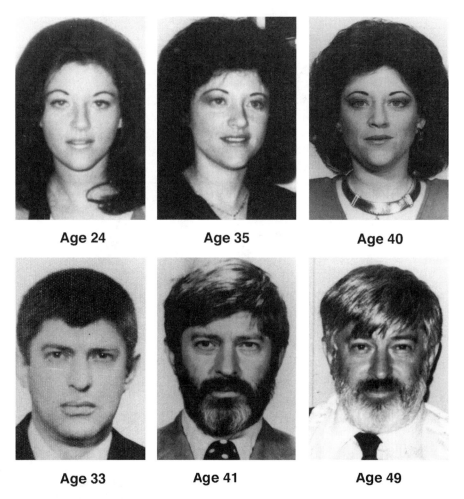

Figure 13.10 Photographic comparisons of the authors over a 16- to 17-year period: Loth at ages 24, 35, and 40 years; İşcan at ages 33, 41, and 49 years.

the sun. In Figure 13.10, photos of the authors illustrate the differences in appearance over an approximately 15-year period.

There are many limitations because photographs are rarely made under exactly the same conditions. Problems are numerous and may include differences in lighting, photographic quality, head position, angle, facial expression, weight fluctuation, balding, and growth of facial hair, among others. Despite the potential drawbacks, this might be the only option if a subject is alive or no corpse exists for comparison. This technique can definitely exclude a person, but in the absence of individualizing traits, a positive match cannot be declared.

Cause of Death

Forensic anthropologists can sometimes determine the cause of death, but only if evidence of trauma or disease is registered in the bones. The expert must first be able to distinguish antemortem lesions that occurred during life from perimortem trauma at the time of death and postmortem destruction after death. Easily recognizable signs of healing and surgical intervention are certain indications that an injury happened at least a few days before death. Perimortem wounds to fresh bone may have different characteristics than postmortem damage to dry bone.[71]

If projectiles (bullets, shotgun pellets, arrow heads, etc.) or their characteristic imprints are embedded in the bones, the trajectory of the object can be tracked to determine if a vital organ or major blood vessel would be transected. Powerful bullets can shatter a skull, but careful reconstruction can usually reveal the entry and exit wounds (Figure 13.11). The presence of beveling at the edges of the wound gives important clues to the angle and direction of entry. Because bone is solid, measurement of the entry wound can indicate the caliber of bullet or size of buckshot. It is also important to analyze the fracture patterns. In cases where more than one bullet is present, the pattern can help designate the point of entry of the first and subsequent shots.

Metallic traces deposited in a cut mark could indicate the use of a knife, ice pick, screwdriver, etc. Blunt trauma can leave its mark on bones in many ways, ranging from incomplete breaks and depressed skull fractures to clean breaks and crushed ribs.

More often than not, a clear-cut cause and manner of death, natural or otherwise, cannot be found in osteologic remains. With the exception of some cancers, few directly fatal diseases in the postantibiotic era invade the skeleton of people living in modern societies. Bullets and knives can kill without damaging bones, strangulation may not be detectable if soft tissue and cartilage have decomposed. Even when perimortem trauma is obvious, it may not be possible to determine if a skull fracture, for example, resulted from a murderous blow to the head, an accidental fall, or followed collapse from a fatal heart attack, especially if months or years have elapsed.

Education and Training

The nature of this field demands a very high level of education and experience. An undergraduate student interested in becoming a forensic anthropologist should build a solid background by taking courses that will give a thorough grounding in biology, anatomy and physiology, osteology, chemistry,

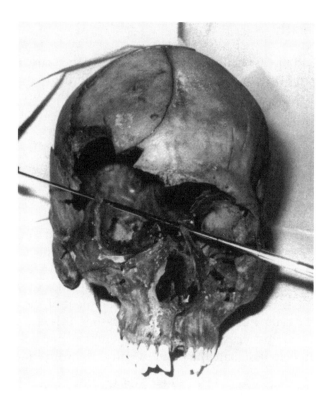

Figure 13.11   Gunshot wound to the skull with rod used to determine pathway of the bullet. Note that the exit wound on the left resulted in destruction of nearly half the face.

archaeology, and cultural and physical anthropology. It is important to join a well respected organization such as the AAFS (in North America) as a student trainee to establish a connection to the field and get to know the experts in it. Graduate work is a must. A Ph.D. plus 3 years of experience is the minimum requirement for eligibility to take the examination for board certification. It is particularly advantageous to choose a doctoral program in an accredited anthropology or human biology department that includes a recognized expert in the discipline who is actively involved in forensic case work.

Conclusions

It should be clear by now that the forensic anthropologist must possess an in-depth knowledge of a wide range of highly specialized technical and scientific subjects. It must also be coupled with experience because one cannot simply pick up a "how to" manual and understand the anatomical and technical nuances necessary to properly analyze a skeleton and its evidentiary context.

The complexity of this discipline makes it imperative that the proper authorities call in a qualified, up-to-date specialist whenever badly decomposed, dismembered, or skeletonized remains are found. This is especially true in today's litigious society where a skilled lawyer can destroy an otherwise airtight case if an expert opinion is weak or lacking.[72] Moreover, an otherwise strong criminal case may be jeopardized if the credibility of the forensic anthropologist is challenged because of a deficiency in training or lack of familiarity with the most current literature and the advantages, liabilities, and limitations of it.

Finally, advances such as electronic mail greatly increase the level of local, national, and international communication among forensic scientists. Electronic discussion lists, such as FORENS-L@ACC.FAU.EDU, allow instant access to specialists in all areas. Many qualified forensic anthropologists are active on e-mail and can direct authorities to the best professional in their area.

REFERENCES

1. İşcan, M. Y., Rise of forensic anthropology. *Yearbk. Phys. Anthropol.*, 31, 203, 1988.

2. İşcan, M. Y., Ed., *Age Markers in the Human Skeleton*, Charles C Thomas, Springfield, IL, 1989.

3. Krogman, W. M. and İşcan, M. Y., *The Human Skeleton in Forensic Medicine*, Charles C Thomas, Springfield, IL, 1986.

4. İşcan, M. Y. and Kennedy, K. A. R., Eds., *Reconstruction of Life from the Skeleton*, Wiley-Liss, New York, 1989.

5. İşcan, M. Y. and Helmer, R., Eds., *Forensic Analysis of the Skull*, Wiley-Liss, New York, 1993.

6. Rathbun, T. A. and Buikstra, J. E., Eds., *Human Identification: Case Studies in Forensic Anthropology*, Charles C Thomas, Springfield, IL, 1984.

7. Stewart, T. D., *Essentials of Forensic Anthropology*, Charles C Thomas, Springfield, IL, 1979.

8. Reichs, K. J., Ed., *Forensic Osteology*, Charles C Thomas, Springfield, IL, 1986.

9. Shipman, P., *Life History of a Fossil: An Introduction to Taphonomy and Paleoecology*, Harvard University Press, Cambridge, 1981.

10. Yoshino, M., Miyasaka, S., Sato, H., and Seta, S., Electron microscopical study on the estimation of the burial time of the compact bone under the ground. *Report of the National Research Institute Police Science*, 38, 1, 1985.

11. Mann, R. W., Bass, W. M., and Meadows, L., Time since death and decomposition of the human body: variables and observations in case and experimental field studies. *J. Forensic Sci.*, 35, 103, 1990.

12. Micozzi, M. S., *Postmortem Change in Human and Animal Remains*, Charles C Thomas, Springfield, IL,1991.

13. Bass, W. M., Is it possible to consume a body completely in a fire?, in *Human Identification: Case Studies in Forensic Anthropology*, Rathbun, T. A. and Buikstra, J. E., Eds., Charles C Thomas, Springfield, IL,1984, 136.

14. Massler, M., Schour, I., and Poncher, H. G. Developmental pattern of the child as reflected in the calcification pattern of teeth. *Am. J. Dis. Child.*, 62, 33, 1941.

15. El-Nofely, A., and İşcan, M. Y., Assessment of age from the dentition in children, in *Age Markers in the Human Skeleton*, İşcan, M. Y., Ed., Charles C Thomas, Springfield, IL,1989, 237.

16. Sundick, R. I., Human skeletal growth and age determination. *Homo*, 29, 228, 1978.

17. İşcan, M. Y., Loth, S. R., and Scheuerman, E. H., Age assessment from the sternal end of the rib and pubic symphysis: a systematic comparison. *Anthropologie* (Prague), 30, 41, 1992.

18. Dudar, J. C., Estimating Adult Skeletal Age at Death Using Morphological and Histological Rib Techniques, M.A. Thesis, University of Guelph, 1992.

19. Russell, K. F., Simpson, S. W., Genovese, J., Kinkel, M. D., Meindl, R. S., and Lovejoy, C. O., Independent test of the fourth rib aging technique. *Am. J. Phys. Anthropol.*, 92, 53, 1993.

20. İşcan, M. Y., Loth, S. R., and Wright, R. K., Age estimation from the rib by phase analysis: white males. *J. Forensic Sci.*, 29, 1094, 1984.

21. İşcan, M. Y., Loth, S. R., and Wright, R. K., Age estimation from the rib by phase analysis: white females. *J. Forensic Sci.*, 30, 853, 1985.

22. İşcan, M. Y., Loth, S. R., and Wright, R. K., Racial variation in the sternal extremity of the rib and its effect on age determination. *J. Forensic Sci.*, 32, 452, 1987.

23. Angel, J. L., Suchey, J. M., İşcan, M. Y., and Zimmerman, M. R., Age at death from the skeleton and viscera, in *Dating and Age Determination of Biological Materials*, Zimmerman, M. R. and Angel, J. L., Eds., Croom Helm, London, 1986, 179.

24. Loth, S. R., İşcan, M. Y., and Scheuerman, E. H., Intercostal variation at the sternal end of the rib. *Forensic Sci. Intl.*, 65, 135, 1994.

25. Bass, W. M., *Human Osteology: A Laboratory and Field Manual*, Missouri Archaeological Society, University of Missouri, Columbia, 1987.

26. Ubelaker, D. H., *Human Skeletal Remains: Excavation, Analysis, Interpretation*, Taraxacum, Washington, D.C., 1989.

27. France, D. L. and Horn, A. D., *Lab Manual and Workbook for Physical Anthropology*, West, St. Paul, 1992.

28. Bennett, K. A., *A Field Guide for Human Skeletal Identification*, Charles C Thomas, Springfield, IL,1993.

29. İşcan, M. Y. and Loth, S. R., *İşcan, Rib Phase Casts: Casts of Age Phases from the Sternal End of the Rib for White Males and Females*, France Casting, Bellevue, CO, 1993.

30. Todd, T. W., Age changes in the pubic bone: I. The male white pubis. *Am. J. Phys. Anthropol.*, 3, 285, 1920.

31. Meindl, R. S., Lovejoy C. O., Mensforth, R. P., and Walker R. A., A revised method of age determination using the os pubis, with a review and tests of accuracy of other current methods of pubis symphyseal ageing. *Am. J. Phys. Anthropol.*, 68, 29, 1985.

32. Murray, K. A. and Murray, T., A test of the auricular surface aging technique. *J. Forensic Sci.*, 36, 1162, 1991.

33. Katz, D. and Suchey, J. M., Age determination of the male os pubis. *Am. J. Phys. Anthropol.*, 69, 427, 1986.

34. Brooks, S. T. and Suchey, J. M., Skeletal age determination based on the os pubis: a comparison of the Acsádi-Nemeskéri and Suchey-Brooks methods, *Hum. Evol.*, 5, 227-238, 1990.

35. Klepinger, L. L., Katz, D., Micozzi, M. S., and Carroll, L., Evaluation of cast methods for estimating age from the os pubis. *J. Forensic Sci.*, 37, 763, 1992.

36. Novotny, V., İşcan, M. Y., and Loth, S. R., Morphologic and osteometric assessment of age, sex, and race from the skull, in *Forensic Analysis of the Skull*, İşcan, M. Y. and Helmer, R., Eds., Wiley-Liss, New York, 1993, 71.

37. İşcan, M. Y. and Loth, S. R., Osteological manifestations of age in adults, in *Reconstruction of Life from the Skeleton*, İşcan, M. Y. and Kennedy, K. A. R., Eds., Wiley-Liss, New York, 1989, 23.

38. Meindl, R. S. and Lovejoy C. O., Ectocranial suture closure: A revised method for the determination of skeletal age at death and blind tests of its accuracy. *Am. J. Phys. Anthropol.*, 68, 57, 1985.

39. Lovejoy, C. O., Dental wear in the Libben population: its functional pattern and role in the determination of adult skeletal age at death. *Am. J. Phys. Anthropol.*, 68, 47, 1985.

40. Sorg, M. H., Andrews, R. P., and İşcan, M. Y., Radiographic aging in the adult, in *Age Markers in the Human Skeleton*, İşcan, M. Y., Ed., Charles C Thomas, Springfield, IL,1989, 169.

41. Stout, S. D., The use of cortical bone histology to estimate age at death, in *Age Markers in the Human Skeleton*, İşcan, M. Y., Ed., Charles C Thomas, Springfield, IL,1989, 195.

42. Ericksen, M. F., Histologic estimation of age at death using the anterior cortex of the femur. *Am. J. Phys. Anthropol.*, 84, 171, 1991.

43. Bang, G. and Ramm, E., Determination of age in humans from root dentin transparency. *Acta Odontol. Scand.*, 2, 3, 1970.

44. Kilian, J. and Vlcek, E., Age determination from teeth in adult individuals, in *Age Markers in the Human Skeleton*, İşcan, M. Y., Ed., Charles C Thomas, Springfield, IL,1989, 255.

45. Charles, D. K., Condon, K., Cheverud, J. M., and Buikstra, J. E., Estimating age-at-death from growth layer groups in cementum, in *Age Markers in the Human Skeleton*, İşcan, M. Y., Ed., Charles C Thomas, Springfield, IL,1989, 277.

46. St. Hoyme, L. and İşcan, M. Y., Determination of sex and race: accuracy and assumptions, in *Reconstruction of Life from the Skeleton*, İşcan, M. Y. and Kennedy, K. A. R., Eds., Wiley-Liss, New York, 1989, 53.

47. Loth, S. R. and Henneberg, M., The Taung Child — it's a boy! Sexually dimorphic morphology in the immature human mandible and its application to fossil hominids. *Am. J. Phys. Anthropol.* (Suppl.), 22, 152, 1996.

48. Weaver, D. S., Sex differences in the ilia of a known sex and age sample of fetal and infant skeletons. *Am. J. Phys. Anthropol.*, 52, 191, 1980.

49. Loth, S. R., and Henneberg, M., Mandibular ramus flexure: A new morphologic indicator of sexual dimorphism in the human skeleton, *Am. J. Phys. Anthropol.*, 99, 473, 1996.

50. DiBennardo, R. and Taylor, J. V., Sex assessment of the femur: a test of a new method. *Am. J. Phys. Anthropol.*, 50, 635, 1979.

51. İşcan, M. Y., Yoshino, M., and Kato, S., Sex determination from the tibia. *J. Forensic Sci.*, 39, 785, 1994.

52. Angel, J. L., The bases of paleodemography. *Am. J. Phys. Anthropol.*, 30, 427, 1969.

53. Houghton, P., The relationship of the pre-auricular groove of the ilium to pregnancy. *Am. J. Phys. Anthropol.*, 41, 381, 1974.

54. Dunlap, S. S., A Study of the Preauricular Sulcus in a Cadaver Population, Ph.D. dissertation, Michigan State University, East Lansing, 1981.

55. Andersen, B. C., Parturition Scarring as a Consequence of Flexible Pelvic Architecture, Ph.D. dissertation, Simon Fraser University, Burnaby, B.C., Canada, 1986.

56. Gill, G. W. and Rhine, J. S., Eds., *Skeletal Attribution of Race: Methods for Forensic Anthropology*, Maxwell Museum of Anthropology Papers No. 4, University of New Mexico, Albuquerque, 1990.

57. Gilbert, B. M., Anterior femoral curvature: its probable cause and utility as a criterion of racial assessment. *Am. J. Phys. Anthropol.*, 45, 601, 1976.

58. İşcan, M. Y., Assessment of race from the pelvis. *Am. J. Phys. Anthropol.*, 62, 205, 1983.

59. Steele, D. G., Estimation of stature from fragments of long limb bones, in *Personal Identification in Mass Disasters*, Stewart, T. D., Ed., National Museum of Natural History, Washington, D.C., 1970, 85.

60. Sonder, E. and Knussmann, R., Zur Körperhöhenbestimmung männlicher Individuen aus Femur-, Tibia- und Humerus-Fraagmenten. *Z. Morphol. Anthropol.*, 75, 131, 1985.

61. Trotter, M., Estimation of stature from intact limb bones, in *Personal Identification in Mass Disasters*, Stewart, T. D., Ed., National Museum of Natural History, Washington, D.C., 1970.

62. Knussmann, R., Toeller, M., and Holler, H.D., On the assessment of body weight. *J. Hum. Evol.*, 4, 497, 1975.

63. Ortner, D. J. and Putschar, W. G. J., *Identification of Pathological Conditions in Human Skeletal Remains*, Smithsonian Contribution to Anthropology, No. 28, Smithsonian Institution Press, Washington, D.C., 1981.

64. Merbs, C. F., Trauma, in *Reconstruction of Life from the Skeleton*, İşcan, M. Y. and Kennedy, K. A. R., Eds., Wiley-Liss, New York, 1989, 161.

65. Kennedy, K. A. R., Skeletal markers of occupational stress, in *Reconstruction of Life from the Skeleton*, İşcan, M. Y. and Kennedy, K. A. R., Eds., Wiley-Liss, New York, 1989, 129.

66. Lan, Y. and Cai, D., Technical advances in skull-to-photo superimposition, in *Forensic Analysis of the Skull*, İşcan, M. Y. and Helmer, R., Eds., Wiley-Liss, New York, 1993, 119.

67. Seta, S. and Yoshino, M., A combined apparatus for photographic and video superimposition, in *Forensic Analysis of the Skull*, İşcan, M. Y. and Helmer, R., Eds., Wiley-Liss, New York, 1993, 161.

68. Grüner, O., Identification of skulls: historical review and practical applications, in *Forensic Analysis of the Skull*, İşcan, M. Y. and Helmer, R., Eds., Wiley-Liss, New York, 1993, 29.

69. Fedosyutkin, B. A. and Nainys, J. V., The relationship of skull morphology to facial features, in *Forensic Analysis of the Skull*, İşcan, M. Y. and Helmer, R., Eds., Wiley-Liss, New York, 1993, 199.

70. İşcan, M. Y., Introduction of techniques for photographic comparison: potential and problems, in *Forensic Analysis of the Skull*, İşcan, M. Y. and Helmer, R., Eds., Wiley-Liss, New York, 1993, 57.

71. Sauer, N. J., Manner of death: skeletal evidence of blunt trauma and sharp instrument wounds, in *Human Identification: Case Studies in Forensic Anthropology*, Rathbun, T. A. and Buikstra, J. E., Eds., Charles C Thomas, Springfield, IL,1984, 176.

72. Galloway, A., Birkby, W. H., Kahane, T., and Fulginiti, L., Physical anthropology and the law: legal responsibilities of forensic anthropologists. *Yearbk. Phys. Anthropol.*, 33, 39, 1990.

APPENDIX
Resources in the Forensic Sciences

WILLIAM G. ECKERT

It is essential that the student of forensic sciences be aware of the many sources of information that can give deeper understanding of the various fields of the forensic sciences and the problems that are unique to these fields. These resources include individual specialists, organizations specialized in a specific field, and the international literature in which there are general reference resources as well as works dealing with specific fields.

General Reference Works

General reference works may be found in the form of reference books especially written as accumulations of technical sources. This is best exemplified by the *Lawyers Desk Reference*, which provides a vast collection of expert witnesses in various fields, medical sources, drug product investigation, biotechnological resources, environmental sources, automobile accident investigation resources, consumer and household product informational resources, industrial third-party injury investigation resources, farm injury investigation resources, railroad accident investigation resources, public utility injury investigation resources, construction and demolition injury investigation resources, admiralty sources, manufacturers of safety equipment, safety organizations and safety libraries, safety standards and codes, governmental information centers, international safety sources, technical safety publications, safety films, hazard and risk recognition, discriminatory torts, swimming pool information, worker's compensation sources, among many other collections of information.

A second important source is the *American Jurisprudence Proof of Facts*, now in its second edition, which deals with specific problems and documents facts essential to a successful, skillfully planned approach to the presentation of the attorney witnesses in the forensic sciences as it brings in the dimension of the legal side of the presentation and offers more understandable insight into the proper presentation of testimony.

0-8493-8101-0/97/$0.00+$.50
© 1997 by CRC Press, Inc.

A third resource, more specifically geared to law enforcement and more especially criminalistics, is the *Semi-Annual List of Selected Articles*. This is a supplement to the *International Criminal Police Review of INTERPOL*, which includes a list of titles and references of important articles dealing with police work and criminal and social matters, selected from the professional journals received at the General Secretariat of INTERPOL (the International Criminal Police Organization) in Lyon, France. In this vast number of periodicals are included the major police publications as well as the forensic science and medical periodicals, and thus a significant collection is accumulated each year. The contents include such subjects of interest as accidents, alcohol, criminal investigation, criminal anthropology, criminal sociology, criminology, counterfeiting, documents, drugs, environmental protection, expert examinations, fire and arson, forensic sciences, medicine and toxicology, forgery, homicides, identification, international law, photography, psychiatry, psychology, sex and morals, suicides, weapons, and explosives.

A fourth resource is the annual publication of the National Library of Medicine called the *Cumulative Index Medicus*. This is a compilation of articles appearing in the thousands of medical and scientific journals received each year in that great repository of knowledge. These are accumulated in a monthly publication known as the *Index Medicus* and then assembled by major and minor subject headings in the *Cumulative Index Medicus*.

A fifth resource is an annual publication of the International Reference Organization in Forensic Sciences and Medicine known as the *International Bibliography in Forensic Sciences*, which includes an indexed collection of the previous year's titles in the forensic sciences gathered from the international literature in medicine, law, and law enforcement. INFORM also publishes compilations of the international literature on specific forensic sciences such as odontology, criminalistics, anthropology, toxicology, legal medicine, serology, psychiatry, thanatology, photography, and questioned documents. These cover 40- to 50-year collections indexed by author and subject. There are also indexed compilations of the international literature dealing with specific problems of the forensic sciences that INFORM has produced. These cover such areas as abortion, aircraft accidents, arson investigation, art forgery, alcohol, alcoholism, autopsy, battered child and infanticide, blood, cadavers, cold injury, dangerous marine animals and foods, diving problems, drowning, drugs and drug abuse, electrical injury, explosives, fat embolism, fingerprints, firearms examinations, firearms injury, focal suicide, geology, hallucinogens, heat injury, home accidents, homicides, iatrogenic problems, industrial accidents, malpractice, medicolegal history, narcotics, paleopathology, penetrating injuries, poisons and poisonings, sex crimes, sports injury, sudden infant death, sudden death, terrorism, trace evidence, traffic accidents, war crimes, and war wounds. In addition, there are collections of major

English, German, and Russian forensic periodicals that have indexed tables of contents available as an additional resource.

Bibliography

American Jurisprudence Proof of Facts, vol. 1–30, San Francisco, 1959, Bancroft-Whitney.

American Jurisprudence Proof of Facts, second series, vol. 1, San Francisco, 1975, Bancroft-Whitney.

Cumulative Index Medicus, annual, National Library of Medicine, Rockville, MD.

International bibliography in forensic sciences annual INFORM-International Reference Organization in Forensic Sciences and Medicine, Wichita, Kan.

International literature compilation (40 to 50 indexed compilations in specific subjects). INFORM-International Reference Organization in Forensic Sciences and Medicine, Wichita, Kan.

Philo, H.M., Robb, D.A. and Goodman, R.M.: *Lawyer's Desk Reference,* ed. 5, Rochester, NY, 1975, The Lawyers Cooperative Publishing.

Semi-annual list of selected articles, supplement to the *International Criminal Police Review,* Lyon, France.

Specific Reference Works

Periodicals

The basic reference sources of the forensic scientist are the periodicals published by national or international organizations. These may be used as the medium for publishing the proceedings of the organizations' national or regional meetings and include review articles, case reports, and original studies carried out by their members. In addition to periodicals published by organizations devoted to forensic medicine and sciences in a specific country, there are communications published on a regular basis by organizations specialized in a specific field of the forensic sciences. Thus, the International Association of Forensic Toxicologists publishes a regular newsletter complete with practical information on newer problems and techniques that have been studied by their members. There is a similar communication published by the International Society of Forensic Odontostomatology. The only international journal of forensic sciences is published by the Elsevier Company in Geneva, Switzerland, and is edited by Prof. Jorgen Voigt of Copenhagen, Denmark. This journal developed out of a need for international media to be developed for proper exchange of information between forensic scientists.

1. *Australian Journal of Forensic Sciences*, editor, Sydney, S.W., Australian Police Journal, Box 45, GPO Sydney NSW 2001.
2. Newsletter, NSW Branch, The Australian Forensic Science Society, Analytical Laboratory Division, Box 162, P.O. Lidcombe, NSW 2141.

Journal of Forensic Sciences
American Journal of Forensic Medicine and Pathology
The Forensic Examiner
Beitrage zur Gericht, Medizin, Institute of Forensic Medicine, Sensengasse 2, Vienna IX, A-1190
Arch. Belges de Medecine Legale et Sociale, Institut de Medecine Legale, Liege University Liege.
Arq. Soc. Med. et Med. Legal Crim., Institute Oscar Freire Rua Todoro Sampaio 115, Sao Paulo (also Revista de Medecina Legal).
Journal of Canadian Society of Forensic Sciences, 56 West Park Dr., Ottawa 15, Ontario.
Revista de Medicina Legale De Chile, Instituto de Legal Medecina, Casilla 6584-Correo 4, Santiago.

Textbooks

The literature in the forensic sciences includes many works written primarily for the student of medicine or law. These are manuals or short textbooks in forensic or legal medicine, and they are found in each country that has a medicolegal investigative center. These are usually related to the medical school as a department of forensic or legal medicine or separate as an institute of legal or forensic medicine in the university or as part of the ministry of justice. These works may be more massive and written for advanced levels of expertise including practicing forensic pathologists and residents of this specialty as well as practicing pathologists. These basic texts are found in many different languages and are listed below. There are relatively few textbooks in criminalistics, toxicology, and other fields including dentistry and anthropology.

Forensic Medicine and Pathology

1. Adelson, L.: *The Pathology of Homicide,* Springfield, IL. 1974, Charles C Thomas.
2. Camps, F.E.: In Cameron, M., editor, *Gradwohl's Legal Medicine,* ed. 3, Bristol, England, 1976, John Wright & Sons, Ltd.
3. Polson, C.J., Gee, D.J., and Knight, P.: *The Essentials of Forensic Medicine,* 4th Edition, 1995, Pergamon Press, New York.

4. Spitz, W.U. and Fisher, R.S.: *Medicolegal Investigation of Death*, Springfield, IL., 1993, Charles C Thomas.
5. Tedeschi, C., Eckert, W.G., and Tedeschi, L: *Forensic Medicine: Study of Trauma and Environmental Hazards*, Philadelphia, 1977, W.B. Saunders.
6. Knight, B. *Forensic Pathology*, New York, 1991, Oxford University Press.
7. Jones, N.L. *Atlas of Forensic Pathology*, 1996, Igaku-Shoin, New York, Tokyo.
8. Plueckhahn, V. Ethics, *Legal Medicine and Forensic Pathology*, 1991, Melbourne University Press, Melbourne, Austraia.

Forensic Anthropology

1. Cottone, J.A. and Standish, S.M.: Year Book Med. Publishers, 1982.
2. Krogman, W.C. and Iscan, M.Y.: *The Human Skeleton in Forensic Medicine*, 2nd Ed., Springfield, IL., Charles C Thomas, 1982.

Forensic Science

1. Fisher, B.A.: *Technics of Crime Scene Investigation*, Boca Raton, FL, CRC Press, 1992.
2. Bodziak, W.J.: *Footwear Impression*, CRC Press, 1990.
3. Cowger, J.F.: *Friction Ridge Skin*, CRC Press, 1983.
4. McDonald, P.: *Tire Imprint Evidence*, CRC Press, 1989.
5. Hilton, O.: *Scientific Examination of QUESTIONED Documents*, CRC Press, 1982, Boca Raton, FL.
6. Lee, H.C.: *Gaeensslen Advances in Fingerprint Technology*, CRC Press, 1991, Boca Raton, FL.
7. Redsicker, D.R.: *Practical Methology of Forensic Photography*, CRC Press, 1991, Boca Raton, FL.
8. Eckert, W.G. and James, S.: *Interpretation of Bloodstain Evidence at Crime Sciences*, CRC Press, 1989, Boca Raton, FL.
9. Farley, M.A. and Harrington, J.J.: *Forensic DNA Technology*, CRC Press, 1991, Boca Raton, FL.
10. O'Connor, J.J.: *Practical and Arson Investigation*, CRC Press, 1996, Boca Raton, FL.
11. Kinnee, K.B.: *Practical Investigation Techniques*, CRC Press 1994, Boca Raton, FL.
12. Walters, S.B.: *Drug Testing in Hair*, CRC Press, 1996, Boca Raton.
13. Clark, F. and Diliberto, K.: *Investigating Computer Crime*, CRC Press, 1996, Boca Raton, FL.

Forensic Pathology — Special Subjects

1. Baselt, R.C.: *Disposition of Toxic Drugs and Chemicals in Man,* ed 4. Foster City, CA, Chemical Toxicology Institute, 1995.
2. Cooper, P.R. (ed): *Head Injury,* ed 2. Baltimore, Williams & Wilkins, 1987.
3. Damask, A.C., Damask, J.B., and Damask, J.N.: *Injury Causation Analysis: Case Studies and Data Sources.* Charlottesville, VA, The Mitchie Company, 1990.
4. Demling, R.H. and LaLonde, C.: *Burn Trauma.* New York, Theime Medical Publishers, 1989.
5. DiMaio V.J.M.: *Gunshot Wounds: Practical Aspects of Firearms, Ballistics, and Forensic Techniques,* New York, Elsevier, 1985.
6. Fischer, H. and Kirkpatrick, C.J.: *Color Atlas of Trauma Pathology,* St. Louis, Mosby, 1991.
7. Guntheroth, W.G.: *Crib Death: The Sudden Infant Death Syndrome.* Mount Kisco, N.Y. Futura Publishing Company, 1989.
8. Kleinman, P.K.: *Diagnostic Imaging of Child Abuse.* Baltimore, Williams & Wilkins, 1987.
9. Knight, B.: *Forensic Pathology.* New York, Oxford University Press, 1991.
10. Knight, B. (ed): *The Estimation of the Time Since Death in the Early Postmortem Period.* London, Arnold, 1995.
11. Limpert, R.: *Motor Vehicle Accident Reconstruction and Cause Analysis.* Charlottesville, VA, The Mitchie Company, 1978.
12. Ludwig, S. and Kornberg, A.E. (eds): *Child Abuse: A Medical Reference,* ed 2. New York, Churchill Livingstone, 1992.
13. Marshall, E.P. and Sanow, E.J.: *Handgun Stopping Power: The Definitive Study,* Boulder, CO, Paladin Press, 1992.
14. Mason, J.K. (ed): *The Pathology of Trauma,* ed 2. London, Arnold, 1993.
15. Mathog, R.H.: *Atlas of Craniofacial Trauma.* Philadelphia, WB Saunders, 1992.
16. Moore, E.E., Mattox, K.L., and Feliciano, D.V. (eds): *Trauma,* ed 2. Norwalk, Connecticut, Appleton & Lange, 1991.
17. National Research Council: *DNA Technology in Forensic Science,* Washington, D.C., National Academy Press, 1992.
18. Raimondi, A.J., Choux, M., and DiRocco, C.: *Head Injuries in the Newborn and Infant,* New York, Springer Verlag, 1986.
19. Schoen, F.J. (managing ed): *Robbins Pathologic Basic of Disease,* ed 5. Philadelphia, WB Saunders, 1994.
    Spitz, W.U. (ed): *Spitz and Fisher's Medicolegal Investigation of Death,* ed 3. Springfield, Illinois, Charles C Thomas, 1993.

20. Sullivan, Jr., J.B. and Krieger, G.R.: *Hazardous Materials Toxicology: Clinical Principles of Environmental Health,* Baltimore, Williams & Wilkins, 1992.

21. Viccellio, P.: *Handbook of Medical Toxicology,* Boston, Little, Brown, 1993.

22. White, T.D.: *Human Osteology,* San Diego, Academic Press, 1991.

23. Saferstein, R.: *Criminalistic Introduction to Forensic Sciences.*

Index